D1441945

# OPERATION SUSANNAH

# OPERATION

*Translated from the Hebrew by Peretz Kidron*

# SUSANNAH

As told to Aviezer Golan

by Marcelle Ninio, Victor Levy,

Robert Dassa and Philip Natanson

HARPER & ROW, PUBLISHERS

1817

New York     Hagerstown     San Francisco     London

This work was first published in Israel by Edanim Publishers.

Library of Congress Cataloging in Publication Data

Golan, Aviezer.
  Operation Susannah.
  Includes index.
  1. Political prisoners—Egypt—Biography. 2. Jews
in Egypt—Biography. 3. Espionage, Israeli—Egypt.
I. Title.
HV9843.G6413  1978     365′.6 [B]     77–3751
ISBN 0–06–011555–6

78 79 80 81 82 10 9 8 7 6 5 4 3 2 1

Dedicated to those who did not return:

Max (Meir) Binnet

Moshe (Mussa) Marzouk

Shmuel (Sammy) Azar

# CONTENTS

*Photo section follows page 178.*

# FOREWORD

I am extremely happy that this extraordinary book has now been translated into the English language so that all who read it may share the personal, almost unbelievable experience of a group of heroic men and a woman in an Egyptian prison. I was fortunate to meet them shortly after their return to Israel.

I must admit I was quite shaken when told that Marcelle, one of the group, wished to speak with me. I envisioned a young woman broken in body and spirit after fourteen years of torture and interrogation. Instead I met a young woman of charm, grace, self-confidence, high intelligence, beauty, and no word of bitterness. As she spoke of some of her experiences, I realized that because of her courage and the way she conducted herself she had practically become the leader of the women's prison. They respected her; even enemies must respect a personality of this kind.

Upon her return to Israel she resumed and completed her studies. She is now married and leads a normal, active life. I must say I have seen many courageous people in Israel—soldiers, their fathers and mothers and young wives—but they were here, among friends, their families were here, the whole nation was with them. But these people were among enemies who sent them to prison and put two of their very good friends to death.

I've spoken about Marcelle first because she was a young woman all alone in a prison of Arab women, surrounded by women guilty of all types of offenses—among them, women assigned to spy on her. It was a privilege to meet her and the men who were prisoners with her; it is a privilege to call them friends. Some married and I attended their weddings. I spoke with these young people who had lived under the most impossible conditions, never knowing whether those who had put them in prison would ever release them, yet still believing in us, never believing for a moment that we had forgotten them. I thought of the Jews throughout Jewish history who faced discrimination, torture, danger, broken in body but never in spirit. I thought of the six million Jews during World War II in Nazi camps, buried alive, tortured, gassed. I thought of the Jews in the Warsaw Ghetto who fought the Nazi tanks.

I listened to Marcelle relate her experiences during the 1967 Six-Day War in the Egyptian prison. She had an illegal transistor radio on which she listened to the news; before going to sleep she would turn on the last broadcast of the Israeli radio to hear "Hatikvah."

I give thanks for Jews like these whose acts throughout the tragic history of the Jewish people made it possible for us today to be an independent Jewish state in our own land.

I must say I've gone through a lot in my lifetime—fifty-six years of them spent in Israel. I've seen acts of great heroism, and I've stood before the people who performed these acts with a feeling of inferiority. I still have the same feeling, today, when I meet any of the group described in this book.

Not only I, but everyone in Israel felt that these were our children when they came home. These are our sons, our children who were in exile, who were in prison, who suffered because they are Jews, because they are Zionists, and because they wanted to be pioneers in Israel together with our young generation. We felt these are our sons that have come back; it was a personal gratification and a personal celebration for each one of us.

I hope those who read this book will find it as fascinating and as exhilarating as I did. In the world in which we live there are often men and women with power but not always with courage. Here is a group that can serve as an example not only to Jews, but to everyone. If only there were more like them, the world would be a better, happier, more decent place to live in.

—GOLDA MEIR

*Tel Aviv*
*January 1977*

# OPERATION SUSANNAH

# 1

# QUIET FLOWS THE NILE

## Introduction

Tens of thousands of Israelis, sprawling in comfort before their TV sets one Friday evening in March 1975, suddenly jerked upright in their seats as three faces appeared on the screen. One was that of a man with graying hair and youthful, alert eyes; the second man had pitch black hair and bore an earnest, melancholy expression; the third was a tall, attractive woman, her bearing proud and erect.

However, it was not their outward appearances that came as such a bombshell to tens of thousands of Israeli homes; rather, it was when the interviewer introduced them: Victor Levy, Robert Dassa, and Marcelle Ninio (the fourth of their number, Philip Natanson, was unable to take part in the program)—the heroes of the 1954 "Cairo mishap."

For over twenty years "the mishap" had throbbed like a festering wound in the living flesh of the state of Israel. It produced recurrent waves of government crises, ruining the careers of statesmen and senior officers; it caused a split in the ruling Mapai party, and led to David Ben-Gurion's final departure from public life. Some considered "the mishap" to have been the "primal sin" that would continue to haunt the state of Israel until its residual trail of injustices was redressed.

Thick tomes have been written about it, in addition to hundreds of newspaper articles; nevertheless, it has remained shrouded in mystery. The writers employed terms such as "the unfortunate mishap," and referred to its participants by code names such as "the third man," "the reserve officer," or "the man." Strict censorship prevented Israeli papers from publishing anything more precise, or even from quoting matters which foreign journals had already made public. The average Israeli possessed no more than a hazy notion that in the year 1954, an Israeli underground cell had been operating in Egypt, carrying out certain actions for which no Israeli body was prepared to accept responsibility, and as a result of which the cell was uncovered, its members arrested and forced to undergo a show trial in Cairo. The final outcome of "the mishap" was tragic: two persons, Yosef (Armand) Karmona and Max (Meir) Binnet (the latter reluctantly acknowledged by Israeli intelligence to have been its emissary to Cairo), committed suicide in the course of their brutal interrogation by the Egyptian police; two more, Dr. Moshe (Mussa) Marzouk of Cairo and Shmuel (Sammy) Azar of Alexandria, were sentenced to death and hanged in a Cairo prison. Israel glorified them as martyrs, their memory was sanctified, neighborhoods and gardens were named after them, as were dozens of children born in the course of 1955. At the same time, it was never publicly conceded that they had died in the service of Israel.

The other six heroes of "the mishap" endured a fate which brought them less prominence: They were sentenced to imprisonment. Two of them, Meir Meyuhas and Meir Za'afran, were released in 1962, after having served seven-year jail sentences. Shrouded in secrecy, they reached Israel where their arrival was not made public and journalists were not allowed to interview them. Sworn to silence, the two men reconstructed their lives to the best of their ability, far from the spotlights of publicity.

That left four: Marcelle Ninio and Robert Dassa, each sentenced to fifteen years' imprisonment; and Victor Levy and Philip Natanson, sentenced for life. Marcelle was on her own, in an Egyptian women's prison, alone among women sentenced for prostitution or murder; while the men—all together in Tura, the prison for men sentenced to hard labor—counted the days which mounted to fourteen long years of alternating hope and despair, as they contended with nauseating conditions and observed the ups and downs of the Egyptian regime. In Israel, "the mishap" periodically flared up, and then died down again. Pinhas Lavon, who held the office of Defense Minister at the time of "the mishap" and was dismissed as a consequence of its failure, fought to clear himself of the blame; he was found innocent—whereupon Ben-Gurion resigned. The whole country was in an uproar. But the four persons who were paying the price with the best years of their lives slipped into oblivion.

Finally, more than fourteen years after their arrest, all four were set free. But they were not yet liberated from the restrictions of anonymity. They reached Israel in secret, in keeping with the Israeli government's promise to Egypt's president Gamal Abdel Nasser that it would refrain from publicizing the matter. The cognoscente were aware of their arrival, some even attended festivities in their honor, but the press was strictly forbidden to mention them; they were nonpersons. Or, at least, so they were before their Friday night TV appearance in March 1975.

For the first time, these unknown individuals—hitherto names without faces—appeared as flesh-and-blood human beings. As tens of thousands of Israelis gazed at their TV screens, they saw two men and a woman who, in addition to their imprisonment, had endured the terrors of enforced silence and anonymity subsequent to their release. After acting and suffering in the conviction that they were emissaries of the state of Israel—a conviction which remained unshaken, in spite of the dreadful price they were forced to pay—they now had some painful and searching questions to pose:

"Why were we sent on a mission, without any prepared escape route?

"Why were we forgotten after falling into captivity?

"Why was our imprisonment not even mentioned in 1956, when Israel held five thousand Egyptian prisoners of war captured in the Sinai campaign?

"Why have we been gagged since our return to Israel?"

Their questions remained unanswered. However, the mere fact of being permitted to pose in public, and of having emerged from their anonymity, seemed to give the foursome a renewed lease on life.

That sensational TV program became the principal topic of conversation among Israelis. It also had a direct impact upon its participants' lives. They received phone calls from friends they had known in their youth in Egypt, and whom they had hitherto evaded, so as to avoid questions and explanations: "We didn't know you were in Israel!"

Victor had a touching experience. "One day, after the broadcast, I was accosted in the street by a man I had never seen before—a Tunisian immigrant. He told me that, in February 1955, his wife gave birth to twins, whom he named Moshe and Shmuel, after Moshe Marzouk and Shmuel Azar, who had been executed a few days previously in Egypt. The twins were now grown men: Shmuel was an officer in the Golani Brigade and Moshe was serving in the navy. On his return home from the 1973 Yom Kippur War, Moshe said: 'Father, I have avenged the blood of Moshe Marzouk, after whom I was named.' "

However, it was Robbie who had the most shocking experience after the telecast: "People asked me: 'After all that, why do you still live in Israel?' "

Perhaps that question supplied the true motive for writing this book—which will relate the details of "the mishap," depict its heroes, explain why they undertook a mission which brought some of them to the scaffold and others to prison cells, and why they still live in Israel and regard the country as their home.

## A Community with Shallow Roots

The foursome—like all the other heroes of "the mishap"—were born and brought up in Egypt, but they never regarded themselves— nor were they ever regarded by others—as Egyptians. They attended Jewish schools, their contacts with the local population were limited, they did not even hold Egyptian citizenship. Some of them retained the nationality of their parents or grandparents who had come to settle in Egypt; others were stateless.

They were typical members of Egypt's Jewish community, which, at the establishment of the state of Israel, numbered sixty to eighty thousand persons, and which was entirely unlike other Middle Eastern Jewish communities.

It was a community with shallow roots. The Jews reached Egypt during the second half of the nineteenth century or the beginning of the twentieth. Some of them settled in Egypt after stopping over while on their way from Yemen or North Africa to Palestine; others were Ottoman Jews, hailing from all over the Turkish Empire which stretched from the Atlas Mountains to the Balkans. Before and during World War I, Egypt became a haven for Jews leaving Palestine; they "went down" to Egypt to avoid starvation, as their forefathers did in ancient times, or to escape induction into the Turkish army. After the world war, Jewish refugees came from eastern Europe, fleeing from the Communist revolution; unable to go on to America or Palestine, they remained in Egypt.

Like other, larger foreign colonies—Greeks, Italians, and Maltese —the Jews resided in Egypt without striking roots there. Very few of them were allowed Egyptian citizenship.

In a mixture of envy and irony, the Egyptians referred to the foreigners as *hawagat* (gentlemen). The *hawagat* lived in their own quarters—in Cairo, Alexandria, and the three Suez Canal cities; they attended their own schools, cultivated their own national folklore, and spoke their own languages, in addition to French, which was "the language of culture," and English, the language of government.

The Jews did not differ from the other foreigners. Many of them were Egyptian-born, like their fathers and grandfathers, and yet they could not read or write Arabic, and spoke no more of the language than was necessary for the simplest daily needs—purchases in the market, vending in their stores, or giving instructions to their Egyptian servants. Nor did they require any more: they attended Jewish schools, maintained by the Jewish community, where the language of instruction was French; when they fell ill, they were attended by a Jewish doctor or admitted to a Jewish hospital, likewise run by the community; they conducted business with Jews or other foreigners; they engaged in sport in Jewish sports clubs such as Maccabi or Hakoach, and whiled away their spare time in exclusive clubs whose Egyptian members constituted an insignificant minority. There was no problem of assimilation in Egypt; in addition to the social and religious obstacles, there was no inducement for the Jews to assimilate.

Their attitude toward Palestine and the Zionist movement was largely influenced by the significant proportion of Palestinian Jews in the community, as well as by the tolerance—perhaps even indifference —which the Egyptians displayed, between the two world wars, toward the *hawagat* and their social activities.

All of Egypt's Jews could have been considered Zionists—or, to be more precise, "lovers of Zion." Some collected money for the Jewish National Fund, others learned Hebrew; they bought Palestinian sacramental wine, some of them went to Palestine on visits, and there were even those who invested money there, buying property for building or an orange grove. To a large extent, this was bon ton Zionism; it was a matter of distinction to adhere to a Zionist organization, to be invited to a reception in honor of a Palestinian football team, or the Tel Aviv Philharmonic Orchestra, or the Maccabi's basketball team of Cairo, the champions of Egypt. In the same way, it was fashionable to visit Jerusalem or attend a Zionist congress. However, this was what Zionist activity amounted to prior to World War II, in those countries where emigration to Palestine was not, first and foremost, a quest for a safe haven.

Thus it remained until 1948, or, 'to be more precise, until the Middle East began to seethe like a volcano, as the United Nations prepared to decide on the future of Palestine.

When fanatical Moslem Brotherhood agitators began to call for a "holy war" for Palestine, and their own neighbors' smiling faces suddenly revealed their anti-Jewish fangs, the Jews of Egypt sensed the oppressive burden of fate, that most prominent characteristic of the Jewish people.

However, the great event was the establishment of the Jewish state, even though it was followed by difficult times for the Jews of Egypt. When the Egyptian army invaded Palestine in 1948, the police swooped down on the Jewish communities in Cairo and Alexandria, arresting hundreds of persons "suspected of Zionist activity," after keeping them under close watch for years. There were even a number of attempts to foment pogroms in Cairo's Jewish quarter. All the same, a spark of excitement flashed through the entire Jewish community: "We have a state, we have a place to go!" was the general feeling. From a vague ideology, Zionism had suddenly become a reality.

After the war, no sooner did the detention camps open their gates to disgorge their inmates than a stream of Egyptian Jews began to head for Israel. Within two years, by the middle of 1950, half of Egypt's Jewish community had departed.

This mass migration was organized and regulated by emissaries of the *Mossad l'Aliya* (Institute for Immigration); wherever Jews dreamed of reaching Zion, the mystery-shrouded Mossad's agents appeared— like the legendary Pied Piper—to lead them to the Promised Land.

The emissaries from Israel were assisted by two Egyptian Jews: Dr. Victor Sa'adiya, a recently qualified young doctor who headed the Egyptian branch of the Bnei Akiva youth movement; and, in Alexandria, Ovadia Danun, manager of a travel agency which served as a cover for Mossad activities and arranged for the emigrants to reach one of the ports of southern Europe.

As for the "field work"—organizing clandestine Hebrew courses, conducting propaganda for emigration to Israel, and training the prospective emigrants—this was done by the illegal Zionist youth movements, which encompassed a majority of Egypt's young Jews, even though membership in any of them carried the risk of imprisonment.

## Six out of Sixty Thousand

This, then, was the background of "the mishap" and of its heroes. "The mishap" actually embraced two separate plots, which unfolded independently in Cairo and Alexandria, intertwined before the military tribunal and on the steps of the scaffold, and divided again as the participants went their separate ways to various prisons.

Marcelle Ninio was born in Cairo in 1929. Her father had fled his native Bulgaria on the eve of World War I to evade conscription; he married an Egyptian woman who bore him two sons. Marcelle was the progeny of his second marriage, after the death of his first wife. He was employed by a French water construction company; among his other undertakings he supervised installation of the water-network in Jerusalem's King David Hotel, where he lived for a year. He considered settling in Palestine, and began down payments on a building lot in Jerusalem. However, failing to find any other employment in Palestine when work on the hotel ended, he returned to Cairo, and stopped his payments for the lot.

Marcelle relates: "I remember him as a pleasant man, full of interest and involvement in his children. He conducted our home in accordance with Jewish tradition; on Friday evening, after he made the Kiddush over the wine, we would stand before him to receive his blessing and respectfully kiss his hand. He died in 1939, when I was ten. My eldest brother was already married, and the second also left home. I was left alone with Mother."

Even during her father's lifetime, their home was not a wealthy one; there was a continual struggle to "get to the end of the month." Now, hard times arrived; her mother was obliged to go out to work.

"She was only forty when Father died," continues Marcelle. "She could have remarried and built up a new life for herself, but refrained from doing so—for my sake: She did not want me to grow up as a stepdaughter. As long as her health permitted, she worked hard to keep me and give me an education. She sacrificed her life for me, and I felt very attached to her."

Mother and daughter moved house frequently: From the roomy apartment in Heliopolis, which they occupied while her father was alive, they moved to a one-room flat after his death. From there they went on to another apartment, close to her elder brother's home; finally, they returned to Heliopolis when a friend of the family moved to Port Said and placed his previous apartment at their disposal without demanding "key money." Marcelle's mother rented out furnished rooms, and their financial situation improved slightly.

These moves forced Marcelle to change schools. At first, she attended the Jewish Abraham Battash school in Heliopolis, and then, successively, a Catholic nuns' school, the British missionary school, and the St. Claire college. She became fluent in English, as well as French, and when she was old enough, she took a summer vacation job, working at the American army Pine Field camp as an apprentice clerk, and then, at a British army base.

Despite her cosmopolitan education, all of Marcelle's friends were Jews; through them, she joined the Hashomer Hatzair youth movement. After a while, her mother's health began to deteriorate. The doctors diagnosed it as a heart ailment (in fact, she was suffering from cancer). With her mother needing her help more and more, Marcelle could no longer attend movement activities nor even dream of going to summer camp in Alexandria. On completing her schooling, she had to find a job, to help her mother.

For some time, her life focused around her work and caring for her mother. But Marcelle was too active to remain content with this for any length of time. In 1947, she joined the Hakoach basketball team of Heliopolis, whose games took her all over Egypt.

In 1948, she was shaken out of her normal routine. War had broken out in Palestine, and there were numerous arrests in Egypt. Many of Marcelle's friends were among the detainees; when they were finally released, it was on condition that they leave the country. There were attempts to attack Cairo's Jewish quarter. Synagogues were set ablaze. Naturally, all this caused some upset, but her most humiliating personal experience was the official ban on the activities of the Hakoach club, while the Heliopolis swimming pool was closed to Jews, with a sign over the entrance proclaiming: "Jews are not desirable."

"All this," relates Marcelle, "came on top of the hatred evident all around, with louts in the street calling after me: *'Ya Sayonia!'* ('Oh Zionist!'). Suddenly, I realized that I did not belong to Egypt, nor did Egypt belong to me . . ."

She rejoined Hashomer Hatzair and even registered for Hebrew classes. "True, without any clear intention of emigrating to Israel—my dreams centered about America—but everyone around me was talking of Israel, and I too was drawn in . . ."

By the beginning of 1951, she was certain that her future lay in Israel. The young man she regarded as her fiancé was a fervent Zionist, and active in the illegal emigration movement; she joined him in his activities. However, when he informed her that with his name on the police's black list he had to leave Egypt immediately and proposed that she join him, she did not for one moment consider the suggestion. Her mother's ailment was worsening. The doctors now suspected the presence of a cancerous ulcer and were considering an operation. The idea of leaving her or of taking her to a strange country was unthinkable.

"We agreed that he should depart immediately, and I would follow him when my mother recovered."

However, her mother's illness dragged on and on. The mother was now too weak to run the household; the lodgers moved out. Marcelle was now the sole breadwinner; she had a well-paid job as secretary to the director of a large British import agency. Marcelle's friends "disappeared" one after another, departing for Israel.

It is easy to imagine Marcelle as she was then: a tall, attractive girl, vivacious and active, and, with that, displaying a highly developed sense of responsibility and duty. "Not for one moment did I rebel against the fate which bound me to an invalid mother. She gave everything she had for my sake; it was only fair that I should repay her to the best of my ability."

Once again Marcelle found an outlet in sports. She played tennis and basketball at the Heliopolis sports club; the swimming pool had also readmitted its Jewish members, after apologizing for the "regrettable unpleasantness." A few of her friends still remained; there were occasional outings to theaters or concerts. Once again her life entered some kind of routine.

And then, one day early in May 1951, Marcelle received a visit from one of her friends, Ninette Pichotto. Ninette was something of a heroine in the small circle to which Marcelle adhered. Two years previously, in 1949, she was arrested (on the unfounded suspicion of being a Communist); a search in her home turned up some "illegal literature"—booklets on socialism which she had used while acting as an instructor in Hashomer Hatzair. This "offense" had gained her a two-month prison sentence.

In the course of the visit, when Marcelle's mother left the room for a moment, Ninette whispered to her friend: "Help is needed. Can you be counted upon?"

"I was sure," Marcelle relates, "that she meant help in organizing emigration, or in Hashomer Hatzair, and I replied in the affirmative."

Cairo was also the birthplace of Dr. Moshe Marzouk, a member of the Kara'ite sect. The Cairo Kara'ites regarded themselves as Jews, and so did the Jewish community as a whole. *Harat el Kara* (the Kara'ite quarter) bordered on the Jewish section in the heart of Cairo's Old City and was a part of it.

Like the rest of the Jewish community, the Kara'ites also dreamed of Israel, and took part in all Zionist activity, whether legal or illegal, even though, in many ways, they sensed themselves less alien in Egypt. They mixed more with the local population, they made greater use of the general education system, Arabic was usually their mother tongue, and they even bore Arabic names. Like the Jews, they too engaged primarily in commerce and crafts; financially, their situation was better than average. They dominated the gold trade—the royal goldsmith was a Kara'ite. Unlike the Jews, many of the wealthy Kara'ites acquired lands and estates in the country, which, like the rest of the effendi class, they cultivated by means of serflike sharecroppers. The Marzouk family also owned a farm in the Nile Delta; it was burned down in 1948, in vengeance for the death of one of the young local villagers during the war in Palestine. For Moshe, this was the handwriting on the wall, a warning that neither Jews nor Kara'ites had a future in Egypt. Not that he needed such a warning; by this time, he was a fervent Zionist.

The Marzouk family came to Egypt from Tunis at the beginning of the century; they still retained their French nationality. They were a wealthy and highly educated family. Leito Marzouk, Moshe's father, owned a pharmacy in the center of Cairo; his mother, one of the first women in Egypt to graduate from a secondary school, was employed as an English teacher. All of Moshe's uncles—Leito's brothers—possessed academic qualifications and were employed by the government as engineers.

Moshe chose medicine. He was a handsome youngster, quiet and introverted; he took great care of his outward appearance, but he was no dandy. His friend Dr. Victor Sa'adiya—Moshe's classmate at the Jewish secondary school, and, later, fellow student at the Kasser el Eini hospital medical school—relates: "He had a sense of style, a kind of chivalry which was very uncharacteristic for an Easterner. He was the incarnation of a gentleman."

Moshe was characterized by his extreme modesty, and the absence of any desire for exhibitionism. In 1948, on receipt of confidential reports warning that the Moslem Brotherhood intended to organize pogroms against the Jews of Cairo, the city's Jewish quarter organized itself for self-defense. Moshe Marzouk was appointed commander, but Victor Sa'adiya—by now his best friend—only learned of this years later. It was not a matter of preserving secrecy; "he was simply incapable of bringing himself to talk about the highly responsible task which had been imposed on him. He was probably afraid of appearing boastful."

Victor Sa'adiya remembers him as being very orderly in everything he did. "His books and notebooks were models of perfection: straight lines, small neat handwriting, without erasures, without notes in the margins. Tidy, everything in its place.

"He had a profound sense of justice, and his personal honesty knew no bounds. When there was something in a lecture which he failed to understand, he stood up and said so. In examinations, when he did not know the material, he wrote nothing. He never tried to 'pull a fast one.'"

When the two boys first made each other's acquaintance, at the Jewish secondary school, Moshe was already a Zionist, and a member of the Dror movement. Under Victor Sa'adiya's influence, he switched to Bnei Akiva.

Nineteen forty-eight was a difficult year for the inhabitants of Cairo's *Harat al Yahud* (the Jewish quarter). As though the extensive arrests were not sufficient, on June 20, there was an explosion in the quarter's Kara'ite section; two houses collapsed, thirty-four persons were killed and sixty injured.

A short time later, there was another explosion, this time, in the scholarly Jews' section of the quarter. Again, dozens of persons were killed.

The Egyptian press ascribed these explosions to an "internal conflict" between Jews and Kara'ites. Heads of the Jewish community denied the report, but the censor prevented publication of their denial. Nevertheless, this attempt to sow dissension between the two communities failed. "We all knew," reports Victor Sa'adiya, "that behind the explosions stood the Moslem Brotherhood, and perhaps, the regime itself . . ."

When life began to return to normal, after the Palestine war terminated in the Rhodes armistice agreements, Victor and Moshe went back to the Kasser el Eini medical school. Victor was soon totally immersed in organizing the emigration of Jews headed for Israel. Moshe too dreamed of emigrating to Israel at the conclusion of his studies.

In 1950, Victor and Moshe graduated. The latter was taken on as an intern at Cairo's Jewish hospital. He gradually made a name for himself as a doctor, and, above all, as an anesthetist with a great future ahead of him. In 1951, he was invited to Japan for further studies, and began to prepare for his departure. He was undecided whether to return to Egypt at the termination of his course or to go to Israel directly from Japan.

It was at this point that Victor Sa'adiya approached him with the tidings that an emissary had arrived from Israel in quest of volunteers for "a special task."

"If it's a movement matter," said Moshe, "do me a favor and pass me over. I'm busy . . ."

However, he changed his mind when he heard that the task was in the service of the state of Israel. He immediately consented to meet the emissary.


In summer, when easterly winds turn Cairo into a furnace and drive its inhabitants from the streets, the air in Alexandria becomes extremely moist, but its sweating inhabitants do not cease their clamorous activity. Unlike Cairo, the oasis-turned-metropolis, Alexandria is a "European bridgehead" in Africa. Alexandria is an ancient city, although nothing remains of its former splendor except for a few old ruins (including the Pillar of Pompeius, and remnants of the Pharos lighthouse, one of the seven wonders of the ancient world). Rebuilt at the beginning of the nineteenth century, the city was laid out on the European pattern, with broad, straight thoroughfares, tall French-style buildings, and a wide avenue along the beach, the Corniche. The city built a large harbor and a cotton exchange; in consequence, Alexandria attracted many of the foreigners who took up residence in Egypt. In its streets, one could hear French, Italian, and Greek, no less than Arabic; its ladies displayed European clothes, as much as those baggy dresses trailing to the ground, which are the traditional costume of Egyptian women. Alexandria exhibited a cosmopolitan energy which overshadowed the slow tempo of the East.

Alexandria was the birthplace of the other heroes of "the mishap" —Shmuel Azar, Victor Levy, Robert Dassa, and Philip Natanson. Their formative adolescent years coincided with World War II, when the city overflowed with tens of thousands of Allied soldiers. The front line was at El 'Alamein, only 90 miles to the west, and German and Italian bombers raided the port nightly.

"The neighbors," Victor Levy remembers, "would say, pityingly: 'Well, the Germans are coming—what will you do?' Indeed, there was concern at home. Father sent Mother to Grandmother in Cairo, along with my three sisters and my younger brother; only he and I remained behind. At that time, he was thinking of withdrawing to Palestine if the Germans continued to advance . . . ."

The fortunes of war changed, and the front receded; Victor's father forgot his worries. But in Victor's mind, Palestine remained a haven for Jews such as himself, for whom the possible arrival of the Germans was a source of particular concern. At the age of eleven, Victor joined Hehalutz Hatzair.

Born in October 1932, Victor belonged to a prosperous family. His Greek-born father was the director of a chemical import firm; his mother was born in Egypt, but she came from a family of rabbis stemming from Jaffa. Their home was a roomy apartment in the Ramleh-Cleopatra quarter, inhabited mainly by Greeks, Italians, and Maltese. Theirs was a traditional Jewish home; Victor attended the Jewish secondary school, with its French teachers. At home, too, they spoke French, only learning Arabic as a duty, for they had no contact with Egyptian children. Hebrew served only for prayer. However, in 1945, Victor was already determined to emigrate to Palestine.

Victor made the acquaintance of Philip Natanson at school. Two months younger than Victor, Philip was a totally different character. He was tall and slim, with a bold look and overhanging forelock, and a weakness for pranks. His father was a Viennese dentist who had settled in Alexandria in 1920 and married there. The family belonged to Alexandria's wealthy class; they lived in the prestigious Stanley Bey quarter, in their own two-story house surrounded by a garden.

For two years, Philip attended a Catholic school—his father favoring the stern discipline imposed by the monks—but to balance out the school's influence, his parents also sent him to the Jewish scout movement. Unlike the Zionist youth movements, the scouts openly wore their movement uniform, but they did not preach Zionism. However, when Philip returned to the Jewish school and became close friends with his classmate Victor, the latter persuaded him to join Hehalutz; Philip carefully kept the matter from his parents.

Robert Dassa, the youngest member of the group, came from an entirely different background. He was the third of five children; his father was born in Egypt, to parents who settled there while on their way from Yemen to Palestine; his Jerusalem-born mother came to Egypt with her family during World War I. Robert's father was a small shopkeeper; his store, like the family's home, was in the lower city, where the Egyptians lived. Robert, a handsome introvert with large, melancholy eyes, was the only member of the group to have grown up among Egyptian children, consequently speaking fluent Egyptian Arabic.

Robert became a Zionist by way of his school—a religious establishment founded by the Chief Rabbi of Alexandria, Dr. Ventura—where the Bnei Akiva movement was active. He received no encouragement from his parents; his father laughed at the *Sayoni* (Zionist) and forbade him to take part in the movement's Saturday outings to Muhram Bey, an area of fields and sports grounds on the outskirts of the city. However, the boy displayed a quiet self-control and an inner fortitude which enabled him to withstand his father's mockery and to become the leader of his group in Bnei Akiva; later, he served as an instructor in the movement.

The three boys—active, though not yet prominent members of their movement—were sixteen years old at the outbreak of the Israeli War of Independence in 1948. Alexandria's Zionist organizations had long been under the supervision of the police's alien section, which was headed by Mamduh Salem (later appointed premier of Egypt after the 1973 war). This supervision was not overstrict: the Egyptian authorities were tolerant toward the *hawagat* with their national and ethnic organizations and scouting movements. However, after the United Nations partition resolution on Palestine aroused turmoil throughout the Middle East, the police established a closer watch. Robert recalls once being accosted by a police officer who was a friend of his father; the officer warned him not to go to Atrin, where Bnei Akiva activities were held. "There will be arrests . . ."

Indeed, there were arrests. On May 15, 1948, Mamduh Salem's agents swooped down on the city, arresting dozens of Zionist activists, including all the youth movements' instructors.

After their release, most of the detainees left Egypt; in fact, they were only released on condition that they leave the country. Taken directly from the camp to the port, where relatives brought them their luggage, they were placed on board a waiting ship. Members of Alexandria's Hehalutz movement got together while under detention and formed a group which, on arrival in Israel, established Kibbutz Yir'on. Victor was determined to join them when the time came. For the time being, these plans were vetoed by his parents, who did not even permit him to take a trip abroad (he was seventeen at the time). But when he announced his intention of studying agriculture, they could not object, even though they knew that he planned to acquire the profession to eventually serve him in Israel. He registered at Alexandria University's agronomy department.

Philip found himself a job as a clerk at the cotton exchange, but most of his energies were channeled into his activity in the Dror youth movement, which had become a target for Communist activists seeking to infiltrate it with the aim of taking it over from within. Philip played a leading role in the shadow war which now began, both in detecting the infiltrators and in neutralizing their influence.

Robert Dassa found a job with a Jewish import-export company. By virtue of his knowledge of Arabic, he was put in charge of the company's correspondence in that language. In the evenings, he studied radio and electrical engineering under a Jewish engineer who had assembled a group of pupils—some amateurs, others in quest of a profession.

The fourth member of the "Alexandria group," Shmuel Azar, did not really belong to their circle; he was four years older than the others. When the group was formed, he naturally emerged as its leader.

Shmuel was a gifted student. His impoverished family lived in the lower city, in a quarter largely inhabited by Egyptians. However, Shmuel's thirst for study, together with his exceptional gifts in various spheres, soon made him one of the leading figures among the city's Jewish youth.

For two years he attended his neighborhood synagogue's *heder* (religious primary school). Then he went on to the Jewish community's "high school," which he attended for free as a scholarship pupil. This was one of the attractive aspects of Egypt's Jewish community: Poverty was no obstacle to a gifted student, and class differences were not noticeable among the school's pupils.

From his early youth, Shmuel was torn between two loves: mathematics and art. But he did not neglect either sphere in favor of the other. He was a talented painter and sculptor, while he was unrivaled in mathematics—in his class, in the school, and, finally, in the whole city. Later, when his excellent grades earned him a scholarship to the French secondary school, he developed a third love—for Jewish studies. He attended an evening class conducted by Rabbi Ventura, where he studied Talmud and Mishna.

His family's poverty was a handicap for him; he could not even afford to buy calipers for geometry lessons. All the same, using a pencil attached to a cord, he drew circles as perfect as those made with the help of a compass, and his diagrams were hung up in the classroom as model assignments.

Shmuel's exceptional brilliance in his studies, and the affection the teachers displayed toward him, did not arouse the envy of his classmates, as sometimes happens in such cases. He was modest and withdrawn, and so kind and helpful that everyone liked him.

When he was thirteen, he discovered his greatest love of all— Zionism. He joined the Hehalutz Hatzair youth movement.

The movement and its clubhouse became the focal points of Shmuel's life. He never missed a single meeting; the clubhouse walls were covered with his drawings and graphics. When only fifteen, he was put in charge of building stage sets for movement festivities. In 1946, he gained his reward: He was selected to join a group of movement activists who were being sent for a two-month training course in *kibbutzim* in Palestine. He returned more enthusiastic than ever, fortified in his determination to build his future in Palestine.

In the meantime, he remained the most active member of Hehalutz Hatzair in Alexandria; contending with his poverty by giving private lessons to classmates, he was still his school's star pupil. That year, he completed his matriculation examinations, his grades gaining him the fifth place among the 3,500 pupils who sat for the examination all over Egypt.

He signed on at Alexandria University's engineering faculty "so that I can serve in the Israeli army as a radar engineer," as he explained to his friends. Once again, his achievements were astounding. Not content with his successes, he extended his interests to psychology, medicine, and economics. His painting was also improving, while he lost none of his enthusiasm for movement activities.

In 1947, as the struggle over Palestine's political future became progressively fiercer, young Jews in Egypt found their routine existence disrupted. This was particularly true of those who came into contact with young Egyptians, as in the universities, where the Moslem Brotherhood was busy recruiting volunteers for the "holy war" in Palestine, while simultaneously conducting a hate campaign against the Jews. In Alexandria, with its mixed population and its strong European influences, the Brotherhood did not possess a strong following—unlike Cairo. However, as the fighting in Palestine escalated, and tempers in Egypt rose, none of the students dared to oppose the Moslem Brotherhood when it began to harass Jewish students. Several Jews were beaten up; later, the Brotherhood sponsored a resolution calling for a boycott against the Jewish students, who were henceforth prevented from entering the lecture halls. Most of the Jewish students gave up and broke off their studies. However, Shmuel, with his quiet courage and his obstinate persistence, refused to give in. He continued his studies at home, without attending lectures or using the university laboratories, entering the university only when he came to sit for examinations. In the latter, however, he again proved himself to be an exceptional student, outshining all his classmates. "That's because I study on my own," he explained modestly, almost apologetically. "Not attending the lectures, it seems that I do not correctly gauge the progress of the class, and I study too much . . ."

The boycott against the Jewish engineering students remained in force for a whole year. Later, it was gradually toned down; when Shmuel sat for his final examinations, in the summer of 1952, he gained the highest grades ever awarded in Egypt to an engineering student.

It was still his dream to emigrate to Israel. The bitter experiences he had undergone during his studies only strengthened his conviction that there was no place for him in Egypt. It was his intention to serve in the Israeli army as an engineer, and, subsequently, to join a *kibbutz*.

However, these plans had to wait. For the past year he had been active in the service of the state of Israel. Early in the summer of 1951, he was introduced to an Israeli emissary, who had asked him to put off his departure for two years, which he was to devote to the establishment of an underground cell in Alexandria.

As was his way, Shmuel replied: "I will do and obey . . ."

### The Emissary from Israel

One morning, late in April 1951, a tall young man with dark hair and a swarthy complexion disembarked at the Cairo airport. His English was perfect. The Egyptian policeman in red tarboosh and faded uniform, who gave a cursory glance at the traveler's British passport, noted that his name was John Darling and that his place of birth was Gibraltar, which explained the man's Mediterranean appearance, contrasting so strangely with his English-sounding name. The passport bore a three-month tourist visa, issued by the Egyptian consulate in London. If challenged, John Darling would have been able to produce documents proving that he was a traveling salesman for a British electrical equipment concern, coming to Egypt to seek markets for its products. However, there was no need; the policeman stamped his passport and, with a languorous gesture, showed him the exit. When the traveler emerged from the terminal building, he was overwhelmed by the burning heat and by a mob of taxi drivers who fought one another furiously for the privilege of driving him into town.

In reality, the new arrival was not born in Gibraltar; the electrical goods agency was no more than camouflage; and his name was not John Darling but Avraham Dar—born in Jerusalem and an agent of Israeli intelligence. The only correct entry in his passport was that referring to his British citizenship; he had indeed inherited British nationality from his Aden-born father.

Avraham Dar had come to Egypt—two years after the conclusion of an uneasy armistice which had ended that country's war with Israel —with the aim of setting up an espionage network. Or, more accurately, not an espionage network, but rather something whose precise nature was not clear, either to Dar or to those who had sent him.

Right up to May 14, 1948, the day the Egyptian expeditionary force invaded the newly born state of Israel, the two countries maintained close, neighborly ties. There was extensive trade between them, wealthy Egyptians came to the hills of Jerusalem for their summer vacations, or, more frequently, for treatment by German Jewish doctors, while tourists from Palestine went to Egypt for the winter. The two countries were linked by a daily train in each direction. For a fare of two Palestine pounds (third class) or six pounds (first class, with a sleeping berth) one could mount the train at Lydda or Rehovot in the evening and find oneself next morning amid the teeming tumult of Cairo's central station. One day after their publication, Egyptian newspapers in French or English were on sale in Tel Aviv, while the Arabic papers were made available in Jerusalem or Jaffa.

The war changed all that. Trains and newspapers no longer arrived from Egypt, nor could Arabic-speaking Jews travel to Egypt to find out what was going on there. During the 1948 war, many Egyptian Jews—primarily Zionist activists—were imprisoned in detention camps; on being released, they began to leave Egypt in large numbers, thereby eliminating another source of information. Many Israeli-paid agents disappeared; during the fighting, they severed their links with Israeli intelligence, and contact with them was not renewed. In 1951, with the war at an end and the political intelligence service regaining the hegemony taken during the fighting by military field intelligence, the Israeli intelligence services' Egyptian Section reassessed the situation and discovered that aside from what could be gleaned from the communications media, it knew nothing about developments inside Egypt.

It was decided to send an agent to Egypt to establish a "base." The task was given to a unit formed during the War of Independence to operate behind enemy lines, where it carried out sabotage attacks and spread false rumors to demoralize the enemy. The unit was commanded by Col. Motke Ben-Tzur, a member of Kibbutz Mash'abei Sadeh; until 1948, he had been a Haganah emissary to Iraq, and during the War of Independence, he served as a company commander in the Palmach's Harel Brigade. As was the custom at that time, he chose another former Palmach-nik for the mission to Egypt. This was Avraham Dar, a sailor and farmer, who had been active in organizing illegal immigration; later, he served in the Palmach's Naval Company, and carried out a number of intelligence missions during the final months of the war. Dar was sent to Britain to prepare an appropriate "background" for himself. Early in the summer of 1951, he reached Cairo.

As instructed, Dar contacted an emissary of the Mossad in Cairo, asking for help in recruiting "a group of loyal and dependable youngsters" for the underground cell he planned to establish.

Ovadia Danun found three of the finest young men in Alexandria: Shmuel Azar, Victor Levy, and, later, Meir Meyuhas, the young director of a metal trading company. Victor Sa'adiya recommended Dr. Moshe Marzouk, Meir Za'afran, and Eli Na'im from Cairo (Na'im hailed originally from Tripoli in Libya; he and his father fled to Egypt during the world war), and his star pupil Robbie Dassa from Alexandria.

Dar required an additional person to maintain contacts with Israel and to undertake liaison between the two cells. The person charged with the task would have to remain in Egypt far longer than the others —for years, perhaps.

A number of names were brought up; finally, they hit upon Marcelle Ninio. She was intelligent and reliable; moreover, owing to her mother's illness, she was not likely to leave for Israel in the near future.

Marcelle's friend, Ninette Pichotto, was requested to sound her out.

Years later, Marcelle recalled: "When Ninette went away, my mother questioned me worriedly: 'What did Ninette want from you?' When I gave an evasive answer, she warned me: 'Keep away from her, she's known to the police!'

"I took no notice. A few days later, Ninette introduced me to Dr. Victor Sa'adiya, who told me of the need for a young woman to undertake dangerous missions, but even then I did not take the matter in earnest. Perhaps this was because I took Ninette as an example. She had taken risks and been caught. She 'sat' for two months. That's not so terrible, I told myself; it is bearable. . . .

"The next day, I again met Dr. Sa'adiya. We met at a street corner, near my place of work, during the lunch break. He arrived accompanied by a short man whom he introduced as 'Martin.' The only hint I had about him indicated that he was an emissary from Israel.

" 'Martin' also spoke of the need for a woman to help in delivering packages, and mentioned the danger involved. 'You are liable to go to prison,' he warned me. But danger is a very abstract concept when one does not face it. I replied that I had thought it over and that I was ready.

"He said: 'Fine!,' noted my phone number at work, and added: 'We'll contact you!'

"A few days later, Sa'adiya contacted me and arranged a rendez-vous in the street again, near the Heliopolis bus stop, but this time it was arranged for the evening, after work. Again, he came to the rendez-vous accompanied by another man.

" 'This is my friend, John Darling,' he said, and immediately disappeared."

To this day, Marcelle has vivid memories of the impression John Darling made on her at that first meeting: tall and elegant in a sports blazer, articulate and very self-confident.

They went to have dinner at the Al Hatti, one of the most prestigious restaurants in Cairo, with crystal chandeliers, gigantic mirrors lining the walls, and a carpeted floor over which tall, white-clad Sudanese waiters glided silently. An orchestra entertained the guests with Oriental melodies. One did not just go to Al Hatti to dine; it was an entire evening's entertainment.

During the course of the evening, John Darling plied her with questions—about her work, her family, her habits. He was blessed with the ability to get people to talk. Marcelle found herself speaking freely, flattered that such a man—without being told outright, she was given to understand that he was an important emissary from Israel—should take such an interest in her.

John Darling did not say much about his mission at that first meeting; he told her only that he wished to establish a cell and needed a woman to maintain contacts. She consented eagerly, and agreed to adopt the roundabout ruse he proposed as a way of legalizing their acquaintance: He would insert an advertisement into the *Egyptian Gazette*—Cairo's English-language daily—seeking a part-time secretary to work between 1:00 and 4:00 in the afternoon, which coincided with the midday break at the office where Marcelle was employed.

A few days later, the advertisement appeared; Marcelle replied, applying for the job, and received a letter inviting her for an interview at Darling's apartment, in a multistory building on Ahmed al-Din Street, not far from the offices of the *Al Ahram* newspaper. Later, he told her that he received about twenty replies to the advertisement, several of the applicants displaying great eagerness to get the post.

Officially, Marcelle's job was to deal with his correspondence. He had already made contact with a number of electrical equipment importers, who showed an interest in the goods he offered. Their letters had to be answered—on a used typewriter Darling had rented for a monthly fee of one Egyptian pound—and filed away. There was not much work to be done; during the rest of the time, they talked—about "the mission," about Israel, and, principally, about Avraham Dar himself. He told her about his farm in Kfar Yehoshua, about his service in the Palmach, and again of his farm and his love for agriculture.

She knew little of his activities during the rest of the week. She was aware that he had begun recruiting people for the cell, but she knew nothing of their identities until the day she came to his apartment and found Dr. Moshe Marzouk there. She knew Marzouk as one of the doctors who had treated her mother at the Jewish hospital. Both Marcelle and Marzouk were embarrassed by the meeting; the only person who showed no discomfort was Avraham Dar (as she now knew him by his true name). Carelessly, he said: "Oh, you know one another? Good, then I don't have to introduce you."

The cell began to get organized. Eli Na'im rented an apartment to serve as a meeting place, and Meir Za'afran, an architect by profession, designed a concealed closet, which was constructed by another one of Victor Sa'adiya's "recruits," a carpenter by the name of Yitzchak Levy, who was shortly to emigrate to Israel, and was accordingly considered to be "dependable."

Dar began to teach Marcelle how to decipher codes and how to process invisible ink. After he left Egypt, he explained, letters from abroad would be addressed to her. Should they contain instructions, it would be up to her to transmit them to their destination. In addition, she would act as the cell's treasurer. Yitzchak Levy constructed a private cache for her, inside the stem of a table lamp, which could be opened by a concealed spring. Here she was to hide the letters she received. However, the lamp did not remain in her possession for long.

"I told Mother that I bought it as a bargain at an auction, but she did not like the lamp, and at the first opportunity, she gave it as a present to my nephew. And, of course, I could not ask for the return of the present without arousing suspicion."

It was in May that Marcelle first learned of the existence of the cell in Alexandria. On arriving at Dar's apartment, as usual, she found a young man whom Dar introduced as Shmuel Azar, the man from Alexandria with whom she would have to maintain contact in the future. During the conversation between Dar and Azar, the name of Suzette Chyprotte came up, and Dar commented: "You will have to keep in contact with her, too. You will receive money through her."

Some time later, early in June, Avraham instructed Marcelle to travel to Alexandria, to meet Shmuel and Suzette, and to make arrangements for future meetings.

After two months with Dar, Marcelle now retained no illusions about the nature of the operation with which she had become involved. She knew she was engaged in a matter which was illegal and perilous and was surprised to find herself totally unafraid. To tell the truth, she was not fully aware of the danger; after all, everything she was doing was so normal and unexceptional.

Today, she cannot help smiling on remembering that she was less concerned about keeping her activities secret from the police than with concealing them from her mother. The mission to Alexandria with which Dar now charged her caused her some difficulty. She recalls:

"It should be understood that in Egypt at that time a respectable girl did not travel alone to another city. True, this was not my first trip to Alexandria, but all my previous journeys had been undertaken with the Heliopolis basketball team, under the supervision of its manager and its trainer; we always stayed at the Swiss Hostel, a very respectable girls' boardinghouse whose manageress was very strict and treated her guests as though they were her own daughters. Men were forbidden to enter the hostel, which was locked punctually at midnight. On one occasion, I stayed late at the home of some friends and arrived after the doors had been locked. All my knocking was to no avail; I was obliged to return to my friends' house; the following morning, I was subjected to a very rigorous cross-examination by the hostel manageress. Still, the place was spotlessly clean, the food was good, and the price relatively moderate. Above all, it was only when she was certain that I would stay at the Swiss Hostel that my mother consented to my trips to Alexandria."

However, this time, she could not make use of the hostel. Avraham Dar insisted that she must not live at a place where she was known. He and Suzette waited for Marcelle at the Alexandria railway station; from there, they drove her to a hotel.

"It was the first time in my life that I stayed at a hotel—and what a hotel! It was in the center of Alexandria's entertainment section, opposite the Atheneus nightclub. If my mother had known she would have died of shame!"

Marcelle herself considered her behavior outrageous and frightfully daring. "I locked the door of my room, I even jammed a chair against it, and all the same, I couldn't get to sleep that night."

The cell in Alexandria was organized in a manner more or less similar to that adopted in Cairo.

Victor Levy was up to his ears in his university examinations. During the past year, his studies had required him to spend lengthy periods in Nile Delta villages, cutting down his activity in the Dror movement.

He did not take part in Philip's struggle against Communist infiltrators into the movement, and got a little bored when his friend insisted on giving him detailed accounts of his battles. To some extent, Victor felt that the movement, and everything connected with it, was a thing of the past as far as he was concerned. He was determined that as soon as he received his diploma—whether or not his family accompanied him —he would leave for Israel, and join Kibbutz Yir'on, together with his fiancée.

Victor was head over heels in love. He had made the acquaintance of his fiancée, Susanne Kaufman, at the clandestine Hebrew course which young Jews organized at the Jewish school, concealing it from the school's director by presenting it as a "geography circle." One day Victor stood at the gateway of the school, watching the pupils of a parallel class leaving at the end of their lesson. Susanne caught his eye immediately.

"In fact," he related later, "I had seen her before, but it never occurred to me that she was Jewish, let alone a Zionist. I took her for a Greek. I asked Philip who she was, and he—always the boldest of us where girls were concerned—simply walked up to her and said: 'Hello, my name is Philip. Meet my friend . . .' "

It transpired that she was the only daughter of Russian-born parents who guarded her jealously. The family intended to emigrate to Israel—which was why Susanne had joined the Hebrew course; but she did not belong to any youth movement. A meeting of Dror was scheduled for the following day, at Sidi Bisher, a suburb of Alexandria. Victor invited her to come along, and she accepted.

Within a short time, two things happened: Susanne became a member of Dror and she and Victor fell in love. "When I told her of my affection and she responded, my happiness was boundless. We were young and enthusiastic, and we were in perfect harmony concerning our future path—life in a *kibbutz* in Israel."

Susanne's family planned to leave in August 1951 while Victor's examinations were due to go on to a later date. They agreed that Susanne should leave for Israel, as planned; when Victor arrived, in September or October, they would get married and join a *kibbutz* together.

"One morning early in June," Victor recalls, "on leaving my parents' apartment on my way to the university, I found Ovadia Danun waiting on the sidewalk in front of the house. 'I have been waiting for you,' said Danun. 'I did not want to talk to you in the presence of your family.' "

Victor was in a hurry, and he suggested that Ovadia accompany him. And so, as they were walking in the street, Danun said: "Look, if

I were to ask you whether you were prepared to dedicate your life to Israel, what would you say?"

Victor was offended at even being asked such a question.

"Fine!" said Danun. "Your contribution is needed for a military operation on behalf of the state of Israel." He did not go into details, but hinted that he was not referring to youth movement work, or help in organizing emigration, but something much bigger.

Hesitantly, Victor said: "You know that I'm ready. But I can't do it before the exams. I would like to complete them."

Danun replied that the matter was not urgent. Victor would have ample time for his examinations, "but I would like to introduce you to an emissary from Israel."

"To our enthusiastic minds," Victor recalls, " 'emissary' was synonymous with 'Messiah'—particularly when it was a matter of contributing to the security of Israel. We were at an age, and in a frame of mind, when we were quite prepared to march blindfolded after 'big words.' "

Victor's excitement and curiosity made it hard for him to concentrate on his examinations. Before he sat for the last of them, he contacted Ovadia Danun and asked him what had become of the promised encounter with the Israeli emissary.

The meeting took place a few days later, at a Greek café on the coastal promenade.

Victor relates: "Ovadia arrived, accompanied by a man I did not know—tall and swarthy, with a pipe stuck in his mouth. Ovadia made the introductions in English, presenting the man as 'John Darling,' and then hurried away. We stood up and strolled along the Corniche promenade, ambling along without any apparent care. Darling now dropped his Oxford English and asked me whether I preferred to speak French. 'What did Danun tell you about me?' he asked. I replied that he had told me nothing. He began to ask about me. And then, as we stood leaning against the promenade parapet, apparently gazing at the amateur fishermen, he told me: 'I am not an English engineer. I am from Israel.' Then he told me all the rest—that he had been a member of the Haganah and Palmach, had taken an active part in the struggle against the British, and in organizing illegal immigration, that he was a farmer from Kfar Yehoshua.

"It all made a tremendous impression upon me.

"We seated ourselves in one of the cafés, at a table on the sidewalk, and continued our conversation. He talked in a roundabout manner— about Israel being a small country, with powerful enemies, obliging us to employ ruses in our war. . . . He spoke about Egypt, and about the probability of a renewed war against Israel. Suddenly, he said: 'If it were possible, during hostilities, to arouse confusion in the enemy's rear, to cause panic in a populous city like Cairo or Alexandria, to undermine morale—that would be an important success.'

"I drank in his words thirstily, even though I didn't yet know what he was driving at. Then he asked me, 'What are your personal plans?' 'To emigrate to Israel,' I replied, telling him of my group which had settled at Yir'on, and of my intention of joining them.

"Enthusiastically, he said: 'That's exactly what I'm looking for! A person like you can lay the foundations for an underground group, recruit people, lease the apartments to serve as their bases, train them. Then, after a time, you can depart for Israel, and the threads linking the group to me and to the person who leased the apartments and recruited the members are severed! That will leave only the group, without any traceable roots. It will be a perfect clandestine group!'

"My heart throbbed vigorously. Here, on a plate, I was being offered everything I had dreamed of: to work for Israel. Before he had terminated his words, I was 'sold' on the idea."

However, Darling confronted Victor with an intolerable demand: He was to cut himself off from his previous existence, from his friends, and, hardest of all, from the movement. "Instead, I had to create a new life, to allow myself to be swallowed up in obscurity, to keep away from anything which might arouse the suspicion of Egyptian counterintelligence." It was easily said, but how could it be done? The movement was precious to Victor, and he was one of the last and most prominent of its leaders. As he visualized his friends' reactions to his withdrawal, he regarded himself as a traitor. However, Avraham Dar insisted that it was essential, and Victor resigned himself to the inevitable.

By a lucky coincidence, Philip's struggle against the Communist infiltrators provoked a crisis that same week. Philip insisted that the Communists be expelled from the movement. The result was a violent disagreement, and Victor took advantage of the schism to proclaim his "profound disappointment" in the movement, and to announce that he was leaving. His companions could not believe their ears. They argued with him in an attempt to dissuade him, but he responded with growing fury, accusing them all of pro-Communist inclinations, and stalked out, slamming the door behind him.

Most surprised of all was Susanne. She listened to his words in astonishment. Nevertheless, when he walked out, she hurried after him. Outside, he told her that he had thought matters over, and come to the conclusion that his membership in the movement had been an error. From now on, he said, he would be free, and not be bound to any organization. If she wished to follow him, her way of life would change completely: They would go out, enjoy themselves. He had had enough of asceticism.

"Every one of my lies seared my tongue. But she followed me, without any argument."

A few days later, Victor was summoned to another meeting with Avraham Dar. This time they met at a chalet in Sidi Bisher, on Alexandria's beach. When Victor arrived, Shmuel Azar was already waiting there.

"Even if I had harbored any doubts about the wisdom of my decision," says Victor, "Shmuel's presence would certainly have dispelled them. Like all the other members of the movement in Alexandria, I admired Shmuel without any reservations. I said to myself: 'If Shmuel is with us, everything's all right.' "

Shmuel was the first of Avraham Dar's recruits in Alexandria. Shmuel was soon joined by Robbie Dassa.

Robbie: "When Dr. Victor Sa'adiya arrived from Cairo and told me that he wished to speak with me in private, I was sure that he wanted to talk about matters connected with Bnei Akiva. However, he surprised me.

" 'It looks as though you will have to leave the movement,' he told me, without any preamble. 'There are matters which are more important. . . .' Then he told me that an emissary had arrived from Israel, and that he needed a number of dependable young people for an operation of which he, Sa'adiya, knew no details. 'If you agree, I will introduce you to him.' "

Robbie was not overenthusiastic. How could he leave Bnei Akiva, of whose Alexandria branch he was now one of the leading members? "How can I explain it to the youngsters I instruct?" he asked, doubtfully.

"Don't worry about that. I'll do the explaining . . ."

Robbie still remained unconvinced. But he consented to meet the Israeli emissary and to hear what he had to say.

They met the following day, at the Monsegnieur café in the Mazzaritta quarter. It was rather a shady place, a kind of nightclub, but it had the advantage of being empty during the day. Dr. Sa'adiya introduced Robbie to "John Darling." They stayed a little longer in idle conversation and parted after agreeing to meet again two days later.

This time, in the absence of Dr. Sa'adiya, "John Darling" spoke more freely. "At first," Robbie recalls, "he got me to talk. He had an exceptional gift for getting people to talk about themselves. He ferreted out details about my family, my activity in Bnei Akiva, my friends, and the neighborhood where I lived, inquired about my relationships with my parents, and asked whether they would permit me to travel abroad on my own. Presumably, he asked that because of my youthful appearance; I looked young for my age."

Gradually, Dar began to talk—in the vaguest terms—about "the mission": setting up an underground cell. As usual, he spoke in a roundabout fashion; without going into operational details, he threw out ideas about the importance of psychological warfare and about the numerous possibilities open to a group of people well rooted in Egypt who spoke the language and could merge with the population, especially if they underwent suitable training.

Robbie was fired by the idea. When Dar brought up the subject of cutting his links with the movement, Robbie no longer objected.

"I was a different person when we parted. Without fully comprehending my actions, I found myself stopping before shop windows, to see whether I was being followed."

At the end of that week, Shmuel Azar contacted Robbie at work. They were neighbors and acquainted with one another, and, like all the other boys in his neighborhood, Robbie admired Shmuel; "but what I liked was that he did not try to contact me at home. If he had come to see me, it would have aroused suspicion."

Shmuel Azar became the contact between Avraham Dar and Robbie. "Without it being specifically stated, I regarded Shmuel as the senior member of the group. Later, when Victor joined, followed by Philip, this was made official: Dar appointed Shmuel to command the cell."

The first task which Dar gave Robbie was to find a meeting place, so as to eliminate the necessity of meeting at street corners or in cafés. It was Robbie who came up with the idea of renting a chalet at the Sidi Bisher beach. There was nothing exceptional about the notion. Every self-respecting Jewish family bought or rented a summer house on the beach, where they could find a haven from the heat of the city; many young men rented such chalets for their own purposes—for parties or for meetings with women.

The two men set off for Sidi Bisher, where they found numerous chalets for rent. Robbie, fluent in peasant Arabic, haggled with the bawabin (caretakers) who represented the owners. Finally, they found a chalet which met their requirements—a wooden structure containing three rooms and conveniences—and rented it for the summer. The chalet became the meeting place and training school for the members of the cell. To remove any suspicion and to confirm the bawab's belief that he was dealing with a bunch of good-for-nothings who wanted a place for their dissipations far from the eyes of their parents, they held a number of parties and dances there.

For some time, Shmuel thought that the cell consisted only of Azar and himself. On Dar's instructions, the pair began to survey points of military importance in the city, paying particular attention to the port. This involved no difficulty; even though the port had been a closed area since 1948 and its visitors were supervised, it was easy to acquire entry permits. The port was the center of all the yachting clubs, and served as the anchorage for boats for hire. Robbie and Shmuel displayed an interest in rowing, their outings occasionally leading them—"by mistake"—into the military area of the harbor.

"Within a few weeks, I changed completely. From a religiously observant youngster, an instructor in Bnei Akiva, I had become a typical Alexandrian playboy, with a chalet on the beach where I held parties and dances; I boasted Greek companions and an Italian girl friend. There were times—admittedly, not often—when I would stop and wonder: 'Is this Robbie?' But my doubts soon dissolved. I was completely captivated by my new life-style."

At the end of August 1951, Avraham Dar departed from Egypt, leaving behind two underground cells in the process of formation, in Cairo and Alexandria. Each cell had a meeting place, fitted out with a secret cache (as summer drew to an end, the Alexandria cell moved its meeting place to an apartment in town, in the Mazzaritta quarter). The link between the two cells was provided by Marcelle Ninio; they received a regular supply of money, by means of the Chyprotte family.

Before leaving Egypt, Dar gave his approval for the recruitment of another member by the Alexandria cell—Philip Natanson, who had been recommended by Victor.

During the final weeks of his stay in Egypt, Dar began to initiate his subordinates into the nuances of clandestine operations. In addition to supplying them with reading material about underground organizations and lecturing them on conspiratorial tactics, he began to train them in simple sabotage techniques, teaching them how to manufacture incendiary materials and explosives from chemicals which were freely available. In the chalet in Sidi Bisher, Shmuel and Robbie—and, later, Victor—engaged in constructing improvised delayed-action devices, consisting of acid sealed into contraceptive condoms; the acid slowly ate its way through the rubber, until it came into contact with another chemical, the resulting reaction causing them to catch fire.

Robbie: "To find out the time required for the acid to eat its way through the rubber, we made countless experiments. We threw the used condoms into the lavatory, often causing blockages in the sewage pipes. We had to call the *bawab* to open the blockage, and I can just imagine what he told his friends about the 'wild orgies' being held in the chalet."

Dar also taught his subordinates how to manufacture "leaflet bombs," to be placed on the roof parapet of a multistory building, with a delayed-action device causing the bomb to detonate some time later, after the person who had laid it had made his getaway.

However, Dar constantly reiterated that all this was no more than the rudiments of the art of sabotage. They would gain a more thorough knowledge of the techniques when the time came for them to go to Israel for proper training.

Now, before his departure, Dar gave his final instructions: He ordered them to keep up their training in improvised sabotage techniques and to continue to study conspiratorial procedures, learning to reconnoiter objectives while concealing their own presence. He told Philip to learn photography and developing, with the aim of making him the cell's cipher expert. But Dar stressed that their most important assignment was to prepare for their departure for training in Israel. They were to obtain passports and seek pretexts to gain an exit permit —together with permission to return subsequently to Egypt.

On returning to Cairo, after meeting Philip, Dar gave Marcelle the Paris address with which she was to maintain contact. He also provided her with invisible ink for writing letters of particular importance. He briefed her again in the relatively simple code she was to use for less important letters and told her that she too should register for a photography course.

The following day, he departed. Seventeen years were to pass before Marcelle saw him again, in Israel.

# 2

## OPERATION SUSANNAH

*Necessary Planning*

After Dar's departure, the members of the Alexandria cell applied themselves vigorously to fulfilling his instructions. Philip arranged to be taken on as an apprentice at Sammy and Sahag's studio, which specialized in wedding photographs. The four cell members met at their Mazzaritta rendezvous several times a week to practice assembling chemical delayed-action devices. At times, when Suzette Chyprotte succeeded in filching a few shotgun cartridges—her father and brother were both keen hunters—the foursome would go off into the desert to practice more "regular" sabotage techniques with the help of the powder they extracted from the cartridges. Suzette, who drove them out in her car, stood watch. But their principal concern was arranging for their departure from Egypt.

The first one due to go was Victor Levy, who was to set out in September. Marcelle arrived from Cairo to rendezvous with Shmuel Azar. Following their meeting, Shmuel informed Victor that the latter had received permission to come to Israel. He was to depart for Marseilles, reporting on arrival to the immigrants' camp, where the security officer would make arrangements for the rest of his journey.

It was not fortuitous that Victor was the first one chosen to go. As a Greek citizen, he had no difficulty in acquiring a passport. Philip and Robbie, on the other hand, were stateless, and would first have to apply for Egyptian citizenship—an almost hopeless undertaking. Robbie was even prepared to do his period of military service in the Egyptian army instead of buying himself out, as the Jews were in the habit of doing, hoping that it would help him to acquire a passport; in response to his summons by the army authorities, he underwent medical tests and was told to return home and await his enlistment papers. The papers never arrived.

Victor had a further advantage. As a graduate of the agricultural faculty, it was easy for him to find a pretext for going abroad—to undertake further studies. That summer, he sent an application to the University of Paris, to study canning. The director of the Alexandria agricultural school backed his application with a warm recommendation, and the reply soon came back—affirmative.

During the period of time which elapsed until his departure, Victor renewed his attempts to persuade his parents that they had no future in Egypt. "But it was to no avail. Life was easy, Father's job was simple and well paid, and it was very tempting to cling to the illusion that matters would remain so in the future. Even when, close to the date of my departure, I warned my father of the possibility that I might not return to Egypt, I did not succeed in getting him to budge from his view."

Victor set sail on the Italian ship *Pace*, which also bore a large group of Jewish emigrants on their way to Israel. The latter underwent strict and humiliating searches in the port: Their suitcases were overturned, books and photographs which lacked the censor's stamp were confiscated. Customs officials tore rings off women's fingers on the pretext that they contained gold exceeding the amount they were permitted to take out of the country. As for Victor, his suitcase was not even opened. Customs agents, who were befriended by his father, had greased the correct palms.

Victor's journey was uneventful, but the atmosphere on board the ship was somber. "It was a refugee ship. Its passengers wondered what awaited them at the end of their journey, and they were full of forebodings."

At Marseilles—wet and gray under October rains—he mounted the truck, together with the other immigrants, and was taken to the "Eilat" camp—a former French army barracks which had served under the German occupation as a concentration camp for Jews about to be sent to the crematoria. The huts with their peeling plaster had changed little since then.

At the camp, Victor was registered as Haim Levin, born in Austria, and began to undergo the "Via Dolorosa" of an immigrant to Israel: medical examinations, forms, more forms, and yet more. This meeting with Israeli bureaucracy did not get him down; he had been forewarned. During this period, he renewed his correspondence with his fiancée, Susanne Kaufman, who had followed the selfsame route herself only a few months ago. He had learned from her what awaited him. "She wrote that she had left messages for me at various places in the camp. And, in fact, on the dispensary wall I found the penciled message: 'I passed through here, Susie.' "

He now wrote her that his plans had changed, and that he intended to emigrate to Israel. Indeed, he felt just like an immigrant. Two days before his sailing date, a group arrived from Egypt, including some members of Dror who were friends of his. They intended to join Kibbutz Ein Hamifratz. "After our joyous reunion, they invited me to join them. I replied that my own group was in Yir'on, and it was them I would join, in due time, but first I intended to enlist in the Israeli army."

On December 7 he set sail from Marseilles aboard the *Artza*. "Together with the other immigrants, I was lodged in the hold, in crowded and uncomfortable conditions; the food was awful. But what a wonderful cruise! This was not a refugee ship, like the *Pace*. This was a ship of immigrants! We danced all night, every night; we sang Israeli songs; our excitement increased with every turn of the ship's screw. When the peak of Mount Carmel appeared on the horizon, at midday on December 12, I trembled with agitation. So did the rest of my companions. Our life's dream was about to be realized. First-class passengers came down to take snapshots of us clinging to the rail, with our eyes on the horizon."

The *Artza* was moored to the pier. Border police, customs officials, and Jewish Agency officials boarded the ship and began to process its passengers. Victor remained on deck. In the midst of the handkerchief-fluttering crowd waiting on the pier, he soon spotted Susanne, standing beside Victor's uncle, an Israeli of long standing. There was a small suitcase beside her: she had come prepared to set off immediately to Yir'on.

"In France, I was told that I would be contacted on reaching Haifa. I waited and waited. The line near the tables of the customs officials was growing shorter; the crowd on the shore was thinning out, and my uncle also had to leave, but Susanne continued to wait. Evening descended, and we were still waiting. I decided that I would wait a little longer and then disembark and head for the *kibbutz*. But at seven o'clock in the evening, someone tapped me on the shoulder; I turned, and saw an officer in air force uniform. He introduced himself: Maj. Elisha. Avraham Dar had sent him my picture to help him identify me."

Elisha swiftly led Victor past the line of officials. He was registered as a new immigrant, unmarried, setting out to Tel Aviv to enlist in the army; he was sprayed with DDT, as was the custom at that time. Elisha took his suitcase, as the two men strode down the gangplank, and then Susanne flung herself into Victor's arms.

"But how was I to tell her? In the end, I summoned up my courage;

taking a deep breath, I told her that I had decided to join the army. Susanne cried: 'What? After I succeeded in persuading my mother to accompany us to the *kibbutz!*' She then delivered herself of a firm declaration: 'I'm not returning home without you!' "

Elisha saved the situation by offering to drive Susanne to Tel Aviv in the military vehicle which awaited them. "On the way, squeezed into the driving cabin of the pickup truck, her anger gradually subsided. Susanne began to brush the DDT from my hair, and by the time we halted at the Hadera crossroads for a cup of bad coffee and a sandwich consisting of thick slices of bread which contained a sliver of something vaguely resembling sausage [it was the austerity period in Israel], our quarrel had been resolved."

On arrival at Tel Aviv, after depositing Susanne at her door, Victor and Elisha drove to a cheap little pension in King Solomon Street. All the rooms were taken, and Victor spent his first night in Israel on a folding bed in the corridor. But this did not mar his festive mood. He found it difficult to fall asleep; impatiently, he counted the hours till daybreak when he could go round to knock on Susanne's door.

Two days later, Elisha found him a furnished room, in the apartment of an army officer and his teacher wife, who were in the habit of helping out Israeli intelligence by putting up its agents. Those were naive times, before the introduction of lavish expense accounts and free access to luxury hotels. Elisha gave Victor thirty Israeli pounds as a "maintenance allowance," told him swiftly that there was an unexpected delay in connection with the course, and added: "You will be contacted. In the meantime—enjoy your vacation!"

He did indeed enjoy his vacation. Susanne also took a leave of absence from her job and the pair spent all the time together; they walked the streets, lounged in the cafés (to this day, Victor remembers the bizarre taste of the coffee substitute, which together with insipid cakes were the only refreshments available in Tel Aviv cafés during the austerity period), squatted on the iron railings outside the Mugrabi cinema, and, after the film, on a bench on JNF Boulevard. Late at night, Victor would take Susanne home and walk to his own room. So it went on, day after day; no one contacted him.

A week later, Elisha dropped in for a brief visit, to ask Victor whether there was anything he needed. A week after that, Victor received another visitor: a colonel in uniform, who introduced himself as Motke Ben-Tzur. He was there, he said, to assure Victor that he had not been forgotten, and that "we are endeavoring to arrange the course for you."

Matters dragged on in this manner for two months. Susanne's leave came to an end, and she was obliged to go back to her job. Victor was now alone most of the time. Every morning he would leave his room and make his way to the Central Bus Station. Here, he allowed blind chance to lead him to some bus or other, which he then boarded and rode to its terminus. In this manner, he arrived in various towns—Rishon Letzion, Hadera, Rehovot, and Natanya—where he would walk about till evening and then return to Tel Aviv. On weekends, Susanne accompanied him on his explorations.

Finally, Motke Ben-Tzur appeared in his room one morning and proclaimed: "The course is arranged!"

The course began at an army camp near Ramleh; at first, Victor was its sole participant. An English-speaking private instructor gave him lessons in sabotage techniques. Victor would arrive every morning by bus ("I made sure I arrived early, to leave time for a military breakfast, which was richer than what was available in town without food coupons"). He studied the traits of various explosives and detonators all day long and learned how to strip down mines and delayed-action bombs and how to reassemble them. He applied himself to his studies with unprecedented diligence. He was now a soldier of the state of Israel, confronted with a mission!

Shortly before Passover, Avraham Dar came to see him at his room in Tel Aviv. The two now met regularly, for friendly conversations, but this time, Dar's visit had a specific purpose. He said: "Another fellow is coming from Egypt; he will take the topography course together with you. We have rented a room for him, not far from yours. I want you to help him get acclimatized."

The next day, he brought the fellow to Victor. In introducing them, Dar did not mention their names. He said to Victor: "This is a friend of mine from Cairo." And to the newcomer: "This is a friend from Alexandria. He knows the way to Ramleh. You will study together and travel together." A few days passed before Victor learned his name: Moshe Marzouk.

Victor: "Every morning we would meet and travel together to Ramleh. At first, our relations were very restrained. He never asked for details about me, and I refrained from questioning him. No one told us, but we alone comprehended that the less we knew about one another the better. It was only later that I found out he was a doctor and that he had been inducted into the Israeli medical corps with officer's rank.

"Avraham asked me to befriend him, telling me that he was lonely. But he was hard to approach. It was only in time, when I got to know him better, that I realized that the wall with which he appeared to surround himself stemmed from an unwillingness to force himself upon others. I brought him to Susanne's apartment—her mother took to him from the first moment—and invited him to join us on our evening promenades in the streets, or outings to cafés."

When Susanne and her mother saw that Victor would not soon join the *kibbutz* and that his sojourn in the city would be a lengthy one, they invested the small sum of money they had succeeded in bringing out of Egypt in buying an apartment, at the corner of Brandeis and Pinkas streets, not far from where Victor and Moshe were staying. This apartment was to become the meeting place for all the members of the network who came to Israel for courses.

Susanne was very quick to pick out the discrepancies in Victor's cover story about serving in the army. She did not leave him in peace until he revealed the truth: that he was undergoing special training in preparation for his return to Egypt, on an illegal mission. When she got over her astonishment, she said simply: "In that case, take me with you." Unable to refuse her, he promised, "I'll try."

At Passover, Avraham Dar organized an outing to Eilat and Ein Gedi for his two subordinates. Susanne was also invited to join the trip, together with the two instructors at the course and their girl friends, as well as a woman officer and soldier, and the drivers of the two military vehicles which had been placed at their disposal. They took arms with them, as well as food for a week (at that time the Negev was an empty wilderness). Ein Gedi was occupied by a unit of the Nahal Brigade, and Eilat was nothing more than a single hut belonging to the navy, and a few tents. Visitors slept on the beach.

For Moshe Marzouk, this outing broke the ice, and he began to open up. Victor: "He was still terribly earnest, and overbrimming with a sense of duty. He was the only one of us who punctiliously carried his gun constantly, as he had been ordered; even when he went to sleep at night he would lay the rifle beside him. At the same time, he now gave an occasional smile, sometimes made some remark about himself.

"I learned from him that he was a Kara'ite; not that it mattered. In Egypt, Kara'ites were considered Jews in every sense, and it was only on arriving in Israel that I found, to my surprise, that this was a matter of controversy here. I also discovered that he loved the Bible, from which he could quote entire passages by heart. No sooner did Avraham utter the name of some place we passed on our trip than Moshe would quote the Bible passage where it was mentioned.

"He loved the country more than anything else. After that Passover outing, we took a number of courses together—electricity, wireless, codes, constructing caches—and our friendship grew. He began to join the 'exploration trips' which Susanne and I undertook in various parts of the country. He'd fix his eyes on some hill and his face would break into a smile of happiness, his eyes glazing over like a lover gazing at his sweetheart."

The two men became inseparable. They dined together, gradually learning how to survive without food coupons under austerity restrictions. "We discovered, for example, that the army canteen in Jaffa served meat on Wednesdays, while the one in Dizengoff Circle on Sundays and Thursdays; that the workers' restaurant opposite the Allenby Street main post office served an egg for breakfast . . ." Having planned out their meals, they crisscrossed the city according to a "food map."

They held many conversations about what awaited them on their return to Egypt. Marzouk, who knew the Egyptians better than Victor, was also more aware of manifestations of anti-Jewish feelings. He was certain that the 1948 war would not be the last one, and that a bitter fate awaited those Egyptian Jews who failed to see the writing on the wall in time.

Not even the July 1952 revolution, which abolished the monarchy and brought to power a group of young and apparently enlightened officers, could alter his somber predictions about Egypt's Jews. "I know the Egyptians," he said. "The revolution will only make their nationalism more extreme and heighten their xenophobia."

At this time, a few days after the revolution, Victor and Marzouk parted ways. Victor was sent to Haifa, for a special course on identifying ships and naval sabotage for which Marzouk, who lived in Cairo, had no use, and was consequently sent on a different course.

This was the last course in Victor's training program. On his return from Haifa he took an examination, at the conclusion of which he was told that he had passed. From now on he was an Israeli officer, with the rank of second lieutenant.

Nine months had passed since his departure from Egypt and he was eager to return. In part, this was out of concern for his family—even though he knew (from his correspondence with them by way of an intermediary in Paris) that they had survived the revolution unscathed—but also because his Egyptian reentry permit would run out in September; and above all, because, after his seven months' training, he now felt ready for action.

With some difficulty, he managed to dissuade Susanne from joining him. He told her that he had undertaken to organize emigration and "self-defense"—matters in which he had engaged in the past and which therefore did not sound so daunting—and that the mission would last for two years. He would return in August 1954, and they would then get married.

As usual, she submitted.

A farewell party was held for him on the terrace of the seaside Kaete-Dan hotel (later to become the Dan luxury hotel). Ben-Tzur attended, as did Avraham Dar, the instructors, Susanne, and Moshe Marzouk. They were served a sumptuous meal, in flagrant defiance of austerity regulations, and much wine was poured; the participants joked and laughed, their forced gaiety attempting to dispel the sorrow of parting and their underlying forebodings. In the course of the evening, someone—Victor no longer remembers who it was that brought the matter up—said that the mission had no code name as yet. Someone proposed a name which was received with general acclaim, accompanied by gales of laughter at the blush on Susanne's face.

The name chosen was Operation Shoshanah, or Susannah; this choice dictated the call-sign which would herald the coded instructions to be broadcast on Israel radio: the American folk song "Oh! Susanna."

On August 7, 1952, a military car came to collect Victor from his pension. From there, he drove to Susanne's home and took her to work, at the El Al offices on Rothschild Boulevard. This time, their parting was brief. Everything which needed to be said had already been said the previous evening, when Victor brought her his suitcase with the clothes he had purchased in Israel and the books he had brought from France. That night they did not go to sleep; instead, they sat dreaming aloud of the future they would build together, in two years' time . . .

After that, the military car drove him to Haifa, where he embarked on the *Negba*, which was about to set off for its biweekly cruise to Marseilles.

## The Underground in Hibernation

Dar's departure did not produce any great change in Marcelle Ninio's way of life. She continued at her work, looked after her mother, met friends. The cell and everything connected with it did not require much of her attention. At regular intervals, she traveled to Alexandria to receive money from Mercedes Chyprotte; once a month, she met Meir Za'afran and Eli Na'im to give them the rent for the Cairo cell's apartment. The rent for the apartment in Alexandria was sent to Shmuel by mail. Aside from that, the cell's expenses were minor. On one occasion, she paid Philip Natanson a trifling sum for some equipment he bought; on another, she was instructed to send a larger sum to the cell in Alexandria, to rent a workshop. Nor was there much mail from Paris.

Of all the members of the Cairo cell, the only one she met frequently was Moshe Marzouk, but these meetings took place at the Jewish hospital, which she now visited often, as her mother's ailment worsened and she was hospitalized for tests with growing frequency.

In October 1951, an emissary arrived from Israel. Marcelle knew of his arrival beforehand; Paris informed her that "Jacques is coming and will bring you regards." Indeed, one day someone phoned to her place of work, saying that he had regards for her from Paris. When they met, he brought her regards from Avraham Dar, and a sum of money. She did not know his true identity, nor the real reason for his coming. At one time, she suspected that he only came to find out "whether we were still in existence." Now she knows that he was an emigration emissary, ordered to take advantage of his visit to Cairo to make contact and find out whether there were any snags.

A further emissary arrived in February or March 1952, not long after "Black Friday," January 26, 1952, when the mobs of Cairo held riotous anti-British demonstrations, and at the same time vented their anger against everything connected with foreigners, setting hotels on fire and looting Jewish shops. This time, too, she received prior notification from Paris: "Emil is coming; he is interested in meeting you." When he phoned and said, "This is 'Emil,' " she was forewarned.

"We arranged a rendezvous at Bijelle's, a small, exclusive café on Kasser el Nil Street. He told me I would be able to identify him by the book open on the table before him and the walking stick by his side. Nevertheless, I had to inspect the café's occupants twice before discovering him hidden in a corner."

This was Max Binnet. He was German-born, had been wounded during the War of Independence, and later became a major in the Israeli air force. He had previously undertaken perilous but successful intelligence missions to Iraq. However, Marcelle did not know all this. Before her she saw a man with blond hair, wearing a suit too heavy and warm for the mild Cairo winter. They began to converse somewhat uneasily. Max Binnet was restrained and introverted; it was only gradually that he opened up, whereupon Marcelle discovered him to be a sensitive man, highly educated, with broad horizons, who loved the Bible and displayed wide knowledge of music.

However, all this did not come out at that first encounter. Without telling her why he had come to Cairo, he informed her that she was to act as his liaison. Instructions would come for him in the letters she received from Paris; when they arrived, she was to transmit them to him by phone without delay. Once a week, she was to come to his apartment to report. He gave her his telephone number and the address of his apartment in the Zamalek quarter (these details led Marcelle to conclude that he had been in Cairo for some time).

At her first visit to his apartment, Binnet gave her a Leica camera to forward to Dr. Marzouk, who in turn would send it to Philip in Alexandria.

As Binnet began to open up in their subsequent meetings, Marcelle learned more about him and his deeds. She discovered that he had indeed arrived in Egypt several weeks before making contact with her. He possessed a German passport and he was masquerading as a German manufacturer of artificial limbs. This cover—which gained all the more credibility because he himself still limped from his 1948 war wound— permitted him to make contacts with the Egyptian army, primarily with those branches set up to rehabilitate war invalids. On one occasion, he showed her a snapshot which presented him standing beside Gen. Muhammed Naguib (then officiating as president of the association of 1948 war veterans) with the two men smiling at one another in great friendliness. Max explained that the smiles were not just put on for the benefit of the camera.

She still had no clear understanding of why he had come to Egypt, but he began to display a growing interest in the activities of the cells. He asked her for a report on her expenses and went over it carefully, requesting a detailed explanation of each item. He even asked her about what was happening within the Cairo cell; on one occasion, when she told him that Meir Za'afran wished to drop out—since he was about to get married, he thought it unfair to his future wife for him to be involved in underground activities and also shoulder his matrimonial responsibilities—Binnet expressed his readiness to meet Za'afran and talk with him.

Marcelle arranged the meeting without attending it; but Za'afran dropped out all the same, and contact with him was broken off.

A short time later, Binnet asked to meet the members of the Alexandria cell, but insisted on one condition: He did not want them to see his face. Following his instructions, Marcelle traveled to Alexandria to meet Shmuel Azar and invite him and Meir Meyuhas to come, at a prearranged day and hour, to the Mazzaritta apartment. Binnet, who had received the key from Marcelle, awaited them there, and talked with them through a half-open door.

Subsequently, he informed her that henceforth he would deal with all financial matters, while the Alexandria cell would maintain direct contact with the address in Paris, freeing her of the need to travel to Alexandria.

If Marcelle had tried to comprehend his actions, she would have noticed that, step by step, he was severing her links with the cells. When Max Binnet was first sent to Egypt, his superiors toyed with the idea of putting him in command of the cells, in addition to his direct task of collecting information. However, after becoming acquainted with the cells, Binnet came to the conclusion that they were structured to operate in channels totally separate from his own line of action. He therefore decided to sever his connections with them; and, since Marcelle had been picked to act as his contact and she already knew him, he also endeavored to sever her links with them.

Marcelle did not pose any questions about his actions. On the contrary; with her mother's ailment growing worse and demanding all her attention, she was glad to be relieved of her trips to Alexandria. She met Dr. Marzouk one more time—Binnet ordered her to bring him a heavy package (which, she later learned, contained a transmitter)—and after that Moshe Marzouk departed for Israel, Za'afran dropped out, and her contact with Eli Na'im was broken off.

As far as she knew, the Cairo cell had become dormant.

After Victor's departure, the Alexandria cell experienced a period of intensive activity, under the leadership of Shmuel Azar. They held training sessions at their apartment or in the desert; they reconnoitered various strategic points in the Alexandria region, particularly in and around the port. Shmuel, Philip, and Robbie became more active in the port-based "yachting club."

Robbie and Philip made efforts to acquire travel documents. They addressed applications to the Paris University electrical engineering department and were answered in the affirmative. Robbie, who was not yet eighteen, even persuaded his father to sign a letter consenting to his trip. Armed with all these documents, they applied for exit permits. However, their applications vanished into the bureaucratic labyrinth of Egypt's shaky administration. Every few weeks they traveled to Cairo, to the Interior Ministry, in the hope of speeding up the processing of their applications—but in vain. Even getting their files brought up from the archives required *baksheesh* to be paid—only to find that no progress had been made on their requests.

In the meantime, they continued to "dig in."

Robbie and Philip were now totally at home in their new non-Jewish social circle. Their apartment in Mazzaritta attained notoriety as a den of iniquity. Shmuel, by nature totally incapable of dissemblement or deceit, did not attend the parties held in the apartment. But during the day he was a regular visitor there. He set up his easel, with an uncompleted painting on it, while other paintings hung on the walls and stood in corners, as a cover in case of an unheralded visit from the aliens police. However, there were no such visits. The apartment aroused no suspicion, and the police had more important matters to concern itself with: in October 1951 the corrupt Wafd party government, trying to regain its popularity by whipping up anti-British nationalist feelings, unilaterally revoked the 1936 Anglo-Egyptian treaty and demanded the withdrawal of the British army from Egypt. The demonstrations which began with the government's blessing were soon taken over by the Moslem Brotherhood and the Communists, and became more and more violent. In the Canal Zone, the Brotherhood and the fascist Misr el Fatah movement launched a guerrilla campaign against British army installations.

Then came "Black Friday"—January 26, 1952—the first rumbling of the approaching tempest. Riotous mobs took over the streets of Cairo for an entire day, looting and setting fire to foreign-owned stores, cinemas, and hotels. For the first time in over twenty years, the army had to be called out of its barracks, to intervene in the riots and restore order. But like the legendary genie, once released, the army could no longer be bottled up.

Even though everyone knew that "things could not go on this way," nevertheless, the July 23 revolution came as a surprise.

Even before the revolution, the British army had consented to withdraw from its Nile valley camps and concentrate its units in the Canal Zone; in consequence, hundreds of apartments and offices were vacated in the European quarters of Cairo and Alexandria. Most of these were taken over by Egyptians, creating proximity—physical but not social—between them and the previous European inhabitants, resulting in friction and clashes.

The revolution heightened frictions. The Egyptians, proud of their victory, began to straighten their backs after generations of humiliation. The age-long term for foreigners—*hawagat* (gentlemen)—took on overtones of contempt. In the cinemas, the new national anthem was played before the movie, and anyone who refused to stand up ran the risk of being torn to pieces by the angry audience. New slogans began to make the rounds—unity of the Arab peoples and restoration of their former glory.

Some of these feelings were directed against the Jews. The heads of the new regime tried to tone things down, and the president, Gen. Naguib, paid a demonstrative visit to the Cairo synagogue on Yom Kippur, but in the streets, the Jews again heard the offensive name first flung at them in 1948—*Sayonin* (Zionists)—this time, with redoubled hostility.

Robbie and Philip personally experienced the change which had taken place, for the revolution led to a reopening of the gates: In August, Robbie was notified by the Interior Ministry that he would receive a travel document valid for six months.

Many weeks were wasted on acquiring an exit visa, thus further shortening the validity of Robbie's passport. The French consulate granted him a visitor's visa for one month only. Philip, on the other hand, gained a student's visa, valid until the end of the academic year.

The two men left Egypt within a few weeks of one another, in

January 1953. With their departure, the Alexandria cell also became dormant.

Victor returned to France in the middle of August 1952, only a few weeks after the Egyptian officers' revolution.

On arriving in Paris, he was instructed to rent a room in a student hostel, to register at the university, to refresh his Parisian French; a week later, he was to report to the Egyptian embassy, to renew his permit for reentry into Egypt, which had expired.

He regarded this as no more than a formality. However, he had not reckoned with the impact of the revolution on the embassy staff. There was an atmosphere of insecurity and uncertainty. No one knew the new rulers, nor what changes they would institute, and in the meantime, no one was prepared to take any responsibility upon himself, not even for a matter so uncomplicated as renewing a reentry permit. His application was sent to Cairo—and no reply came back.

The matter was drawn out for seven months, and in the meantime, Victor's French residence permit ran out. He became "illegal." Someone came up with the idea that it would be easier to renew his permit of residence if he applied in Marseilles. He went there, staying at a small hotel which the police were not in the habit of visiting, and taking care not to approach the transit camp for emigrants to Israel.

It was a miserable period. "There is nothing as depressing as winter in Marseilles. Everything is somber and damp, the rain drips incessantly, and I was so lonely! Without papers, without anything to do— I sensed myself so worthless! I wandered from one cinema to the next, so as to spend my hours among people, even if not in their company. Every now and then, I went to the Jewish Agency official who was supposed to take care of my papers; his answer was always, 'Not yet.' I became desperate."

Victor's contact informed him that Moshe Marzouk had also completed his training and had arrived in France. He was living in Montpellier, at the medical school, and was soon to return to Egypt. Victor went to visit him.

"Before me, I found a new man. There was a woman with him— a tall, smiling Australian woman, whose acquaintance he had made on board ship, between Haifa and Marseilles. It was love at first sight for both of them. They could not tear themselves away from one another. All three of us traveled to Paris together; all the way, they sat embracing one another unashamedly. Moshe's restraint vanished as though it had never existed. He was overjoyed, and he shared his happiness with the whole world."

At Montpellier, Victor met another old friend, Johnny Mazza, a classmate of his at the Alexandria agricultural school, who had come to France for further studies in his specialty, viniculture (vine-growing). Johnny had not been a member of any Zionist youth movement in Alexandria. "He belonged only to the scout movement, but he made no secret of his sympathies toward us, and all in all, he was an excellent fellow." Victor soon discovered that Johnny, who had left Egypt after the revolution, possessed a rare "asset"—a perfectly genuine permit to return to Egypt at the end of his course, in a year's time. "Instantly I hit upon the idea: Why not recruit him? He displayed all the traits we needed: He was unconnected with any Zionist organizations and had a good cover to explain his prolonged residence in Egypt."

Before approaching Johnny, Victor consulted his contact in Paris. He was told: "Wait. We will check on him." A few days later, he got the green light. Victor returned to Montpellier and headed for Mazza's room, where he presented his proposal. He asked Mazza to give up his proposed course in viniculture. Instead, he would go to Israel to train in an entirely different sphere, one requiring the sacrifice of his personal career in favor of rendering the state of Israel services which involved difficulty and danger.

Johnny Mazza was not a spontaneous character. He asked for time to think it over. However, a few days later, he phoned Victor in Paris: "I agree." Two weeks later, he was in Israel.

Johnny underwent a fuller and more thorough course than Victor's and returned to Egypt a year later. He was in line to take Victor's place in the Alexandria cell after Victor's eventual departure for Israel. However, he arrived at a time when the cell had already launched the operations which led to its downfall; for various reasons, Johnny did not take part in them. Nor did he have time to make the acquaintance of "Paul Frank," the Israeli emissary. Perhaps that was the reason he was saved.

In the meantime, Victor had returned to Paris, where he gave no rest to the visa official at the Egyptian embassy. The reply to his application had yet to arrive. Time lay heavily on his hands. He had been ordered to shun the company of Zionists and Israelis, and he had no other friends. He made the acquaintance of a Jewish female student and fashion designer with Communist leanings; she and her friends became his social circle. He began to attend Communist meetings, and joined their protest rallies and demonstrations outside the American embassy (at this time, the world was in uproar over the execution of the Rosenbergs, the American "A-bomb spies").

Victor's Israeli contact man, Raoul, having completely lost hope of Victor's papers ever arriving, suggested that Victor travel to Germany, learn German, build up a new background for himself, and then head for another Arab country, possibly Syria. However, Victor replied that if he did not succeed in returning to Egypt, he would prefer to return to Israel and remain there.

"I was quite close to doing so. Robbie arrived from Egypt, followed two weeks later by Philip; while they waited for their journey to Israel to be arranged, we whiled away the time together—famished. At this time, our money ran out and Raoul disappeared. We spent hours planning how to manipulate the Jewish female student into inviting us to her studio, where there was always a pot of soup bubbling on the stove."

One day, Victor set out as usual to the Egyptian embassy in the Avenue Victor Hugo, firmly resolved that this would be the last time! If he got yet another negative answer he would not return again; instead, he would join Robbie, who that same morning had been instructed to go to Marseilles, and from there to Israel.

"And precisely that day, the visa clerk received me with a broad smile: *'Monsieur,* today we are getting rid of you. The papers have arrived!' "

Robbie was forced to wait twenty-one days in Paris before his journey to Israel was arranged. Of this period, with its tensions and privations, he remembers above all his gnawing impatience. "My French visa was for one month alone, my passport would become invalid in two months' time. Every day was therefore precious and time was being wasted on pointlessly waiting for a berth on a ship. Frequently, I would ask myself: 'Why don't they send me by air?' " He began to wonder whether the whole matter was as important as he imagined. This suspicion was dispelled the moment he arrived in Israel. He was immediately flung into an intensive whirl of training.

In consideration of the short time he had left, a separate course was organized for Robbie. It was very intensive; he hurried from lesson to lesson, without a break, six days a week. Saturdays were devoted to touring the country. Robbie took four such trips and the sights he saw "were etched in my memory and became the spiritual sustenance which supported and fortified me during my fourteen years in prison. I would conjure them up, repeatedly, drawing from them the strength I needed to hold out."

On those evenings when he was free of Hebrew lessons, he would go—alone at first and then later accompanied by Philip—to Susanne's apartment, which became their second home. When they returned to their shabby hotel room, they would lie there, talking at length—about what they had learned and above all about what they would do on returning to Egypt.

Robbie: "The intensive training course had its effect. I sensed that I was maturing rapidly—that I was changing, becoming a soldier. I had still been told nothing of what I would be expected to do in Egypt. However, I said to myself: 'I am learning sabotage; Mazza is doing a wireless course. Isn't this an indication of the tasks awaiting us?' I was prepared."

However, toward the end of his training, at his sole meeting with Motke Ben-Tzur, when the latter suddenly asked, "Why don't you remain here and we'll think of another mission for you?" Robbie's old doubts and suspicions revived. He replied vigorously: "Unthinkable!" Years later, he conceded: "The mere fact that the question was posed seemed to detract from the importance of everything I had done and was about to do."

Early in March 1953, Robbie embarked on the *Artza;* five days later he landed at Marseilles, staying there for three days before boarding an Italian ship and setting sail for Alexandria. He almost missed the sailing. When he reached the pier, the gangplank had already been raised, and it was lowered specially for him. If he had come a few moments later, who knows what might have happened . . . for this was his last opportunity to return to Egypt. His Egyptian passport expired on March 21— the day his boat docked at Alexandria.


Victor returned to Alexandria in March 1953, preceding Robbie by a few weeks. Philip only joined them seven months later, on October 5, 1953.

In Paris, where Philip stayed for a few weeks to acclimatize himself, he made the acquaintance of a Dutch female student, and the two fell in love. Philip proposed, she consented; on his return to Egypt, he asked his superiors for permission to marry her. Victor sent his request on to Israel, but the reply was: "It would be better for him to wait." Philip submitted, but kept up his correspondence with his fiancée until the day of his arrest. She continued to write to him subsequently, but there was no reply. Six months later, she sent an agitated letter: "What has happened? Why is there no answer to my letters?" Again, there was no reply, and she ceased writing. Years later, she sent him an invitation to her wedding, without any accompanying letter. But Philip's parents, wishing to spare him any additional burden, did not forward the invitation to the prison.

Prior to Philip's return, his companions had engaged mainly in "striking roots." They found various jobs; Robbie with a Jewish firm which imported raw materials for the soap industry (a possible source of chemicals which could be of use to the cell) and Victor in a company importing diving equipment from Italy. They found a circle of friends, mostly non-Jews. They rented another apartment in place of that in Mazzaritta, which had been given up during the period when Shmuel was on his own. The new apartment was on Amiri Hospital Street, near the Ramleh quarter's tram stop—a centrally placed area teeming with traffic—in a multistory building with numerous exits (a valuable feature in a city where the gatekeepers were all police informers, instructed to report on the tenants' comings and goings). The apartment was rented by Shmuel Azar, whose departure for Israel had already been approved, and only postponed for a few months to permit him to conclude his work as a "monitor" at the Jewish community's secondary school.

Shmuel, a proficient amateur radio operator, had set up a camouflaged transmitting aerial on the roof of the building. When the job was completed, Victor traveled to Cairo to meet Dr. Marzouk (who had also returned from Israel and resumed his work at the Jewish hospital), from whom he picked up the tiny transmitter which Marzouk had received by way of Marcelle.

With the transmitter, they also received instructions: twice a week, on Wednesdays and Fridays, at six in the morning, Victor was ordered to transmit a Morse call-sign. At noon on the same days, he was to listen in on a prearranged wavelength. If his transmission had been received well, a reply would be transmitted back to him.

Aside from this exchange of signals, several times a week a special transmission was broadcast for him: Morse signals at dictation speed, for practice. He took great pains over his exercises, and his speed improved from nineteen to twenty-six words a minute.

Victor's trip to Cairo, to pick up the transmitter, was almost the sole contact between the cells in Alexandria and Cairo. This was preceded by another contact, when Victor, shortly after his return to Egypt, traveled to Cairo to ask Marcelle whether she was prepared to go to Israel for training. ("It was only then that I learned of Victor's return to Egypt," relates Marcelle. "I asked him about his stay in Israel, and he replied evasively: 'It was all right.' I did not inquire further.") As for going to Israel, Marcelle, who was bound to her mother's sickbed, replied: "Not now."

There was a further contact, when Moshe Marzouk came to Alexandria to meet his sweetheart, whose ship cast anchor there for one day on its way to Australia. At the same opportunity, he contacted Victor and delivered a second transmitter, which Shmuel installed in Victor's parents' apartment.

That was all. The two cells had no further contact.

In Cairo, Marcelle had now totally severed all her links with the other members of the cell. She still met Dr. Marzouk at the hospital. This was only natural, for on returning to the hospital, he resumed his treatment of her mother, and they also met socially; but he told her nothing more of what was happening in the cell. Her activities were confined to serving as Max Binnet's contact, and here, too, her duties progressively dwindled.

Binnet left Egypt in June 1952—a few weeks before the officers' revolution, which made his friend Muhammed Naguib the first president of the Egyptian republic—and did not return till the beginning of 1953. That, at all events, was when he renewed his contacts with Marcelle.

This time, he brought his wife and baby daughter with him—although Marcelle knew nothing of this—and with the possible aim of protecting them, he refrained from meeting Marcelle at his apartment. He would phone her to ask whether there was any mail for him; if there was, he would arrange a rendezvous at some street corner, where he picked her up in his car. While he drove around the city, she would hand over the messages she had received for him; after conversing a little, he would stop near a bus stop and let her out.

Throughout the entire period following his return, right up to their detection, she met him only three or four times. She did not know where he lived, nor his telephone number; she did not even know whether he resided in Cairo or only came there for regular visits. She did not ask; she knew it was better not to.


On Philip's return, the Alexandria cell came back to life. In addition to his romantic memories, he had brought a film from Paris with detailed instructions for the manufacture of high explosives. In a storehouse on the roof of Philip's parents' apartment, they set up a workshop, where Philip and Victor began to practice mixing the materials, according to instructions. Shmuel and Robbie engaged in similar practice in the cell's apartment. Paying careful attention to the rules of secrecy they had learned in Israel, they refrained from meeting in public places; when they did happen to meet, each one ignored the other.

After his photographic training in Israel, Philip had become a much-sought-after photographer, and tried his hand at art photography. Several of his photographs won prizes in amateur competitions, and he now applied for a license to open a commercial photographic studio in one of the rooms of the cell's apartment in Amiri Hospital Street. Philip also served as the cell's cipher expert, who conducted its correspondence with Israel. In addition, he got a job as a clerk at the cotton exchange, which gave him free access to the port area.

The port attracted the attention of all four members of the cell. They signed on as members of the "yachting club," where they rented lockers; after learning the search procedures at the port gateway, they smuggled in explosives and concealed them in their lockers, "for whenever they're needed."

They did not let any opportunity slip by. When the papers reported that an American company was shooting a movie, *Abdullah the Great* (on the life of King Farouk)—adding that the Egyptian government had permitted the producers to make use of Farouk's yacht, *Mahroussa,* aboard which the deposed king was sent into exile—Victor and Philip joined dozens of other applicants for jobs as extras in the film. Victor got a role; he appears in the film for a few seconds, resplendent in a captain's uniform. But more than the glamour of "stardom," which he gained among his friends, he was gratified by the fact that the *Mahroussa* lay at anchor alongside the Egyptian navy's submarine base, and that during breaks in the filming, he could stand on the deck of the royal yacht and peer at the top secret installations of the naval anchorage.

(Years later, while Victor was serving his sentence of life imprisonment in Tura, the worst prison in Egypt, his fiancée, Susanne, chanced to enter a Parisian cinema and was astounded to see Victor's face on the screen. She went to see the film four times in succession.)

Following instructions from Israel, Victor also engaged in recruiting work. He enlisted two additional friends: Jacques Danon, the son of an agronomist who managed a farm for its absentee owners, and also owned a farm of his own, in the Delta, forty miles from Alexandria; and Jacques Farhi, a pharmacy student in his final year at Alexandria University, who had free access to the university laboratory. Victor had specific tasks in mind for these two: He intended to ask permission from his superiors in Israel to construct a large arms cache at the Danon farm, while he planned to make use of Jacques Farhi to gain access to the university laboratories. Consequently, neither of the two was brought into the cell's regular operations.

Johnny Mazza had returned from his training course in Israel bearing a letter appointing him as Victor's deputy, with the aim of replacing him when Victor departed for Israel; but Johnny too was not brought into the cell's current operations. He was about to get married, and as he was to take over Victor's job, he was given a kind of "honeymoon vacation."

In consequence, when the emissary arrived from Israel, Mazza was not introduced to him; nor were Farhi and Danon. These were the only three members of the network who did not fall into the hands of the Egyptian counterintelligence.

*The Underground Awakens*

The emissary from Israel arrived at the end of June 1954.

To this day, the circumstances of his mission as well as his precise task remain part of the mystery shrouding "the mishap," provoking the question which has yet to be answered: Who gave the order?

The background to his mission is clearer. Early in 1954, the Egyptian officers' regime suffered a shakeup. On launching their revolution a year and a half earlier, the officers had not intended to take over power. They wished only to remove the corrupt politicians. "However," as Gamal Abdel Nasser was to relate, "when we began to seek out honest politicians to whom to hand over power, it transpired that there were none; they were all corrupt!" and consequently, the officers' junta remained in power.

Gen. Muhammed Naguib, their nominal leader, did not belong to the junta. The thirteen unknown officers who constituted the Revolutionary Council, chose him—a senior officer, a hero of the 1948 war and a popular figure inside and outside the army—in order to exploit his popularity for their revolution. They appointed him president, but his was a figurehead role. In February, deciding that they had no further need of him, they deposed him. However, vigorous protest demonstrations at home, and sharp reactions from abroad, forced them to restore him to office a month later. On the surface, Naguib's position appeared firmer and more influential than before his dismissal.

Whether out of a belief that Naguib's position was firm or from a desire to strengthen his rule, whether glad of an opportunity to divest itself of the heavy burden of empire or under the pressure of President Eisenhower and his Secretary of State, Dulles, who adopted a policy of wooing the Arab states, Britain now consented to terminate its seventy-two-year-long presence in the land of the Nile. Negotiations settled the conditions for the British army's withdrawal from its bases in the Canal Zone; the evacuation agreement was due to be signed on July 27, 1954.

The forthcoming agreement between Britain and Egypt, whereby the Egyptian army would take over the military installations which Britain had built up over decades in the Canal Zone—camps, airfields, giant stores, and up-to-date workshops of all kinds—was regarded in Israel as an ominous development.

Even worse, the political developments expected to follow the agreement—closer relations between Egypt and Britain, at a time when the United States had begun openly wooing the Arabs, with Secretary of State Dulles staking his political future on the Baghdad Pact, and appointing the pro-Arab Henry Bayrod to head the Middle

East Department—all these seemed likely to aggravate Israel's political isolation.

Was it possible to halt the wheels of history? Some of Israel's defense chiefs inclined to an affirmative answer. They believed that if Egypt's military regime were shown up as insufficiently reliable to be entrusted with the Suez Canal, the world's most important waterway, and if its rule within Egypt were also shown to be shaky, the British might reconsider their decision to leave Egypt and the American policy makers might abandon their illusions about basing "the southern tier" on the Arab states and upon the Baghdad Pact.

Who were the persons who held these views? This too is one of the questions buried deep beneath the mounds of conflicting testimony relating to "the mishap." After the collapse of the network in Egypt, an attempt was made in Israel to examine the background of, and the motivation for, the operations in Alexandria and Cairo (and to discover who was responsible for them), but no one stepped forward to accept responsibility. Consequently, there was no one to defend the operations in Egypt, which came to be regarded by public opinion as an adventurous, irresponsible, and pointless act of folly.

One thing is clear, at all events: The Israeli cabinet was not the body which decided on this course of action. To the premier, Moshe Sharett, "the mishap" came as a complete surprise. The question: Who gave the order? has remained open to this day. One fact is certain beyond any doubt: Early in the summer of 1954, a decision was taken in Israel that this was "the emergency," in anticipation of which Avraham Dar had established the underground cells in Cairo and Alexandria three years previously. The commander of the "special task force," Col. Motke Ben-Tzur, received the order: "Go ahead!"

It was Ben-Tzur who chose the emissary who would be charged with directing operations in Egypt.

The emissary was Avraham (Avry) Seidenberg, a tall, powerful, handsome man with blond hair. Born in Austria, during the War of Independence Seidenberg had served as intelligence officer in the Palmach's Harel Brigade, and it was there that Ben-Tzur first met him. Ending the war with the rank of major, Seidenberg was posted to Haifa, where he got involved in an affair involving looting of war booty—a refrigerator taken from an abandoned Arab apartment. He was court-martialed and sentenced to be cashiered. His attempts to rehabilitate himself in civilian life failed, and he also suffered matrimonial upsets—his wife was about to divorce him. At this time, desperate and with nowhere to turn, he met his former comrade in arms, Motke Ben-Tzur, who recruited him into the intelligence service. At that time, Israeli intelligence was very active in Germany, tracking down Nazi war criminals and checking possible collaboration between them and the Arabs, and Avry's external appearance made him the incarnation of a "pure Aryan."

He was sent to Germany, to establish a new identity—that of a former SS man, a fanatical Nazi unable to adapt to life "under the yoke of occupation"—and to infiltrate the ranks of Nazi underground organizations, a task in which he was successful. After acquiring documents under the name of "Paul Frank," he set out for Egypt early in March 1954. He chalked up a number of successes, uncovering the underground route by which wanted Nazi war criminals slipped through to the Arab states, as well as supplying the first reports about Egyptian efforts to establish an arms industry with the help of German experts. Even though his reports were not complete, and always displayed some defects, his superiors were impressed by his successes.

One day in May 1954, "Frank" was summoned to Paris, for a meeting with Motke Ben-Tzur. Here "Frank" was given a new task: to take command of the cells established by Avraham Dar three years previously. According to testimony presented to the Dori-Olshan committee of inquiry in January 1955, "Paul Frank" was charged with organizing operations which would make it clear to the whole world that Egypt's new rulers were nothing but a group of foolhardy extremists, unreliable and unworthy of taking charge of an asset as important as the Suez Canal. Furthermore, it was to be demonstrated that their grasp on power was uncertain, that they faced powerful internal opposition, and that, consequently, they were unworthy of being counted upon as a dependable ally.

It was Philip, the Alexandria cell's cipher expert, who received the letter from Paris which heralded the arrival of an emissary from Israel. He took the letter to Victor, and the two deciphered it together. It stated: "Robert will come to visit Henry on June 18. We hope the meeting is successful, and that you make him welcome."

"Henry" was Philip's code name.

Philip: "This was the signal we had been waiting for. While still in Paris, on my way back from Israel, I was informed that an emissary would soon arrive from Israel, whereupon we'd commence operations. It was agreed that on arrival, the emissary would contact me at my parents' home, because we lived in an area inhabited by numerous Europeans, and the appearance of a stranger would not attract attention."

The emissary did not arrive on the eighteenth. However, a few days later, while Philip was sitting in the ground floor guest room, playing with his two large dogs, his mother was upstairs, and there was no one else at home, the doorbell rang. Philip opened the door to confront a tall blond man, elegantly dressed. With no preamble, the newcomer said: "I am Robert."

"We have been waiting for you for days," replied Philip, pacifying his fretful dogs. When they sat down in the salon, Philip's mother came down to see the new arrival. Philip introduced "Robert" to her as an old friend; she shook hands, said a few polite words, and went out.

Philip displayed his photographic studio to the visitor, who inspected it with an expert eye. "Robert" expressed his desire to meet Victor, requesting that he await him the following day, in front of the Rialto cinema. Philip offered to join them, but "Robert" said he preferred to meet Victor alone.

When "Robert" stood up to leave, Philip also got up to see him out. But "Robert" said: "Don't trouble yourself, I'll find my way out." Philip: "To me, his words sounded like more than any mere expression of politeness; he did not *want* me to accompany him. All the same—or, perhaps, precisely for that reason—I hurried to the window. I saw him enter a car parked outside—an open green Plymouth with diplomatic plates. Two children were waiting for him in the car."

Philip's senses were alerted. That day, meeting Victor to tell him about the visitor and to invite him to the rendezvous the following day, Philip tried to drop some hints about the puzzling aspects connected with "Robert"—his belated appearance, the car with its CD number plates, and with two children sitting in it—all of which seemed to indicate that "Robert" was not a new arrival in Egypt. But Victor was too enthusiastic at the appearance of the long-awaited emissary to pay attention to any reservations. His enthusiasm grew following his meeting "Robert."

Victor waited outside the Rialto cinema and at the appointed time, three o'clock, a green Plymouth halted beside him. Victor immediately recognized the car, which fitted Philip's description. This time, too, two children were in the back seat. The driver opened the door and beckoned to him to enter.

When the car moved off—Victor noted that the driver seemed to know his way around in the heavy traffic of downtown Alexandria— "Robert" said, in English: "I bring you regards from your friends. Also from your girl friend."

Victor: "Instantly, I warmed toward him. I asked: 'Did you see her?' but he had not met her. However, he was well acquainted with Avraham and Motke Ben-Tzur. I asked him about the children, sitting silent and polite, in the back: 'Are they yours?' and again, he replied in the negative. He said that they were the children of a German admiral,

Baron Bechtoldsheim, who served as an adviser to the Egyptian admiralty. He related that he was staying at the baron's home, and indeed, we drove there to an attractive villa in Mazzaritta. He took the children up to the house and immediately returned to the car. I guided him to the cell's apartment in Amiri Hospital Street."

On the way, "Robert" talked extensively about himself. He related that he had come by car from Libya, by way of the Western Desert, that he had already made himself at home among Cairo's Nazi colony, that he shared an apartment with another Nazi in the Zamalek quarter, and that he was befriended by Zecharia Muhi el-Din, a member of the Revolutionary Council, as well as the Cairo police commissioner, whom he had "eating out of the palm of his hand" and consulting him on everything.

On arrival at the apartment, "Robert" gave Victor the things he had brought: new crystals for the transmitter, a new cipher based upon a pocket edition of *Moby Dick,* and new radio frequencies. They were written out on a sheet of paper, openly and uncoded, *in Hebrew!* Victor's amazement grew. Was he not afraid of carrying such a dangerous document around with him?

"Robert" examined the transmitter in the apartment, and questioned Victor about the cell's other means of communication.

"We are going into action," said "Robert." "Fast and hard."

"When?" Victor asked, thrilled.

"Yesterday! Time is pressing." He added that on July 23, the anniversary of the revolution, they had to carry out an operation that would "turn their festivities into a day of mourning."

Victor grew serious. "Our equipment is primitive," he said, "the delayed-action devices we manufacture are unreliable. In Israel, we were promised that when it was time to begin operations, we would be supplied with proper equipment—at the very least, delayed-action detonators."

But nothing could mar "Robert's" astounding self-confidence. "As to that—don't you worry! I'll get detonators. I have a German friend who will supply them, any amount we need. I'll also get hold of explosive charges. I know of an Egyptian army explosives store at Sakra (near the Pyramids). You and I will eliminate the guard and break in. Have you ever killed anyone? No? Then I'll deal with the guard alone. But you will be present, to gain experience . . ."

Victor's head whirled. Many long and bitter months later, in the dock of the Cairo military tribunal, when Marcelle Ninio asked him in a whisper about this "Paul Frank" whom the prosecutor mentioned so frequently, Victor, still under the impact of his meeting with the man, replied: "He's a terrific fellow!"

On taking his leave of "Robert," Victor immediately headed for Philip's apartment, to share his excitement with his friend. "Now we'll go into action!" he declared festively. Immediately, he began to enumerate "Robert's" virtues—his daring, his resourcefulness, the amazing contacts he had already made, in Cairo and Alexandria.

Philip's reaction was a little cool. "If we are going into action," he said, "we must first remove the workshop from my home." This was a matter he had frequently mentioned in the past. They had already decided that the workshop in Philip's house was to serve solely for experiments and training; when the time for action came, it would be removed elsewhere, so as not to endanger his parents.

Victor answered that he would consult "Robert."

However, a few days later, Victor notified Philip flatly that, for the time being, until they found suitable premises for the workshop, it would remain where it was. That was an order.

In that same conversation, Philip brought up the subject of preparing passports for the cell members, in the event of an emergency which would oblige them to make a rapid getaway. He said: "If we are beginning operations, we have to prepare a retreat route. That's elementary in every operation." The passports on which the cell's members had gone to France were taken from them on their return; in any case, they were no longer valid.

Victor replied: "You're right. I'll talk about it with 'Robert.' "

He discussed it, and came back to Philip with "Robert's" reply— the matter presented no difficulty. "Robert" had a good friend—an important person—who could arrange visas for transit into Libya at a few hours' notice.

However, Philip was not disposed toward relying on this mysterious "friend." He mentioned the matter of the passports to Victor several times during the next few days; each time, Victor replied: " 'Robert' has promised to see to it . . ." but there were no passports forthcoming, right up to the end.

Two days after his first meeting with "Robert," Victor set off to Cairo for a second meeting, as had been agreed between them. The purpose of his journey was to receive delivery of the delayed-action detonators which "Robert" had promised.

"We met in front of the Groppi café, but we did not go inside. Instead, we went over to a small café on the other side of the street. 'Robert' explained that the Groppi—one of the best-known cafés in Cairo—was frequented by many of his German acquaintances, and it would be unwise for him to be seen in my company."

Seated in the smaller café, Victor learned that he would not receive the detonators he had come for. "Robert's" German friend had been rushed to the hospital, suffering from a sudden attack of appendicitis. "Time is pressing," "Robert" said. "I picked up a message from Israel, ordering us to launch operations without delay. We shall have to begin with the means available."

Victor still had not the faintest shadow of suspicion.

They set off. First, they headed for the Italian hospital where "Robert" visited his German friend while Victor waited in the car; from there they drove on to Alexandria.

"On the way, 'Robert' opened up completely. He told me that he had left his wife and son behind in Israel, that he missed them greatly; he brought out photographs from his inside pocket and displayed them proudly, like any father. He told me that he lived in Haifa, and had studied mechanical engineering at the Technion. He told me of his deeds in the Palmach, during the British mandate and the War of Independence. There and then, he switched on the car radio and turned the dial to 'Kol Yisrael,' mentioning offhandedly that he received his instructions from Israel by way of the radio, through prearranged signals planted in the women's hour and the classical music requests program. He also mentioned his tasks in Egypt, though no more than a hint. He said: 'You people will do your job, but the really hard work will be left to me.' "

That same day, at the Alexandria cell's apartment, "Robert" met Shmuel Azar, who must have made a deep impression upon him, because henceforth, he regarded Shmuel as head of the Alexandria cell and consulted him on every matter. "Robert" repeatedly told Victor of his admiration for Shmuel's personality and intelligence.

During that meeting in the apartment, "Robert" notified his two subordinates that he had chosen the first target for the cell's operations: the Alexandria central post office. If they were surprised by the choice —his talk of "doing something which will cause some noise" had led them to expect a more spectacular objective—they did not show it. Robbie Dassa, who was not present at the meeting but heard of it from Shmuel Azar, says quite simply: "It never even occurred to us to question his decisions. He was the commander and we were his subordinates." However, "Robert" did not rely solely on the obedience of his underlings; he explained his choice. The purpose of the operation was to create the impression—inside Egypt and abroad—that the officers' junta faced internal opposition. Consequently, the operation's impact would not be measured by the material damage it caused, but rather by the public reverberations it would evoke. Therefore, it had to take place in the center of the city, where there were lots of people, "to produce uproar and give rise to rumors—so that the operation can't be concealed by the censorship."

Victor: "I liked his way of thinking. I thought to myself: 'In spite of his courage bordering on foolhardiness, he is a sensible man.' "

They began to make plans: Who would carry out the operation? "Robert" wanted all the cell members to take part—including "Alex" (Johnny Mazza's code name). Victor explained that "Alex" was on leave until after his marriage. However, "Robert" insisted. He demanded a meeting with "Alex," to persuade him to break off his vacation. Then he calmed down, and said that he only wished to meet Alex, so that he could identify him in the future.

"Arrange a rendezvous with him," he ordered Victor, "and I will stand nearby. Perhaps I'll take a picture of him."

However, when Victor phoned Johnny Mazza that evening and summoned him to a meeting the following day, "Alex" said that he was busy; it was the day before his betrothal. "Robert's" anger on being told of "Alex's" refusal came as a surprise to Victor—but he was not suspicious. "With some difficulty, I convinced him that the matter was not worth getting so worked up about, and that the four of us would suffice for Operation Post Office."

They decided to carry out the operation on Friday, the Moslem day of rest, when the post offices closed early. The idea was that the incendiary devices would ignite after the post office closed, when it was empty. The day chosen was Friday, July 2, 1954.


On the appointed day, the four men assembled at their apartment. They immediately began to pack the incendiary materials into cans of Vim. The delayed-action fuses would be constructed and assembled at the last moment.

It was approaching midday, when the post office was due to close.

Philip was the first to set off, carrying a package which was already addressed and, furthermore, to forestall any suspicion, stamped. He was followed twenty minutes later by Victor and Robbie, carrying similar parcels.

Robbie: "We hired an Arabiyah *hantur* [horse-drawn carriage] and ordered the driver to head for the Corniche. About two hundred meters from the post office, I said good-bye to Victor and got out. As I entered the post office, my heart thumped violently.

"In the parcels department, I found three large mailboxes: one red, for airmail; the second green, for express packages; and the third gray, for ordinary packages. Each of the boxes bore a sign indicating the times when they were emptied. I glanced at it. The next collection time was only the following morning. The post office was about to close, in another few minutes. Out of the corner of my eye, I saw Victor enter hastily.

"I dropped my parcel into the gray box and walked out."

It had been previously agreed between them that Robbie would return an hour later, to watch and report. The hour dragged on endlessly; to while away the time, Robbie walked all the way to the Ramleh station and back again.

"When I approached the post office, the street was cordoned off by a line of policemen, and a fire engine was standing on the sidewalk opposite the post office. A group of curious bystanders had congregated near the police cordons, and they whispered excitedly among themselves. No one knew for sure what had happened."

However, Robbie did know. The operation had succeeded!

The following day, July 3, when "Robert" arrived from Cairo, Victor met him at the cell's apartment and reported in detail on the previous day's events. "Robert" responded enthusiastically: "Wonderful! And now a bigger operation, in Cairo and Alexandria simultaneously! We shall strike at the American libraries!"

Philip and Victor were chosen to carry out the operation in Cairo, and Azar and Robbie in Alexandria. Robbie objected, claiming that he could carry out the operation on his own, and that there was no need to involve Shmuel only a month before his departure from Egypt. The others inclined to agree with him, but it was Shmuel Azar himself who dismissed the idea. He said: "If the operation in Cairo calls for two people, the same goes for the operation in Alexandria." Nothing could dissuade him from taking part in the operation. In the end, the others agreed.

Philip brought up another question: Why should the Alexandria cell undertake the operation in Cairo? Why should the Cairo cell not take on the job? Victor replied that the Cairo cell was no longer in existence. Indeed, he believed this to be the case. Shortly before, when he met Moshe Marzouk to receive delivery of the second transmitter, Marzouk explained that he was dropping out of operations. To Victor's questions, he replied laconically: "I've had a row with Motke Ben-Tzur." Victor did not question him further.

The second operation was scheduled for July 14—Bastille Day. In Alexandria, with its many French residents, the day was almost a national holiday. That evening, dozens of private and public parties and festivities would take place and Philip and Victor took this fact into account in planning their alibis. If everything worked out according to plan, they would have time to get back to Alexandria early enough to make their presence noticed at one of the parties.

That morning, they left for Cairo by train. They were scheduled to meet "Robert" at six o'clock that evening; they would head for his apartment and prepare the delayed-action devices in spectacle cases;

later—so he had promised while the operation was being planned—he would drive them to the American library.

However, on meeting "Robert," their plans changed.

"My apartment is 'out of bounds,' " he told them. "I found a microphone concealed underneath the refrigerator, and for the past two days there has been a plainclothes detective outside the house." On observing their worried looks, he hastened to reassure them. "I don't believe that I am under suspicion; I think it is the man I share the apartment with who is the suspect."

In place of his apartment, he drove them to the Gzira area, where the prestigious Nile bank sports clubs were located. He drove wildly, almost running over a pedestrian who was crossing the street. Philip made some comment about his driving, and "Robert" asked him, with a trace of a sneer in his voice, whether he was nervous. "Don't forget, there are explosives in the car!" Philip replied, angrily, and "Robert," now making no attempt to conceal his scorn, retorted: "You really are nervous!" Philip bit his lip and made no reply.

"Robert" halted behind a tennis court, which was deserted at this time; while he sat at the wheel of the car, keeping watch, Philip and Victor knelt in the back seat and assembled the bombs. It was very hot, and both of them sweated profusely. In a conciliatory gesture, "Robert" held out his handkerchief for Philip to wipe his face.

The American library was a large wooden structure, adjoining the American embassy at 6, Sheikh Brakat Street, near Liberation Square. They got there a few minutes before the appointed time, at 7:30 in the evening.

Philip: "This time I was calm. In the Alexandria post office I imagined that the bomb would burst into flame in my hand at any moment. Now I already knew there was no danger of this happening. There were few people in the reading room, and no one took any notice of us. We took our leave of one another, each of us heading for a different hall. Pretending to glance at the titles of the books on the shelves, we laid the bombs, in their spectacle cases, in the gap between the books and the wall."

On leaving, they no longer found "Robert" outside. They stopped a cab and managed to get to the station on time to catch the 7:50 train. A few hours later, they were in Alexandria. Victor hurried home, dressed up in his finery, and was only slightly late for the Bastille Day fireworks show at the St. Stephano hotel. If any of his acquaintances wondered at Victor's noisy joviality, they probably attributed it to the champagne which was flowing freely and never suspected that this gaiety was deliberately designed to impress itself on the memories of those about him.

The operation in Alexandria had also gone off without a hitch.

Shmuel and Robbie reached the American library, in the basement at 2, Fuad Street; they laid their spectacle cases—one in the reading room next to a pile of journals, the other in the library, on a bookshelf—and made their exits without attracting attention.

The following day, at two o'clock, they met at their apartment. On the way, Victor passed Fuad Street, where there were clear signs of the fire which had occurred. There were still pools of water in the street, with scorched pages fluttering around. He found further testimony to the success of the operation on reaching the apartment. Shmuel greeted him by flourishing a local paper, the only one to report the fire in the library. True, there were only a few lines, containing not the slightest hint that this might have been an act of arson—the fire was blamed on a short circuit—but all the same, it was reported.

Later, "Robert" arrived from Cairo, full of praise. "Fine work! Cairo and Alexandria simultaneously—that's got to arouse some attention!"

"Robert" related that he was with Zecharia Muhi el-Din when the latter was informed of the fire at the American library in Cairo, and the two men immediately headed for the scene in the minister's car. "Robert" took snapshots of the blaze, simultaneously making angry sounds to demonstrate his displeasure at the dastardly deeds of the arsonists.

Victor and Philip listened thirstily while he depicted the flames leaping out of the library windows, and the confusion as the firemen looked for fire hydrants. Years later, during their confinement in prison, having lost some of their blind faith in the daring and probity of their commander, they began to find discrepancies in his story. His descriptions of his close contacts with the Egyptian Interior Minister appeared particularly questionable.

There were other acts of "Robert's" which puzzled the members of the Alexandria cell—even then, in July 1954, when they were still borne aloft by their jubilation at the success of their first operations, and while they still retained their unreserved faith in the daring commander sent to them from Israel.

Two or three days after "Operation Libraries," Victor set out for Cairo, to reconnoiter the objectives chosen for the forthcoming operations. While there, he met "Robert," who told him proudly: "It's not just you people who are active, I am also!" He related that the previous evening, while driving along the Gzira road, a police jeep came toward him from the opposite direction, and signaled to him to halt; "Robert" slowed down, and then, when the jeep was near, he tossed a bomb into it and stamped on the accelerator, speeding away with the police jeep going up in flames behind him.

"I believed him," Philip said, years later. "It never even occurred to me to doubt the veracity of his story, even though the Cairo papers made no mention of the incident. A resentful thought flashed through my mind: 'Why are there no bombs available for *us?*' "

At that meeting "Robert" gave Victor a letter to deliver to Philip, who was to encode it and send it on to Paris. When Philip got down to the job, he found that the letter dealt with matters unrelated to the activities of the cell. It contained the names of fifteen or twenty Nazi German scientists who had found refuge in Egypt, and listed their present addresses and occupations. Most of them had found work in the Egyptian arms industry, and were engaged in weapons development.

Philip: "Clearly, this was important, confidential information. Consequently, I was surprised at his sharing the secret with us, when, furthermore, he had already told us that he had his own channels of communication with Israel, through which he got his instructions. I asked myself: 'Why did he not send this message off directly?' His behavior seemed to run counter to all the conspiratorial rules we had been taught."

But above all, Philip was astonished at another of "Robert's" orders, also transmitted by way of Victor: "Robert" instructed Philip to keep a copy of every letter he sent to Paris or received from there.

Philip found this order so strange and illogical that he took it upon himself to disregard it. Of all the incoming correspondence, he retained only the film he had brought with him from Israel—which contained the instructions for manufacturing explosives—and a microcopy of one letter bearing the key to a new cipher. As for the outgoing letters, he destroyed them after encoding them and sending them off. He retained only one—a letter from "Robert" in which he reported that he was staying at the Cecil hotel in Alexandria, and which contained a number of details concerning his transmission times. Philip got this letter just before setting out on the third operation, the one which led to the cell's capture. Philip concealed the letter in his photographic laboratory, placing it inside an envelope full of photographic paper until there was time to encode it. When the police later searched his house, they failed to find the letter. When Philip's parents came to visit him in prison, he managed to whisper to them to destroy the letter—and they did so.

"All the same," concedes Philip, "even though I was less overwhelmed by 'Robert's' personality than, say, Victor, it never crossed my mind to suspect him. I regarded his acts and his instructions as imprudent, as erroneous—but no more than that."

"Robert" scheduled the cell's third action for July 23, Revolution Day. "This should be the biggest one of all!" he told the Alexandria cell members when he met them at their apartment.

Their first action had struck at one target; the second, two. Now, however, "Robert" wanted to attack five targets and, as before, he wanted to strike simultaneously in Cairo and Alexandria. The objectives he had chosen included two cinemas in Cairo, two in Alexandria, and the Cairo railway station.

"We shall attack cinemas which are foreign-owned, or which show Western films," he explained, "and then the blame will fall on the Moslem Brotherhood or the Communists; we shall choose centrally placed cinemas, so that our attacks can be seen and heard. Not even the censors will be able to keep the public ignorant of fires breaking out in four cinemas!" The fifth target, the railway station, required no explanations. It was the busiest place in the city, particularly on Revolution Day, when tens of thousands of peasants would come into the city to watch the military parade.

Together with Victor, who came up specially from Alexandria, "Robert" chose the two Cairo cinemas to be singled out for attack; they also toured the railway station, the junction of all of Egypt's railway lines. On their return from the station, "Robert" asked casually: "Do you know the Cairo cell's people? Do you think we can make use of them?"

Victor was doubtful, saying that to the best of his knowledge, the Cairo cell had ceased to exist. But he added: "Are you interested in meeting them?"

"Robert" replied in the affirmative, and they set off for the Jewish hospital. However, Dr. Moshe Marzouk was absent at the time; when Victor began to ask when he was due to return, "Robert" interrupted him: "Leave it. It's not important."

However, he expressed a wish to meet Marcelle. They headed for her house, but she too was out. Victor gave "Robert" the phone number of her office, and returned to Alexandria. Later on, the members of the Alexandria cell were to torment themselves with the question: How did the Cairo cell come to be embroiled in the calamity which befell them in Alexandria? They themselves had not given their interrogators so much as a hint about the existence of a further cell in the capital. In fact, they were not even interrogated on the subject. As for the members of the Cairo cell, they had done nothing which could put the police on their trail. How, then, were they detected? It was only years later, when they had finally grown used to the notion that one of their number may have betrayed them, that Victor remembered that visit to Cairo, and the interest which "Robert" displayed in Moshe Marzouk and Marcelle Ninio.

*Calamity*

In Alexandria, feverish preparations were afoot for the third operation. Once again, they went out on a "shopping expedition," acquiring chemicals, Vim cans, and spectacle cases. They divided out the tasks. It was decided that this time, Robbie and Shmuel would operate in Cairo, while Philip and Victor were responsible for the Alexandria operation.

Everything was ready for Friday, July 23.

That morning, the four of them met at the apartment. Robbie, who intended to stay over in Cairo till Sunday morning, brought his pajamas and toilet requisites. Shmuel Azar, who was to return to Alexandria the same evening, did not bring any personal belongings. He would carry the cheap cardboard suitcase, bearing no identification marks, which was to be deposited at the station's left-luggage bureau. The suitcase contained a bottle of acid, some condoms to be used for assembling delayed-action detonators, two spectacle cases containing inflammable material, and two cans of Vim filled with homemade explosives; the rest of the space in the suitcase was stuffed with old newspapers and clothes.

They set off on the ten o'clock train, arriving in Cairo at 2:30. As planned, they headed for a small hotel, the Hotel de Rose on Suleiman Basha Street. No sooner had they locked themselves into their fourth-story room than they set about assembling the bombs.

Keeping to schedule, at 4:30 that afternoon they went down to meet "Robert," who was waiting in his car outside the hotel. "Shmuel recognized him," relates Robbie, "but as for me, this was my first sight of him. I saw a powerful man with blond hair, wearing sunglasses. He beckoned to us, and we both got into the back seat. Immediately, he started up the car."

On their way to the railway station, "Robert" said that he would deposit the suitcase in the cloakroom. However, by the time they reached the station, he had changed his mind. "I'd rather *you* deposited it," he told Robbie, who, offering no objections, took the suitcase and handed it in to the left-luggage bureau, while "Robert" and Shmuel waited in the car.

After that, "Robert" drove them back to their hotel, where he left them. "Before parting, 'Robert' made certain that our plans were unchanged, with Shmuel returning to Alexandria that same evening, while I remained in Cairo over the weekend."

The two men went up to their room to prepare the delayed-action devices for the spectacle cases. On completing their task, they descended and walked together toward the nearby cinema section.

"Near the Rivoli cinema, Shmuel left me and went to the ticket counter. It was the last time I saw him until we met again in prison. I walked on to the Radio cinema, where I brought an expensive ticket for the balcony. The cinema was half empty; Cairo people are late risers, and the first showing is not popular there. When the lights went out, I laid the spectacle case on the carpet beneath my seat; in the interval which followed the newsreel, I walked out, as though intending to buy refreshments—and I did not return. I ripped up my ticket and went to buy a ticket for the nearby Metro cinema, keeping it as an alibi in case of need."

The following day, Robbie rose early, bought all the morning papers and read them through, line by line—and found nothing! Not a word about conflagrations in the cinemas—neither in the Rivoli nor in the Radio. In Alexandria, too, the newspapers reported nothing exceptional.

Later on, he traveled to Heliopolis to visit a girl friend; together they headed for the Barrage (a dam on the Nile which was a favorite picnic site for the inhabitants of Cairo). That evening, they went to a movie; once again, Robbie was careful to keep the tickets for his cover story. The next day he again went over the newspapers—and still there was nothing. No cinemas had gone up in flames in Cairo or Alexandria, and there had been no explosion in the railway station.

Robbie: "I spent a very tense day. I wanted to return to Alexandria, to meet my companions and find out what had happened. At five o'-clock that afternoon, I went to the railway station, to discover that I had arrived late; the next train would leave only at eight o'clock in the evening and I had arranged a rendezvous in Alexandria with a friend at ten. Accordingly, I went to the bus station. I began to sense a feeling of unease, as though I was being followed. However, I did not succeed in picking out who was shadowing me.

"I got on the bus. A man sat down next to me. I recognized him —he had been standing behind me in the line by the ticket office at the railway station. Had he too preferred to take the bus rather than wait for the next train? I was uncertain. He began to talk to me, in English. He turned out to be a merchant from India. All the way he talked about this and that, while I had to make an effort to focus my attention on his words. My uneasiness grew from minute to minute.

"By the time we reached Alexandria, my sense of unease had become clearly defined: I was worried. I was worried about what awaited me at home. Consequently, I was glad to accept my traveling companion's invitation to join him in a cup of tea at a café near the bus terminal. After that, I went to our prearranged rendezvous, but my companions had not arrived. I strolled along the Corniche. To my misfortune, I did not see a single acquaintance. No one but prostitutes, policemen, and amateur fishermen. My fear of returning home became stronger.

"In the end, I was left without any rational reason for postponing my return. Near midnight, I reached my street.

"The street was dark and silent. A single car was parked opposite our house. I told myself that all my fears had been nothing but a trick of the imagination, and entered the doorway. Instantly, two shadows broke away from the wall and came after me. Before I understood what was happening, they had grabbed my elbows. I saw other men leaping from the parked car and surrounding me.

"They took me up to our apartment, where they identified themselves as agents of the Muhabarat [military intelligence]. My weeping mother was alone in the apartment. My father, she managed to tell me, had been arrested on Friday night."

The events which led to the arrest of Robbie Dassa on Sunday night and to the downfall of the whole Alexandrian cell began forty-eight hours previously, when Philip and Victor had a mishap on their way to their own objectives in the Alexandria cinema quarter.

Was the mishap the true source of the calamity? To this day, there is no clear answer to that question. The only answers are those which can be deduced from circumstantial evidence.

The advance planning, in which "Robert" took part, singled out the two largest cinemas in Alexandria—the Metro and the Rio—as the targets of the operation. They also decided on the mode of action: The bombs, again packed in spectacle cases, were to be placed in the cinemas' washrooms, inside the flush tanks. This was decided with the double aim of allowing Philip and Victor, having laid the bombs unseen, to leave the cinemas before the explosion and of ensuring that they would cause little damage, and not endanger innocent persons. After all, that was the purpose of the operation—not to cause damage or casualties, but to demonstrate the existence of an internal opposition movement in Egypt.

"Robert" departed—possibly returning to Cairo—while Philip went out to buy the cinema tickets. At the Metro, he had a surprise; the ticket desk displayed a Sold Out sign. There was another cinema nearby, the Amir; the Richard Widmark film playing there was one that Philip had already seen. "At least I won't have to regret missing the movie," he thought, and decided to buy a ticket for the Amir. On returning to the apartment, he reported the change of plan to Victor, who received it without objection.

This seemingly unimportant detail is of considerable significance: Before the military tribunal which later tried the members of the network, the prosecutor—for some unaccountable reason—presented a policeman who testified that on Friday evening, July 23, he had been ordered to take up a post outside the Metro cinema to protect it from terrorists. Outside of the four members of the cell, the only person who knew that the Metro was the objective was "Robert."

After placing the delayed-action detonators into the spectacle cases, which they then waterproofed by slipping them inside a condom, the two men left the apartment at six o'clock in the evening. The following is Philip's account of what happened:

"The streets teemed with throngs of revelers, and the crowds grew denser as we approached the cinema section. I noticed fire engines parked at the intersections, and I whispered to Victor: 'They're expecting us.' The thought cheered me. If they were waiting for us, that was a sign that they were worried.

"Victor's target, the Rio cinema, was the first one we came to. I intended to leave him there, but I changed my mind at the last moment and decided to remain until I saw him go inside. The cinema was half a story above the street, with about fifteen steps leading up to the entrance. We began to walk up precisely when the doors opened and the audience from the afternoon performance began to pour out. It was hard to move forward in the face of the stream of people.

"We reached the foyer. In front of me, I saw a man wearing a *galabiyeh* [the long robe worn by Egyptian peasants] with a jacket over it, and for some reason, the thought flashed through my mind: 'a plain-clothes detective!' for that was their usual garb. At his side, striding straight at me so that I had to turn aside to avoid running into her, was a woman in a yellow dress. That was the precise moment when I sensed a wave of heat searing my right thigh. Instantly I understood what had happened. The bomb, which was in my trouser pocket, had ignited!

"I wanted to shout to Victor, 'Run!' but I could not get the word out of my mouth. I heard him ask anxiously: 'What's the matter? What happened?' I must have groaned, or perhaps my face twisted with the pain. I remember the expression of alarm on the face of the woman in yellow, as she tried to draw back. Everything happened in a flash. I tried to pull the spectacle case out of my pocket, but it was too late; flames were leaping out of my trousers and my hand was burned. I squeezed my thigh with all my strength, in a vain attempt to stifle the flame before the bomb could ignite—but it was in vain.

"Then came the explosion. The woman's yellow dress was spattered with black stains. She shouted and drew back while I fell down.

"There was a brief moment of oblivion, and then I found myself lying on the ground, surrounded by a circle of people with startled expressions on their faces, not daring to approach.

"My first thought was: 'My leg's gone!' One at least. I did not dare to look down at my legs. I began to glance around me, searching for my amputated foot. Then I gave a second look, closer to me. Everyone was fixing me with frightened stares, without saying a word; there was a profound silence, you could have heard a fly buzzing. I now looked down and saw both my legs. I could not believe that they were still attached to my body. Carefully, I jerked one and then the other—and both of them responded. My trousers were totally burnt and through the holes I could see the blackening skin on my thighs. My arms were also scorched right up to the elbows, and seemed to be covered with black spots. These came from the aluminum powder in the bomb, which, on ignition, had formed tiny crystals that splattered all over me.

"It's strange how swiftly a man's mind works at such moments of shock. I thought: 'I can't run away. I probably can't even manage to stand up. In other words, I'm finished. The only thing left to do is try and gain time, to give the others time to get away.' My mind was not sufficiently clear to think whether there was anywhere they could get away to. With a feeling of relief, I discovered that Victor had disappeared.

"A police sergeant appeared, followed by a plainclothes detective. The man dressed in the *galabiyeh,* whom I had identified as a plainclothes detective, also approached. Somebody in the crowd shouted: 'Take care! He may have another bomb!' I heard the sergeant reply: 'Don't worry, don't worry. We were waiting for them. These are the people who set fire to the American library.'

"I was dragged aside, near the wall. A young man in European clothes, one of the cinema employees, asked: 'Can I help in any way?' I told him to call a taxi to take me to a hospital. The police officer intervened: 'There's no need. An ambulance has already been called.'

"He told the young man to move away, and asked me for my name and address. I knew there was no point in lying, because my identity card was in my trouser pocket. I told him my name and the street where I lived. But when I realized that he was not asking for my identity card, I gave the number of a house at the other end of the street. 'Let them search,' I thought. Meanwhile, time will pass.

"The plainclothes detective asked whether I was alone. I replied in the affirmative. I'm sure he had seen Victor beside me, but he probably didn't want to mention the fact, for fear of being rebuked by the officer for letting Victor get away.

"By the time the ambulance arrived, about a quarter of an hour later, a large crowd had collected, hundreds of people. The officer and the sergeant grasped me on both sides, lifting me up and supporting me while I paced slowly toward the street. The crowd surrounded me, noisy and excited. Someone I knew, a young Jew from Port Said, walked alongside us, asking repeatedly: 'What can be done for you?' I did not reply, for fear that he would also be arrested. Only when I was lifted into the ambulance did I cry out: 'Tell everyone what you have seen!'

"I was brought to the Amiri hospital. While I was in the ambulance, the officer rummaged through my pockets and brought out my bunch of keys, including the key to the cell's apartment as well as the key to the locker in the 'yachting club.' As soon as we reached the hospital, he and the sergeant left me and departed (as I learned later, to search my house), and I was left alone with the detective in the *galabiyeh*. I was taken into a large hall, full of patients, and laid on a bed near the entrance.

"I lay there in misery, without being treated, until an idea came into my mind. I began to shout that I demanded to be transferred. I hoped to be moved to one of the European-run hospitals, where I might perhaps find someone who would help me get away. But my shouts were ignored.

"Only half an hour later did a young orderly come over to me and give me an injection. But the pains did not subside. I continued to shout, and the orderly returned to give me a second shot—morphine this time. Then my scorched clothing was cut off me, I was dressed in a pajama top, and moved to another bed, further from the entrance. I lay there, with the lower half of my body naked and uncovered, unable even to cover myself with a sheet, because of the pain of the burns. While I was lying there, aching all over, with the morphine beginning to lie heavy on my eyelids, a man in a bright red shirt appeared at the foot of the bed. He gave me a prolonged stare, and then, without a word, went away again. It was only some months later, when I met him a second time, that I discovered his identity: He was an agent of the Muhabarat.

"After his departure, some police interrogators arrived—about a dozen of them, wearing civilian clothes. They surrounded my bed and began to fling questions at me from every side. 'Where are the others?' 'How many of them are there?' 'Where are the other bombs?' 'Where were you on July 14?' 'When were you in Cairo?' . . .

"There were threats, too. 'If anything happens before you talk, we'll kill you!'

" 'Talk before the other bombs go off!'

"As they were all asking together, I could choose whichever question was the easiest to answer. I replied: 'I don't even remember what I ate for breakfast, and you ask me about July 14?' For that, I received a slap across the face. Luckily, the morphine was beginning to take effect, and I didn't feel the blows.

"I was taken to the operating theater, and a doctor arrived. I recognized him immediately. He was an Egyptian who had recently moved into our neighborhood. With a pair of pincers, he began to pull the aluminum splinters out of my wounds. In the meantime, the morphine had worn off and I groaned with pain, while at the same time, the interrogation went on uninterrupted. One of the interrogators—later I learned his name: Captain Kamel—grabbed my hair and yanked it hard.

" 'I want a lawyer!' I cried.

" 'That means you admit your guilt?' Kamel interrupted me.

" 'No! I want to lodge a complaint about you mistreating an injured man!'

"I was taken back into the ward. The district prosecutor came, accompanied by his clerk; they placed their chairs beside me, spread out their interrogation forms, and began: 'Your name, father's name, age, address.' The clerk muttered to himself *Sin* [for *sual*, question] and *Gim* [for *gawab*, answer] as he noted down the interrogator's questions and my answers.

" 'Where were you going?'

" 'To the Amir cinema.'

" 'What were you doing in the Rio, then?'

" 'I stopped to look at the publicity stills outside, and somebody bumped into the box of matches I had in my pocket, causing them to catch fire.'

"And so it went on and on.

"Later, after dark, the officer who had confiscated my keys came back, apologizing to the others for his tardiness: 'There were some enormous dogs there which wouldn't let us in.' I comprehended that he had been at my home. Indeed, he pulled out a batch of snapshots and spread them out on the bed. As it happened, all of them depicted friends who had meanwhile left Egypt. I identified them by name, but each time I was asked as to their present whereabouts, I would reply: 'Switzerland, Spain, abroad . . .'

" 'Don't you have any friends in Egypt?' asked the interrogators angrily.

"An officer entered and whispered something in the prosecutor's ear. The latter beckoned to his clerk and both of them arose to go. The interrogation was at an end. They wanted me to get up as well. The doctor objected, but they took no notice of him. I was carried to a car, and we drove to the Atrin police station. Henceforth, our file would be referred to as 'Atrin 10.'

"I was taken into an office occupied by two officers in civilian clothes. One was gigantic and enormously fat, the other of medium height and thin; the latter ordered me to sit down facing him, saying: 'The governor of Alexandria is here. This is your chance to talk, before you get into trouble. Where are the others?'

" 'What others?'

" 'Don't play the fool! If anything happens, you'll pay for it with your life!'

"The fat one broke in: 'It won't work this way. Give him to me!' And before I could turn, a powerful blow flung me against the wall. It was followed by another blow; then he grabbed me by the shoulders and banged me against the wall again and again. He slapped and punched me, drawing involuntary grunts of pain from me. He was foaming at the mouth, his shirt had been yanked out of his trousers. His face was flushed and he panted heavily. Silently, I prayed: 'Let him have a seizure!' but the only thing I said out loud was: 'I want a lawyer, I'm being mistreated!'

"There was a knock at the door. The thin officer went out, returned, and I was dragged into the next room. A swarthy man in uniform, with a red general's insignia on the collar, was sitting behind an enormous desk: the governor.

" 'Here he is, *ya sad't el basha* [Your Honor, the *basha*].'

"He threw me a chilly look. 'Ready?'

"I was dragged outside, where a line of about ten vehicles was waiting. I was put into one of them, together with two officers, and with screeching tires and sirens wailing, the column moved off. On the way, the questions were kept up: 'When were you at the post office? When did you go to the library?'

"I replied: 'What post office? Which library?'

" 'Stop pretending!' one of them said. 'The object which exploded in your pocket is exactly identical with those that went off last week at the American library, and before that, at the post office.'

"I did not have time to reply. The convoy halted, outside my parents' house. We got out, and one of the interrogators grabbed my burnt arm and twisted it behind me, pushing me toward the doorway. Someone came toward us: 'Put out your cigarettes! No smoking!'

"I deduced that they had found the incendiary materials.

"The house was overflowing with policemen and detectives, in and out of uniform. They took me straight to the garden, and to the workshop in the garden hut. This too was so crowded there was no room for me, and I remained standing on the threshold.

"The policemen had piled the table with Vim cans, chemicals, and the fine scales I used for weighing them. With each item they found, they asked me: 'What's this? What's it for?'

"I told them that I was experimenting in manufacturing dyes.

" 'Sure,' said the governor sarcastically. 'There's a good market for them, praise be to Allah.'

"Together with their other trophies, they also confiscated the gardening implements, as well as a fork and spoon. (How *they* got there

I do not know; they were later among the exhibits presented at the trial.) The policemen tried to pull up the floor; they searched among the roof tiles and drilled holes in the walls in their quest after concealed caches. They found the notebook where I had written down the formulas for manufacturing explosives, which I copied from the microfilm I had brought from Israel. 'What's this?'

"I told them I had copied them from a chemistry book I chanced upon.

"They finished tearing the hut apart, and then headed for the house. We went from room to room. Everything was topsy-turvy. We went up to the second floor, to my photographic laboratory, and there it began all over again. They pulled out every drawer and emptied out the contents. 'What's this? And this?'

"The laboratory contained photographic materials—hundreds of feet of film and packets of photographic paper; inside one of the latter I had concealed 'Robert's' most recent letter, which I had not yet had time to send off, and which bore 'Robert's' address. There was a nerve-wracking moment, but they failed to find the letter. Neither did they identify the jar containing mercury fulminate for detonators, nor the one with invisible ink. Taking them for developing materials, they left the jars aside.

"We went to the next room—mine. There were thousands of photographs and negatives there, as well as Victor's matriculation certificate, which remained in my possession after I had photocopied it for his university application. There were dozens of snapshots dating from my period of activity in the movement, as well as various festivities in which I had taken part. There were negatives, including the sheet of instructions I had brought from Israel. They leafed through the photographs, but soon realized they were too numerous to examine carefully. They packed everything into a suitcase, also taking my enlarger, my dryer, as well as all the cameras they found. Afterward, at the trial, the prosecutor made frequent mention of the sophisticated 'espionage camera' they found in my house. However, when it was presented as an exhibit, it turned out to be nothing more than a simple, cheap box camera. My Leica must have been 'taken over' by one of the police officers.

"As we were about to leave the house, we were joined by another detective. This was Maj. Said Fahmi of the Alexandria political police, who was to head the team of investigators working on the 'Atrin 10' file. Suddenly, he flung a question at me:

" 'Do you know Victor Levy?'

"I thought he had noticed Victor's matriculation certificate among my papers, and was trying to gauge my reaction to a 'shot in the dark.'

" 'I know lots of Victor Levys,' I said. 'For example, the racing cyclist.' To tell the truth, I did not know him, but his name was familiar to me, as it would be to any other young Egyptian who took an interest in sport.

" 'I mean the Victor Levy who lives in Cleopatra.'

" 'Oh, that one. Of course. We went to school together from the age of nine.'

"I felt dejected. How had they arrived at Victor?

" 'Are you interested in seeing him?'

" 'Now? Why now? What's the time anyway?'

"It was 1:30 in the morning. The time had come for us to go. I was ordered to get dressed. I knew that I'd be spending a long time in custody, so I chose a strong pair of jeans. Putting them on was agony, because the burns on my thigh had not been dressed yet. I also put on a clean shirt and shoes, and we left. In the course of the three hours we spent in the house, I had seen no trace of my parents. It transpired that they had been taken to the Muhafza [secret police headquarters] for interrogation. I was glad of their absence; I would not want them to see me in my present sorry condition.

"I was driven to the Muhafza and taken into one of the offices. There were three desks there, each one bearing the name of its occupant, from which I learned the names of my interrogators, Said Fahmi and Yusuf Fauzi. There were two armchairs facing the desks. On one of the desks stood the suitcase with the photographs taken from my home.

"They began to interrogate me, with two interrogators flinging their questions at me in turn, asking me mainly about additional bombs. Their questions were backed up by threats: 'If they go off, we'll execute you!'

"While they were talking, the telephone rang. I could hear what was said at the other end: A bomb had gone off in the Radio cinema in Cairo.

"If looks could kill, I would have died on the spot. Said Fahmi flushed and paled, opening and closing his mouth, then he grabbed his name plate off his desk. I could now see the other side, which bore the Koranic exhortation: 'Patience is a virtue,' and he was about to fling it at me. However, regaining his self-control, he put the plate back on the desk. Several moments passed before he calmed down sufficiently to resume his questioning. I was well aware that the real interrogation was just beginning. All the same, I felt encouraged. At least the Cairo operation had succeeded.

"Finally he asked: 'Did you hear?'

" 'No,' I said innocently. 'What happened?'

" 'A bomb went off in a cinema in Cairo!' he yelled.

" 'What does that have to do with me? After all, I'm here!'

"Once again, his face flushed and he had to fight down his fury. In the end he calmed down, went to the door, ordered someone in the corridor to bring some sandwiches, and returned to his desk. We began to go over the snapshots one by one and I was ordered to identify the persons appearing in them. I noticed that when he came to snapshots of Robbie, he laid them aside without asking questions. I thought to myself: 'That must mean that he's known to them.'

"Again, the telephone rang. Another bomb had gone off, in Cairo's Rivoli cinema.

"This time, the tidings did not provoke any outburst. The two interrogators stared at me for a long time, without a word. Finally, Fahmi said: 'You had the chance and you didn't talk. Never mind, we have enough evidence against you to have you hanged.'

" 'You decided from the outset to victimize me! You didn't find any bombs in my home, only dyes.'

" 'We found cans of Vim, like the kind we found at the post office; on you, we found the remnants of a spectacle case, of the kind that set fire to the library. That's enough! You're young, you're not responsible for your actions, but you were living in your father's house. He's responsible for you! We'll hang him!'

" 'I'm too young? My father's old! I want a lawyer!'

" 'You're not entitled to a lawyer!'

"Said Fahmi asked me: 'Do you want to meet your parents?' I replied in the negative.

" 'Why not?'

"I held out my burnt arms. 'I don't want them to see me like this. After my burns are dressed, I'll be glad to meet them.'

"However, he went to the door, beckoning to someone. They came in—Mother weeping, Father furious. 'What have you done?' he shouted at me.

" 'I didn't do anything. A box of matches caught fire in my pocket and they're making a big fuss about it.'

"I did not succeed in convincing him. In the course of the next ten minutes, both of them tried to preach to me. 'Help the police and they will help you.'

"Finally, I said: 'If you want to help me, get me a lawyer.'

" 'But they say martial law is in force and you're not entitled to a lawyer,' said my father.

" 'Don't believe them. Go to a lawyer.'

"They left, and the interrogation was resumed. I was worn out, my burns were painful, and my head was dizzy, but I sensed satisfaction. I was gaining time!

"We went back to the snapshots.

"In the early morning, I requested to go to the washroom. In the corridor, my father came toward me; he, too, like me, was escorted by a policeman. He had not been released yet. Passing by me, he hissed at me in a whisper: *'Assassin!'* and my heart sank.

"After relieving myself and washing my face, I started on my way back to the office. In the corridor, I had another encounter, this time with Victor. He came toward me, dragged along by two policemen. His appearance here was a blow to me. I was fighting tooth and nail to gain time for him to get away, and here he was, in custody, just like me.

"On seeing me, Victor halted.

" 'Did you say I did something?' he flung at me with a show of hostility.

" 'Of course not!' I replied.

"He was led away."

### In the Custody of the Detectives

Victor will never forget the scene at the entrance to the Rio cinema; every time he recalls it, he shudders at the thought of how a man could be doomed in a single moment.

One moment they were walking along, side by side, purposefully, full of confidence. And the next moment . . .

"Suddenly, Philip let out a stifled cry. 'What's the matter? What's wrong?' I called, and as I spoke, I realized that a calamity had occurred. A flame burst out of his trousers. A man wearing a *galabiyeh* grabbed my arm. I drew back, wrenching my hand away.

" 'He's on fire!' I shouted. 'Call an ambulance!'

"Philip was rolling on the ground, trying to stifle the flames which were leaping from his clothes. The crowd drew back. A woman shouted. There was a moment of confusion and panic."

Amid the uproar, at the same time as he was filled with concern for his friend, a thought flashed through Victor's mind: the second bomb! What if it also went off? He had to get rid of it!

He stepped back into the crowd. Everyone, including the plainclothes detective in the *galabiyeh,* had their attention focused on Philip, on the ground. No one noticed Victor as he slipped outside.

How does one get rid of a bomb which is about to go off when one is in the crowded center of a city? Victor looked for a sewage drain, but he could not find one. He continued to stride along the teeming streets until he came to the Corniche. That too was crowded. He walked up the Corniche toward Mazzaritta; gradually, the crowd thinned out. Only a few amateur fishermen stood near the railing with their rods. There, Victor flung the bomb into the sea.

Now that he was no longer on the alert in case the bomb in his pocket caught fire, he could turn his attention to thinking about what had happened, and what needed to be done.

Later, when the members of the Alexandria cell reconstructed the events of that "Black Friday"—among the other incidents of "the unfortunate mishap"—they would relive the terrible confusion they experienced when the calamity occurred. Preparing for an eventual calamity is an important part of the training which any underground agent should receive. He has to have a cover story, with every detail corroborated, so as to give him a chance to stand up to police interrogation, even if only briefly; he has to learn to face cross-examination; he should be instructed what to do to cover his tracks; not to mention a prearranged escape route, when all else fails. There are occasions when none of these precautions is adequate; however, by preparing for the worst, the underground agent fortifies himself to face calamity and endure the shock of seeing everything collapse around him.

The members of the Alexandria cell had not received such training. When disaster struck, they had nothing to fall back on, other than their own instincts and resources. It was this instinct which guided Philip, in custody, to try to gain time; it was the same instinct which told Victor, pacing the promenade in an anxious daze, that above all, it was essential to cover their trail: Everything suspicious must be removed from the cell's apartment.

He hastened to the apartment. There, he took the remaining bombs and the chemicals and flushed them down the toilet. He stripped down the transmitter and concealed it. He looked around, to ensure that he had not left any incriminating traces. Everything was "clean."

The next step was to warn his companions. Four persons possessed keys to the apartment: Philip, Shmuel Azar, "Robert," and Victor himself. Philip had been caught. As for "Robert," Victor was scheduled to report to him the following day, not at the apartment but at a small café on Missla Street. Would it occur to "Robert" to come to the apartment? Probably not; but Shmuel definitely would come. Victor therefore wrote a short note: " 'Henry' [Philip's code name] is dangerously ill. For your information," adding the time and place of his scheduled meeting with "Robert." He pinned the note to Shmuel's easel. If he came, he would certainly see it.

What next? There was the store hut and the laboratory in Philip's home, in the Stanley Bey quarter at the other side of the city. Victor boarded a tram going in that direction.

An hour and a half had passed since Philip had burst into flame at the entrance to the Rio cinema; when Victor reached Barbazeh Street, where Philip lived, darkness had fallen. However, from the corner of the street, he could make out two cars parked in front of number 13, with several men in civilian clothes standing nearby. Victor's senses were highly alert. He remembered that the Natanson family did not possess a car and no one lived opposite them. The other side of the street was occupied by a large garden belonging to a villa further down the street; the wall surrounding the garden did not have an opening opposite the Natanson home.

Instinctively, Victor turned on his heel and returned to the tram stop. He decided to go home. There, too, he needed to "clean up" and remove the transmitter.

Mireille, Victor's elder sister, was at home when he arrived. "Philip has been arrested," he told her laconically. He did not go into detail, nor did he mention the possibility that he too might be arrested, but his actions spoke for themselves. Before the worried gaze of his sister, he took the transmitter out of the closet and dismantled it into two sections. He concealed the transmitter in a cache he had previously prepared, inside a thick medical textbook. He hid the book inside the sewing machine. "If anything happens," he instructed his sister, "tell Roger [their younger brother] to throw the contents of the book into the sea."

Roger indeed did so; consequently, the prosecutor was unable to prove that Victor had been in radio contact with Israel, thereby possibly saving Victor from the scaffold.

After that, Victor went over all the papers in the house, destroying anything which might arouse suspicion. There was only one item he forgot—a letter notifying him of "Robert's" arrival in June.

It was unbearable to sit at home, facing his sister's worried gaze. "I went out. But where could I go? To the apartment? Perhaps the police were already there. I wandered aimlessly around the streets. What should I do? Where should I go? Should I try to flee? Where to? And how, without documents or money? I had no more than thirty pounds in my pocket. Finally, after midnight, I made my decision: I would return home. Let fate bring what it would."

He approached the house cautiously, but he saw nothing suspicious. Their home was in a seven-story residential block, in a busy street. Outside the house, dozens of cars were parked, as usual. The Nubian *bawab* (concierge) was standing on the pavement, near the entrance; when Victor approached, the man gave him a broad grin, turned, and entered the stairway. Victor followed him; as he crossed the threshold, hands grabbed at him from behind. He tried to struggle, calling to the *bawab* to help him, and then he heard someone say: "See whether he has a gun." Someone else growled furiously: "You wanted to burn the whole country, did you?" Now he knew; it was the police.

Victor: "The scuffle in the stairway must have been audible in our apartment. My father opened the door and called: 'Victor, is that you? What's going on there?'

"I thought to myself: 'Anything is better than getting them embroiled.'

" 'It's all right,' I replied, 'it's the police. I'll see what they want.' "

His two captors took him out into the street. There they asked him: "Do you know Philip Natanson?"

"Of course, I know him from school, an unstable fellow. What's he done now?"

"As if you didn't know!"

"Really, I don't know what you're talking about."

"You'll be told at the Muhafza!"

"At police headquarters, I was taken into an office. After a moment, a middle-aged man, elegantly dressed, walked in; without a word, he slapped me twice. Instinctively, I lashed out, kicking him in the ankle, shouting: 'Scoundrel, how dare you!' but the two burly men behind me grasped me while the man punched me repeatedly until my face swelled up. It was only then that one of the policemen said: 'Are you crazy? That was Col. Samir Darwish [the commander of the Alexandria police force]!' Then he walked out, still not uttering a word.

"I sat there for about an hour, between the two silent policemen. After that, I was taken to a neighboring room, followed by a tall, heavily built man in civilian clothes. He sat down at the desk which bore the sign Sar [Maj.] Mamduh Salem. The name was familiar to me. He was the head of Alexandria's aliens police. It was his department which had kept watch on the Zionist youth movements. Twenty years later, he was to be appointed prime minister of Egypt.

"He sat there for a few moments without saying a word; suddenly, he seized an ashtray from the desk and flung it at me, followed by pens, pencils, anything he could get his hands on. All this was accompanied by curses and shouts: 'You want to burn down the whole of Egypt! Dirty traitors!'

"I feigned innocence. 'What do you want?' adding indignantly, 'Ask me civilly and I'll answer you.'

" 'All right. Do you know Philip Natanson?'

" 'Yes, I do.'

" 'Do you know that he was caught trying to set fire to a cinema? And that you are suspected of abetting him?'

" 'I don't know. Even when we were at school together, he was a bit of a nut. And aside from that, there's almost no contact between us. We went to the movies together a couple of times; together with a whole group we share a chalet in Sidi Bisher. We meet there at parties, that's all.'

"He began to question me about the chalet's other visitors. I reeled off dozens of names—a few Jews but most of them non-Jews—none of whom was connected to the cell. Later I learned that they were all arrested for questioning.

"My comprehensive replies calmed him down. At two-thirty in the morning, he said: 'Good. Let's go to the chalet.'

"I continued to play my role. 'Listen, that's not very nice. Maybe one of the group is there with a girl.'

"He brushed this off with a wave of the hand, and we set out in three cars. I was in the back seat of the first one, squeezed in between two detectives. The chalet was empty. The policemen conducted a thorough search, demolishing walls and pulling up the floor, but found nothing. We returned to the Muhafza; for an hour or two, I was left alone, with a policeman, in one of the offices. Then I was again brought before the interrogators. While being led down the corridor, I saw Philip; he was sitting on a chair near the door of the washroom and his appearance was pitiful; his arms were covered with ugly burns, and his face was twisted in pain. I flung myself at him in feigned anger: 'Are you crazy? What kind of trouble have you got me into? Did I do anything?'

" 'I didn't say you did anything,' he replied.

" 'Then tell them!'

"Even though we had not arranged it beforehand, Philip instantly understood my intention and played his part to perfection. Mamduh Salem, standing at the door of his office, heard every word. Whether or not he was taken in I cannot be certain.

"After a further brief series of questions, a policeman escorted me to a room at the end of the corridor; it contained no chairs, only desks. I sat on one of them, and began to contemplate my situation. Matters were grave, without any doubt, but I still had some hope of fooling them.

"At six o'clock in the morning, I asked to go to the washroom. In the corridor I ran into my father. When I failed to return home, he had come to inquire about me, but no one gave him any clear answer to his queries. 'Are they beating you?' he asked, his expression furious. Poor Father! He was so confident, so accustomed to seeing matters working out in accordance with his wishes. 'Shall I go to the consulate?'

" 'No. There's no need. I didn't do what they accuse me of.' (Out of the corner of my eye, I saw Mamduh Salem again standing in the doorway of his office.) 'They'll soon clear it up. You can go to work, without worrying.'

" 'But are they beating you?'

" 'No, they aren't beating me.'

"Mamduh Salem, who spoke French well, intervened: 'Monsieur

Levy, you can go. You see that everything is all right. By midday, your son will be home.'

"I sent Father on his way with an encouraging smile. It was the last time I would see him until the trial. I was taken back to the room, where I remained until four in the afternoon. The policeman guarding me was relieved at intervals; each time a new guard arrived, I would shower him with questions: 'How long will I be detained? What's going to happen?' but they knew no more than I.

"In the end, an officer arrived. 'Come along, Philip wants to talk to you.'

"I was indignant. 'I have nothing to talk to him about.'

"All the same, I was taken out into the corridor, to find Philip coming toward me, limping and burned. The police escorts drew back a little, leaving us together."

That first meeting with Victor, in the corridor leading to the washroom, had fundamentally changed the situation, from Philip's viewpoint. Hitherto, his principal aim had been to gain time so as to enable his companions to make their getaway. But Victor was in custody, and the police also seemed to know about Robbie (as he guessed from his interrogators' indifference when they came across snapshots of him). In that case, there was no point in playing for time. On the contrary, something needed to be done to halt the interrogation, or perhaps to divert it in another direction, on a false trail . . .

As yet, he did not know how that could be done. When he was brought back to the interrogation room, he turned mutinous: "I won't talk until you release my parents and bring me a lawyer!"

The interrogators tried to bargain with him. "You are not entitled to a lawyer. First tell us everything, and then, when we block all your operations, we'll release your parents."

"And what will you do with me?"

"We'll detain you for some time, not long, a few months . . ."

"Will you deport me?"

"Do you want to be deported? Why? After all, this is your home."

"My home? But when I applied for Egyptian citizenship, I was turned down. What prospects are left for me in Egypt now? Who will give me a job?"

It went on like that for several hours. In the end, Said Fahmi suddenly said: "If you wish, we'll let you meet Victor Levy. He'll also tell you you have no right to a lawyer."

Philip agreed instantly. Perhaps together, the two of them would come up with some idea.

At this time—it was Saturday afternoon—the corridor was crowded. The policemen escorting Victor and Philip stepped aside, and the two were left face to face. Looking at one another, each thought how bad the other looked. It was evident that both had just endured some difficult hours.

Philip began to speak immediately in a semiwhisper.

"We're caught," he said. "I was caught in the act, and they also found the store in my home. There's no point in denials. At least, let's save the others. I suggest we confess and take the blame for everything."

Victor hesitated for a moment, but then he said: "All right. I agree. The two of us did everything."

"No, they know there are three of us. They found three overalls in the hut. And they know about Robbie. We will have to give his name as well."

This was too much for Victor. "Out of the question! Only the two of us."

"But there was the operation in Cairo!"

They argued for a few moments, until Victor was convinced. Then he said: "If they ask us for our motives, we'll say that we're Communists, Egyptian patriots, and we wanted to speed up the departure of the British."

"Not Communists!" Philip amended. "Socialists. The Communists don't believe in terrorism."

"Communists, Socialists, it makes no difference! Leave it to me to explain." Victor was confident that his Communist contacts in Paris had given him sufficient acquaintance with Communist dialectic to permit him to stand up to interrogation. In case of need, he could even give the names and addresses of active Egyptian Communists who had found asylum in France.

They were separated.

On being brought back to the interrogation room, after waiting all night, Philip said: "I'm prepared to believe your promises; I'll talk, but if I do, will you release my parents?" They promised to do so.

"And will you deport us?" This, too, they promised.

"When?"

"Within four to six months. All right?"

"And will you take me to the hospital?"

"As soon as you complete your statement."

He pretended to believe their promises.

"Good. In that case, I confess to having laid the bombs in the post office, in the American library, and in the cinema."

"How many of you were there?"

"Three—I, Victor, and Robert."

"Robert Dassa?"

I was right, thought Philip, they know about Robbie.

"But that is impossible!" said Yusuf Fauzi. "At least five persons were needed to carry out the operations you mentioned."

"Why? There were three bombs in the post office; each of us laid one. Victor and I set fire to the Cairo library, and Robbie acted alone in Alexandria; this time, Robert acted alone in Cairo—as you can see by the times: First he went to the station cloakroom, then to one cinema, and finally to the other. If more than one person had been involved, all the bombs would have gone off simultaneously."

"Which of you was in command?"

"There was no one in command. We were all equal."

"What did you aim to achieve?"

Philip explained: "We wanted to exert pressure on the British to leave immediately."

"In that case, why the attacks on the American library?"

"To make sure the Americans didn't come in, in place of the British."

(This was the first mention of the story that the operations were directed against Britain and the United States. Philip made it up on the spur of the moment and the Egyptians seized on it, finding it so plausible that they continued to adhere to it, even when they found out that Philip's "confession" was a pack of lies. This account was also presented at their trial, where the prosecutor depicted the attacks as a provocation aimed at sowing dissension between Egypt and the West—without troubling to explain how attacks on a post office, cinemas, or a railway station could serve such a purpose. However, with no denial from Israel, the story took such a firm hold that there were those in Israel who feared that "the mishap" could disrupt Israel's relationship with the United States.)

The uniformed policeman who was standing by could not contain his admiration.

"By Allah!" he cried. "If there had been at least one true Egyptian among you, we'd say that you were heroes, like the *fedayeen*. . . . But you yourselves are foreigners!"

"True, but we wanted to prove that we're patriots!"

The interrogators seemed satisfied by his answers; nevertheless, Philip was relieved when they switched their questioning back to the practical details of the operations. He was not very confident of the "ideological explanation" he had presented.

By evening, his interrogation was completed. He was taken—without being shoved or cuffed this time—to a room at the end of the corridor, where he found two desks and a chair upon which a plainclothes detective was dozing. On one of the desks, curled up and dejected, lay Victor.

Victor's interrogation had also been completed. On being requested to sign the statement, he had refused on the grounds that it was written in Arabic. The only thing he gained from his refusal was a flurry of blows until he signed.

Philip laid himself down on the other desk. They conversed in a whisper, each one telling the other of his experiences. Philip said that the microfilm he had brought from Israel, with sabotage instructions, was in his apartment, and he feared it would fall into the hands of the police. Victor replied: "Never mind, we'll get over that." At this point, the policeman woke up and ordered them to be silent.

Finally, they fell asleep.

In the morning—it was now Monday—Victor was escorted to the washroom. There, at the end of the corridor, he ran into Robbie, his face swollen from the beatings he had endured. There was a detective beside him.

Walking past him, Victor whispered in French: "Only three. You, in both Cairo cinemas. We're Communists."

Robbie wanted to say something, to object, but there was no time. However, from his expression, Victor knew that he had understood.

At first sight, it would appear that the Alexandria cell was uncovered as a result of the mishap which befell Philip Natanson at the entrance of the Rio cinema, but there can be no doubt that the accident was a cover which the Egyptian police used to conceal their prior knowledge about the cell and its members, as well as the operations planned for July 23. This is confirmed by the fire engines standing by in the cinema section in Alexandria, and by the police sergeant who told the agitated crowd surrounding Philip: "We were expecting them!"

But there are further indications, all of which, taken together, led the three to conclude that there was a double agent within the cell. Perhaps the most obvious proof comes from the circumstances under which Victor and Robbie were arrested. Victor was picked up at midnight on Friday, July 23, before Philip ever mentioned his name. Robbie, admittedly, was taken into custody on Sunday night, on his return from Cairo; but the police raided his home, arresting his father, on Friday night, long before Victor and Philip met in the corridor at the Muhafza and decided to take the blame, together with Robbie.

Many years passed before any of the three ever dared to mention the horrifying possibility that one of their number was a traitor. (Israel's intelligence community had reached this conclusion far earlier.) But at this time, nothing could have been further from their minds.

Robbie was in a daze when he was torn from the arms of his weeping mother and taken away to the Muhafza. True, one of the detectives told his mother: "Have no fear, he'll be back within an hour!" but after hours of foreboding, he refused to snatch at this hope. However, on the way to police headquarters, he had time to think matters over, to reconstruct the sequence of events since his departure for Cairo, and to reach the conclusion that matters were not hopeless. He knew that his home was "clean," containing nothing incriminating. His stay in Cairo was also completely "covered"—he had picnicked with his girl friend at the Barrage, taken her to a movie—and there was no shred of proof that he had done anything else. He prepared himself for his encounter with the interrogators.

The first of these was Samir Darwish, head of the Alexandria police force. He went about matters in his own way: Before even asking Robbie the first question, he struck him with several violent blows to the face. This had always proved an effective method against most persons brought to him for interrogation. But Robbie closed up like a clam.

Later, he was to say: "I don't know whether I would have been able to withstand systematic scientific torture. It is normal to believe that the human mind is capable of thinking up tortures so diabolical as to be unendurable. But beatings are a different matter altogether. They are bearable. They only strengthened my determination to hold out, and my confidence that I was capable of doing so, particularly when I found out that they had suspected all sorts of things, but had no real proof."

Under the flurry of blows which descended upon him, Robbie woodenly repeated his prepared cover story: He had gone to Cairo to meet his girl friend and had spent the weekend in her company. They had gone to the Barrage and to the movies. Here were the tickets, as confirmation. And if that wasn't enough, why didn't they ask the girl herself?

On discovering that the beatings did not produce their usual result, Samir Darwish altered his approach. He lit a cigarette for Robbie and said: "Look, we can prove your guilt without any confession on your part. We'll make a microscopic examination of the dirt under your fingernails, of the dust in your trouser pockets. We'll definitely find incriminating traces. But it will be easier for you if you talk."

With that, the interrogator reverted to his systematic beatings. One of his assistants, a burly thug called Kamel, began to punch Robbie persistently and viciously. Blood ran down his mouth and out of his nose, and he was certain that at least one of his ribs was broken.

Kamel was followed by another thug, who twisted Robbie's arm behind his back until he was certain it was about to break. The pain was awful. However, he succeeded in enfolding his mind within a kind of dull armor which the physical pain failed to penetrate. One of them later said to Victor, with no small measure of wonder: "What kind of man is that friend of yours? Is he a beast or a human being? None of you has endured what he's been through, but he won't talk!"

"What else could I answer?" Robbie said, years later. "My only course was to act dumb and obstinate. My interrogators flung at me: 'You're an Egyptian, you've drunk the waters of the Nile [a popular expression for a true Egyptian]; how could you raise your hand against your own country?' What could I say? Could I say that I did what I did out of loyalty to my own country—a different country? Every word I said could only cause harm. The best thing was to say nothing, and just repeat: 'I don't know . . .' "

At four in the morning, his interrogation ended, and he was flung into a cell in the basement, where the police were in the habit of leaving drunks to sober up. It was a large room, high-ceilinged, with an iron-plated door and no windows. The room was stifling in the July heat; and worse, filled with the powerful stench of urine and vomit left behind by countless drunks who had failed to find their way to the *kardal* (the bucket which served as a toilet) near the door.

The *kardal* was the room's sole furnishing, aside from a jug of malodorous drinking water and the *borsh*, a filthy, dilapidated mat spread on the floor.

"When they bolted the iron door on me, I felt terrible; it was as though I had been locked out of the world, and buried in this stinking vault, illuminated by the murky light of a single bulb. My shirt was torn; my trousers bloodstained. Blood was oozing from my nose and ears, and my whole body was swollen from the beatings I had suffered. I took off my shoes and put them under my head; then I stretched out on the *borsh*. I did not believe that I'd be able to fall asleep, but I dozed off straight away. I dreamed that rats were scuttling around me and all over me, and it wasn't just a dream. . . .

"When I was awoken, I thought I had slept for no more than five minutes. However, it was ten o'clock, Monday morning. Once again, I was brought before the interrogator.

" 'Are you ready to talk?' he asked me. Instantly, my mind enfolded itself within that same dull, impenetrable veil. 'No!' I replied, and tensed myself for the blow. But the detective who was present in the room said: 'Look, Victor and Philip have already confessed. Do you want to see their confessions?'

"I refused, whereupon he said: 'All right, we'll let you meet them.' Again, I refused. 'They're no friends of mine!' I declared. All the same, they took me out into the corridor and Victor came toward me.

"When he whispered to me, my first reaction was: 'Are you crazy?' But I did not have time to reply. He was taken away.

"I pondered over what Victor had said. His words were not to my liking. True, we had fallen into enemy hands, and a confession was inevitable. However, I could not remain true to myself while pretending to be a Communist. I would have been more responsive if I had been able to declare that I'd acted on behalf of the ideal in which I really did believe—on behalf of the state of Israel.

"Consequently, when the interrogator again asked me: 'Are you ready to talk?' I again replied in the negative. The detectives tried to 'influence' me. Above all, they wanted to know whether I had 'left anything else' in Cairo. They warned me: 'If it explodes—we'll kill you!'

"I remained firm in my refusal, but all the time, I was weighing Victor's proposal. I began to see the logic of it—even though, in my heart of hearts, I was indignant that we had not decided to resist to the end. I was convinced that one could stand up to the interrogation, as long as one sealed one's consciousness to the pain and the humiliation. . . .

"When I said that I was ready to talk, Philip and Victor were brought in, and they took down the testimony of all three of us together. Victor dominated the interrogation, 'guiding' us to such an extent that he answered questions directed at Philip or me, whereupon the interrogator shouted at him: 'Shut your mouth, you. It wasn't you we asked!'

"Our line was that in the course of his studies in France, Victor had become a Communist, and on his return to Egypt, he had led us two in his wake. Victor gave the names of two or three well-known Egyptian left-wingers living in Paris. He appealed to Philip to 'back him up': 'Do you remember Mustaki, the one who took us to the library?'

"Philip 'remembered'; he also 'remembered' meetings with Communist girls, which he described in great detail. The interrogators drank his words in thirstily. This was precisely what they loved!

"When we signed our statements, the atmosphere in the room became almost friendly. Nevertheless, I felt despondent, dejected by the awareness that, despite everything, I had 'broken' and confessed, and furthermore, I sensed that this was not the end of the episode. It was only the beginning. . . ."

Were the Egyptians really foolish enough to believe that they were dealing with a "Communist underground"? If so, how does this fit in with the hypothesis of a double agent operating inside the Alexandria cell?

This apparent discrepancy has an explanation, confirmed by subsequent events, inside Egypt and abroad. The explanation is that the double agent was not in contact with the aliens police or the civilian counterintelligence, but with the Muhabarat, the military intelligence service. At that time, these bodies were in open rivalry. Most of the higher police officers, having been appointed before the revolution, were suspected of being secret supporters of the *ancien régime,* or at least, were considered untrustworthy. As for the military intelligence and its subordinate internal security division, this was not merely an integral part of the new regime, but belonged to its most extreme wing, which strove to extend the influence of the revolution over every aspect of life in the country.

It is a reasonable assumption that if the military intelligence had chanced upon information indicating the existence of an Israeli underground network in Egypt, it would have told the civilian police no more than the latter required to put an end to the operations of that network. The military intelligence would have kept the rest of the information to itself—both with the aim of protecting the double agent and also with an eye on future steps, not the least of which was to discredit the civilian police.

## Everything in Ruins

The three men were transferred to Kum el Dik, a detention center for foreigners, which was situated in Atrin. This is a small, two-story prison, with about ten cells on each floor, and a large courtyard surrounded by a wall with an opening toward the street. Most of the prisoners detained there were Turkish or Lebanese sailors who had jumped ship, or Moslem pilgrims from North Africa on their way to or from Mecca, who tried to stay over in Egypt without a residence visa. These persons were detained here until their deportation.

It was a fairly comfortable prison; each of the three men was placed in a separate cell—Victor and Philip at the front of the building, near the prison office; Robbie at the other end, near the washrooms. The walls were thin, and one could hear whatever was said in the courtyard. There was even "musical entertainment," a radio operated at full blast (only during news broadcasts was it turned down). Robbie spent hours at a time peering through the spy-hole at everyone entering and leaving the washroom. Having discovered where the three men were imprisoned, their parents, though forbidden to see them, insisted on the right accorded to every prisoner prior to his trial, to receive his food from outside. For a daily payment of thirty piastres the trio received their meals from a restaurant facing the prison. They were also permitted cigarettes, although these were kept by the guard on duty in the courtyard. Whenever they craved a smoke, they were obliged to bang on the door and call him—it being the custom to offer him a cigarette, too. If he was in a good mood, he would "forget" to lock the cell door, permitting the prisoners to see one another and exchange grins of encouragement.

The interrogations continued. Every morning they were taken to the Midan Sa'ad Zaglul Aliens Court. (In fact, this was an ordinary court, with only its name remaining as a reminder of Egypt's "capitulations" period, when foreigners were entitled to trial before a special court, in accordance with the laws of their own country.) Here they were questioned by a team of Muhafza interrogators headed by Maj. Said Fahmi, while court clerks recorded their testimony. The questioning was still harsh, and accompanied by an occasional slap, but this was done more out of routine than in anger, for they were now considered "cooperative." A police expert set off some of the explosives found in Philip's home and emerged, blackened and dazed, muttering: "No doubt about it, a very dangerous substance." But even then, the interrogators remained relaxed. They were even gratified, for the greater the menace of the "Communist underground" they had uncovered, the greater the glory they would reap for having "cracked" it.

A few days later, however, everything changed.

Philip: "It happened on Thursday, our sixth day in custody. We were taken for interrogation, as usual, but on the way to the court, I noticed that something out of the ordinary was afoot. The guards who came to escort us seemed angry, and as they took us to the cars, they gave us more than our normal portion of shoves and kicks. But they said nothing till we arrived at the court. There we were taken into a room, not that of the prosecutor, where a table was piled high with dozens of envelopes containing the documents and photographs confiscated from my home. When Said Fahmi began to empty them out onto the table, my glance froze on two postcard-size negatives, which I immediately recognized as the film of instructions I had brought from Israel, side by side with the negative of the letter from Paris containing the key to the cipher.

"I stole a glance at Victor. He was white as a sheet.

"Either because he did not yet grasp the importance of the negatives or from a desire to trick me, Fahmi began by questioning me about other photographs. I had to make an effort to concentrate on his questions. While doing so, I slid my hand toward the nearest negative, the one with the instructions, and tried to scratch away the writing with my fingernail. Naturally, I failed.

"However, while everyone's attention was focused on me, Victor seized on the opportunity: His hand rested on the negative of the letter, and when he bent down to tie up his shoelace, the negative vanished from the table, without anyone noticing."

Victor: "As soon as I saw the negative of the letter on the table, I knew that the game was up. The letter's contents would blow our cover story about being an independent Communist underground. The frequencies testified to our radio contacts with Israel. Furthermore, the letter mentioned the cell's apartment, whose existence we had hitherto succeeded in concealing from our interrogators. I resolved at all costs to get hold of the letter.

"While everyone was looking at Philip, my hand 'roamed' over the table and on encountering the film, pushed it off the edge. When I bent down to tie up my shoelaces, I slipped it into the cuff of my trousers. After that, I asked permission to go to the washroom. Fahmi was so immersed in his questioning of Philip that he did not even look at me. Impatiently, he told the uniformed policeman: 'Take him!'

"I opened the door to go out, fancying that I had succeeded, when behind me, I suddenly heard Fahmi's voice: 'Just a moment. There was a black film here, and I can't see it!'

"We went back to the table. All of us, interrogators and detainees, began to thumb through the pile of documents and films, without success.

" 'Don't drive me out of my mind!' roared Fahmi. 'The film was here.' He ordered us to be searched, but nothing was found. Then one of the interrogators said: 'Maybe it fell on the floor?' They bent down to look under the table, they lifted the carpet, and while they were doing so, one of them noticed the edge of the negative sticking out of my cuff.

"There was a sudden silence. Fahmi grabbed a Coca-Cola bottle and for a moment, I thought he was about to smash it over my head. But he controlled himself, and only hissed, with venomous hostility: 'For that, you will be executed!' "

Everything changed. The three prisoners were handcuffed and separated. While Robbie and Philip were escorted back to the Kum el Dik prison, Victor was taken to the Muhafza.

"We thought that Philip was the leader," Fahmi spat at him furiously. "Now we know it was you . . ." and punched him in the face. The other three interrogators joined in. Without asking him any questions, they punched him savagely until they had vented their fury. Then, they threw him, bleeding and dazed, into the stinking dungeon in the basement.

"One of my more useful characteristics," says Victor, "is that at times of tension, I find refuge in sleep. That's what happened now. Unable to see any way out of my new predicament, I fell asleep.

"The next morning, I was awakened by the flies which swooped down on me at first light, and gave me no further rest.

"The flies were the only creatures to display any interest in me that day. The iron-plated door remained locked, as though I had been forgotten, or else, which was nearer to the way I felt, I had been buried alive. At one point, a policeman heard my banging on the door, which he opened with curses and oaths, and prodding me from behind, led me to the washroom. He brought me back, and again, the door was locked behind me. Later, it was reopened for a moment; a dry pitta [Arab bread] and a hunk of cheese were tossed in, to land on the filthy floor. Aside from that, no one took an interest in me, no one asked me anything, they didn't even trouble to beat me.

"The night was worse. I think that must have been the worst experience one can undergo. As darkness descended, the rats emerged from their holes.

"I have a deathly fear of rats, and that fear pursued me throughout the years I spent in Egyptian prisons, all of which teem with these disgusting creatures. That night in the Muhafza, I heard their squeaking; later, they became more daring and approached near enough for me to see them. They were revolting beasts, as big as cats. I trembled with the fear that they would touch me; I did not believe I'd find the courage to close my eyes. Nevertheless, I did finally fall asleep.

"The following morning—I had to make a tremendous effort to recall that it was Saturday, July 31—the door opened and a policeman stood in the doorway. I was so pleased to see a human being, I almost kissed him. He beckoned to me to come outside, and led me to an office, where I found Said Fahmi alone.

" 'Do you see this sheet of paper?' he greeted me when I stood before him. 'That's my report on what happened the day before yesterday.' Indifferently, I muttered that I could not read Arabic.

" 'This piece of paper could take you to the scaffold,' he continued, and waited for me to respond. I made no answer. 'But we're humane,' he continued, 'and here's the proof!' and he ripped the paper into shreds. 'But from now on, behave yourself! We know that you are the head of the group; you must tell us everything.'

"His threats of the scaffold did not frighten me. I told myself that if he had torn up the report, it was not out of mercy toward me, but rather out of fear that his superiors would rebuke him for his negligence in letting me lay hands on the negative. I continued to feign indifference.

"He now called in the whole team of interrogators. Kamel began to slap me on the face, slowly but persistently, and with every slap, he muttered: 'Now we want the true story.'

"I gritted my teeth and said nothing. Later on, when the three of us got together again, we compared notes on the interrogations we had faced, and how we had stood up to them. Philip related that, with every blow, he let out a cry; he claimed that his cries gratified the interrogators, who did not hit him much. For some reason, I could not bring myself to act in this manner. My obstinate silence seemed to heighten their anger.

"Fahmi stood up and walked out, whereupon the others did not rest content with slaps. By the time he returned, an hour later, I was swollen and weak.

"Fahmi brought the negatives, blown up to the size of a sheet of paper. He said: 'Now we'll sit down and read this together. What is this?'

"It was the page of instructions for manufacturing bombs.

" 'I found it in the library,' I said, trying to stick to my story.

" 'No,' said Fahmi. 'There's a letter here,' and he held out the photocopy of the letter from Israel which Philip, on 'Robert's' instructions, had refrained from destroying. Fahmi himself began to read, and he soon came to the portion which mentioned the apartment at 18, Amiri Hospital Street. 'What's this? What apartment is this?'

"I said that it was a bachelor apartment which I had rented together with a friend. At this point, the interrogation was broken off, and they hurried to the apartment."

The apartment was searched thoroughly, but they discovered nothing. They failed to find the cache containing the transmitter; every other incriminating object had been removed by Victor prior to his arrest. However, when the detectives questioned the building's caretaker, they learned that the apartment had been rented by a certain Shmuel Azar.

That same day—eight days after the abortive action at the Rio cinema—Shmuel Azar was arrested.

How had Shmuel Azar spent those eight days? Another six months were to pass before his companions were to hear the story from him. That was at the commencement of the show trial in Cairo, the first occasion when all the arrested members of the network were confined together and got the chance to talk to one another.

This was when Shmuel Azar told them his story.

He had, indeed, reached the apartment on Saturday, the day after the arrest of Philip and Victor. On entering, he found the note which Victor had left on the easel. Shmuel did not precisely comprehend what had happened (the newspapers made no mention of the events at the Rio cinema), but from the note, he understood that Victor wanted him to come to the rendezvous with "Robert" at the café on Missla Street.

When Shmuel arrived, "Robert" was waiting there. Shmuel

showed him the note referring to "Henry's" illness. It was clear: Philip had fallen into the hands of the police.

But what had happened to Victor? "Find out and let me know," "Robert" ordered. They arranged to meet again in two days' time.

That same day, Shmuel went to Victor's house. It was Victor's sister Eugette who opened the door. She had never met Shmuel, but she sensed that the delicate-featured young man was a friend of her brother's. "Victor was arrested yesterday," she told him.

By Tuesday morning, when he met "Robert" again, Shmuel had also learned of Robbie's arrest. He reported his findings to "Robert," who looked very worried.

"I hope they don't incriminate me," he said. "I trust Victor, but what of Philip? I'm sure he'll talk."

"In that case," said Shmuel, "the most logical thing is to go away."

"Robert" thought it over for a moment and then indicated his agreement. "All right," he said. "Pack your things and I will arrange for your departure from Egypt. Tomorrow morning I'll come to collect you."

The following day—by now it was five days after the mishap at the Rio—"Robert" appeared outside Shmuel's apartment at six o'clock in the morning. Shmuel was waiting for him with his suitcase packed. However, "Robert" told him, confidently: "I have read the transcripts of their interrogation. They are pretending to be Communists, and they're standing up to the questioning. I'm sure they won't break, so there's no immediate danger, and it wouldn't pay to run away. We'll make our getaway after we succeed in getting them out of prison." He indicated that he had a plan of action for accomplishing this.

Shmuel was still worried.

"There's no cause for concern," "Robert" reassured him. "No one suspects you. But to make quite certain, I'll post people outside your home, to inform me if anyone starts to take an interest in you. They'll be disguised as policemen, so if you see them, don't be afraid."

They agreed to meet again, in three days' time. Shmuel returned home feeling embarrassed and foolish. He had told no one but his sister of his forthcoming secret departure from Egypt, and brother and sister had held an emotional leavetaking. Now he had to return home and explain that it had all been a mistake.

For Shmuel, the three days which elapsed before his next meeting with "Robert" passed amid a mixture of anxiety and hope. However, when he met "Robert," on the morning of Saturday, July 31, the latter had no news, only the promise that the operation to rescue the arrested members of the network was imminent. "Robert" asked Shmuel about his plans for that day and the next few days. Shmuel replied that he was

going straight home, and he would wait there.
At midday, the detectives came to get him.

Victor encountered Shmuel Azar at Muhafza headquarters, in the corridor outside Said Fahmi's office. During a break in Victor's interrogation, while he was waiting outside, Shmuel was brought in, handcuffed to a policeman. During the brief moments that they waited together, they conversed in French. Victor tried to persuade his friend to deny any charges, and to put the blame on him. "Tell them that you sublet the apartment to me and that you know nothing of what went on there," he begged Shmuel. "We're in it up to our necks whatever happens, and what you say won't make matters any worse for us. But as for you, the only thing linking you with us is the lease on the apartment."

But it was in vain. Shmuel Azar was incapable of lying, and, being aware of the fact, he did not even try. As soon as Said Fahmi began to question him, Shmuel said simply that he was a full accomplice in everything his companions had done. "We are Jews and Zionists," he said proudly, "and we acted on behalf of the state of Israel." They were all taken back to prison; henceforth, the interrogation focused on Shmuel Azar.

At Kum el Dik, no trace remained of the former relaxed atmosphere. The interrogators were furious with the three prisoners for having misled them, and probably feared for their own fate when it was found out how easily they had permitted themselves to be taken in by the yarn about the "Communist underground." The guards, too, now behaved differently: Any request, even if one of them wanted to go to the washroom, was answered by beatings. They were completely isolated; even the criminals brought to do cleaning work in the detention center avoided any contact with them. "But the most painful thing," recalls Philip, "was hearing Shmuel's cries of pain, which filled the prison. His interrogation was conducted in the prison office, on the second floor, and went on for twenty-four hours. Even when we blocked up our ears, we could hear his cries."

No one can stand up to an interrogation accompanied by torture, when his interrogators know what they are about. Now that the interrogators realized that they were dealing with an Israeli underground cell, they were not choosy about the means they employed. In the end, Shmuel Azar broke down, although even then, he did not forfeit his pride or his chivalry, and he took full responsibility for everything the cell had done. But in the course of his interrogation, he let fall a hint that Victor had visited Israel.

"At that, the interrogators came back to me. Hitherto, I had prayed for the moment when the door would open and I'd gain a moment's respite from my loneliness; but now, hearing the key turn in the lock, I experienced a sense of horror. I felt the pain of the blows even before I was beaten. What was worse, now I knew that they had discovered yet another detail."

At this stage, the interrogation no longer consisted of questions. The interrogators would fling a statement at the prisoner, who had no choice but to confirm it, while trying to smooth matters over a little.

Victor: "When I was first confronted with the fact that I had undergone military training in Israel, I could not avoid confessing that I had been to Israel; but I denied receiving military training. One of the interrogators, Kamel, let fly with a powerful blow which broke one of my teeth, but I remained adamant in my denial. I insisted that while I was in France, a Zionist youth movement had offered me a trip to Israel, and I had fallen for the temptation. But while I was in Israel, I only went on tours and visited *kibbutzim*. Later, I learned that my companions had told the same story, even though we had not previously coordinated our accounts. It may have been this unanimity which convinced our interrogators of the truth of the story. The fact is that at our trial, no mention was made of military training in Israel."

As blows showered down upon them from all sides, the three men were forced to think up their answers instinctively, for their minds were dulled by the beatings, the shouts, and the atmosphere of terror under which the interrogation was conducted. Under the circumstances, it was amazing how they managed to skirt the truth, and to make use of their interrogators' knowledge of some facts to conceal others.

Victor: "They knew that my fiancée was living in Israel; consequently, I told them that this was the sole reason I accepted the proffered trip to Israel, where I was approached with tempting offers to work for Israel on my return to Egypt. I cut down my stay in Israel to a mere two months, which is too short for thorough military training. To prove that I did not undergo military training in Israel, I pointed to the negative they had found with the instructions for the manufacture of explosives. If we had been trained, I said, there would have been no need of instructions. In the meanwhile, they searched my home again, and this time, they found one half of the concealed radio; but they only found the receiver, for my brother had in the meantime thrown the transmitter into the sea. When I was questioned as to whether we had radio contacts with Israel, I was able to reply: 'How could we have? We didn't have a transmitter, we could only *receive* broadcasts . . .' "

However, that second search at Victor's home turned up the letter from Paris which said: "Robert will come to visit Henry." Victor could not deny the existence of the letter, but he tried at first to feign innocence and to claim that it referred to Robert Dassa—Robbie got a savage beating for denying that he knew what the letter meant—but in the end, Victor had to admit that someone had come from abroad, but he knew nothing about the man, other than that his name was "Robert." Azar was also beaten into admitting that he had met the man, but he too refrained from divulging any details about him. Even though the members of the network were convinced that "Robert" had made his getaway, they displayed considerable self-sacrifice in refusing to divulge any detail about him. They regarded this as a kind of duty to which they were honor-bound; he was their commander and an emissary from Israel. Consequently, his safety was more important than theirs.

The first time Philip was confronted with the letter found in Victor's house and asked when "Robert" arrived in Egypt, he tried to evade the question by claiming ignorance. He was told: "We broke two of Victor's teeth for trying that one. It says here that 'Robert' will contact you at your home." He had to admit that a certain "Robert" did visit his home, and that he came by car; after a further series of punches, on realizing that he would not be able to evade the issue, he "confessed" that it was a dark Buick. But he made no mention of the diplomatic plates, nor of the two children sitting in the back of the car.

However, as their interrogations dragged on, and their powers of resistance were worn down by their ill treatment, they became less and less capable of withstanding the interrogators' technique of confronting them with the alleged confession of one of their number. They tried to adopt a policy of conceding whatever the interrogators already knew, without providing additional information, but they could not always adhere to this principle.

One day, on arriving at the Muhafza, Victor met Meir Meyuhas. The latter's links with the cell had diminished; in effect, he had broken off his contacts over a year before. Victor did not succeed in entering into conversation with him, to find out what he had been arrested for, and what he was being interrogated about.

A day or two after the arrest of Meyuhas, Moshe Marzouk was also taken into custody. Victor was brought to the prison office and there, sitting on the floor, was Marzouk, his feet swollen from *falakas* (beatings on the soles of the feet), with ugly burns beneath his arms (the interrogators in Cairo set fire to the hair in his armpits), and his clothes covered with clotted blood.

"I tried to pretend that I did not know him, but he gave me a sad glance and said: 'You can see what they're doing to me. I couldn't hold out. I confessed everything. I told them that I know you.' "

However, Marzouk had also instinctively concealed the fact that they had been inducted into the Israeli army and undergone military training in Israel.

Dr. Marzouk's arrest came as a shock to the Alexandria cell. A long time would pass before they could talk with one another and discover that none of them had informed on the Cairo group, and even then, they were too naive and trusting to ask: In that case, who *did* inform on them? Now, at Kum el Dik, they could not even find out how Dr. Marzouk had fallen into captivity, for their interrogations now focused on a new question—the Cairo cell—and they were subjected to a new series of savage and violent interrogations.

Victor: "One night—I had long lost all count of the days during this terrible period—I was taken to interrogation. This time, the questions probed a new direction:

" 'What do you know about Max Binnet?'

"I was able to reply in all sincerity that I had never heard the name.

" 'And what about 'Emil'—don't you know him?'

"I did not. They gave me a terrible beating, but I couldn't answer differently. I really did not know him. They showed me a German passport, and the photo inside it: 'Who is this?' I replied that I did not know him.

" 'But he's already in our custody! You can confess!'

"I could not, because I did not know what to confess. But I got the awful feeling that everything was in ruins, even more so than I had imagined. I tried to find some comfort in the fact that they had failed to arrest 'Robert.' But this German, Max Binnet, who was he, and what part did he play in the whole affair?"

The following morning, Philip was summoned to the prison office. Yusuf Fauzi, one of the investigators in charge of the "Atrin 10" file, was waiting there, with a menacing expression on his face.

"Who is 'Emil'?" he asked without any preamble. "Do you know him?"

Philip replied in the negative.

"We've caught him!" said Fauzi. "He's a big fish!" and added that if 'Emil' had not been caught, all of them would have been executed.

On being taken back to his cell, Philip saw 'Emil.' The door of his cell was ajar; the cell was bare, with no bed, and 'Emil'—unshaved, dressed in crumpled khaki clothes, with the encrusted blood on his face testifying to the "treatment" he had undergone—was sitting on the floor. As Philip passed, the man lifted his eyes and gazed at him. Philip did not know him. Only later on, in Cairo, was he to learn that this was Max Binnet.

That same evening—or it may have been another evening—Victor saw a woman guard standing on the parapet of the second-floor corridor, chatting loudly with the guard in the courtyard below. Victor was dejected enough to be prepared for the worst. He thought: "A woman guard? There must be a woman prisoner then. Perhaps it was 'Claude' . . . ?"

## The Fatal Leap

It was not "Claude." But "Claude"—Marcelle Ninio—had also been dragged down in the general calamity; she too was in the hands of the Egyptian police. The circumstances of her arrest are an important link in the chain suggesting the presence of a double agent inside the network. None of the men hitherto arrested had so much as mentioned Marcelle's name during the interrogations; furthermore, they had no reason to do so; they had had no contact with her for over a year.

The last of the Alexandria group to meet Marcelle was Victor, shortly after his return to Egypt, when he came to ask her whether she was prepared to go to Israel to undergo military training.

Marcelle met Dr. Marzouk later, but this was only when she came to Cairo's Jewish hospital, to visit her mother. At these encounters, they spoke of nothing other than her mother's deteriorating health. Marcelle's mother died at the end of 1953, whereupon these meetings also came to an end.

Her mother's death left a vacuum in Marcelle's life. For so many years, her life had revolved around her ailing mother; and now, nothing. She was left on her own.

She continued to occupy the large apartment in Heliopolis, which she shared with a lodger, Armand Karmona, a divorcé in his fifties, who suffered from partial paralysis in one leg; he was employed as an official at the Heliopolis railway. He was the last of the lodgers who had lived in the apartment during the lifetime of Marcelle's mother, though he moved elsewhere temporarily when her deteriorating health prevented her from running the household. He was on affectionate terms with Marcelle, treating her as a second daughter (a married daughter of his had recently emigrated to Israel). When Marcelle's mother was hospitalized for the last time, he came back to live in the apartment, out of affection for Marcelle—"to save me from my loneliness at this time." This generous gesture was to cost him his life, as an innocent victim of "the mishap."

Marcelle held onto her job at the English import-export company. However, her work and the company of an elderly railway official did not suffice to fill the emptiness of her existence. She had completely broken off her contacts with the underground cells; Max Binnet did not contact her very often. She met him no more than once during the first half of 1954, the period preceding her arrest. She tried to fill the vacuum with various activities: she engaged in sports, exercised, played basketball, and went out to social functions. However, it all seemed superficial and worthless. With thoughts of leaving Egypt, she initiated efforts to acquire a passport, but the bureaucratic walls were too thick to be pierced, and even her employer's intervention was of no help. "I reached the stage where I was prepared for a fictitious marriage with anyone possessing an exit visa." However, there was no one like that among her acquaintances, and she carried on her humdrum existence.

At the end of July, she took a short vacation, with the intention of spending a few days at the seaside, at the chalet belonging to the family of her friend Renée Hefetz.

That day, after a long interval, Max Binnet phoned her. Today, she can only guess that having read the newspaper reports of events in Alexandria, he wished to gauge her mood. But he said nothing, only asking how she was.

She made some offhand reply.

"Good. Can we meet on Friday?"

She said that Friday was out of the question, because she would be out of town.

"When will you be back?"

"On Sunday."

He told her he would contact her on her return, and hung up.

Marcelle departed.

Ras el Bar is a beautiful resort, situated where one of the branches of the Nile runs into the Mediterranean. It is a picturesque resort, with small houses, rows of thatched-roof huts, a casino, and an amusement park. Cars are not allowed into the resort, where transportation is provided by horse-drawn carts and small motorcycles. The bay, where the Nile waters run into the sea, is always calm and inviting.

It was here that Marcelle first heard of the arrests in Alexandria. It was the topic of the day among the Jewish holiday makers. The young people living near her hosts' chalet were surprised by her expression of amazement.

"What? Didn't you hear? It was in all the papers yesterday! Here" —and they showed her a copy of an Alexandria evening paper, whose front page carried the Interior Minister's statement:

"A group of Zionist arsonists has been uncovered; it laid incendiary bombs in the Alexandria post office on July 2, and in a library belonging to a foreign embassy. Philip Hermann Natanson and Victor Levy were apprehended on July 23. A third accomplice, Robert Dassa, was also caught. All three of these young Jews are well-known Zionists, with files in the police aliens department."

Throughout the course of that miserable weekend, Marcelle felt the ground burning beneath her feet. She tried to convince herself that it was inconceivable, that there was some mistake which would soon be cleared up. All the same, she desperately wanted to return to Cairo.

On arriving, she immediately wrote to her contact address in Paris. "The twins Pierre [Victor] and Henry [Philip] have caught a contagious disease, and it is to be feared that Roger [Robbie] has also caught it. They cannot be contacted at present since they are in isolation because of their sickness."

After sending off the letter, she "cleaned up" her apartment, destroying the code and anything else which might reveal her contacts with the underground.

While she was so engaged, she received a phone call from Max Binnet.

Again, he asked her how she was.

"Not too good," she said, hoping that he would understand her meaning. But he preferred to ignore the hint, possibly fearing to speak openly over the phone.

"We have to meet," he said. "But the trouble is, I'll be busy all week. What about next Sunday? Eight o'clock in the evening?"

Their meeting did not take place. Their next encounter was to take place six months later, in the dock of the Cairo military tribunal.

"The next few days," Marcelle related later, "were awful for me. I did not know what was happening, I did not comprehend the purpose of the acts of arson for which the three Alexandria members had been arrested. The whole affair vanished from the newspapers with the same suddenness that it had appeared. Worst of all was my isolation. I had no possibility of contacting Max Binnet; I did not dare to approach Moshe Marzouk. As for 'Robert,' the emissary from Israel, I didn't even know of his existence. (When I was questioned about him after my arrest, I didn't know what to answer.) I had to go on with my daily routine, to go to work every morning, to meet acquaintances. All the time—even as I continued to hope that it was all just a mistake and tried to reassure myself that there was no longer anything to link me to the underground —my ears were listening for the heavy footsteps of the detectives coming up the stairs. If I had possessed a passport, I would have picked up and gone. There was nothing more to keep me in Egypt. But I didn't have one. If I had had a place of concealment, I would have gone into hiding. But there was none, nothing had been prepared for the eventuality of a mishap . . ."

Reconstructing the timetable of events can show that these days—which Marcelle spent in solitary torment with her fears, without anyone to consult—were also the crucial period when she could have been rescued, if only rescuers could have been found.

Philip Natanson and Victor Levy were arrested in the evening and night of July 23; Robbie Dassa two days later, on July 25; and Shmuel Azar on July 31. There were no further arrests until August 5, when Meir Meyuhas was arrested in Alexandria and Moshe Marzouk in Cairo. This was the breathing space which the four Alexandria detainees gained, by standing up to brutal torture and by taking upon themselves all responsibility for the operations of the underground.

What use was made of these precious days? None whatsover. And what was "Robert" doing, that "Robert," whose presence in Egypt was jealously concealed by the detainees? Aside from his two meetings with Shmuel Azar and his "plans" for a daring raid to rescue the three men from prison—which Shmuel later related to them—we have nothing to go on other than what the prosecutor told the Egyptian military tribunal, and what "Robert"—alias "Paul Frank," alias Avry Seidenberg—told on returning to Israel.

Before the military tribunal, the prosecutor depicted "Robert" as a daring agent who did not lose his nerve, even when the network he headed disintegrated completely; even though he knew that the secret of his presence in Egypt might be revealed to the police, who could come knocking at his door at any moment, he nevertheless remained in Egypt for a further full fourteen days, and, with a coolness which the prosecutor characterized as "diabolical," concerned himself with . . . selling his car (whose description might also have reached the police)!

"Robert's" story on returning to Israel presented a similar account. He remained at his post, right up to the last moment, seeking ways to help his arrested subordinates, until he felt the net tighten around him. Even then, he brought out whatever he could rescue—the transmitter he carried on him.

Naturally, there was no way of verifying his story; at the time, no one even thought it necessary to do so. "Robert" got a hero's welcome as "the sole ember saved from the blaze." It was only a year or more later that second thoughts led to a reexamination, which showed that "Robert's" sole action during those fourteen crucial days was the sale of his car.

It was further noted that he left Egypt on August 5, the day that the second round of arrests commenced. And some people began to ponder aloud whether there was any significance to the proximity of the two events.

For Marcelle in Cairo, the days crawled past with a maddening slowness. Every morning, she examined the newspapers, to find nothing, no hint or mention of the "Zionist underground" in Alexandria. Her meeting with Max Binnet was scheduled only for next week. She did not know how to pass the time till then.

Consequently, when Armand Karmona offered her his place on a weekend outing to Ras el Bar, organized by the Heliopolis railway's works committee, she was inclined to accept his offer. At least, it would give her something to occupy her mind and take her attention off her concerns. Karmona continued to persuade her. "For me, the outing is only a burden," he said. "It's hard for me to drag my bad leg through the sand dunes, and I don't particularly enjoy swimming. But you'll enjoy it." Thinking that her reservations stemmed from a reluctance to go off with a group of strangers, he promised that one of his friends would look after her and protect her from the harassment to which a solitary girl might be subjected.

Finally she accepted the offer.

The railway employees' outing set off by bus at midday, on Friday, August 5. At five, it reached Damieta, pausing for a short rest. "While people were buying peanuts and lemonade through the bus windows, my eyes idly scanned the teeming crowd at the station. My gaze chanced upon a man in European dress, wearing trousers and a shirt, who was standing opposite my window, transfixing me with a piercing, angry stare. I thought to myself: 'What is he looking at? And why is he so angry?' Then the bus set off on its way."

By the time they reached Ras el Bar, she had forgotten the man. The group was housed in a hotel, Marcelle sharing a room with two women administrative employees. Immediately after unpacking her suitcase, she set off for the chalet of the Hefetz family, where she spent the evening. The next day, after a swim in the bay, she returned to the chalet. A few young Jews, who were staying nearby, sat around licking ice cream and gossiping. Marcelle's glance wandered out of the window and fell upon two men standing on the sidewalk outside the chalet, staring at her challengingly. "It's because of my bathing suit," she told herself. That evening, when the whole party headed for a dance at one of the nightclubs and she again noticed the two men, she still suspected nothing.

The group of railway employees was scheduled to set out for Cairo on Sunday, straight after lunch. "In consequence, I lunched at the hotel. I met an acquaintance from Cairo, Marcel Weiss, and joined him at his table for a short talk. On rising to return to my table, I noticed the same two men, sitting at a corner table, not taking their eyes off me.

"I was annoyed, but I resolved not to make a fuss. I went up to my room to pack my things and came down to the foyer with my suitcase. Karmona's friend, the one who was looking after me, was already there waiting for me. We stood waiting for the bus, when the loudspeakers boomed: 'Victorine Ninio—telephone!'

" 'Victorine' was the name I was given at birth. After a severe sickness as a child, my parents, following the Jewish custom, gave me an additional name. Consequently, I thought it must be a friend of mine wanting to say good-bye. I went up to the counter, whereupon the two men appeared and seized me.

"This unheard-of deed—laying hands on a foreign woman in public —so astounded me that my first reaction was spontaneous: 'Take your hands off me!' I shouted. 'How dare you!'

" 'Shut up, "Claude"!' one of them replied, with a frightful expression in his eyes. 'We're better than those Jews of yours!'

"When I heard him say 'Claude' I comprehended my situation. Only members of the underground knew me as 'Claude.' "

At nine o'clock that evening, she was brought to the Muhafza in Cairo.

The three-hour train ride from Ras el Bar was one long nightmare. The two plainclothes detectives gave her endless descriptions of what was in store for her in Cairo—beatings, torture, rape. They cursed her in a manner she had never yet experienced. She made no reply, pretending not to understand Arabic, but she could not keep down the flush of anger which covered her face, whereupon her two escorts launched into a description of the manly endowments of the twenty Sudanese waiting for her in Cairo. She sat there, trying to close her ears and protesting at their disgusting words. She kept telling herself: No, such things are impossible; people are not treated that way in the twentieth century, not even in the torture chambers of the Egyptian police! But doubts began to prey on her mind: Who knows? By the time they arrived, her nerves were completely shattered.

At the Muhafza, Marcelle was taken to the office of the duty officer. There were six men in the room, all in civilian clothes. She was told to sit in a straight-backed chair, and one of the men, seated behind the desk, began:

"We know everything. About Moshe Marzouk and the people in Alexandria; about Eli Na'im, Meir Za'afran, and 'Emil.' Who is 'Emil'?"

On hearing these words, her head spun. How had they arrived at "Emil"? She bit her lip and said nothing. One of the men standing beside her slapped her face hard: "Talk!"

"I want a lawyer," she muttered. Again a slap landed on her face. She began to cry, but her tears had no effect upon them. The slaps rained down, one after the other, from left and right. One of them brought his open palm down on the nape of her neck.

When they tired of slapping her—Marcelle was quite dazed by now —they pulled up a stool; one of the interrogators grabbed her hair and yanked her against the back of the chair she was sitting on, a second one seized her shoulders, a third man rudely caught hold of her legs and pulled off her shoes. Convinced that she was about to suffer the rape with which she had been threatened, she put all the force of her lungs into an ear-piercing scream. A powerful blow from an open palm cut off her scream in the middle. They placed her bare legs on the stool; one of the interrogators held them while another began to strike her on the soles of her feet with a thin bamboo cane. The *falakas*— the most notorious form of torture employed in the Middle East—landed on her feet, each blow causing a sharp, stabbing pain which seemed to pierce her mind. After each blow, came a question: "Who is 'Emil'?" "What do you know about the people in Alexandria?" "Talk, you dirty spy!"

"I screamed, I wept, I may even have fainted. I don't remember. Every now and then, they would stop the *falakas* and try persuasion. When that failed, they tried threats. Again, they threatened me with rape, with execution. And again, the bamboo cane whistled through the air . . ."

After three hours of this treatment—strong men have been known to break after half an hour of the "cane treatment"—she had turned into a bundle of shrieking nerves, shuddering with pain at the mere sound of the cane's swishing. "I can't stand it anymore," she groaned.

They left her alone for a moment, to regain her senses. Then they began a new line of questioning: "Who is Eli Na'im?"

Later, when she regained her strength and tried to reconstruct the details of that awful interrogation, she wondered about the questions. They knew perfectly well who Eli Na'im was; in fact, he was already in their custody. She concluded that it was not information they were after, or no more than confirmation of details they already knew, but rather, they aimed to "break" her, as an end unto itself. The Muhafza agents were in the habit of boasting that anyone who underwent their "interrogations" would never be the same again.

However, this conclusion came later; there, at the Muhafza, she sensed only one single desire: to halt the swishing of that cane, whatever the price.

Eli Na'im? "We made use of him to rent an apartment for us. But we left the apartment long ago, and we broke off all contact with him. . . ."

"And Meir Za'afran?"

"He was a member for some time. But he dropped out, of his own accord."

She told them about Avraham Dar, and everything she knew about Dr. Sa'adiya, going into the minutest details; she knew that they had both long left Egypt, and she tried to make her stories about them as lengthy as possible, so as to postpone, for as long as she could, the questions she really feared.

However, these also came.

" 'Emil'? Who is 'Emil'?"

It transpired that she was not yet completely broken. She still retained enough willpower to tell herself: Him—no!

She replied that she did not know. Where does he live? She did not know that either.

Once again, the cane was lifted; she cringed with pain and burst into tears. "Truly, I don't know. We used to meet in the street." Suddenly a thought flashed through her mind: They were due to meet at eight that evening! When he saw that she did not turn up, perhaps he would understand that some calamity had occurred, and make his getaway? Deep in her heart, she prayed: Let it be. Then came a second thought: If he is going to escape, every moment I can gain for him is of importance.

But the interrogators were persistent. "How were your meetings arranged?"

"By phone," she replied.

"What is his telephone number?"

She did not know. Again, the blows rained down and the cane whistled; she burst into hysterical tears, until they were convinced that she really did not know.

"How did he come to the meetings?"

"By car," she admitted.

"What make? What number?"

She did not know. Again, the *falakas* and slaps hailed down on her, her hair was pulled, until she broke down completely, unable any longer to control her tears.

The next morning, she was awakened and taken to a car waiting in front of the building. Her legs were so swollen that two detectives were obliged to prop her up. They drove to the railway station, to the Alexandria platform. She was placed inside a third-class compartment, completely empty. But at the other end of the compartment, sitting between two policemen, she saw Meir Za'afran, also swollen from the beatings he had received. His appearance came as no surprise to her; right at the start of her interrogation, she had been told that he was in custody and had confessed everything. It transpired that they had told him the same about her.

"He lifted his eyes and gazed at me, but I did not respond. I curled up in a corner, depressed and in despair. I was dazed by the sadistic cruelty of my interrogators. I was incapable of grasping the fact that in the twentieth century, one of God's creatures could be capable of such barbarism. These were the people among whom I had lived, with whom I had made conversation or exchanged jokes. I felt a terrible disgust— with my interrogators, with the whole of humanity, myself included, because I had been like clay in their hands, because I had cried whenever they wanted me to cry and screamed whenever they wanted me to scream. My human dignity was fatally injured. When I remembered that I was still in their hands, I did not want to go on living. I think it was then I began to think seriously about suicide."

Her thoughts may have been evident. Her two escorts did not burden her by talking, but they did not leave her on her own for a single moment. When she asked to go to the washroom, one of them preceded her, making sure that its window could not be opened easily; after that, he stood before the open door without budging.

She was interrogated again at the Alexandria Muhafza. "They didn't use a cane here, but I was so badly beaten that one slap was enough to make me scream."

The Alexandria interrogators were better informed than their Cairo colleagues. They did not fire blind, they did not ask her to tell them anything; they told her, asking for no more than her confirmation and the completion of various missing details. They knew about Avraham Dar, but ordered her to tell them how she met him and who introduced them. Naturally, they knew about Victor and Philip and Shmuel and Robbie, and about the chalet at Sidi Bisher and about the apartment, but they wanted to know whether she had ever been to the chalet? She confessed that she had. Then they wanted to know how she received the money which she transferred to the Alexandria cell. She replied without hesitation; the Chyprotte family had left Egypt long ago.

But now, for the first time, she heard a new name: "Robert." Immediately, she said: "Robert Dassa." But they broke in: No, there was another Robert, who arrived recently from abroad. She had nothing to tell them about him. They hit her again, but she was still unable to reply. She got a further beating when she failed to answer their questions about the firebombs.

Her interrogation went on throughout most of the day. That evening, an interrogator came from the prosecutor's office; she was again questioned, while he wrote down her replies.

During the night, she was ordered to get up. She was taken down the corridor, until her escort halted before a bolted door. They unlocked it and opened it wide. Inside, she saw Meir Za'afran sitting on the floor, and opposite him—her heart sank at the sight—was Max Binnet. He, too . . .

"Do you know them?" she was asked.

She answered in the affirmative. Immediately, she was taken away.

"I was taken to an empty office at the end of the corridor: a long room with a single window. Two guards escorted me there; as I entered, they bolted the door. I sank down on a chair, totally exhausted. It was my second night without food or sleep.

"I wanted to sleep, but my two guards began to give me 'psychological treatment.' 'If you don't talk,' they told me, 'there are twenty men ready to jump on top of you, one after the other.'

"I don't know whether they were instructed to terrorize me or whether they did so on their own initiative. But their words fell on fertile soil. By now, I believed them to be capable of anything.

"I made no reply. My gaze fixed itself on the window; with a show of innocence, I stood up and approached it. The window looked out on a paved inner courtyard, about twenty feet down, which served as a parking lot. The policeman read my thoughts: 'God help you if you try anything!' he shouted, and yanked me back. He took my chair, moved it away from the window, and ordered me to sit down. Then he closed the window.

"I sat there silent and dazed. The guard's words had revived all my fears and pains. To go through another interrogation like that . . . perhaps they would indeed bring those twenty Sudanese? I couldn't take any more. I didn't want to . . . it would be better to die.

"From that moment on, I waited for an opportunity.

"After some time, one of the guards stood up and went out. The second one pulled up his chair and sat close to me. There was one single thought running through my mind: If only he would move away from me . . .

"It happened! Somebody knocked at the door. The guard walked over—without taking his eyes off me—and asked who was knocking. I did not hear the reply. My guard said something else, and bent down to unbolt the door, and turned his eyes away from me.

"In a moment, I was on my feet. With three strides I crossed the room and with a 'fish leap,' as though I were jumping in a diving competition, I flung myself at the closed window.

"When I awoke, in violent pain, I was being carried to a dilapidated leather couch in a room which was unfamiliar to me. The pain was unbearable. Later, they told me I was only saved from death by a miracle. I fell a few inches from a sharp iron rod embedded in the paving of the courtyard. As it was, I had a fractured skull, a second fracture in my elbow, eleven of my ribs were cracked, and my hip was crushed. Blood was oozing from my ears and nose, and I was probably bleeding internally, too. The concussion had affected my sight; for a number of days I saw double.

"I was surrounded by detectives. I don't remember whether a doctor was brought to me at the Muhafza or whether I was taken to him. My next memory is of the hospital. I came round as a doctor was bending over me, giving me an injection. Then I was taken to the operating theater and wrapped in bandages. They took no notice of the fracture in my arm; perhaps they had not noticed it. Beside me, in the operating room, was a Muhabarat agent dressed in a doctor's white gown; he did not cease asking me questions, even while the anesthetic began to take effect. (Later, when I regained consciousness, one of the nurses 'confided' to me: 'You talked while you were under the influence of the injection and he wrote everything down.' It was all part of the psychological warfare which they continued to conduct against me, even when I was in the hospital.)

"As I began to sink into oblivion, the last thought that flashed through my mind was: 'At least I am rid of them. They won't follow me into here.' "

While Marcelle was in the hospital in Alexandria, tossing between frightful pain and unconsciousness, "the mishap" claimed its first victim, with the death of Armand Karmona, the kind-hearted, lame railway official.

It was only a few days later that Marcelle learned of his death, when she had recovered somewhat from her injuries. The Alexandria *wakil niaba* (prosecutor general) came to the hospital to ask her why, if Karmona had no links with the underground cell, as she claimed, he had committed suicide? She could only turn her face to the wall and cry bitterly over the departure of a good friend.

Seemingly, it was Karmona who told the detectives that Marcelle had gone to Ras el Bar for the weekend. When asked for her whereabouts, he saw no reason to conceal the fact. It never even occurred to him that she was wanted for any crime. But the detectives did not rest content. On Tuesday, two days after Marcelle's arrest, they returned to the apartment in Heliopolis.

Earlier that evening, Karmona spent some time at a club in Heliopolis, playing cards with friends. He did not appear frightened, only somewhat depressed. He told his friends that he was looking for an apartment; he did not wish to remain in the Ninio place after Marcelle's arrest. It was too gloomy, living alone in that big apartment.

Later that night, neighbors heard shouts from the Ninio apartment. They went down and found the police there.

Gruffly, the policemen ordered them to clear off if they didn't want trouble, and they went away.

The following morning, one of the neighbors living on the third floor looked out of her kitchen window, which faced the window of the Ninios' bathroom, and her scream of terror aroused the whole neighborhood. Through the window, she could see a man's body, hanging.

It was Armand Karmona. Did he kill himself? Or perhaps he died under the police "interrogation," and they faked the suicide to conceal the causes of his death? It is an open question, which will never be answered.

# 3

## HELL ON EARTH

### The Great Hangman

The atmosphere at Kum el Dik grew progressively more somber.

The prison's walls constantly reverberated with the cries of one or another member of the network undergoing interrogation in the office on the second floor while his companions cringed in their cells, shuddering with every cry, as they imagined what their friend was enduring.

Robbie: "At the same time the guard's radio in the courtyard was emitting ululating Arab music, or Koran readings. What was worse, adding insult to injury, were the humorous radio programs. We were in a terrible mood."

They now grasped the full extent of the disaster. The cells had been uncovered, all their members had been arrested and forced into a full confession, withholding only a few details concerning their contacts with the state of Israel, Egypt's enemy. They had no need of their interrogators' curses and threats to comprehend that their deeds could be depicted as acts of treason, punishable by death.

Philip sprawled in his cell, dolefully toying with fanciful escape plans. He counted the number of bars in the window, measured their thickness, and gauged the time necessary to file them through, if only he had a file. Or else he saw himself luring the guard into the cell, overpowering him, and taking his keys; he would then release his companions from the other cells. One of them—probably Robbie, who could best masquerade as an Egyptian—would put on the guard's uniform and call the sentries at the gate to enter the courtyard, one by one . . .

Philip's burns were becoming infected, but it was only by threatening to go on a hunger strike that he managed to have himself taken to a hospital occasionally for his dressings to be changed.

Robbie made friends with one of the other inmates, a Turkish seaman by the name of Abbas, who had spent the longest time at Kum el Dik; he had been there for forty days, waiting for his papers to arrive so that he could be deported from Egypt. Thanks to his "seniority" in the prison, he enjoyed certain privileges: his cell door was left unlocked during the day and he was free to wander around the courtyard. Every now and then, Abbas would bring Robbie scraps of news concerning him or his companions. Robbie suspected the man of doing so on behalf of the prison authorities, the information being aimed at further demoralizing the prisoners. Nevertheless, one evening, when Abbas whispered through the locked door that he had heard the prison officers say they were about to "liquidate the Jewish group," Robbie was inclined to believe him.

The following day, Victor vanished.

That same day, Philip was taken for further interrogation at the Muhafza. "On my return, I passed Victor's cell, and saw that it was empty. In exchange for a cigarette, Abbas told me that Victor and Azar had been taken away that morning under escort, and no one knew where to.

"The following day, Robbie's cell also remained empty.

"Finally, my turn came."


Victor was taken away from Kum el Dik on August 14. He remembered the date because it was the birthday of his youngest brother, thirteen-year-old Roger.

One morning, when the prison commander was making his daily tour of the cells and his mood seemed more pleasant than usual, Victor approached him with a request: to permit Roger to come and see him, as a birthday present. The officer replied: "All right. Tomorrow, I'll let him in."

But the following day, at six in the morning, the door of his cell opened. "Out! You're moving."

"Where to?" he asked, but there was no reply.

A detective in civilian clothes arrived, and Victor was handcuffed to him. At the prison office, he regained all the possessions which had been confiscated from him—money, watch, comb; while he was standing here, Shmuel Azar was also brought in, similarly handcuffed to a detective.

They were taken aboard a truck; within minutes, they found themselves at the railway station.

"I felt a lump in my throat and my heart was heavy. I was being banished. After all, Alexandria was my city; my parents and friends were here. Where were we being taken? No one told us a thing.

"I looked toward Shmuel standing with his escort some way away. The fact that I was not alone was some encouragement, but not sufficient to overcome my disquiet."

The fear which Victor bore in his heart throughout the journey increased when the train entered Cairo. Instantly, he was surrounded by a mass of detectives, who prodded and cursed him as they escorted him to a waiting car. Cairo's police were well known to be more savage and brutal than their Alexandria colleagues, whose behavior showed the influence of their contacts with Europeans. The policemen in Cairo made no secret of their hatred for foreigners.

His eyes were blindfolded with a strip of cloth, and they drove off. After a time, the car halted, he was ordered out, and dragged along for some distance by his escort. When the blindfold was finally taken off his eyes, he found himself in a hut within a military camp. He stood there, still wearing the handcuffs, until the arrival of a swarthy officer in lieutenant's uniform, with a cane under his arm, who gave an order, whereupon the detective unlocked the manacles. Unthinkingly, Victor said, "Thank you," and instantly, the cane came down on his shoulders. The officer turned and strode away wordlessly, while a red-headed sergeant with a pointed moustache subjected Victor to a flurry of slaps, shouting: "Don't you know that you are not to address an officer?"

The sergeant searched him thoroughly, confiscating everything he found; after Victor put his clothes back on again, his hands were handcuffed behind his back. His eyes were blindfolded and he was marched away.

When the blindfold was taken off and he was left alone, with his hands still manacled behind his back, Victor looked around. He was in a high-ceilinged cell, larger than that in which he had been detained in Alexandria. The cell was in the corner of a building and each of the two outside walls had one barred window; a wooden beam lay across the two windowsills (instantly, the thought flashed through Victor's mind: "Is that for a hanging rope?"). The walls, once whitewashed, had gradually turned a filthy gray; halfway up the wall there was a black line, like a notice of bereavement. The cell's iron door had no window. On the crude concrete floor there was nothing but a water jug, a black rubber bucket for his toilet needs, and a dilapidated *borsh*. That was all.

The change was bewildering. Suddenly, everything was quiet. Nothing could be heard from the other side of the door, neither footsteps nor human voices. From afar, he could hear a bugle's flourishes, repeating the same call over and over again, with an infuriating monotony.

What is this place? thought Victor, fearfully. Where have they brought me?

The place to which Victor had been brought (to be followed by all the other male detained members of the network) was the Sigan Harbi (military prison). In the Egypt of 1954, the mere mention of its name was enough to send a shudder of horror down the backs of one's listeners. In the years to come, that horror was to grow sevenfold.

The Sigan Harbi was in the center of Abbassiya, the large British-built military camp near Cairo. From this camp, the British army had maintained its control over the Egyptian capital, and thereby over the whole of the Nile valley. During the world war, Abbassiya had housed many of the installations and offices of the Allied armies' Middle East command.

After the British withdrawal, the camp served a similar purpose for the Egyptian army, housing its high command and the garrison protecting Cairo. It was from this camp that the Egyptian units set out on July 23, 1952, to launch the military coup which put an end to the monarchy.

Learning a lesson from their own coup, the heads of the revolution made sure that the units stationed at Abbassiya would loyally maintain their grip on the fickle and undependable city of Cairo. As for preserving discipline within the army itself, this purpose was served by the Sigan Harbi, a group of five large blocks, each one consisting of a square two-story building with an internal courtyard, in the center of which stood a structure containing showers and washrooms. Each block constituted an independent prison unit, guarded by its own sentries and administered by military guards. The whole block was surrounded by a high wall, with sentinels on duty day and night; the night guards were reinforced by a large number of soldiers who slept at the base of the wall. It was the best-guarded prison in Egypt; however, it was not this feature which gave the place its terrifying reputation, but rather what went on within its walls.

Prior to the military coup, the Sigan Harbi was an ordinary military prison housing soldiers who had committed offenses against military law; so it remained at the beginning of the revolutionary regime, but not for long. In the behind-the-scenes struggle in progress between various Egyptian power groups, the civilian police and the prison service were regarded as followers of the *ancien régime*. Most of their senior officers had been promoted to their posts under the monarchy, and were suspected of loyalty to the politicians who had appointed them, and who had now become "enemies of the regime." In consequence, supervision of internal security gradually passed from the police to the Muhabarat, the military intelligence, and convicts considered "dangerous to the regime"—civilians included—were confined in the Sigan Harbi.

With a growing number of persons being held in custody without trial, the Sigan Harbi took on additional importance. As a military prison, it was not subject to civilian law; a person confined there had no right to go to court and demand an explanation for his detention; he was not even entitled to see a lawyer. Even the civilian prison regulations, with the bare minimum of rights they granted to inmates of ordinary prisons, did not apply here. The prisoners were entitled to nothing more than whatever the Muhabarat officers and guards were gracious enough to allow.

The guards were all regular soldiers, selected for their task for a number of traits. The first of these was unswerving loyalty to the regime, or, to be precise, to Gamal Abdel Nasser in person. They were brainwashed until it was firmly fixed in their minds that they were the defenders of their leader's safety and welfare. A majority of them were illiterate villagers from the Delta and Upper Egypt, chosen deliberately to forestall any dialogue with their charges, most of whom belonged to the more educated classes. Most of the guards had no idea of the charges for which their prisoners had been brought here; they knew only that anyone sent to the Sigan Harbi must be an opponent of Abdel Nasser, and they could, consequently, vent all their anger and sadism on him. They had explicit instructions to ill-treat their prisoners and they obeyed, not with any objective in mind, nor with the purpose of extracting information or confessions from their prisoners, but with brutality as an end unto itself, for the purpose of breaking the prisoner, to confirm the terrifying reputation of the prison as a place from which no one emerged quite the same as when he entered. Like every Egyptian soldier, the guards hated and feared their officers. But when they got their hands on a convicted officer (such reached the Sigan Harbi in large numbers), they ill-treated him doubly. Even though the guards were observant Moslems, they did not even spare ministers of religion, who were incarcerated en masse after the regime turned on the Moslem Brotherhood.

When Block 4 filled up, a few weeks after the arrival of the detained network members, the screams of tortured convicts echoed ceaselessly day and night, mingling with the bugle calls which drifted in from the nearby training camp for buglers.

The Sigan Harbi "terror factory" was supervised by Emir Alai (Brig.) Hamza el Bassiuni, a tall, fleshy man with gray eyes, who came of Mameluke origins and was a born sadist. He gave his guards a free hand, and the latter would boast to the prisoners: "If we torture you to death, the *basha* will give us promotion." El Bassiuni himself would prowl the five blocks of his prison like a predatory devil, holding a *kurbatz* (a long Sudanese whip made of rhinoceros hide). He was followed by two enormous wolfhounds, "Leila" and "Lucky," who were as cruel as he; he was in the habit of setting them on to attack the prisoners. This was "the great hangman"; it was into his hands that the arrested members of the network were delivered.

That first day at the Sigan Harbi, Victor was left alone in the empty cell, with his hands manacled behind his back. The door remained locked. He tried to peep through the keyhole, but all he saw were two rows of locked cells facing him, and part of the internal courtyard. There was no one to be seen in the courtyard; the prison appeared deserted.

He laid himself down on the *borsh*. He may have fallen asleep. Later, he kicked at the door; it opened immediately, as though the guard had been lurking behind it all the time. A powerfully built young soldier charged into the cell and punched Victor in the face. "It's forbidden to call the guard here!" he roared. "It's forbidden to talk altogether!"

Victor said that he wished to go to the washroom.

"Not now!"

"What about food?"

"I'd know!" he said, bolting the door. His speech and behavior were savage and rude; he had been trained to terrify and break his charges. Victor swore that he would not allow himself to be broken.

That evening, the same soldier returned, unlocked Victor's manacles, and led him at a run to the washroom in the courtyard. He stood there urging him to hurry and then took him back to the cell where he put the manacles back on his wrists. "Sit down. But sleeping is forbidden! If I catch you sleeping, you're in trouble!"

Depriving prisoners of sleep is a well-known form of "treatment" designed to break their willpower. Victor had heard of this, and concluded that the interrogators would arrive shortly. He sat waiting, hungry and full of foreboding. Outside, it was beginning to get dark, and the cell was lit up by a naked bulb hanging from the ceiling. Every few moments, the guard's shadow flitted over the peephole in the door.

Now Victor heard cries, and identified Shmuel Azar's voice. The shouts came from above, from the second floor. After a time, they died down, and again there was an oppressive silence, broken only by the calls of the sentries: "Number one, all present and correct," "Number two, all present and correct," and so on, up to fifteen—the number of sentry posts on the wall. These calls, mingling with the cries of prisoners being interrogated, became the background music which accompanied their nights throughout their period of imprisonment at the Sigan Harbi. Whenever one of the sentries was late in giving his call, indicating that he had dozed off, the red-haired *shawish*—sergeant—(named Abdul Gawad, as they soon discovered) would beat him ferociously.

As Victor sat there, fighting off his desire to sleep, the bugs made their appearance. They marched along the walls in endless processions; he now realized that the black marks on the whitewashed walls were the bodies of bugs squashed by some previous inmate. Every now and then there would be a light thud as one of them fell to the floor, where they discovered Victor's bare feet and attached themselves to them. He could see the creatures swelling up with his blood. He shook them off, stepped on them, but others came to take their place. Even if he had been permitted to sleep, he would not have dared.

It was an awful night.

At four in the morning, the door opened. His manacles were unlocked and he was taken at a run to the washroom. In the five minutes he was permitted to stay there, Victor had time to empty out his *kardal*, relieve himself, take a swift shower to wash off the crusted blood left by the bugs—wiping himself down with the filthy rag which was also to serve him for washing down the floor of his cell—and refill his jug of drinking water; then he was taken back to his cell at a run, the manacles were replaced, and the door locked.

He tried to doze off, but morning brought swarms of flies which gave him no rest. Every now and then, the guard would appear at the peephole, growling: "You were asleep, I saw!" Hunger gnawed at his insides; he had eaten nothing for forty-eight hours.

That night, he again heard Shmuel Azar shouting in the cell above.

The following day, his third at the military prison, a soldier brought him a slice of bread. "That's from our rations," he said, "but today there'll be food for you as well." Indeed, at three in the afternoon, Victor received his first "meal": a sickening stew of greasy eggplant and one dry pitta. His manacles were taken off to permit him to eat; they were not replaced.

That night, the cries came from various directions. Shmuel Azar's shouts still came from above, from the second floor. But Victor soon identified the voice of Moshe Marzouk, coming from somewhere to his right; later, there were shouts from the left, and Victor identified

Philip's voice. Gradually, the shouts died down, and silence reigned again.

And then it struck Victor that he had not heard Robbie's voice. "What have they done to Robbie?" he thought anxiously.

The object of Victor's concern, Robbie, was within shouting distance of him. He too grieved and worried about the fate of his companions, as their shouts reached his ears. "When they came to take me from my cell at Kum el Dik, on the morning of August 15, I sensed a double anxiety. First, there was my fear of change, of any change. This was a fear I was to experience frequently in the course of my imprisonment. For a prisoner, routine, even if it is a painful routine, is somehow reassuring. You get used to a place and its ways, you make contacts, you get yourself organized; you permit yourself to be deluded by the continuity of your routine. And then, along comes a change, and again you confront the fact that you are nothing more than a leaf blown about in the wind, your fate is in the hands of some officer, and any passing fancy of his can overturn your existence.

"My other fear was more concrete: What awaited me at the end of the journey? I could still hear the words of Abbas, relating what he had heard from the prison officers.

"I was taken to the railway station on my own. But after some time, another prisoner was brought along, like me, handcuffed to his guard. This was Eli Na'im, from Cairo. At that time, I was not yet acquainted with him. We were not permitted to converse in the train, and on arrival in Cairo, we were put in different vehicles. In the car, I was blindfolded. The soldiers who received me at the railway station remained silent throughout the drive.

"We drove for about half an hour. When we halted, someone seized my elbow and ordered me to jump off the truck. I heard a shout: *'Inteba!'* ['Attention!'], and guessed that an officer was approaching. In the coming months of our confinement at the Sigan Harbi that cry echoing along the corridor was to serve us as advance warning of the arrival of an officer, and usually, of trouble.

"Still blindfolded and manacled, I was marched along a courtyard and then a corridor, until I was ordered to halt. Then I heard a door being bolted and I was left alone, shackled and blind, my senses alert to pick up any sound which might disclose where I was. I was filled with concern for my companions. At that moment, I would even have welcomed their cries of pain, as long as I knew they were still alive.

"Two hours later, a soldier returned and took the cloth off my eyes. I found myself in a relatively clean room, with a table and chair, as well as a bed which even had a sheet on it. A few hours later it transpired that I had been mistakenly brought to Block 1. This error was typical of the atmosphere at the Sigan Harbi. The military guards had not the faintest idea of the accusations against their prisoners, nor did they care. ... Even after my transfer to Block 4, which housed the most dangerous enemies of the regime, most of the guards did not connect me with the other members of the network, whom they considered as *hawagat*, while they regarded me as an *ibn balad* [native]; I spoke Egyptian Arabic and I even resembled an Egyptian in my appearance.

"The cell where I was confined after my transfer to Block 4 was larger than that in Block 1. But it contained no table or chair, or bed with sheets; there was nothing but a filthy *borsh* spread out on the concrete floor. It was a corner cell, with two windows in separate walls. The soldier who had brought me ordered me to stand facing the wall, without budging. With that, he left me. He did not even trouble to bolt the door, and I remember myself thinking: 'That's so as to waste no time, when they come for me.'

"Night had fallen, and there was a profound silence all around. However, after a while, I heard awful cries coming from somewhere nearby. I could not identify the voice. After ten minutes, the cries ceased, but they were instantly renewed, from a different direction. I began to count the minutes till my turn came, and when nothing happened, I tried to convince myself that the cries were nothing but a trick to break my spirit.

"That night I was not molested. I can only assume that I was left in peace as a result of the same error which caused me to be sent to Block 1 at first. Apparently, I had yet to be registered in the 'work schedule' of the torture experts. Only the guard came around every half hour, to make sure that I was still standing with my face to the wall.

"At four in the morning, when it was still dark, I was taken to the washroom at a run, the guard prodding me from behind with a stick. As I ran, I tried to look around. The prison appeared deserted; there were only a few soldiers standing around at the corners of the courtyard.

"At eight in the morning, the prison came to life. From the corridor I heard a shout of '*Inteba!*' and a Sudanese officer entered my cell, accompanied by a group of soldiers.

" 'Do you need anything?' he asked.

" 'No. Nothing. Only the handcuffs.'

"He ordered them to be removed. 'Do you want anything to eat? What do you want?'

"A thought flashed through my mind: a final request before my execution. I replied: 'Whatever you give me.'

"He turned to the soldiers. 'Bring him halva and cheese.' Then, to me: 'Is that all right? Olives, perhaps?'

"He went out, but I didn't get to see any food. It was only the next day, forty-eight hours after leaving Alexandria, that I received my first food in Cairo—half a pitta and a hunk of halva. That day, when the sentry opened the door to glance at me, I saw Shmuel Azar, without his spectacles, dressed only in an undershirt, being taken to the washroom at a run. Later, I also saw Philip, in an undershirt and shorts, crossing the courtyard.

"On seeing them, I felt better. They were still alive. . . ."

Philip was next to the last one to be transferred from Alexandria to Cairo. Blindfolded at the Cairo railway station, like his companions before him, he did not know where he was being driven to. Only when he was taken off the truck at the end of the journey did he hear one of the Alexandria policemen who had escorted him say something about the Sigan Harbi, to which his colleague replied: "No one comes out of here alive. . . ." These words were to echo and reecho through his mind in the course of the coming weeks. There were even moments of weakness, when he imagined that he had reached the end of his tether, and thought indifferently: If only death would come. . . .

But the beginning was not ominous, possibly because of the inflamed and ugly burns on his arms. When the duty officer came to his cell (after Victor had been treated to the usual run down the corridor, blindfolded and manacled, with the guards urging him on with their canes), Philip complained about the handcuffs, and the officer ordered them removed.

"I must have looked so wretched that he took pity on me. He asked me if I wanted anything to eat, and when I replied in the affirmative, he sent a soldier to bring me a plateful of cold lentils. He even added apologetically that this was all there was.

"Wishing to seize on this moment of warmth, I asked about the fate of my companions. He replied severely: 'You don't ask questions here!' I was soon to learn that even this gruff answer was relatively merciful. Impertinence such as I had just displayed in addressing an officer without being asked was usually punished with great brutality.

"I was left to myself, wondering where I was and what had befallen my companions. That evening, I was taken out to the washroom, to find that I was in a two-story building with a square internal courtyard. I counted the doors: nine on each side; multiplied by two stories, multiplied by four wings—that made seventy-two cells in all. Only six of them were illuminated, all corner cells. I guessed that it was in these that my companions were confined.

"The previous mildness vanished on my return to my cell. When the door was bolted behind me, I lay down on the *borsh*, trying to fall asleep, but the bugs gave me no rest. Inadvertently, I let out a curse. Instantly, the door opened and a soldier charged in furiously. I stood up, but he gave me a punch which knocked me down again.

" 'What did you say?' he barked, adding a kick in the ribs for good measure.

" 'I was cursing the bugs,' I stammered, and received another kick. 'It is forbidden to curse the bugs; they belong to the prison!'

"This was the beginning of a series of beatings which went on without respite, until the prison filled up with members of the Moslem Brotherhood, leaving the guards too busy to deal with us. Till then, they used to beat us on any excuse; they beat us whenever we were supposedly interrogated by agents of the Muhabarat; they beat us during the nightly tours of Hamza el Bassiuni, the prison governor; they beat us without any reason, whenever we happened to be within reach of a guard's arm or leg.

"But the worst was when Hamza came on one of his nightly tours. I could gauge his approach by the sound of doors being opened and closed, and by the cries of my companions as they were beaten. I would lie on my *borsh*, trying to stop my ears, and count: 'Now they're in Marzouk's cell, that's Victor's voice . . . they've reached Azar. . . .' "

Victor was "honored" with the first of Hamza el Bassiuni's visits on his third night at the Sigan Harbi. In the course of the coming months, there would be numerous visits of this kind, no less terrifying, but the first remained branded in Victor's memory.

"The shouts all around died down. I was sitting on my *borsh* trying to unravel what I had heard, concerned about Robbie, whose voice I had not heard. Suddenly, the cell door opened and a group of men rushed in. They were headed by a tall, fleshy man, with gray hair and gray eyes. A scar ran down his cheek, giving him a most ferocious expression. His shoulders bore an eagle and three stars, the insignia of an *emir alai*.

"I stood up. Immediately, I got a punch in the stomach from the red-haired sergeant, Mahmud Abdul Gawad, who hissed: 'Officers are to be saluted!'

"I saluted.

"The officer asked: 'Is everything all right? Is there anything you want?'

"I complained about the bugs. He turned to one of the soldiers and commanded: 'Clean the *borsh* for him!' and to another soldier: 'Disinfect the cell!' A third soldier took out the water jug and the *kardal*. But the smiles on their faces as they cleaned out my cell should have forewarned me.

"They went out and locked the cell. I heard them advance along the corridor. A door opened, I heard cries. Then the door was locked again. Then another door was opened. . . .

"At last, the tour ended. I heard footsteps in the corridor approaching my cell.

"Seven or eight soldiers burst into my cell, grabbed hold of me. Before I could realize what was happening, a rope was looped under my armpits, and the other end was flung over the beam which lay between the two windows; I was yanked up and left dangling in the air. Then they all began to beat me with clubs and sticks.

"Suddenly, there was a roar. The fat man had returned; standing in the doorway, he yelled: 'Dirty sons of bitches, let him down! What are you doing? Do you want to leave marks on him?'

"They let me down. I was on the verge of unconsciousness, and my senses were completely dazed. Mahmud, the red-haired sergeant, tore my shirt off, wrapped a towel around my chest, and then replaced the rope, laying it over the towel. I was blindfolded, and pulled up again; once again the blows rained down.

"Before I was blindfolded, I took the first beating without making a sound. I was even surprised by my own powers of resistance. However, with my eyes blindfolded, it was ten times worse. You don't see the blow coming down, and your body is unprepared. I let out an awful scream.

"Apparently, my screams satisfied them. They halted their beating and went out, leaving me blindfolded and dangling in midair.

"After a while—an hour? two? I lost all count of time—one of them came back and let me down. I fell, unable to control my legs. He ordered me to get up. I tried to, but instantly, my legs gave way again. Then he beat me with a club, and I remember nothing more till the next day.

"Only one thing pierced the haze of oblivion: the cries of Philip, Marzouk, and Azar (who, it transpired, were treated to a 'welcoming ceremony' similar to mine), and other voices which I did not identify, but not that of Robbie."

## Lots of Stick, Few Carrots

Robbie had a stroke of luck; he fell sick. When he awoke, on the third day after his arrival in Cairo, he was burning with fever. He did not touch the bowl of lentils he was brought; when the guard asked why, Robbie told him he felt unwell. The guard did not dare call the duty officer, the Sudanese captain, but when the latter conducted his routine evening tour of inspection, he gave instructions for a doctor to be called. The doctor arrived, accompanied by the prison governor, Hamza el Bassiuni.

The doctor took Robbie's temperature and declared: "He has to be taken to the hospital." But el Bassiuni looked angry, and beckoned to the doctor to come outside with him. On their return, the doctor canceled his instructions for Robbie's hospitalization; instead, he left twelve aspirin tablets with the guard, with orders to give one to the patient every two hours. Hamza ordered the filthy *borsh* to be replaced by a mattress.

The following day, the doctor returned, again accompanied by el Bassiuni. Robbie complained that he could not sleep because of the bugs, whereupon Hamza gave orders to have him transferred to the neighboring cell "until your cell is disinfected." He told the guards to whitewash the cell and spray it with insecticide. "God help you if there's one bug left!"

Robbie never knew whether the order was carried out, because he was not transferred back to the cell; he remained in the neighboring one, without a mattress.

That night, frightful shouts came from the cell Robbie had just vacated. He thought it was Victor's voice, but the questions put to the new inmate, which Robbie could hear clearly, were unconnected with the network. Robbie guessed that the man undergoing interrogation was a cavalry officer (the cavalry rallied to Gen. Naguib when an attempt was made in February to overthrow him; Naguib was restored to office, but the regime instituted a purge of the cavalry corps, many of whose officers were secretly arrested). The next morning, when Robbie was taken out to the washroom, he passed by the open door of his former cell. He saw numerous cigarette butts on the floor, two chairs, and a rope dangling from the overhead beam. Later on, when Robbie came to know the customs of the military jail, he comprehended why el Bassiuni had had him transferred to another cell. The corner cells in the prison were reserved for "hanging torture" and el Bassiuni did not wish to "waste" such a cell on a sick prisoner who could not be strung up.

To this day, Robbie does not know the precise nature of his ailment; it lasted for about a week, saving him from the "hanging" which was a kind of "reception ceremony" accorded to every new inmate of the military prison; it also gave him a respite from the beatings and interrogations to which the other members of the network were subjected. He was left in peace. The sentry on guard outside his cell—a smooth-cheeked young soldier, about nineteen years old, with a small bird tattooed in blue at the corners of his eyes, marking him as a member of one of the Upper Egyptian Said tribes—did not speak to him. But if Robbie ever asked him anything, the young man would order him to be silent: "You heard what the officer said; it is forbidden to speak!" Robbie lay on his *borsh*, dispiritedly listening to the monotonous bugle calls repeated over and over again with maddening persistence; at night, he would hear the sentries call: "Number one, all present and correct!" "Number two, all present and correct!," mingling with the cries of those being "interrogated." The hours crawled by, filled with anxiety and foreboding.

Because he was sick, the guards were less strict with Robbie. The sentry in the corridor did not trouble to lock the door of his cell, and at times—particularly when there were no officers in the block—did not even close it. In the morning, when he was taken out to the washroom, the guards did not make him hurry back to his cell, as they did the others. There were occasions when the sentry did not even trouble to accompany him, whereupon Robbie seized on the opportunity to dawdle beside the water taps, taking a long time to wash or rinse out his handkerchief, until the next prisoner was brought out. (Before the prison filled up with Moslem Brotherhood convicts, the prisoners were taken out to wash one at a time, to prevent their meeting.) In this manner, he successively met each of his companions. He did not yet venture to talk to them, but there was some encouragement and comfort in exchanging glances with them.

As for the others, their first weeks at the Sigan Harbi were to remain etched in their memories as the worst period of their prolonged imprisonment.

The arrested members of the network had become pawns in a power struggle between the civilian police and the military intelligence, the Muhabarat. The latter, determined to prove the ineffectiveness of their rivals, endeavored to make the prisoners reveal "new facts" which had been overlooked by the civilian police. This was done by the well-tried techniques of torture and inculcating fear.

Philip, curled up tensely on his *borsh*, listened to the cries which marked the interrogators' progress from cell to cell. "Then I heard the rattle of a key in the lock, and they were in my cell. Hamza el Bassiuni at their head, his eyes flashing in expectation, the scar on his cheek giving his face a frightening expression; he was followed in by six to ten soldiers; instantly, I was in their grasp, and the blows rained down, accompanied by shouts of, 'Talk! Tell us everything you have concealed so far!'

"It was not an interrogation. They took no interest in my replies, they asked no questions, they only beat me. But the next day, the

Muhabarat interrogators arrived. From now on, I was able to recognize an unchanging pattern: Whenever I received a nighttime visit from Hamza and his thugs, I knew that this was a 'softening-up operation' in preparation for an interrogation the next morning."

The Muhabarat investigators came for Victor the day after his "ordeal by hanging," when he was still swollen and in pain.

"In the afternoon, the door opened and a number of soldiers burst into the cell, followed by two Muhabarat agents in civilian clothes. One of them, very thin, was elegantly dressed in a pressed, expensive suit. His colleague was stout and blue-eyed. They stood before me. 'Your name?' and before I had time to reply, blows fell on me from all sides. 'Now, talk!'

" 'What can I tell you? I've told everything.'

"The thin officer seized my shirt collar, ripping it open and baring my chest. Then he pulled out a spring blade and began to draw its razor-sharp point over my skin, lightly, without pressing. In a moment, I was drenched with blood.

" 'If you don't talk, I'll cut your ear off. What were you doing in the Canal Zone? And on the bridges?'

"He did not wait for my answers. Glancing at his watch, he said: 'It is now three. At five, I'll come back. Till then, you have time to think it over. . . .'

"He left me dazed and bewildered; my knees were trembling. What did they want? What bridges? I had never been to the Canal Zone! I lay down on the concrete floor (my *borsh* had not been brought back after my 'hanging treatment') and tried to think. But that was impossible: The cries were now coming from the neighboring cells, and they drove me out of my mind."

The two officers did not return. But hours passed before Victor calmed down, realizing that he had just been subjected to yet another trick aimed at breaking him psychologically.

After that, a week went past without any interrogation, but the beatings did not cease. Every now and then, soldiers would burst into his cell and beat him, with no apparent purpose, until they had satisfied their sadistic instincts. The ban on sleeping remained in force. At intervals, the guard would charge into the cell, yelling furiously: "I saw you sleeping!" and his cane whistled through the air. "I would sit on the floor, leaning against the wall, awakening with a start from a momentary doze, and pray for the morning to come."

But the morning did not bring any relief. Five minutes to relieve himself, wash briefly, and fill up his water jug, and he had to sprint back to his cell. Despite their growing weariness, the prisoners ran with all their might, prodded from behind by their guards, while on the way, they had to run the gauntlet of other guards, each of whom added his quota of kicks or punches as he passed. If anyone fell and the water spilled out of his jug, he was left without any water till the following morning.

In the course of the day, there was another torment the guards had invented. They would burst into the cell and shout: "Stand up! Face to the wall! Arms up! Stand there like that! If you lower your hands, God help you!" Then they went away, leaving the door wide open.

Victor: "How long can you stand with your arms up? Ten minutes, twenty. Then you begin to lose all sensation in your hands, and the pain in your shoulders and fingertips is so fierce, you begin to think that beating is better, so you lower your hands. At times, nothing happened, because the guard had gone away and did not return. But you are so terrified of the beatings that after a rest of a minute or two you raise your hands again. But there were times when the guard would lurk behind the door. . . ."

Philip thought up a way of finding out whether the guard was nearby. He would save up a few crumbs of his pitta, pushing them out beneath the door into the corridor, which was open to the courtyard. As long as there was no one there, sparrows would swoop down to pick up the crumbs. But if the sentry was lurking behind the door, they would stay away. If they flew off in sudden panic, this would warn Philip that the sentry was approaching, and he would hasten to raise his arms.

It was no small sacrifice for Philip to give up part of his meager rations of food to the sparrows. He was constantly hungry, even more than his companions.


Robbie's mysterious ailment led the doctor to suspect that it was caused by the prison staple, the greasy mess of lentils. A day or two after he fell sick, instructions were given for the network prisoners to be fed with rations brought from the nearby military hospital. This was a rather more "European" diet—an egg, jam, butter, American cheese, at times, even boiled chicken. But the *shawish*, Abdul Gawad, intercepted the deliveries, which he shared with those of his guard cronies who hailed like him from the Delta town of Mansura. The prisoners received only the scraps. But the *shawish*, fearful of being found out, would tour the cells every day and inform the prisoners: "If the officer asks you what you ate today, tell him you had chicken, butter and jam, and cheese. God help you if you tell the officer you didn't get all that!"

But Philip did not even get the leftovers; from the very first day, he had invoked particular hostility on the part of the guards.

Robbie: "Philip—the *mahrua*, the burnt one, as the guards called him—was more European in appearance than the rest of us, and perhaps that is why they treated him worse than us. But he didn't make things easier for himself. He always felt an inner urge to answer back, to have the last word. His sharp tongue often got him into trouble."

In consequence, Philip was punished by being deprived of the hospital food, and he continued to receive the ordinary prison rations. In time, he grew accustomed to its greasy taste, and even came to like the sharply flavored vegetable stew. But during the first period, he was weakened by hunger, sleeplessness, and the repeated beatings he suffered.

"They succeeded in making me break down," conceded Victor. "After a week without sleep, with next to no food, and constant beatings, I reached a stage of apathy. One evening, when two soldiers broke into my cell, one brandishing a knife and the other holding a pistol, shouting: 'Your time has come! Choose how you want to die!' I replied indifferently: 'You can decide. I don't care.' Even the blows I received for my insolence did not hurt me that much."

Robbie recovered. He had been saved from the "reception ceremony" and the guards, having yet to discover his links with the *hawagat,* did not give him the "special treatment" they lavished on his companions. Nevertheless, the "normal treatment" was bad enough. And when the Muhabarat interrogators arrived, they did not pass him over. Like his companions, he underwent the "knife interrogation," which left scars on his chest.

The art of interrogation requires periods of rough treatment to be followed by milder methods. The "knife interrogators" departed and did not return. Their places were taken by two other officers, more pleasant in their bearing.

Victor: "After a week of hell, I was told one day: 'Stand up! Go and wash yourself! An officer wishes to see you.' By now I was in such a state that I no longer feared this ominous summons. What more could they do to me?

"I was blindfolded and shoved on my way. When the blindfold was removed, I found myself in an office of some sort, facing two civilians.

" 'Sit down. You are Victor Levy? Do you want a cigarette?'

"All the fears to which I fancied myself to have become immune now returned. I turned down the proffered cigarette. 'What do you want of me?'

" 'Relax, relax. From now on, my friend and I are in charge of your interrogation. The people here wanted to use force to make you talk, but we believe in peaceful methods. You are an educated man, and you understand your situation. What is the point of concealment? We are sure that you will tell us everything.'

" 'I told everything in Alexandria,' I replied.

" 'What you related there doesn't interest us. Here, you'll tell us everything, all over again. Remember, we have the power to grant you hell or paradise. It depends on you.' "

"He had Shawish Mahmud Abdul Gawad called in, and made a great show of telling him: 'From today onwards there are to be no more beatings. He is like my brother. . . .'

"And then, turning to me, he continued: 'Now go back to your cell, and write everything down. You will receive a table and chair, a pen and paper, and you can write in peace.'

" 'What I related in Alexandria?'

" 'Everything.'

" 'In English or in French? I can't write Arabic.'

" 'English is better. Is there anything else you want?'

" 'No, thank you. Oh, yes. I want to send a letter to my parents.' Over and above my physical sufferings, I was tormented by worry for my parents. They were probably heartbroken with sorrow and uncertainty.

" 'That's difficult. I can't promise. All the same, write the letter, we'll try and get it sent. But there is one thing you ought to know. My friend and I have saved your lives; the others were not content with torturing you, they wanted to kill you. We had to put up a stiff fight to take over the interrogation.'

"I left them, bewildered and confused. I knew that this was just another trick; after breaking us physically with the stick, they were now dangling the carrot in front of us. But my heart was foolish enough to desire, there was such a longing to believe in the humanity of man . . .

"By the time I got back to my cell, my *borsh* had been brought back; I even received two blankets, and a chair and table were standing there. I sat down and wrote out my account. It was a wonderful day. I wasn't beaten once, and I was permitted to sleep undisturbed all night.

"The following day, I handed in the 'manuscript.' Later, I was again summoned to the two interrogators. 'You did not write enough about your training in Israel. You must give more details.'

" 'What training? I visited *kibbutzim!*'

"They did not push the point. They went on to other topics on which they wanted further information. Years later, when we talked about the subject in prison, it struck me that throughout my interrogation by the Muhabarat in Cairo, I was never once questioned about

'Robert'—'Paul Frank.' In Alexandria, the police had questioned me at great length about him, but the Muhabarat officers didn't say a word about him.

"One day, three or four days after the commencement of the 'new regime,' I was again taken to an office, more luxurious this time, that of the prison governor. An officer in a resplendent uniform, whose insignia was hidden by a towel wrapped around his shoulders, glowered at me. He was holding my 'manuscript.'

" 'All this,' he barked, 'is nothing but a pack of nonsense. What is behind your gang? You're spies! What did you tell the enemy? Who were the officers you met in Israel? Remember, your life is in my hands!'

"I tried to stick to my story. But he shouted: 'Go on! You are great scoundrels! What were you taught in Israel? Where?'

"Later, I saw the man's picture in a newspaper, and thus discovered his identity. He was Emir Alai Nuri Mansour, the head of military intelligence.

"He questioned all my companions in a similar fashion. When we met again, at the Istianuff prison in Cairo, Moshe Marzouk told me that Nuri Mansour held a long conversation with him, at the end of which he said: 'Your state will vanish. If it weren't for the June 1948 ceasefire, Israel would not be in existence by now.' 'And if it weren't for the 1949 ceasefire, what would have been the fate of Egypt?' retorted Marzouk promptly, whereupon the brigadier flung himself at him, punching and kicking him, with all the other men in the room joining in. They did not rest content with that; on being taken back to his cell, he was strung up for six hours, for having dared to offend the *basha*.

"My own interrogation passed off uneventfully, but it obviously did not satisfy him; the table and chair were removed from my cell, and the beatings were resumed."

The others had similar experiences.

When Philip Natanson was ordered "to write everything," he feigned innocence and wrote down his curriculum vitae, for which he was beaten brutally. On one occasion, he was summoned to the prison office, where an interrogator he had not previously seen questioned him at length about the developing techniques he had been taught in Israel. Another interrogator spread out a map of Israel and asked him to point out the site of any military camp he had seen there. Experienced enough not to refuse, he pinpointed a military camp in the vicinity of every town in Israel.

One day, after not having been mentioned for weeks, "Robert's" name came up again. Philip was taken out of the prison. When his blindfold was removed, he found himself standing before a car parked between two barracks. "Is this 'Robert's' car?" he was asked. When he replied that it was not a Buick and its color was not green, he was beaten.

A few days later, he was again taken to identify a car. This time it was a Buick and its color was green, but it was not "Robert's" car. There were ten persons standing nearby, one of them no more than a boy. Another, wearing an expensive silk shirt, showed signs of having undergone a rough interrogation. Could Philip identify any of them? Again, he got a murderous beating when he replied in the negative.

In the end, they found "Robert's" car. Robbie was the first one called to identify it.

"One day, two of 'our' interrogators from Alexandria turned up, Yusuf Fauzi and his assistant, Kamel. I was glad to see them, as though they were relatives. They said that they had found 'Robert's' car, and wanted me to identify it. I replied that I had never seen it. Nevertheless, I was taken to look at it. I was also shown a snapshot of him, which I also failed to recognize."

After Robbie failed to satisfy them, Philip was summoned to identify the car.

"I recognized it immediately, even though its green paint had been stripped off, as though it were about to be repainted. It was 'Robert's' Plymouth. But when asked whether I recognized it, I replied in the negative. Then I was shown a snapshot of a group of people and asked whether I recognized 'Robert' among them. I pretended indecision.

" 'All your companions have identified both the car and the man!' a Muhabarat officer shouted at me. 'Is this him?' and he pointed at 'Robert' in the picture. I was obliged to concede that he did look like 'Robert.'

" 'And the car?' asked the officer.

" 'I only saw it once, from the window of my home, and then it was painted, not like it is now.'

" 'It doesn't matter,' he said. 'In any case, we've finished off the car's owner. We found him in a hotel, and when we tried to arrest him, he pulled out a gun and ran away. We pursued him through the streets of Alexandria and shot him dead.'

"His words rang true. I knew that 'Robert' had a gun; the car also looked as though it had been in a collision, and the whole story seemed to fit 'Robert' as we perceived him.

"My heart sank, but I shrugged with pretended indifference: 'Unfortunate,' I said.

" 'What's unfortunate?' he shouted.

" 'It's unfortunate about him. He was so young and good-looking . . .'

"He nodded. Later, when I recalled the expression on his face, I was sure that he said to himself: 'What a naive fool!'

"We remained there a little longer while they wrote out the identification report. It was hot, and one of the soldiers was sent to bring lemonade. I found myself standing beside Yusuf Fauzi; he whispered to me: 'Did you believe him? Don't believe it! That man is as courageous as a wild animal! He had the courage to remain in the country for fourteen days after your arrest, and he even sold his car before leaving Egypt.'

"I took a second look at the Muhabarat agent who was busy writing his identification report. Suddenly, I comprehended why he looked familiar: This was the man in the red shirt who had stood at the head of my bed in the Alexandria hospital, after my arrest, the one who gave me a long, searching look and then went away without saying a word.

"At my side, Fauzi whispered: 'These Muhabarat people. They think they're smart! What did you tell them? You shouldn't tell them more than you told us; it will only get you into trouble!' "

As for Philip, he was already "in trouble." His refusal to identify "Robert's" car had put him in the Muhabarat's black books, earning him several weeks of "special treatment." The sentry outside his door roughed him up with greater frequency than previously; he was forced to stand with his hands above his head for hours at a time; if he fell asleep at night, the sentry would kick him awake; if he did not fall asleep, he was beaten nevertheless. His rations were reduced, and the food was worse than ever—only some thin, murky soup, and not always as much as that. At times, he got a plateful of *maluhia* (a popular Egyptian soup made from the sour leaves of a wild plant)—"and that was a real feast!"

His burns troubled him more than his hunger. The wounds did not heal up. Every few days, an army medical orderly—a different one each time—would be brought to bandage him. Before his arrival, the guards would warn him: "If you complain, you'll die!" While the bandages were being changed, Shawish Abdul Gawad stood behind the orderly, sliding his finger around his throat threateningly.

"I did not complain. What was the point? Just for telling the orderly that his salves were not doing any good, I was given a murderous thrashing. The salves really were of no use. My wounds remained full of pus for months before they finally healed up.

"There were moments when I wanted to die. But they soon passed. Although I was broken physically, I was spiritually mutinous. I was resolved to survive—in spite of everything—and to live for the day when I could tell of the horrors we had experienced. I was particular to exercise each day, to keep myself in shape. I made efforts to keep count of the days, as a way of preventing myself from losing touch with reality. During the brief time that the table stood in my cell for me to write out my confession, I managed to pull out a loose nail, with which I scratched a line on the wall for every passing day of imprisonment. (At first, I scratched the dark portion of the wall, but the guards noticed the lines and beat me for making them, though they failed to find the nail. Later, I moved my 'calendar' to the whitewashed portion of the wall.) I applied my mind to repeated reconstructions of the events preceding my arrest. I sensed no remorse, only regret at having failed. I told myself: 'If I had to do it all again, I would do it better!' "

One night, some time later, the prison reverberated with the cries of terror which heralded a "reception ceremony" for newcomers.

At that time, the prison had begun filling up with arrested members of the Moslem Brotherhood, while the members of the network had all been transferred to the second floor and housed in one wing, in adjacent cells.

Robbie: "When the doors were opened in the morning, we were all at the openings, risking the guards' wrath and poking our heads out in an effort to see what was happening in the courtyard. From door to door, the whispered message was passed on: 'Jews from Cairo. One of them is Meir Za'afran's father.'

"Weeks later, when the newcomers were about to be released, Meir was permitted to see his father briefly; it was only then we discovered who they were and what they were arrested for. They too were victims of 'the mishap.' "

This is the story: While in Paris, Moshe Marzouk met an acquaintance, a former resident of Cairo, who asked him to take one hundred Egyptian pounds for his brother who had remained behind in Egypt. He gave Moshe his brother's visiting card: César Cohen, employed at the Zilcha Bank, married with two children. Moshe met him, gave him the money, and forgot all about the episode. However, the visiting card was among his belongings when he was arrested, and the police found it.

César Cohen was called in for questioning. When asked about Marzouk—he knew that Moshe had been arrested on suspicion of grave crimes—he denied any connection with him, whereupon he was tortured so brutally that, not content with "confessing" to being a "Zionist agent," he went on to denounce a whole "network" of other "spies"— all the employees of the Zilcha Bank, including Meir Za'afran's father, and a number of other prominent members of the Jewish community, forty-two in all.

"They were all interrogated under torture; we heard their cries every night for a week, until the interrogators concluded that César Cohen's 'testimony' was nonsense, whereupon they left their prisoners in peace. On the eve of the Jewish New Year, they were all released, with the exception of César Cohen. The interrogators were so furious with him for misleading them that they planned a particularly cruel punishment for him. Not content with keeping him in custody, they informed him that he had been sentenced to death. They staged a whole execution ceremony; he was led out into the courtyard at dawn, a firing squad lined up before him, he was blindfolded and the order was given: 'Fire!' "

The rifles did not fire, but César Cohen was never the same again. His nerves gave way, and he acquired a severe stutter.

## The Moslem Brotherhood

Inside Egypt, the power struggle intensified. On the surface, President Muhammed Naguib's position seemed firmer than ever, particularly after the signing of an agreement with Britain, whereby the British army would complete its withdrawal from Egypt within twenty months. But in the background, the security services had succeeded in destroying Naguib's power bases within the army. They now turned on the most important force outside the ranks of the army—the Moslem Brotherhood.

The Brotherhood is an extreme religious movement which supports a return to the principles of "pure Islam." Its ideology is pan-Moslem, regarding all believers as a single nation, and refusing to recognize their division among separate sovereign states. For some reason, the Brotherhood found fertile soil for its ideas in Egypt, where it became a mass movement of great influence. However, the Brotherhood never became a party, and never ran for election with the aim of gaining the power needed to carry out its ideals. It operated by preaching in the mosques and, frequently, by acts of terror. Brotherhood agents assassinated several Egyptian premiers and statesmen whom the movement had denounced as "sinners."

Even though the Brotherhood gave its blessing to the officers' revolution, and Col. Mohana, one of the thirteen original members of the Revolutionary Council, acted as its unofficial representative, it soon found out that the new regime was no more inclined than its predecessor to subject Egypt to religious law. On the contrary, the officers' revolution aimed at bringing the country into the twentieth century. The ways parted: Col. Mohana was the first member of the Revolutionary Council to be "purged." The Brotherhood's preachers in the mosques soon began to deliver sermons against the "unbelievers" who had taken power in Cairo. The heads of the revolution, fearing that the

Brotherhood would take the side of President Naguib in any open confrontation, decided that it was essential to crush the Brotherhood and destroy its power before they could get rid of the President.

On September 26, 1954, they got their opportunity.

Col. Gamal Abdel Nasser, then Vice President and head of the Revolutionary Council, was addressing a mass rally at Midan Menashia in Alexandria, when, from a house overlooking the square, someone opened fire at the speaker's rostrum. The shots missed, and the would-be assassin was arrested. His name was Handawi Dawir, and he was an active member of the Moslem Brotherhood's "Secret Arm."

In time, the Brotherhood was to point out that, from the window where Dawir was standing, the distance to Nasser's rostrum was over eighty meters, while Dawir was only holding a pistol. They contended that Dawir would not have been able to hit his would-be victim. Consequently, his act—if indeed he perpetrated it—was nothing but a provocation staged by the secret police.

Be that as it may, the Midan Menashia incident gave Nasser's supporters the opportunity for a double campaign: on the one hand, they instituted extensive acts of repression against the Brotherhood, with the aim of eliminating its influence, and, at the same time, they could build up the image of Nasser, hitherto fairly unknown to the masses and overshadowed by the much more popular Naguib. Editorial writers informed their readers how fortunate it was for the Egyptian people that Nasser had been spared from assassination; the popular singer Um Kultum wrote a song of thanksgiving, whose text, freely translated, was as follows:

"O Nasser, model of nationalism, your salvation at Menashia was the finest hour of the nation . . ." The song was broadcast on radio stations throughout the country, several times a day. This mass hysteria was carefully fostered until, by October, public opinion had been prepared for the second—and final—overthrow of Gen. Naguib. He was placed under house arrest, while Gamal Abdel Nasser took his place as the head of state.

The ups and downs of Egypt's political life find faithful reflection inside its prisons. In the course of their fourteen years in jail, the imprisoned members of the network were able to follow the political upheavals which overtook the country by the successive waves of prisoners who were "housed" in the prisons. Whenever Cairo fell out with Moscow, the prison filled up with Communists. When the squabble was patched up, their places were taken by journalists with pro-Western leanings. Any decline in the standing of some member of the Revolutionary Council was accompanied by the arrest of his followers and confidants.

Now, at the beginning of September 1954, it was the turn of the Moslem Brotherhood.

The first indications of the change in the military prison came one evening, when the members of the network, hitherto dispersed all over the prison, were ordered out of their cells and concentrated in one wing of the second story, in adjacent cells.

Robbie: "We didn't know the reason for this until, that night, the prison reverberated with cries and shouts. I was horrified. I feared that there had been another wave of arrests against Jews. But the next morning, when I went down to the courtyard, I saw them. They looked most wretched: beaten and bruised, their clothes torn, their heads shaven, as well as their beards and eyebrows. The loudspeakers were playing Um Kultum's song: 'O Nasser, model of nationalism,' and these miserable wretches were ordered to join in the song. Anyone who didn't sing, or didn't do so loudly enough, was beaten."

At this time, Robbie had achieved a kind of semiofficial status in the prison. The guards had grown used to his prolonged stay near the water taps in the morning, and when he sought justification for his dawdling by cleaning out the washroom on his own initiative, they did not object. On the contrary, hitherto, this unpleasant task had been imposed upon them and they were glad to be rid of it. In consequence, Robbie was the first one to be taken out of his cell in the morning, and he remained beside the faucets until his companions had completed their toilet, when he remained behind to clean up after them.

As the prison filled up with Brotherhood members (three hundred arrived on the first evening; by the end of the week, there were eight hundred of them crowded in Block 4 alone; altogether, the Sigan Harbi housed over five thousand Brotherhood members), Robbie was charged with a new task: He assisted in handing out rations to the cells. Two guards carried the pot filled with stew, while Robbie followed, carrying the pitta in a blanket.

"The prison turned into a purgatory," he relates. "New prisoners were brought in every day. Daily, inmates were taken to the Muhabarat for interrogation, returning in an awful, sickening condition—blood pouring from their mouths, their teeth smashed; frequently, their flesh was scorched by red-hot irons, or their foreheads showed the marks of the 'nail belt,' a terrible torture device which the interrogators tightened about their victim's head until his eyes popped out . . .

"Nor did they fare much better in the prison. Every night, Hamza el Bassiuni and his henchmen toured the cells and the cries ascended to the heavens . . ."

There was one group which suffered a particularly bitter fate. A few days after the onset of the campaign against the Brotherhood, a group of its members attacked a police station, with the aim of releasing some of their comrades imprisoned there. The attack failed, and the attackers were caught. They belonged to the "Secret Arm." When they reached Block 4 after being interrogated by the Muhabarat, there wasn't a part of their bodies which did not bear marks of their ordeal. After that, at night, they received visits from Hamza el Bassiuni.

Robbie: "Next morning, when the doors of their cells were opened and they were called out to the washrooms, not a single one of them came out; they were incapable of standing up.

"I had no sympathy for the Brotherhood or its aims; they were the most extreme in their enmity toward Israel and the Jews. But when the prison gates close behind a man, he leaves his past outside. He becomes a fellow sufferer. At least, that was the way I felt as I stood by that open door and saw that no one came out. I was unable to stand by idly.

"The guards were not paying any attention to me, so I went inside the cell. One by one, I pulled them to their feet and propped them up as they tottered out, semiconscious, beaten and bleeding. I helped them to the faucets where I washed the blood off them and bathed their wounds. I even helped them pull off their trousers to relieve themselves. One of them, Yusuf Tla'at—I later learned that he was one of the heads of the 'Secret Arm'—gazed at me with pain-filled eyes and asked me who I was. I said: 'A Jew.' The surprised expression on his face was my reward.

"But, in fact, the real reward was the knowledge that I, a prisoner at the mercy of the guards, was able to help and encourage him. I muttered in his ear: 'Hold on. You can stand up to it. Look, we also suffered the same treatment!' I said it to him, but the words helped to strengthen me."

Each morning, Robbie accompanied the guards as they opened the cell doors. "The sights I saw were horrifying. The overcrowding was awful; at times, twenty men were housed in a single cell. The shaved heads, the faces dehumanized by having their eyebrows shaved off; the encrusted blood, and, most frightening of all, the awful fear in their eyes . . ."

When the prisoners completed their early morning wash, Robbie was left on his own in the courtyard to clean out the washrooms. He soon found an assistant, a young Jew by the name of Uri. He was from Alexandria, a little older than Robbie. Uri had emigrated to Israel straight after the War of Independence. While there, he incurred a psychological disorder and was committed to a psychiatric hospital, but he escaped, obsessed by a single notion—to rejoin his brother who had stayed behind in Egypt. He made his way to the Gaza Strip, where he was arrested on suspicion of espionage; he underwent terrible tortures, which could not have improved his mental state. Finally, the Muhaba-rat tired of him and sent him to the Abbassiya military prison.

When the guards of the Sigan Harbi got to know him, they permit-ted him to remain in the courtyard, where he ambled about with his face set in an idiotic smile, which changed into an expression of terror whenever one of the guards addressed him. The guards treated him as a plaything, sometimes ordering him to stand in the courtyard and shout at the top of his voice: "May Ben-Gurion die!" At times, in quest of a more sadistic form of amusement, they would order him to beat the Moslem Brotherhood prisoners.

Uri spent three years at the Sigan Harbi before being shipped back to the Gaza Strip to be court-martialed. He was sentenced to life impris-onment; only in 1973 was he released and sent back to Israel.

After cleaning the washrooms, Robbie would return to his cell, the nearest one to the stairs. The guards were not strict about locking his cell, but, as a precaution against an unexpected visit by the duty officer, Robbie would pour a bucketful of water into the corridor, in front of his cell. The sparkling pool of water reflected the image of whoever was coming up the stairs. If it was an officer, he would hasten to close the door.

At ten o'clock, he would be called to help in giving the prisoners their rations.

Food was also utilized as a way of abusing the prisoners. At times, the guards would give a single bowl of soup and a sole pitta to a cell which housed sixteen or twenty men. They would then instantly lock the door. Alternatively, they would shout: "If anyone wants some more, he can come outside." If someone accepted the invitation, he would get a bowl of soup, but then, carrying it, he would be forced to run the gauntlet between two rows of guards who showered him with kicks and blows of their canes. Rarely did he manage to get back to the cell with any soup.

At times, the guards on their rounds would leave out one of the cells. Robbie soon learned the reason for this: One of the inmates had died in the course of his nighttime ordeal. Later, at the end of their rounds, the guards would come back to the cell and drag the corpse outside.

There was usually food left over, and Robbie contrived to get an extra portion to Philip, who was always hungry. At times, he gave food to the Brotherhood members.

Robbie began to befriend the Brotherhood prisoners, above all, the extremists, the members of the "Secret Arm." They were young and highly educated. Among their number there was a judge, an architect who had studied in the United States, a number of lawyers—with a blind faith in their ideals and their leaders. In prison, their eyes were opened; and the fact that the only person who helped them was a Jew —after they had been taught to hate and despise Jews—may have been an additional eye opener.

They told him that those Brotherhood members housed in Block 4 were the movement's leaders, including its *murshid al am* (spiritual leader) Hassan el Hudeibi, later sentenced to death (his sentence was commuted to life imprisonment), as well as Nasser's would-be assassin, Handawi Dawir.

Dawir was given "special treatment" of a particularly diabolical nature. On el Bassiuni's orders, Dawir was the only Brotherhood prisoner who was never beaten. He was given a cell of his own, on the ground floor; a chair was placed outside, and Dawir sat there from morning to night in the cool breeze, reading a paper and smoking, while his companions flitted past, staring at him with murderous eyes. They could see clearly that Dawir had betrayed and denounced them, and these special privileges were his reward. They could forgive him for denouncing them; they knew that certain forms of torture could break the bravest of men. But to receive the reward for his treason and enjoy it openly? More than one member of the Brotherhood secretly swore that if only there were an opportunity, he would give his life to wreak vengeance on the traitor.

There was no need. The regime broke its promise to reprieve Dawir, and he was executed, together with five of the heads of the "Secret Arm" whom he had denounced.

One of those executed was Yusuf Tla'at, the man whom Robbie had helped in his hour of need. But before his execution, Tla'at passed the word around among his companions: "Robert helped us, he is one of us." When the network prisoners later reached the Tura prison, where a large group of Brotherhood prisoners were confined, they found that the rumor had preceded them. The *murshid al am* personally invited Robbie to his cell, "to thank the man who helped our martyrs."

With the arrival of the Brotherhood prisoners, things became a little easier for the arrested members of the network. There is something horrifying and humiliating in the thought that the sufferings of one human being can lighten the burden of another. But the fact remains that having found new victims, el Bassiuni and his henchmen left the ten Jewish "spies" in peace. The latter did not escape an occasional kick or swipe of the cane if they passed within range of some bored guard, but they were no longer subjected to deliberate torture. Robbie, in his role as "caretaker," was free to come and go, at least, during the morning, as long as there were no officers in the block. And in the course of time he managed to get Philip to assist him. It all began with a duty sergeant, a little milder than the others, seeing Robbie bowed down by the weight of the pitta he was carrying; taking pity on him, he told him to call one of the prisoners to help. Robbie called Philip; after that, whenever that sergeant was on duty, Philip was sent to help Robbie in carrying pitta, or in cleaning up the washrooms.

However, not even routine could dull the sense of horror which constantly haunted the members of the network.

"It was enough to see the tormented faces of the Brotherhood members, when their cells were opened in the morning, for me to think: 'That's probably the way I look . . .' "

Soon they encountered another horror: "the pool"—the most sickening implement of torture to emerge from Hamza el Bassiuni's twisted mind. Inside one of the ground-floor cells, a meter-high double wall was built and waterproofed. After that, Robbie and Philip were kept busy a whole day, carrying buckets of water, until they filled the pool; when it was full, the Brotherhood members were flung inside. Standing waist-deep in water, they could neither lie down nor even sit. They were forced to stand there, day after day, their feet swelling up. They relieved themselves into the water, which they then had to drink, because they were not given any drinking water. Some of them held out for six or even eight days before losing the will to live and collapsing into the "pool" (whereupon they were dragged out, if the guards got there in time). Even the strongest of them were broken by the "pool"; they were brought out, crippled and deranged; many of them incurred incurable heart ailments.

### Lights in the Darkness

Robbie: "It was impossible to escape from that purgatory, even when the cell door was locked behind me and I remained alone, trying to erase the horrors I had seen. I tried to force myself to think of something else. But what? It was only natural that my thoughts should carry me back to the past, conjuring up memories of my dear ones—family and friends. Instantly, I was beset with worry about their fate, until I forced myself to return to present realities—to the locked cell door, the walls stained with the bodies of bugs, the cries of torment coming from outside.

"On one occasion, I was sitting in my cell, woolgathering, in a daydream, when suddenly I discovered that I was totally incapable of remembering my brother's name! I was overcome with fear. Was I losing my sanity? My temporary mental blank soon passed, but not the fear. That moment of oblivion brought it home to me: Outside the prison, life was going on, but I had no part in it. I was fated to a living death in this prison cell, or others similar to it, and I had better forget about any other existence. I could not contain the tears which poured from my eyes. I sat on the *borsh* behind the locked door, and wept as I had not wept since my childhood."

Of all the changes which followed the arrival of the Brotherhood members in the Sigan Harbi, the most significant for the members of the network was that they were now housed in adjacent cells on the second floor. Robbie had the first cell, near the stairs; beyond him César Cohen, then Eli Na'im; Meir Meyuhas then Meir Za'afran; Philip, Shmuel Azar, Victor, Max Binnet, and, in the last cell, Moshe Marzouk.

Victor: "After the arrival of the Brotherhood members, the guards no longer troubled to lock our cell doors after bringing round our rations. This may have been a way of saving time and trouble when they returned later, with Robbie, to collect up the empty bowls. The doors remained open and, with only two guards stationed at the end of the corridor, we hastened to seize the opportunity. I remember the first morning as I approached the open door with beating heart and a dull sense of apprehension; nevertheless, I couldn't help poking my head out of the doorway. I saw heads sticking out all along the corridor. Shmuel Azar's head appeared at the doorway to my right; to my left, an unfamiliar face, Max Binnet. We exchanged smiles.

"With time, we grew more venturesome. We gulped down our food, standing in the doorway, begrudging every moment; as soon as we saw the guards' attention directed elsewhere, we began to converse.

"It was in this manner that I made the acquaintance of Max Binnet. It was a hurried meeting, our conversation was conducted in staccato whispers, with one eye on the guard at the end of the corridor. But we continued to converse for a long time, until, line by line, I managed to sketch a full portrait of his personality.

"Binnet was profoundly depressed, as his expression revealed. I considered it my duty to cheer him up, telling him: 'We'll overcome. We have to hold on.'

"But he shook his head in despair: 'They know that I'm an Israeli officer.'

"The next day, or the day after, he told me that his wife and daughter had been with him in Egypt, but they left some time before the network was uncovered. When the calamity occurred, he cabled them not to return. He was grateful that at least they were safe.

"He talked a lot about his little daughter, and his eyes would fill with tears, while his voice shook.

"On another occasion, he told me that he wrote poetry. He found a stub of pencil in the washroom, which he managed to conceal from the guards; for paper, he used empty cigarette packets. (Toward the end of our confinement at the Sigan Harbi we were permitted to buy cigarettes with our own money from the prison canteen.) Once, he flung me a poem he had written. The words are etched in my memory to this day, and I think they depict him better than I can. Moreover, they explain the manner of his death.

> Life itself is nothing
> But how you live is everything.
> Death itself is nothing
> But the fear of death is everything.
> Faith itself is nothing
> But the faith in God is everything.

"In time, our conversations grew lengthier. Binnet told me a little about his life in Israel; about his love of music—he played both piano and violin—and of the Bible, long passages of which he could quote by heart. But death came up repeatedly in his conversation. He told me over and over again that he was resolved to commit suicide. He was certain that the Egyptians would execute him in any case. He said: 'You can hope, but I will be killed.' I did my best to dissuade him, to give him hope, but as it turned out, I failed. One morning, when they began to take us out to the washroom, I heard shouts coming from Binnet's cell; later, looking through the peephole, I saw him being dragged along the corridor toward the stairs. He was brought back an hour later, his face showing marks of a beating. In the afternoon, I asked him what happened. He told me that he had tried to commit suicide by tying his shoelaces tightly around his wrists, so as to halt his circulation, but the guards found him in time.

" 'Now,' he said resolutely, 'I shall fast until death.'

"Again I tried to arouse his hopes, but in vain. He stopped eating, but the guards discovered his intentions when they found his food in the *kardal*. He was beaten and fed by force, until he agreed to give up his suicide attempts. 'But if I'm sentenced to death,' he said, 'I won't give them the pleasure of executing me.'

"My conversations with Azar, my other neighbor, were less gloomy. Azar was full of optimism. Perhaps, like me, he felt that he ought to be cheerful. I taught him the Morse code. His swift grasp had not been affected by his suffering, and within two days, he knew the code by heart. After that, we used to hold long Morse conversations till late at night, tapping lightly on the wall between us with buttons we ripped off our shirts. We tried to guess what was in store for us, we exchanged information about the day's conversations with the guards, we encouraged one another. When there was nothing left to talk about, we invented a game, a kind of Scrabble in Morse. We would choose some letter, and compete in finding words which began with that letter. Anything to keep up our contact, for a few moments longer, to ward off the loneliness of our cells. Solitude and separation from our companions—these were our worst enemies.

"Aside from Robbie, and, very rarely, Philip, I had no contact with my other companions, except for an exchange of glances along the corridor during mealtimes. I would see Moshe Marzouk at times, as he was being taken at a run to the washroom in the morning, but I only saw him through the keyhole, with the cell door dividing us. It was apparent that he had suffered more than the rest of us. He walked with a limp, the *falakas* having left their marks on his feet; his back was strangely twisted. Remembering him as he used to be—dignified, his back as straight as a ramrod—my heart sank. But when our glances met, as we stuck our heads out of our doorways at mealtimes, he always smiled, although it was a forced smile. More than any of us, he was well acquainted with the people in whose hands our fate lay, and he was therefore well aware of the danger to our lives. As for me, when the forecasts of our execution immediately on reaching Cairo proved false and when I learned from our interrogators' remarks that we would face trial, I began to regard the future in a more optimistic light. I remember a number of brief conversations with Shmuel Azar about the trial awaiting us. Shmuel was certain that we would get no more than five years. Trying to enter into his optimism, I replied: 'In that case, we'll hold out.'

"The future did not worry us, but the present did. A man needed all his spiritual powers so as not to sink into the chasm of evil and viciousness which surrounded us, and to keep his sanity and humanity in the face of the bestial cruelty and sadism which, even when they passed us by, always threatened to drag us down.

"One day, I was taken at a run from my cell, to the office of the duty sergeant, on the ground floor. Gawad was there, together with a number of guards and one of the Brotherhood members, a stout man, swollen all over from the beatings he had received, and with a look of fear in his tear-filled eyes.

" 'And now,' said Gawad as I entered, 'a Jew will beat you, you son of a bitch!'

"Gawad turned to me: 'Hit him!'

"I drew back. 'I'm a prisoner like him. Why should I hit him?'

" 'That's an order!'

"I continued to refuse. The Brotherhood man's frightened expression softened a little, but when Gawad noticed this, his anger grew. 'He'll hit you,' he told his victim, and then, to me: 'Hit him, you dog!'

" 'I'm not a dog, and I won't hit him!'

"At that, they all flung themselves at me. I took the beating without uttering a sound, and only my hate-filled eyes spoke for me. My silence angered the guards even further, and they stepped up their beating until even the Brotherhood member cried out: 'Leave him alone!' and burst into tears. But they continued their beatings until I fainted.

"When I came round, I was lying on the ground, and one of the guards who had been beating me—one of the worst—was wiping my face with a damp cloth, muttering: 'Get up, *hawaga,* wake up!' He supported me to the chair, and stood there until I recovered, wiping the blood off my face with a damp cloth.

"To this day, I don't know whether I gained his esteem by refusing to raise my hand against a fellow prisoner or whether the whole episode was contrary to orders, and he feared that I would denounce him to one of the officers, but that guard never beat me again. On the contrary, he seemed to be trying to gain my friendship. When he was on duty in our corridor, he would open the door of my cell, talking to me about his village in Upper Egypt, about his homesickness, about his hatred for the army and its officers. It was the first time I had a chance to observe the violent class hatreds lurking within the Egyptian army."


"Amid this darkness," Victor recalls, "there were some gleams of light. Suddenly, without giving any reason, without any idea of the whys and wherefores, one of the officers made a humane gesture which warmed our hearts and gave us the strength to hold out."

One day, books were given out to the prisoners. Philip received the novel *Colombe* by Prosper Merimée; he had such a craving for the printed word that he read it through three times on the first day. Robbie received a thick medical almanac, full of Latin terms, while Victor's trophy was a Bible in French.

Victor had not been brought up at home to read the Bible, but in the solitude of the prison, he was capable of reading the print on cigarette packets. Accordingly, he flung himself at the Bible, reading it through in ten days. He immediately began again with Genesis, and so on.

But this was not reading for its own sake. Victor was captivated by the Book of Books. "I found it full of treasures—beauty and nobility. Every chapter conveyed a message. I relived the deeds of my people's ancestors, its kings and heroes; I found the noble words of the prophets applicable to our own circumstances. I cannot find words to convey what the book became for me: a faithful friend, to whom I could pour out my heart."

Later, at the Tura prison, the convicted members of the network instituted a Sabbath eve ceremony. They would save up their food all week so as to make the Sabbath meal more festive, but the high point of the ceremony was the collective reading from the Bible, with Victor, the "expert," explaining the passage and trying to convey to his companions something of the feelings it aroused within him.

That allocation of books was not the last ray of light to flash through the darkness of their prison.

One day, Victor was summoned to the office of Hamza el Bassiuni, in the office wing which was a separate part of the prison block. He had only been there twice previously; that was when he was taken blindfolded for interrogation by Muhabarat officers. Now, at this third summons, he felt a sense of foreboding. Every break in routine was ominous. He was not even reassured when the guard refrained from covering his eyes; anxious and uncertain, he entered the governor's office. Behind the desk sat el Bassiuni, the same stocky, terrifying figure with the awful scar, and smiled!

"You have a visitor," he said. "Your sister is here. I don't want any scenes. Tell her you're all right, and that's all. D'you understand?"

In his astonishment, Victor was incapable of replying. El Bassiuni went on, impatiently: "Tomorrow is your birthday, have you forgotten? That is why I gave permission. Give her a kiss and let her go. Quick!"

He got up and walked out, and in came Mireille, Victor's elder sister!

"We flung ourselves into each other's arms. I was dazed; she tried to cheer me up, murmuring, 'Happy Birthday!,' but her tears welled up. 'Did you read the newspapers?' she said hurriedly, as though she had learned the words and was afraid she would not have time to say them. 'They want to sentence you to death. Don't believe it; it'll be all right!'

"I tried to reassure her and, through her, our parents; she did the same for me. I said: 'It's all right here. Don't worry about us. It's like a youth camp. . . .' "

He longed to extend her visit, wishing it would never end. But Hamza's warning words—"one kiss and that's all!"—hung over him menacingly, like a dangling sword. But stronger than that was his wonder: How had she succeeded in coming?

"Mireille told me, with a mixture of laughter and tears, while she kissed and stroked me. Every day, our parents went to the Interior Ministry and the Muhafza, demanding to know where their son was. But they received no reply. And then, a report in the newspapers: The prosecutor would demand the death penalty for those accused in the Zionist plot. This was how they found out that a trial would be held, and that we were being detained in a military prison. They began to seek ways of reaching me.

"We had a neighbor, an Egyptian air force officer. Our relations with him were cool but respectful. Even after my arrest, he did not refrain from greeting my parents. In their distress, they decided to approach him.

"He told them the location of the military prison, and even revealed how they could get to it: They should go to the Abbassiya camp and head for the military hospital, the only installation in the camp which civilians were permitted to enter. On going through the hospital to its back exit, they would arrive at the gates of the prison.

"That was precisely what Mireille did. With a courage stemming from a sense of 'nothing to lose,' she banged on the gate and asked to see the governor. And this cruel being, Hamza el Bassiuni, unexpectedly softened up. . . .

" 'He even promised that if we send you winter clothing, he will allow it in!'

"Mireille's story awoke memories from the distant past. I had concealed the transmitter crystals among my winter clothing; they might be found.

"As I was giving her a parting embrace—el Bassiuni was already standing in the doorway—I whispered to her: 'Among the winter clothes . . . an envelope . . . throw it into the sea!'

"She understood.

"I was taken back to my cell, carrying a birthday cake Mireille had brought me, my head floating in the clouds. A miracle! The wall which had surrounded me for the past three months had been pierced! I had seen one of my beloved ones, someone from the living world! Long after the cell door was locked behind me, I was unable to calm down. I paced the cell like a lion in its cage.

"Mireille contained her tears until I disappeared from her view. Then she burst into bitter weeping. And no wonder; my appearance— my head shaved, thin, showing marks of the suffering and humiliation I had undergone—revealed the truth, in spite of all my efforts to conceal it.

"El Bassiuni tried to cheer her up. 'You see? He's all right! But know this: I let you in as an act of leniency. There are no visits here. Don't come again.' As she was about to go, he added, apparently on second thoughts: 'You'd better get him a good lawyer!'

"In spite of el Bassiuni's warning, Mireille came once more. This was a week after the first visit. Suddenly, I was called to the office: a visit.

"It turned out that when my father discovered how Mireille had succeeded in seeing me, nothing could stop him. He and Mireille reached the prison gate and asked to see el Bassiuni. My father was confident that he would succeed in convincing the man to let them in.

"By a stroke of luck, el Bassiuni was away from the prison at that time. In his place was his deputy, a Copt officer by the name of Fuad. When my father and sister were brought before him, he was about to send them back where they came from, but my father hurriedly said: 'El Bassiuni gave permission,' and my sister added, 'Yes, when I was here last week!'

" 'El Bassiuni gave you permission to enter?' repeated Fuad incredulously. 'In that case, all right; but only for a quarter of an hour.'

"In this manner, and probably for the first time in the history of the Sigan Harbi, I received two visits in the course of one week.

"Naturally, this too was a most emotional reunion, with all of us putting on an act. I pretended that I was comfortable in prison, and they feigned indifference to the impending trial. Father told me that he had engaged a lawyer, and that my companions also had lawyers. He brought us all winter clothing, which he left with Fuad (later el Bassiuni permitted the clothes to be taken to our cells; he may have feared that if they were deposited in the prison store, they would reveal that there had been an illegal visit). After that, we stood there, our glances fixed on one another. I could not help noticing that Father's erect figure had bent since I last saw him, and that his eyes had lost their vivacity. Then Fuad indicated that the visit was at an end."

The Egyptian Interior Minister's announcement of the impending trial of the "Zionist spies" was published in *Al Ahram* on October 25, 1954. In fact, it was an excerpt from an interview which Zecharia Muhi el-Din granted to an American radio correspondent. He said that the prosecution had proof that the group—which had committed acts of arson in the American libraries in Cairo and Alexandria and attempted to damage foreign-owned cinemas—was directed by Israeli intelligence, and that its purpose was to disrupt Egypt's relations with the United States. "They will soon be placed on trial and we shall present our proof," he said.

*Al Ahram*'s correspondent added that the prosecutor would demand the death penalty for the accused.

This publication constituted part of the secret struggle going on, within the Egyptian establishment and abroad, for the lives of the arrested members of the network.

Immediately after receiving the first news of the calamity in Alexandria, Israeli intelligence, without waiting for a full report from "Paul Frank," went on the alert for a rescue operation.

In all the world's capitals, action was taken to mobilize the support of persons with contacts in Cairo. The British Jewish M.P., Maurice Auerbach, a friend of Nasser, flew to Cairo and came back with encouraging tidings: There would be no executions.

The Israeli ambassador in Rome, Eliyahu Eilat, heard a similar statement from a high-ranking Egyptian representative.

In Paris, Gideon Rafael, Director General of the Israeli Foreign Ministry, on a secret mission to make contact with the Egyptian authorities with the aim of settling the Arab-Israeli conflict, told his collocutors that there would be no settlement in the shadow of the scaffold.

There were additional intermediaries: Nehru, prime minister of India, promised to "say a word" in Cairo. There were also promises from the French, and the Americans made a half promise that President Eisenhower would intervene.

One of the last emissaries to set out for Cairo was Roger Baldwin, president of the Human Rights League in the United States. He met with Nasser, who gave him to understand that the sentences on the network members would be mild. At the same time, in reporting on his conversation with Nasser, he made a comment which should have set alarm signals jangling in Israel. He said that the Egyptian officers' junta was "in a delicate situation." Death sentences had recently been imposed and carried out against leading members of the Moslem Brotherhood. They would therefore find it difficult to discriminate in favor of "Israeli spies."

Information about the other part of the struggle—that within the officers' junta—was obtained only indirectly, and a long time later. Some of this information was picked up by the convicted members of the network, when, as long-standing inmates of the Tura prison, they befriended other convicts who had formerly belonged to the Egyptian establishment. These persons included a relative of the brothers Salah and Gamal Salem, members of the Revolutionary Council, and Mustaffa Amin, formerly publisher and editor of the daily *Achbar al Youm*. The stories gleaned from these persons showed the military junta to have been divided in its views on the way to handle the "Zionist underground." There was a group of moderates which, hoping for a favorable outcome to the secret meetings with the Israeli representatives, did not want to harm the prospects for a settlement by making the sentences too stiff. On the other hand, there was an extremist group, headed by Gamal Salem, which called for the execution of the whole group, without even troubling to put them on trial.

The disagreement became very heated. According to one report, Gamal Salem warned that if it was decided to free the prisoners, he and his men would force their way into the Sigan Harbi and he would execute them personally!

In the end, Nasser settled for a compromise. The prisoners would not be summarily executed; instead, there would be a show trial, to be exploited for anti-Israeli propaganda. But to give satisfaction to Gamal and his colleagues, the prosecution announced that it would demand the death penalty.

A month passed and the chilly winds of autumn began to blow. And then, on November 29, all ten prisoners were summoned to the office. They were handcuffed and led outside, where a covered truck awaited them.

They clambered in. Two soldiers took up positions at the rear, and the truck moved off. Still overawed and cowed by the Sigan Harbi, the prisoners did not dare to break the silence, not even when their truck emerged from the Abbassiya camp and drove through the streets of Cairo. But their eyes sought the opening between the two soldiers, and they gazed outside at the cloudy skies, the upper sections of apartment blocks, with women on the balconies hanging out their laundry or beating rugs, reminders of a world from which they had been excluded.

The truck halted in the center of Cairo and four of the prisoners were ordered to climb down: Meir Meyuhas, Meir Za'afran, César Cohen, and Robbie Dassa.

"We were glad for him," relates Victor. "It was clear that the first three would get off with a light sentence, or perhaps none at all, because their links with us were fairly remote. If Robbie had the good fortune to be attached to them, all the better! We smiled our farewells to him. But I thought I detected a look of sadness in his eyes, maybe even of apology, as though he were ashamed of his good luck."

The remaining six—Philip, Moshe Marzouk, Shmuel Azar, Eli Na'im, Max Binnet, and Victor—were driven further, into the old quarter of Cairo. The truck finally halted before a gloomy four-story building, the Istianuff (Appellants) prison. The appeals court was close by, and the Istianuff prison housed convicted persons while they were appealing their sentences, or prisoners facing trial on grave charges.

The gate opened and they were led into a dark corridor lit by electric bulbs even though it was the middle of the day. After handing over their charges to the prison service guards, the soldier escorts departed back to the Sigan Harbi, but the six prisoners still remained anxious and fearful. Silently, they marched to the office. Silently, they undressed to be searched. Still in silence, they followed the guards to the wing set aside for them. Six cell doors were opened. With a last farewell glance at one another, they stepped inside and the doors were locked behind them.

Victor: "I looked around. Through the door, whose top half consisted of a barred opening, some murky light stole in from the corridor. The walls were damp and filthy. Near the top of one of them, just below the ceiling, there was a small barred window, through which I could make out a patch of cloudy sky. The floor was black tar. Everything was black and filthy. Touching the wall, my hand came away black with dirt. The cell's 'furnishings'—a *borsh,* a ragged blanket, a canvas *kardal*—helped to complete the gloomy atmosphere."

The atmosphere was most appropriate; although they were not yet aware of the fact, the six men were in Istianuff prison's death row. Over the years, hundreds of condemned men had spent their last hours here, awaiting their final encounter with the executioner. Among them, a few years earlier, were two young Palestinian Jews—Eliyahu Hakim and Eliyahu Bet-Tzuri—sentenced to death and executed for the assassination of Lord Moyne.

# 4

## IN THE SHADOW OF THE SCAFFOLD

*A Very Special Prisoner*

After her attempted suicide at Muhafza headquarters in Alexandria, Marcelle was taken to the El Muwassat hospital—the most expensive in the city. It was a private hospital, staffed by Europeans; prior to the revolution, one wing was reserved for King Farouk, who was in the habit of besporting himself there with the Swiss and German nurses. After the revolution, this "royal wing" was kept for distinguished foreign patients in whose welfare the regime was interested. During Marcelle's period of hospitalization, the "royal wing" was occupied by the Mahdi of Sudan. This hospital was hardly the appropriate place for a prisoner; indeed, the police officers originally intended to take her to the general hospital. But the Muhabarat men objected, pointing out that it would be impossible to keep her isolated in the general hospital, which was always full of visitors. In El Muwassat, she was given a room of her own, with a sergeant and two policemen taking turns guarding the door.

For a few days, she was left alone. All she remembers of those days are violent pains, doctors bending over her with syringes, and sinking into oblivion as the injections took effect. Gradually, the pains subsided; her smashed hip was restored to its place with the help of heavy weights; and she was encased in a plaster cast from hip to knee. Gradually, she began to take an interest in what was happening about her, and to converse with her guards. One of these, Sgt. Haj el Saffer, did not conceal his liking for her. He was a middle-aged man, and strictly religious, never omitting one of the five daily prayers, even if he happened to be on duty at the time. For all his piety, he was addicted to hashish, and always a little "high." He always carried a "finger" of hashish in his sash, and he frequently offered some to Marcelle: "Try it, it'll help your pains." When she refused firmly, he brought her sweets and chocolate instead; he showed a fatherly solicitude in making sure that she ate up all her meals. "You've got to eat and get better," he would tell her. Whenever he completed his guard duty, he would come in to bid her farewell, asking: "What shall I bring you tomorrow?"

After some time, her interrogations were resumed. The questioning was conducted by a Muhafza interrogations officer and by two Muhabarat agents: a redhead with blue eyes, by the name of Sa'ad, and the swarthy Mahmud Abdul Aziz. Each time, they would appear with some exhibit or other: on one occasion, a pair of spectacles, apparently belonging to Max Binnet; on another, a snapshot of a baby girl, possibly his daughter. They may have expected her to display some agitation at seeing these objects, but she remained indifferent. She had never met Binnet's wife and daughter, and did not even know of their presence in Egypt.

The interrogations ceased, and whole weeks passed without her seeing anyone except for her guards, the doctor, and the German head nurse, a massive blonde with a surly expression, whose appearance and behavior made her resemble the SS women in the European extermination camps. With nothing else to do, Marcelle began to leaf through her guards' Arabic newspapers; after a time she succeeded in reading them.

"On the whole, I took no interest in the news. I was in a kind of unthinking state. I had not regained my will to live, nor did I believe that I could expect to live. I was certain that as soon as I was well enough to stand up, I would be executed. I didn't even think of a trial. I was sure they had enough evidence against me to settle my fate without any trial. On October 25, when one of the guards brought me a copy of *Al Ahram*, and I read the Interior Minister's statement that the Zionist spies had been shown to have worked for Israeli intelligence, and that the prosecution would therefore demand the death penalty, I took his words at their face value: that there was a man who held my fate in his hands, and he would decide, for better or worse. I never even imagined that he would be lenient. I was totally indifferent. Occasionally, my thoughts would stray to my companions, who faced a similar fate, and I accepted that, too."

Three months had passed since her arrest. On November 14, the plaster cast was taken off and she stood up. Her feet scarcely bore her. She waddled like a goose, each step an agony. But within two days, she was able to step from her bed to the washbasin in the corner, without feeling dizzy or faint.

That same day, the guard on duty came into the room, his eyes red and tear-filled.

"What's wrong?" she asked him in wonder.

"I have come to beg your forgiveness," he said. "If I have offended you or insulted you or given you trouble, forgive me . . ."

She understood his meaning, knowing that the Moslems, like the Jews, are in the habit of begging forgiveness from those who are about to die. Quietly, she asked: "You have not offended me nor insulted me. But what is the matter?"

He told her: "Instructions have arrived to prepare you for your departure. Tomorrow you will be executed, and I don't want you to meet your Maker with any resentment against me in your heart," and he wept aloud.

"I remember, I didn't even get worked up. The guard's words were no more than confirmation for what I inwardly knew. I thought: 'Well, this is the end.' I tried to think back over my short life, everything I had experienced and everything I had missed. I think I tried to dredge up some feeling of regret, of self-pity, but there was nothing like that within me. Nor was there any sense of relief. Just a profound sense of emptiness."

That afternoon, they came for her. Two plainclothes detectives carried her few possessions and supported her down the hospital steps to a police car. When they arrived at a prison surrounded by a wall— it was Kum el Dik, the foreigners' prison, but she did not know it—she was certain that this was her place of execution.

She was led into a large room on the second floor, near the office of the prison governor. The latter, having been instructed not to leave her alone for a single moment, now took up his post in the same room.

Nighttime brought a stalemate. Marcelle wished to go to bed, but the governor refused to leave the room, nor even to turn off the light for a moment. She refused to undress in his presence. In consequence, they sat there gazing at one another, until the governor finally said: "If you're not going to bed, let's at least while away the time with a game of cards." He gave orders for a Greek prostitute to be brought in from the neighboring cell, called for a pack of cards, and invited them to play.

"It was a peculiar feeling to be spending my last night on earth playing rummy with a whore and a jailer. I remember, I even smiled . . ."

In the morning, they stopped playing. Marcelle washed in the basin in the corner, combed her hair, and waited. At seven o'clock, an officer came with two policemen; the governor indicated that she was to go with them.

"To the execution chamber?" she asked, trying to sound calm and indifferent.

"Execution? Of course not! You're being taken to a prison in Cairo."

She was still convinced that the scaffold awaited her at the end of her journey. The train ride, in a sealed coach empty of all passengers other than herself and her escort, was agonizing.

Her injuries made it hard for her to remain seated for any length of time, but whenever she tried to alter her position, or stand up to stretch her limbs, the guards would spring up warily.

There was a car waiting for her at the Cairo station; when it halted, she immediately recognized the building before her, Sigan Misr (Cairo prison), at the bottom of Citadel Hill.

"This is journey's end," she told herself as the cell door swung behind her.

The sense of anticipation as she awaited her fateful encounter with her executioner grew sevenfold with her arrival at Sigan Misr. Cairo's central prison consisted of four three-story buildings, each of which fulfills a separate purpose. The one where she was confined was reserved for prisoners awaiting trial, but she was not aware of the fact. While the prison officer was examining her papers, presented to him by her police escort, her eyes darted about, looking for the scaffold.

The duty officer's room opened into the internal courtyard, with a wall in its center which divided the building into two halves—that beyond the wall serving as a women's detention center. She was led there, still limping painfully.

A harsh-faced woman guard—the *sit a-raissa*, or supervisor—received her at the gate leading into the women's section. "You're the *gassussa* [spy]?"

Marcelle glanced about her. She saw two women prisoners cleaning the courtyard. They were dressed in prison uniform, dresses of rough blue material, unbelievably filthy, tied at the waist with a rope. The two women were barefoot and their hair was entangled, giving them the appearance of fairy-tale witches. A third prisoner, in a somewhat cleaner dress, stood beside the supervisor; she was the latter's *nabatshia* (servant). As Marcelle was to learn, this was an important post in the prison hierarchy, usually filled by women sentenced to short terms. The supervisor conducted a body search, while the *nabatshia* rummaged through Marcelle's half-empty suitcase, which contained nothing but the few summer clothes she had taken for her weekend at the seaside.

When the search was completed, the supervisor asked: "Do you have any money?" She did not; the five Egyptian pounds she had taken with her to Ras el Bar disappeared while she was at the Muhafza in Alexandria, together with her snapshots.

"That's a pity," said the supervisor. "If you don't have any money, you can't be a detainee." Her words were not an indication of the corruption in Egyptian prisons; rather, they reflected the existing legal situation. Under prison regulations, a prisoner awaiting trial had the right to buy food outside the prison, as well as certain rights such as sleeping on a bed and retaining civilian clothes. But anyone who did not possess the ten Egyptian piastres needed to pay for these privileges was treated like a convicted prisoner, or worse.

A list was made of Marcelle's possessions, and her suitcase was deposited in the store. Then a woman guard escorted her to the showers to wash and change into prison uniform.

A number of women prisoners worked in the clothes store. Later, when Marcelle got to know them, she was to discover that the prisoner in charge of the store was a murderess, while her two assistants had been convicted for dealing in hashish.

Marcelle was dismayed at the thought of undressing in their presence. She argued that she had already showered that morning, in Alexandria, but the woman guard would not give way. Every prisoner had to take a shower on entering the prison. That was the law.

One of the hashish dealers, Kamella, flung her the blue prison dress, and a pair of "underpants"—a coarse cloth sack with two holes for the legs. The revolting contact with this "uniform" shook Marcelle out of her apathy. "I won't put this on!" she shouted, and burst into tears.

The others held a consultation. The murderess stroked Marcelle's head. "I'll give you my dress," she promised. "I'm clean . . ."

The discovery that even such tough, coarse women displayed some sensitivity cheered Marcelle, and she stopped crying. She put on the murderess's dress, which was, indeed, cleaner than the filthy uniforms in the store, wearing it on top of her own underclothes and blouse. Then she joined the other women in eating the stew they had cooked up. After that, she sat and waited.

At three o'clock in the afternoon, the prisoners were led out into the courtyard. These were the privileged inmates: Communists, well educated, coming from "good families," with the influence and money to buy whatever could be bought in an Egyptian prison. They occupied small single cells on the ground floor (while the "criminals" were housed in large dormitories in the upper stories), they were not obliged to work, and, aside from mealtimes, when they were locked into their cells, were free to stay in the courtyard.

Marcelle sat looking at them, and suddenly saw a familiar face. This was Joyce. Marcelle's brother had been her teacher, and they had made each other's acquaintance through him. They embraced one another, and Joyce brought her a cup of tea (having been in custody for some months, she had managed to acquire certain luxuries, such as a private kettle and a primitive heater). They had time to exchange a few words before a guard ordered Joyce away, with the rebuke: "It is forbidden to talk to *that* one."

But that brief meeting sufficed to cheer Marcelle up, and also to sadden her. This was her first contact in months with someone from her own world.

She found it hard to sit still for a long time. She stood up and limped over to the door of the storeroom. While she was standing there, another prisoner ignored the guards' shouts and came over to her. This was Aliya Tawfik, the wife of Yusuf Sadik, a leading member of the officers' junta who still had influential friends outside, even though his leftist views had caused him to fall from favor and be placed under arrest. (At this time, Gamal Abdel Nasser was looking toward the United States, and negotiating with Secretary of State Dulles for American aid in constructing the Aswan Dam.) Aliya had attempted to mobilize her husband's friends on his behalf, in the process making such a nuisance of herself that she was sentenced to a year's imprisonment. But even in prison, her spirits did not fall; she dominated her surroundings and displayed contempt for the guards, who did not venture to rebuke her.

Aliya addressed her: "You're the spy? How are you?" Aliya soon became Marcelle's best friend. She believed that justice would triumph in the end, and her husband would be restored to his former high position; but that belief took far longer to realize than she expected. Sadik was released a few years later, but it was only after the death of Nasser that Anwar el-Sadat restored his rights. When Sadik died shortly afterward, Sadat ordered him to be given a state funeral.

In the evening, the prisoners were taken back to their cells, and Marcelle was led to hers. "It was after dusk, and the inside of the cell was quite dark. When the door was opened, I saw a black tarred floor, still damp after having recently been washed; a water can stood in the corner, next to a *kardal*, a tin mug, a *borsh*, and two blankets. I halted in the doorway: 'It's dark in here,' I complained, 'and wet . . .' The guard gave me a shove forward and locked the door."

The cell contained an iron bedstead, on hinges anchored into the wall; but it was raised and padlocked to the wall. Beds were only for those who paid.

"This was the first time since my arrest that I was locked in. In the hospital, the door was open, with a guard standing in the opening. Now I was left on my own. It was an awful feeling . . ."

No sooner were the cells locked than the prisoners began to let off steam. One called to her friend in the neighboring cell; another one sang; a third banged her tin mug on the cell door, asking for a match. One woman let off a stream of curses which made Marcelle blush in the darkness of her cell. "Her words sounded so awful, I blocked up my ears."

From seven o'clock till ten, the radio boomed throughout the prison, the loudspeakers turned up so high that it was out of the question to fall asleep. Nor did the stinking blankets or the hard floor make it any easier for Marcelle. Her back was aching, and she tossed from side to side, trying to find a less painful position. Even laying both blankets beneath her did not make it any the easier.

Early the next morning, her cell door was opened, and she was led to the washroom. Rising early was an exclusive privilege of the "politicals," who thus enjoyed the washrooms while they were still clean from the previous evening.

In the washroom, Marcelle made the acquaintance of the other "politicals." Most of them were Jewish, but from a desire to "identify with the Egyptian people," they had resolved to speak Arabic exclusively. They were reserved in their attitude toward Marcelle, the "agent of capitalist Israel"; the only exceptions were Joyce, and, of course, Aliya.

On discovering that Marcelle had no money with which to buy food from the outside, Aliya undertook to give her some of her own. This was done by means of the *nabatshia*, the criminal convict who served the "politicals" and cleaned out their cells. Being the only one permitted to go from cell to cell while their occupants were in the washroom, the *nabatshia* smuggled food to Marcelle, her filthy prison dress concealing pitta and cheese, a hard-boiled egg, and—most precious of all to Marcelle—a little tea in a bottle (Egyptian convicts do not receive a warm drink in the morning).

Marcelle reached the Sigan Misr on a Thursday. The following day, Friday, the day of rest, only the "politicals" were allowed out of their cells, and even they stayed out only till midday; after the midday meal was given out, they were locked in their cells. In these long, drawn out hours of solitude, Marcelle's thoughts reverted to the scaffold. She was convinced that she would soon be executed.

The following morning, Saturday, she was taken to the prison dispensary on the second floor, for a checkup. "Two of us went to be examined. I was accompanied by Saida, a hashish dealer who had tried to escape by jumping out of the window when the policemen came for her. She broke her knee and limped on her left leg while I limped on the right. And so we limped along, supporting one another up the stairs to the dispensary." (Saida was later sentenced to life, and was with Marcelle throughout her fourteen years of imprisonment.)

The prison doctor, Dr. Mustaffa, was "short, bespectacled, shy, and very pleasant." However, when Marcelle, following the advice of Joyce and Aliya, complained that her injuries made it impossible for her to sleep on the floor, and asked him to admit her into his tiny three-room "hospital," he refused.

The "hospital," serving principally as a maternity ward, was the domain of Sit Fatma, a fat old nurse, evil and hardhearted. When her patients cried out with labor pains, she slapped them, growling: *"Then, you enjoyed yourself, and now you're shouting?"*

Dr. Mustaffa explained what Marcelle herself had already guessed: Since she was considered a "very special" prisoner, he had strict instructions to grant her no privileges whatsoever. Nevertheless, he took the risk of giving her the red card of a *mulahza* (person under medical supervision) which carried with it the greatest prize of all, a straw-filled palliasse to sleep on.

"Even though the straw had the irritating habit of sliding into one of the sack's corners, and though I didn't get a sheet or a pillow till the very end, I was overjoyed."

Life at the Sigan Misr followed a regular routine: In the morning, the prisoners were allowed out to the washrooms while the *nabatshia* cleaned out their cells. They were then confined to their cells again till ten o'clock, when they were allowed out into the courtyard for half an hour. They went out again in the afternoon. Joyce received visitors once a week, and food parcels twice a week. The other prisoners also received their food from outside, and all of them, even the hostile Communist women, gave Marcelle part of their food.

No one came to visit her. One of her brothers had left Egypt two years previously, and the other, Yitzchak, was afraid to come into contact with her, nor did she want to get him involved. He was already suspected by the police because of his Communist leanings in the past. Consequently, when asked about her family, she replied that she had none.

About two weeks after her arrival at the Cairo prison, she was given her indictment, written in Arabic. Her fellow prisoners translated it for her.

Some doubts had begun to overshadow her previous certainty that she would soon be executed. But now, on reading the indictment, the doubts faded. Such grave charges could bring no sentence other than death. Only now, the scaffold would bear the trappings of legality.

Her companions told her that an accused person who did not have a lawyer would be defended by an appointed attorney. But the days passed and no one contacted her.

Matters remained like that, till the day she was informed: "Tomorrow, your trial begins."

## The Execution

To this day, Robbie is convinced that it was an administrative error which led to him being separated from the other prisoners. At the time, he sensed regret and humiliation.

"Not only were my three companions strangers to me, while my best friends remained in the truck, but these three [Meir Meyuhas, Meir Za'afran, and César Cohen] had nothing to do with the cells or with the matters for which we had been arrested. Having been arrested by error, they were filled with a sense of the injustice to which they had been subjected. As for the rest of us, being aware of the reasons for our imprisonment fortified us. We were strong and determined to hold out."

The four of them were brought to the Sigan el Mahata (the railway station prison), a medium-sized building in the center of the city, with a garden around it, surrounded by a wall. The jail used to serve as a municipal detention center, until the trials of leaders of the Wafd party, and of King Farouk's confidants, including Saraj al-Din—the Interior Minister and Nahas Basha's brother-in-law—as well as Farouk's secretary, Karim Tabt. When these men were given long prison sentences, the question arose: Where were they to be confined? All had been immensely rich, and even though their property had now been confiscated, they had succeeded in concealing considerable sums of money. Knowing what went on in Egypt's prisons, the officers' junta foresaw that the prisoners would use their money to gain control of any ordinary prison, turning it into a center of plots and intrigues against the regime. It was consequently decided to house them in a special jail, and the choice fell on the Sigan el Mahata, which was placed under the command of Sag (Maj.) Abbas Kut'b, a veteran prison officer and the scion of a prosperous Mameluke family. (Up to 1936, only members of wealthy families owning more than five *fedan* of agricultural land could become officers in the army and police.) The officers' junta considered Kut'b sufficiently trustworthy and honest for the post; he was one of the few officers appointed prior to the revolution to continue his advancement subsequently. By 1968, he was the director general of the prison service.

However, for all his honesty and reliability, Kut'b could not overcome the tradition of Egypt's prisons, whereby money can buy anything. Under his supervision, the Sigan el Mahata became a comfortable pension, the fond dream of those convicts who did not have the good fortune to be sent there. Saraj al-Din was given a comfortable top-story room with a small kitchen where he could make coffee at night. One of his household servants, dressed in a pure white *galabiyeh,* stood by to serve him up to the time the gates were closed at night; he would bring Saraj his food from home, serving it in silver dishes. The other "important prisoners" also acquired extensive rights, including the right to visits from their wives or mistresses. These privileges were paid for in cash, and more than one prison officer set himself up for life in the course of one or two years' service at the Sigan el Mahata. (As a means of reducing corruption and to prevent prison officers from "digging themselves in" in their posts, they were moved about at frequent intervals. However, this only induced them to hasten to make the most of their chances, before being transferred.)

Robbie knew nothing of all this when the door of his new cell closed behind him for the first time. "But it didn't require much intelligence to grasp that I had come to a place utterly unlike the Sigan Harbi. The difference was apparent, right from my reception by the duty officer. The place was comfortable, and so was the cell itself—roomy and airy, with a large window which let in the sounds of the street, the creak of trams, the voices of passersby, the calls of a watermelon vendor . . ."

True, the cell's furnishings did not differ much from those in the Sigan Harbi—the same patched *borsh,* the *kardal,* and the jug. At the Sigan el Mahata one could obtain a bed, cigarettes, food from outside —at a price. But Robbie had no money.

For about two weeks, from November 29, the day the group was transferred from the military prison, until December 11, Robbie felt like a beggar in a palace. All about him, he saw comfort and luxuries, but he himself had no part in them. In the morning, when his cell door was opened, he was taken to a nearby washroom, to wash, empty out his *kardal,* and refill his water jug; after that, he returned to his cell. He went through the same procedure in the afternoon, after which his door was locked for the night. Then, when the prison emptied of its staff, with the sole exception of the duty officer and his assistant, "that's when the rich prisoners began to have fun." They would welcome their lady guests to their cells, or else they would all gather in one of the cells for a *hafla* (party) or a game of cards.

In the course of these first two weeks, Robbie did not once meet his three companions. "Even though their cells were close to mine, and they passed my door whenever they went to the washroom, they made no attempt to contact me. They were too wrapped up in thoughts about their bitter fate and their anxieties . . ."

At Sigan el Mahata, Robbie had his first encounter with convicted prisoners, in blue uniforms. "They would be brought every morning from the Sigan Misr to do cleaning jobs. Their appearance was very

depressing: They were barefooted, their heads shaven, very thin, almost famished. When they finished their work, they would sit beneath
my window and talk, while they waited for the truck to take them back
to the Sigan Misr. For me, their conversation was a kind of peephole to
a strange and unfamiliar world, the world of prison. They talked about
their release; one of them was due out the following week, at the end
of his fifth term for pickpocketing, and had no intention of abandoning
his 'profession.' They talked about various prisons, their advantages and
drawbacks. When speaking of Tura, they showed fear, and their words
remained etched in my memory."

Friday was the worst day; Robbie did not leave his cell at all. For
the other prisoners, it was visitors' day; their families came, and children played in the garden. But Robbie only heard their voices, and his
heart filled with yearning.

Matters remained unchanged until December 9. That morning,
the duty officer brought him two sheets of paper, written in Arabic: the
indictment. The gravity of the charges came as a shock to him, but
nevertheless, he sensed a feeling of relief; this meant that there would
be a trial. However, a few hours later, he forgot all that. For the first
time, he received visitors.

"With the completion of the indictment and a date having been
fixed for the beginning of the trial, on December 11, my parents were
given permission to visit me. My mother and father came, accompanied
by the lawyer they had hired for me, a certain Ali Mansour.

"The meeting was very emotional. Ali Mansour introduced himself,
said that the trial was to start in two days' time, on Saturday, but that
I wasn't to worry; at normal times, under civil law, I could expect a
prison term of between six months and three years, and he hoped that
the military tribunal would not be more severe."

"But I paid no heed to his words; my attention was focused on my
parents. What deep imprints the past months had left on their faces! I
tried to calm them, telling them that I was well and lacked nothing. But
my appearance did not back up my words. I was wearing the same
summer clothes I had on when I was arrested; since then, I had laun-
dered them numerous times, till they were ragged. My mother began
to weep.

"The duty officer, in whose room our meeting took place, said:
'Bring him a suitcase with clothes, so he doesn't appear in court looking
like a beggar. Bring him some money, too. How can he survive in jail
without money?'

"Instantly, my father took out all the money he had in his pockets
and handed it over to the officer."

At the end of the visit, which left Robbie agitated and overwrought, he returned to his cell to find that he had now acquired a new status: that of "a prisoner with money." A bed, table, and chair were brought to his cell, as well as a white enamel wash bowl and cigarettes. At midday, his food was brought in from outside: meat, rice, vegetables, and fruit. "I never liked Egyptian cooking, but now, after months of eating nothing but prison rations, these were the greatest delicacies."

Now that he had cigarettes, the *nabatshin* made sure they emptied out his *kardal* and refilled his water jug, while the guard came along to talk to him and fill him in on prison gossip. A veritable revolution!

On Saturday morning, December 11, two police officers in resplendent uniforms arrived to take the four accused to court. Robbie was the first one to be brought to the room of the duty officer, who was sitting there, drinking his morning coffee and reading the newspaper. The headline said: SIX MOSLEM BROTHERHOOD LEADERS SENTENCED TO DEATH HAVE BEEN EXECUTED!

Robbie felt sorry for the six men, whom he knew from the Sigan Harbi. Along with his regrets, he also had an ominous sense of depression. "If that was the way they treated Brotherhood members, native-born Egyptians, what will they do to us?"

Meyuhas and Za'afran arrived, followed by César Cohen. They exchanged muted greetings. Six policemen closed about them and led them to the waiting car.


All the vague fears which filled the hearts of the network's members ever since they were taken from the Sigan Harbi to some unknown place took on a very clear form the moment they marched through the gateway of the large, dismal building which bore the sign: "Sigan Istianuff" (Appellants Prison).

Philip: "After a punctilious search in the prison office, we were taken through a creaking iron door to a dark corridor. Our previous prisons all had an open inner courtyard, but not this one. It was a large, four-story building, with cells along the sides. There was a courtyard in the center, but it was covered over, giving no view of the sky; iron gangways on each floor linked the sides; there were guards on the gangways. The stairs by which we climbed to the second story were also of iron, and our footsteps rang out. As we passed by the cells, we heard the buzz of conversation, unlike the Sigan Harbi where there was always a deathly hush, broken only by the cries of those undergoing interrogation. I thought to myself: 'A real prison, like in the movies!'

"We walked past prisoners in ragged blue uniforms, with numbers on their chests; they were barefoot, and engaged in washing the floor. We reached a row of cells with barred doors. I could make out the occupants of the first two cells; they were dressed in red! In popular Egyptian slang, 'dressed him in red' means 'sentenced him to death'! Marching beside me, Shmuel Azar whispered: 'They execute people here!'

" 'Nonsense!' I replied, trying to encourage him, but the guard ordered me to be silent: 'It's forbidden to talk!' "

In spite of the guard's rebuke and the proximity of the men in red, Philip felt encouraged. Later, he was to explain: "The moment we were brought into the Istianuff jail, I knew that we were back within the realm of the law, and we could no longer be mistreated in the manner we had to endure in the Sigan Harbi. Now I was certain we would be placed on trial, and consequently, I was not frightened by my neighbors."

Furthermore, he soon made their acquaintance. They belonged to a gang of robbers, one of whose exploits, in a famous Cairo nightclub, took place before the arrest of the network. That robbery caused a great shock, because two of the club's employees were murdered. In the end, the gang was caught and put on trial, and its two leaders were sentenced to death. These were Philip's neighbors.

Philip: "The sentence had not broken their spirits. They conducted loud conversations through the barred door, swapping jokes with one another and, after they got to know me, with me. One had a very pleasant voice, and knew all the Italian songs; every evening, he gave us a 'request program.' "

(The two robbers were executed the same day that Moshe Marzouk and Shmuel Azar mounted the scaffold. They were taken away to execution in turn: a robber, a "spy," a robber, another "spy" . . .)

From his cell at the beginning of "death row," near the stairway, Philip could watch the prisoners arriving and departing. On arrival, they wore white uniforms, but before going up to their cells, they were made to take off the white clothes and put on the dirty blue uniforms. "The following morning, I saw them descending to the ground floor, and stopping again to change. I understood. These were prisoners who had appealed their sentences. On being taken to court, they were dressed in clean uniforms, for appearance' sake. In Egypt, everything is done for appearance' sake."

That night, he heard the sounds of the prison. The prisoners on the top floor were housed together in a large dormitory, not in individual cells; from up there came a despairing cry: "Guard, they want to rape me!" By his voice, Philip guessed that he was a young boy. Then Philip heard the guard's indifferent reply: "So what!" and he felt thankful that he and his companions were considered dangerous enough to be housed in separate cells, even if they were on "death row."

The adjoining cell was occupied by Moshe Marzouk, and the next ones by Max Binnet and Shmuel Azar. There were not enough cells for all of them, and Victor and Eli Na'im were housed in "ordinary" cells, whose doors were solid except for peepholes.

It was a rainy day when they arrived, and the cell was very cold. Victor tried to sit on the floor, but the cold forced him to stand up. He approached the door and looked through the peephole; when a guard passed, he called through the locked door: "I wish to go to the washroom."

"Here you go out at fixed times. Use the *kardal!*"

The guard's reply was sharp, but Victor comforted himself with the thought that at the Sigan Harbi he would have been beaten for voicing such a request.

(There were beatings at the Istianuff jail: Victor saw a prisoner beaten to death after being caught stealing bread while the rations were being given out. But the members of the network were not beaten; they were to go on trial in public, and the prison authorities were ordered to make sure that they "looked good.")

At midday, there was a great noise and uproar. Close to the peephole, Philip saw prisoners emerging from the cells facing him; after a time, he saw them returning, carrying a large blackened pot. A small barefooted prisoner used a large ladle to pour the contents of the pot into a row of soup bowls, lined up on the floor. The guard then opened the cell doors. Each prisoner came at a run to where the food was being given out, took his soup bowl, and returned at a run to his cell. However, for those in the condemned cells, the food was brought to them.

"When my soup bowl was held out to me, filled with a sticky lentil stew, I asked the guard: 'What about a spoon?' but he locked the door without replying. How was I to eat? In my pocket, I had a half-empty cigarette packet; removing the remaining cigarettes, I used the packet to fish out the food. But after dipping it in twice, the cardboard grew soggy. Left with no other alternative, I 'drank' the stew."

At four o'clock in the afternoon, the door was opened again and he was let out to the washroom. On the way, the guard opened additional cells and their inmates filed out, each one carrying his *kardal.*

"We soon turned into a procession of barefooted, filthy prisoners, covered with sores and stinking. They looked at me—the only one in civilian clothes—as a weird phenomenon, a *hawaga,* while I regarded them as creatures from another world. Hitherto, I had had no contact with such as them; at most, I passed them by in the street where they were begging for alms. When we were led into the washroom, to relieve ourselves together, I felt as though I had fallen into a sewer. I said to the guard: 'I've finished.' "

On returning to his cell, he found a bundle lying in the doorway: a *borsh* and a blanket, neither anything more than filthy rags. It was the custom that when the cells were opened in the morning, the prisoners would place their bedding in the corridor, where it was left till their return from the evening *"kardal* procession." But the orderlies used the blankets as floor cloths to clean the corridor, and they ripped pieces of the *kardal* for use as wicks, dipped in oil, for heating or lighting.

When he spread out his "blanket," Victor found it completely blackened and giving off a stench of kerosene. "Is this thing a blanket?" he flung at the guard who came in response to his banging on the door. "That's all there is," the man replied, through the locked door, and went away.

That night, as the cold grew more intense, Victor got over his feeling of revulsion and wrapped himself in the stinking blanket. But he did not succeed in falling asleep. The following day, he demanded to see an officer, but it was Friday, the day of rest, and there were no officers in the prison. At ten o'clock, the doors were opened, but only for a *"kardal* procession." Later, the other prisoners were taken to prayers, while the members of the network were left locked in their cells all day.

It was only on Saturday that Victor got to see the duty officer. To his surprise, the officer agreed and immediately gave orders for him to be issued a new blanket. After that, when he was ordered to take it out into the corridor, he objected: "If I take it out, it will be used as a floor cloth. Is that what I was given a new blanket for?" Again, to his great surprise, his demand was met. The blanket remained in his cell.

The following day, he became more venturesome. He asked to be taken to the washroom on his own, after the others had finished. Yet again, his demand was granted. The duty officer gave orders for the members of the network to be taken out one at a time, and not as part of the general *"kardal* procession."

Encouraged by this response to his requests, Victor prepared a further list of demands that night, and waited impatiently for morning to arrive, when the cells would be opened and he could ask to see the duty officer.

However, morning came and the door remained locked. All night, the prison had buzzed like a beehive, but now, there was complete silence. Filled with curiosity, Victor looked out through the peephole. "On the stairway, I saw a group of jailers, together with officers and some civilians. Then two guards appeared, leading a prisoner dressed in red uniform. Then I understood; it was an execution."

Indeed, Monday was execution day. A black flag was hoisted above the prison, and the relatives of the sentenced man congregated at the gate, to receive his body. Inside the prison, the tension was enormous. The prisoners crouched behind the locked cell doors. With bated breath, they pricked up their ears to hear the sounds from outside, as a man was taken to his death . . .

The execution chamber was on the ground floor, and the stairway faced the peephole in Victor's door. He could see the condemned man stumble down the stairs, supported by two guards, and followed by a whole retinue of officers and civilians, the latter including the doctor, the *kadi* (Moslem judge-cum-spiritual leader), a court official, journalists, and photographers, until they disappeared into the corridor below.

Half an hour later, they returned, and another man in a red uniform was led out of his cell.

Suddenly, from afar, Victor heard screams of despair. "Torture!" he thought for a flash, until he noticed that the screams were coming from outside the barred window, and hence, from outside the building. Later on, he learned that these were the mourning shrieks of the executed man's relatives, when the official announcement of the execution was hung on the gate.

All that morning, at half-hour intervals, the march of the condemned men to the execution chamber went on. When the hangings terminated and the cells were reopened, Victor remained silent. All the demands he intended to present had been banished from his mind.


Two or three days later, a guard came to take him to the office. *"Ziara!"* ("a visit").

In the duty officer's room, Victor found himself face to face with his father, mother, and sister.

"I flung myself into their arms. Mother was crying. Father was earnest: 'Do they beat you?' he wanted to know, and I replied: 'No, they don't, everything is all right.' Anything to reassure them, to smooth out the worried wrinkles which had appeared on their faces. Suddenly, Father said: 'Don't worry, d'you hear? If you read that you are to be executed, don't believe it!' Poor Father. He thought we were permitted to read the papers. He went on: 'We've hired a lawyer for you. Don't worry. We'll make a fuss. I'll go to the consulate. It'll be all right.' Mother was crying, while the duty officer tried to calm her down; and my sister only stroked me wordlessly."

Finally, the duty officer gave them some practical advice. "If you send him money, he'll be able to receive food from outside. And next time you come, bring him warm clothes."

The others also received visitors and money (with the exception of Eli Na'im; the day they were transferred from the Sigan Harbi, his father died, and he had no other relatives in Egypt). Now they had money to their credit at the prison office, their way of life changed. Instead of prison rations, they received warm meals from an outside restaurant; they could buy cigarettes at the prison canteen, and possessing cigarettes changed their status. The prisoners doing cleaning duty would say entreatingly: *"Hawaga,* got a cigarette?" and in exchange, they would sweep out their cells, bring them water, and tell them prison news.

"That was the way I found out about the expected arrival of the condemned Moslem Brotherhood leaders. When they came, I saw them through the peephole. I knew one or two of them from the Sigan Harbi. Unlike us, they were tried by a military tribunal behind closed doors, so that there had been no need to 'beautify' them. Consequently, they still showed the marks of their terrible sufferings, and their appearance was wretched. I met one of them, the lawyer Abdul Kader Udda, on the way to the washroom. His forehead was 'adorned' by a ring of wounds, from having an iron belt tightened around it. He was a big man, and the red uniform he wore was too small for him. His feet were bare. He looked up at me and said: 'You see how we're treated . . . I hope your fate is better . . .'"

The following day, they were executed. From seven in the morning until ten, the condemned men strode, one at a time, to the execution chamber—six hangings on a single day (only their spiritual leader, Hassan el Hudeibi, had his sentence commuted to life imprisonment). News of the execution of the Moslem Brotherhood leaders was carried over the grapevine to all the prisons in the country; at the Sigan Misr, where hundreds of the dead men's colleagues were confined, there was uproar in the men's section, while Marcelle recalls that the Communist women prisoners observed a minute's silence to commemorate "the victims of the regime."

Philip was a witness to the execution of the Brotherhood leaders. The previous night, he caught cold; usually, the prisoners were not allowed out of their cells till the hangings terminated, but he was so insistent in his demands to be taken to the doctor that his wish was granted. "I soon grasped the difference between this prison and the Sigan Harbi: Here, you could make demands, and when they were refused, you could carry on arguing." He put up an argument at the dispensary, too, until the doctor gave him a chit for an additional blanket. On his return from the dispensary, he found himself opposite the corridor leading to the execution chamber, precisely as the first of the condemned Brotherhood members was brought there.

"There were many persons standing there: the prosecutor, the prison service *kadi,* journalists, photographers, and policemen, as well as civilians whose functions I did not know, and a group of senior army officers. The condemned man stood between two policemen, while the prosecutor read out the sentence. All the while, photographers were taking pictures of the man, from front and back, closeups and long shots, till one of the officers growled at them, ordering them to desist. After that, they led the condemned man into the execution chamber, and I was taken away."

The last of six men to be executed was kneeling in prayer in his cell when the two policemen came for him. Philip heard them call to the prison governor that the man was still praying, and the reply: "All right, we'll wait a little." But five minutes later, the governor's voice was impatient: "Hasn't he finished yet?" and when told he had not, he ordered: "Take him by force!" Philip saw the man, dangling like a limp rag between the two powerful guards, being carried moaning toward the stairs. At that moment, Philip vowed: "They won't drag me in that manner!"

"Ever since I gave my consent for the explosives laboratory to be set up in my home," he explained years later, "I knew that if caught, I was liable for the death penalty. But when I was caught, I felt that the deed for which I had been arrested did not warrant such a severe punishment. If I was sentenced to death, it would be unfair. After seeing that Brotherhood member being dragged to his death, I resolved that if my turn came to follow in his footsteps, I would at least do something to justify the punishment, I would fight the executioners to the last ounce of my strength. Perhaps I would even succeed in killing one of the officers."

He began to exercise in his cell, to regain his physical fitness. He exercised several hours each day, until he felt that he was regaining his old strength. He was now sure that he could put up a good fight against his hangmen before they could place the noose around his neck.

Each member of the network displayed a different response to the "procession to the scaffold." But for all of them, the march of the condemned men down the stairs, accompanied by the chorus of shrieks and moans from outside, was a horrifying experience which haunted their dreams. They asked themselves: Will our end also be like that? And as the thought sent shivers up his spine, Victor repeated to himself! "Don't panic! We will overcome!"

*The Trial*

What came to be known as "the Cairo trial" commenced on December 11, 1954, in the central chamber of the Court of Grave Crimes in the old quarter of Cairo.

It is now known that the verdict was predetermined, as a compromise between the military junta's extremists, who demanded the blood of all the accused, and the moderates, who preferred to win the world's sympathy for their regime by a more humane approach. This was confirmed by the court's presiding judge, Gen. Fuad el Digwi, when he fell into Israeli captivity during the 1956 Sinai campaign while serving as the military governor of the Gaza Strip. He told his Israeli interrogators: "The verdict was dictated to me by my superiors, who decided how many were to be sentenced to death, how many to imprisonment, and for what terms."

The two-week-long "judicial process" was nothing more than a well-staged performance. It had two purposes. Abroad, it was to stress the story that "Israel tried to undermine Egyptian-American friendship"; at home, it would show that the regime's severity was not confined to the Moslem Brotherhood alone. Since it was a show trial, it was given unusual publicity. In the days leading up to the trial, the Egyptian press was full of articles depicting the "Israeli spies" as a great danger to the country, and editorials demanding exemplary punishments for all the accused, whom the press found guilty long before their trial commenced.

This organized incitement had its effect, above all, on the families of the accused. The vicious press attacks, with the demands for death sentences on their dear ones, inevitably cast them into deep depression, as they succumbed to awful premonitions. But when the trial began, and they came to court every day, they always displayed smiles of encouragement. Whenever they had a chance to exchange a few words with their sons during intermissions, they uttered nothing but words of encouragement and confidence. The accused did the same. They had no need to read the newspapers to understand the gravity of their situation. For months, the threat of execution—even without trial—had been hanging over them. Now, in the Istianuff prison, they were almost literally living in the shadow of the scaffold, constantly haunted by the "procession of the condemned" which they had witnessed. All the same, when they confronted their families in the courtroom, when they exchanged glances or a few brief words, they always made an effort to be encouraging, reassuring, and calm. It was a mutual deception, heartbreaking but noble.

Robbie and his three companions from the Sigan el Mahata were the first to reach the courthouse in Saida Square, in the Moski quarter. As they approached, they could sense the unusual preparations for the trial. The small square usually teemed with litigants and their relatives, lawyers, clerks, and—as in any place in Cairo where there is a crowd —with vendors proclaiming their wares, shoeshine boys, and carriage drivers whose horses are bedecked with colored feathers. But this time, it was empty. Dozens of policemen, standing shoulder to shoulder, blocked the way before a crowd of curious onlookers who gathered behind them. Only persons with some special reason for attending the court were allowed past.

There were many such. When Robbie and his companions were led in, the courtroom was packed to overflowing. Robbie immediately picked out his own parents, and those of his companions from Alexandria. There were other persons there with expressions of suffering on their faces, and Robbie guessed that these must be the relatives of the Cairo members. But in addition, there were many others whom he did not know. There were dozens of journalists, Egyptian and foreign. There were also consular representatives from those countries whose citizens were among the accused: Germany, France, and Greece. There were foreign lawyers and representatives of international humanitarian organizations, mobilized by Israeli emissaries who hoped that their presence would ensure a fair trial. There were also dozens of local lawyers and court officials, who abandoned their business in other wings of the building so as to come and satisfy their curiosity about this much-heralded trial.

Robbie looked about him. It was a large hall; at one end, there was a raised platform bearing an elongated table and five chairs. The wall behind the judges' table bore a metal bas-relief of the scales of justice, with a Koran passage etched underneath. To the right, there was a dock enclosed in netting to a man's height, with two wooden benches inside it.

No sooner were Robbie and his companions led into the dock than Marcelle was brought in, wearing white prison uniform and limping badly. Robbie smiled at her. Three years had passed since his sole encounter with her, on one of her visits to Alexandria, but his heart fell on seeing her. He wanted to whisper some words of encouragement to her, but he did not dare: "I was still under the influence of the Sigan Harbi."

Marcelle was led into the dock, but after a whispered consultation among the police officers, she was taken out again. A bench was placed in front of the dock for her, and she sat there, her gaze wandering over the crowd in search of familiar faces. She recognized Moshe Marzouk's mother, who smiled at her; but she did not see her own brother.

After that, the six men confined at the Istianuff jail were brought in. Victor: "At first, there was the joy of meeting Robbie and Marcelle. But then my eyes encountered my parents and I felt a pang of sorrow. How anxious and worried they looked! My mother's glance fell on the manacles on my hands, and instantly, tears sprang into her eyes. I pushed my hands between my knees, to hide them from her, and tried to catch her glance, trying to look confident, to tell her: 'Don't worry!' "

The defense lawyers—those hired by the families as well as those appointed by the court—approached the dock to make the acquaintance of their clients. The most prominent of them was the one engaged by the Marzouk family, Ahmed Rushdi, a famous jurist and the head of a large lawyer's office, who had previously defended Wafd cabinet ministers. He was the only one of the defense lawyers who refused to be overawed by the presiding judge, Gen. Digwi, and ventured to argue with him. In time, he became the effective leader of the defense lawyers. There was another prominent attorney, ex-general Abbas Hilmi Zaglul, defending Max Binnet. In the distant past, while he was still serving in the army, Zaglul was Digwi's immediate superior, and hoped that this fact would be of help to his client.

All the other attorneys—Ahmed Fahmi Rifat and Ali Mansour, defending Victor and Robbie; Ahmed Mukhtar Kudeb, defending Meir Za'afran and César Cohen; Hassan el Gidawi, appointed by the court to represent Shmuel Azar, Philip, Meir Meyuhas, and Eli Na'im; and Yusuf al Gariani, Marcelle's lawyer—were most deferential to Digwi. They did not as much trouble to defend the accused as try to convince the court that they disassociated themselves from the deeds attributed to their clients.

A uniformed official banged his staff on the wooden floor and roared: *"Mahkameh!"* ("The court!") Everyone arose, and the judges entered.

They were headed by Fuad el Digwi, who had already gained fame through a number of political trials over which he had presided, and Victor recognized him from the pictures which had appeared in the press. Digwi was followed by Kaimakam (Col.) Abdul Munam Shazli, Ka'id-Ginah (Wing Comm.) Samir Abbas, Kaimakam Abdul Muhsan Hafez, and Bichbashi (Lieut. Col.) Ibrahim Saami. Military tribunals were usually composed of three officers and two civilians. The present composition—five officers, and of such high rank—was designed to stress the gravity with which the regime regarded the accused.

Digwi opened the session. Instantly, Ahmed Rushdi arose to request a postponement, claiming that he had met his client that morning for the first time and had consequently been unable to prepare the defense.

Digwi promptly demonstrated how he intended to conduct the trial. "Does your client's negligence entitle him to a postponement?" he roared. "Respected sir, sit down and permit me to conduct the trial!"

The prosecutor, Muhmad Facri el Nabi, now stood up and read out the indictment.

Military trial number 678, 1954.

The prosecutor general of the Supreme Military Tribunal accuses:

1. Avraham Dar, known as John Darling, an Israeli army officer, in absentia

2. Moshe Marzouk, twenty-eight, a doctor at the Jewish hospital in Cairo

3. Shmuel Becor Azar, twenty-four, teacher

4. Victor Moise Levy, twenty-one

5. Victorine Ninio, known as Marcelle, twenty-four

6. Max Binnet, thirty-seven, an employee of the Anglo-Egyptian Company

7. Paul Frank, in absentia

8. Philip Hermann Natanson, twenty-one

9. Robert Nissim Dassa

10. Eli Jacob Na'im, twenty-two

11. Meir Yosef Za'afran, twenty-six

12. Meir Shmuel Meyuhas, twenty-nine

13. César Yosef Cohen, thirty-three.

The aforementioned accused committed crimes as defined in Article 48 of the Penal Code and the Interior Minister's Explosives Order. Therefore, in accordance with the order of January 26, 1952, proclaiming the existence of a state of emergency, and the decree of March 26, 1954, proclaiming the continuation of the state of emergency, and of Military Order number 10, ordering persons accused of these offenses to be tried before a military tribunal, the prosecutor general requests the Supreme Military Tribunal to try the accused for the aforementioned offenses.

The prosecutor now went on to give details of the charges.

Accused number one organized and directed groups in Alexandria and Cairo for the purpose of carrying out criminal acts. These groups received their instructions from an enemy government, the government of Israel. Accused number one was an officer in its army. The groups maintained radio contact with the enemy government for the purpose of transmitting state secrets to it, and of receiving its instructions, with the aim of helping it to attack Egypt. The group also intended to spread unrest in Egypt by laying explosives in the American information office in Cairo and Alexandria, in a number of cinemas and other public places. Accused numbers two, three, four, five, six, and seven took part in these groups. Accused number two was head of the Cairo group, accused number three, head of the Alexandria group, until he handed over his post to accused number four. Accused number five was the secretary of the group and conducted its financial affairs. Accused numbers six and seven supervised the activities of the groups in place of accused number one, after the latter left Egypt.

Accused numbers eight to thirteen took part in the aforementioned criminal activity.

At this point, the prosecutor stopped reading and addressed the court: "Because of the confidential nature of the offenses attributed to the accused, the prosecution requests that the continuation of the trial be held 'in camera [without the presence of the public].' "

Naturally, there was no prospect of this request being granted. From the start, the trial was designed as a showpiece. However, as it was now ten o'clock and time for a coffee break, Digwi proclaimed an intermission for consultation.

In the course of the half-hour-long intermission, the defense lawyers hastened to the enclosed dock, and the families of the accused also seized on the opportunity to approach their dear ones, to thrust sandwiches or bars of chocolate into their hands, or just to stroke them. Uproar broke out around the dock.

Amid the uproar, Yusuf al Gariani managed to whisper to Marcelle that it was her brother who had appointed him. "My first reaction was one of anger. I asked: 'Why didn't he come here?' But I instantly regretted my question, and my anger was replaced by a genuine, profound sense of well-being. In that case, he was well! When I failed to see him in the courtroom crowd, my first thought was: 'He's been arrested!' After all, we had been told repeatedly that our families would be made to suffer."

Marcelle exercised a magnetlike fascination on the photographers. Yusuf al Gariani liked to have his picture taken, and his principal activity during the trial was during the intermissions, when he would hasten to place himself alongside Marcelle, while the photographers milled around, seeking a new angle from which to take their pictures.

"I was constantly hungry," she relates. "Such is my nature. At moments of tension, I get a craving to eat. My companions soon grasped this, and when their parents brought them sandwiches, they would give me some. As a result, almost all the courtroom photographs published show me chewing, with Gariani standing beside me in the pose of a great movie lawyer."

In fact, he was far from being a great lawyer. His contacts had enabled him to build up a modest practice, principally among the teachers in Cairo's foreign schools. That was how Marcelle's brother came into contact with him. He almost never intervened in the court's proceedings. When his turn came to deliver his summing up, he caught cold and lost his voice. The court showed patience, postponing his summing up for two days, but in the end, Digwi brusquely ordered the attorney to "speak up or shut up." Gariani mumbled a few sentences in a hoarse, almost inaudible voice.

But Marcelle forgave him, out of gratitude toward him for serving as her contact with her brother. Gariani told her that her brother did not want to come to the court, for fear of being arrested, but was prepared to do anything he could on her behalf. She said: "Tell him I need money and clothes. If he can't come, you will have to come to the prison and hand in the money for me." Indeed, that same afternoon, Gariani came to the Sigan Misr, bringing a suitcase full of clothes (they belonged to her sister-in-law, for her own home had been locked up by the police, and he was not permitted to enter). He also paid the "prison tariff"—ten piastres a day, and another twenty-five for meals from outside—for the whole period of the trial. Now that the money had been paid in, the bed in her cell was unlocked, and she even received a mirror.

Victor was also approached by his attorney, Ali Mansour. The noise around the dock was so great that there was no possibility of conversing. At his request, Victor was allowed out of the dock, and the two men stood talking near the prosecutor's table.

"Your parents appointed me," the attorney told him. "You ought to know that if this case were being tried before a civilian court, you would be liable for a sentence of imprisonment of between six months and three years, at most. But this is a military tribunal, and the judges don't know the law. There's no way of knowing how they will act. All the same, they're fair men. I shall try to explain the law, and ask that you be judged accordingly."

But when it came his turn to address the judges, he began with a lengthy preamble which stressed that a lawyer resembled a doctor, and that it was his professional duty to respond to anyone who approached him. Consequently, the fact that he had consented to defend a man accused of crimes against the state should not be interpreted as proof that he identified with the accused or his deeds. On the contrary, he was an Egyptian patriot and a loyal citizen, etc. At long last, he began to cite the civilian law, whereupon Digwi broke in, shouting: "Are you trying to teach me the law? That's very good. Ali Mansour teaching Digwi? . . . Sit down!" and Mansour sat down. For a long time, he sat there, wiping the cold sweat which was pouring down his pudgy face.

The judges returned after a recess and Digwi read out their decision: For the time being, the court saw no need to proceed in camera. If the need should arise, the prosecutor could present his request again, and the court would decide.

One after another, the accused were asked: "Guilty or not guilty?" One after the other, they stood up and, obeying their lawyers' instructions, proclaimed: "Not guilty." Only Moshe Marzouk said: "I admit the facts, but not my guilt."

Robbie expresses his companions' feelings: "The question put us in a quandary. This feeling of unease, of dishonesty, of being untrue to ourselves grew stronger in the course of the trial, when our turns came to mount the witness stand, to take the oath, to tell our stories and face cross-examination by the prosecutor. We knew what we had done, and we were not ashamed of our deeds. On the contrary, as long as I could remember, I had dreamed of serving the state of Israel, and that was what I had had the good fortune to do! I regarded myself as a soldier who had carried out the task imposed on him. But I couldn't say that . . ."

Throughout the period that they were in Istianuff prison, in anticipation of their trial, they had awaited some sign from Israel to guide them in their line of defense before the court. No such sign came. Two days before the trial, Max Binnet received a visit from an English lawyer by the name of Wilson, supposedly sent by his wife. After the visit, Binnet sent his fellow prisoners some of the bananas and apples the man had brought. On the rind, he scratched the date: December 11, which they understood to mean the date their trial was scheduled to open. But that was the only sign they received.

Robbie: "It was an embarrassing situation. The Egyptians accused us of betraying our homeland. To this, there could only be one answer: Egypt was not our homeland! Israel was our homeland! But we could not say that. The state of Israel disassociated itself from us, denying that we had anything to do with it, and consequently, we could not claim that we *did* belong.

"At that time, as we sat in the dock, we could not comprehend Israel's denials. The prosecutor said that the whole purpose of our operations was to stir up trouble between Egypt and the United States and that was a downright lie! We were the first to hint at such an aim, in the course of our interrogation by the police, but that was when we were pretending to be Communists. But we did not hear that Israel denied this story. It was only years later that we were to learn that Israel failed to deny the story for the simple reason that no one in Israel took the responsibility for our actions or presented a different explanation for them. Everyone wriggled out. Everyone hastened to blame someone else for 'giving the order.' In consequence, not only were we left open to charges of treason, without being able to defend ourselves, but the state of Israel forfeited the chance of defending itself against charges of stirring up trouble between Egypt and the United States.

"To tell the truth, that was not the sole explanation for our behavior. There was a further reason: our parents. We saw them sitting before us in the courtroom, aging daily out of anxiety for our fate, bowing under the burden of their concern. They read the vilifications in the press, they heard Digwi curse and rave, while in the neighboring courts, members of the Moslem Brotherhood were being tried at 'assembly-line' tempo. Each day, eighty to a hundred Brotherhood members were tried and given draconic sentences: life imprisonment, twenty years, fifteen years. For a five-pound contribution to Brotherhood funds, a pharmacist got life imprisonment. Our parents could not avoid comparing their trials with ours. Consequently, when my lawyer said, just before putting me in the witness stand, 'The only thing left is to save you from death, for the sake of your parents,' adding: 'And the only way to do that is to present you as foolhardy children, throwing the blame on those who misled you,' I consented. I told myself that if I cannot stand up and say proudly: 'Yes, I did what I did as an act of conscience and faith,' it doesn't make any difference *what* I say. I remember that when the time came for me to stand up and give evidence, Victor whispered: 'Cry, cry . . .' As I strode the twenty or so paces from the dock to the witness box, my only thought was: 'How can I make myself cry?' As it happened, the tears came of their own accord. But they were not tears of fear or remorse, as they were depicted in the press; rather, they were tears of frustration. My frustration grew when I heard my attorney take advantage of my outburst to depict us as 'children who played with fire.' To this day, it grieves me to think that we were presented in such a light."

### The Death of Max Binnet

The trial entered a regular routine. The prosecution began to present its witnesses—thirty-four of them. There was a clerk from the Alexandria post office who had been burned by the incendiary bombs (his injuries were slight, but the prosecutor presented him as having been crippled by "the vicious gang"); there were assistants from the opticians' shops where the spectacle cases had been bought; the policemen who arrested Philip at the entrance to the cinema.

The defense lawyers did not cross-examine the prosecution witnesses very much, but even so, they found little difficulty in showing up contradictions in their testimony. However, whenever that happened, Digwi would intervene, rebuking the lawyers and ordering them to be silent. In general, he conducted the whole trial with one eye on the press gallery. Whenever one of the witnesses said something of significance (when Shmuel Azar, for example, admitted that he was a graduate in radio engineering despite his companions' pleas to present himself as a mechanical engineer), Digwi would turn to the journalists with a triumphant expression and repeat: "Radio engineering! Did you hear?" When the defense counsel complained that the press reports of the trial had already found the accused guilty and asked for the court to intervene and restrain the journalists, this gave Digwi the opportunity to deliver an eloquent speech about the freedom of the press in Egypt.

The defendants comprehended these exchanges only in part. "They spoke *nahwi* [literary] Arabic," recalls Marcelle, "and I did not understand most of what they said." As for the others, their attention was focused on their parents. Philip was the only one to notice the words "from intelligence sources" which were reiterated in the testimony. When an Alexandria police sergeant testified that he had been posted to protect the cinema section on Revolution Day, Ahmed Rushdi wished to know why he had been sent there, of all places, whereupon the prosecutor arose and declared that the Alexandria police had acted on information coming from "intelligence sources" whose identities he did not find it necessary to reveal. The police's success in linking Marcelle to the Alexandria group was also attributed to the same sources, as well as the discovery of "Paul Frank's" car. Philip found himself wondering as to the nature of these "intelligence sources," and for the first time, it crossed his mind that his arrest and the uncovering of the network may not have come about solely as a result of the mishap he suffered at the entrance to the Rio cinema. But that was no more than a passing thought, and he did not take it further—for the time being.

The six men detained in the Istianuff prison had undergone a significant change in their conditions since the opening of the trial. Victor, whose parents visited him the day before the first session of the court, seized on the opportunity to ask the duty officer for permission to share the meal they had brought him with his friends. The officer thought for a moment and said: "Not today. But tomorrow, when you return from the court, I'll give orders to have you all confined together."

So it came about. From that day on, on returning from the courthouse, all six of them were taken to Victor's cell, where they stayed together till "Lights out," when the guards would come and take them back to their own cells.

"Those hours," recalls Victor, "were some compensation for the frustration, the humiliation, and the rebukes we endured in court. We got to know one another."

Without any doubt, it was an unusual group. Their devotion to their ideals had not been shaken in the slightest, despite their months of suffering and the knowledge that more was in store for them. "Not a single one of us expressed any sorrow or regrets over what we had done," affirms Victor.

They conversed at length about what they had experienced. They tried to reconstruct their actions, to uncover what it was that had brought about their downfall, but they failed. Whenever they seized on some thread which might have led them to the answer, some sixth sense caused them to draw back.

Shmuel Azar related what happened to him after the arrest of all his companions in the Alexandria cell left him on his own. He told of his meetings with "Robert," of their escape plans. His words conveyed great resentment against "Robert": "He abandoned me. He could have got me out of Egypt, and the Cairo people, too, but he did not comprehend that the net was tightening around us. He was too sure of himself." Philip too had his grudge against "Robert"—for failing to trust him and for suspecting him of being likely to denounce the network. "If he feared that I wouldn't stand up to the interrogations," he said in an offended voice, "why didn't he arrange for the escape of those of you who had not yet been arrested? And why did he remain in Egypt for another two weeks?" Seven years were to pass before he dared to answer his own questions.

They talked a great deal about the trial and its probable outcome. But they always spoke hopefully, optimistically. On one of her visits, Shmuel's sister told him that Israel sentenced a group of Egyptian students to five years in prison for espionage, and even though the Egyptian press published harsh attacks on the severity of the sentence, everyone hoped that the members of the network would receive similar terms. On his return, Shmuel said: "Suppose they sentence us to five years of hard labor? So what! We'll build up our muscles!" And Moshe Marzouk added: "Even if we get twenty years, that's still not the end of the world. Perhaps we'll be pardoned. It's all a matter of politics."

To what extent was their optimism genuine? "At times, it was feigned," Victor concedes, "particularly if we had just experienced an especially bad day in court. But even on days like that, we adhered to our hopes, even if it was only a pretense. Each of us regarded himself as responsible for his companions, and did everything he could to keep them from despair."

Even in prison, Shmuel's fingers had not lost their amazing skills, and, using bread soaked in water, he modeled some beautiful chessmen. "When we're released," Victor would promise, "we'll take them out with us, and every year, we'll hold a chess tournament, the 'Istianuff tournament.'

"The best days," he recalls, "were Fridays, when the court did not sit, and we could spend the whole day together, locked in my cell. At times, we would run out of cigarettes, and then we would smoke butts we had previously discarded, holding them with a pin. Shmuel would try to teach us mathematics, lecturing us on the theory of relativity and explaining how television works. Moshe frequently quoted from the Bible he had in his possession. His love for the Bible had grown even stronger, and he used to say that if he were given the opportunity, he would dedicate his life to a thorough study of it. 'You can find all the answers to any question in here,' he used to say. Philip told jokes, and we made fun of the beard he was growing."

Philip had decided to grow a beard so as to dispense with the services of the prison barber, and also in preparation for his escape from prison, which he never stopped thinking about. He hoped that the beard would help him to confuse his pursuers when his getaway was discovered. By the end of the trial, his beard was quite thick. But then, on the eve of judgment, Victor said: "They'll sentence us to prison, and we'll get sent to some place teeming with lice. . . ." Philip took his advice and shaved off the beard.

They had many matters to engage their attention. One day Moshe told them that on the wall of his cell, he had discovered a Hebrew inscription: *"Shema Yisrael . . ."* and they spent many hours trying to guess which Jew awaiting execution could have written it. Finally, they agreed that it must have been one of "the two Eliyahus"—Eliyahu Hakim and Eliyahu Bet-Tzuri—who assassinated the British Minister of State, Lord Moyne, in 1944, and were executed at the Istianuff prison. No other Jew had been executed in Egypt during the past twenty years.

One day, Moshe told of his encounter with the Copt prison doctor, Dr. Snafero. They had studied together at the Cairo medical school, and, like all the other students, Dr. Snafero was full of respect for Moshe's ability, regarding him as a man with a great future. Now, when Moshe was taken to the dispensary to receive a visit from his family and the two men met, Dr. Snafero asked only: "Why?" Moshe shrugged and said: "It happens . . ."

Dr. Snafero's brother was a fighter pilot in the Egyptian air force. During the 1948 war, he set out on a mission over Israel and failed to return. He was reported missing, and, after a suitable length of time, presumed killed. But Dr. Snafero refused to believe in his death. He was convinced that his brother had bailed out, fallen into captivity, and subsequently—perhaps because he fell in love with an Israeli woman— decided not to return to Egypt. Now, on discovering that Moshe, his fellow student, "had connections with the Israeli government," he asked his advice on whether he would be permitted to go to Israel, to seek his missing brother. Would the Jews kill him? Moshe advised him to go to some European capital and contact the Israeli consulate there. Dr. Snafero took his advice, but only a few years later, when he went to Sweden and met Israelis, making inquiries about his brother. But he stopped short of going to Israel, possibly because, in the meantime, he had made the acquaintance of a Swedish woman and married her, and finally settled in Sweden.

But before that, his path was to cross that of the members of the network once more. Like them, he was transferred to Tura prison, and one day, Philip appeared for "sick call." On learning the identity of the prisoner before him, Dr. Snafero whispered to him: "I knew Moshe Marzouk. We were friends. He was a wonderful man." He added that he had been ordered to attend Marzouk's execution, but he refused: "I couldn't . . ."

Amid this group which took refuge in its optimism, always endeavoring to present a cheerful appearance, Max Binnet stood out by his doleful expression. The oldest member of the group and its leader by virtue of his rank, he did not permit himself to fall into any illusions. While his companions reassured one another that they would hold out, even if they were to spend twenty years in prison, he would smile sadly: "You, perhaps, you are all young. But I won't hold out."

He was well aware that his situation was worse than that of the other accused. He was an Israeli, an officer in the Israeli army; during his interrogation, he had admitted having been sent to Egypt as a spy. Furthermore, his age made it impossible for him to hope that the court would treat his deeds as "adolescent mischief." His only hope was that his lawyer would convince the court that, in view of the armistice in force between Israel and Egypt, he could not be sentenced to death for espionage during wartime. However, when his lawyer arose to present this claim, Digwi interrupted rudely, whereupon the lawyer walked out of the courtroom in protest and did not return. After that, Binnet knew that there was no hope.

However, it was not the thought of the grave punishment in store for him which got him down; rather, it was the thought of the "disgrace" he would undergo when he mounted the witness stand. Victor, who was closer to him than the others, heard him say several times: "I won't give them that pleasure. In any case, I don't have a chance. I'll kill myself."

Remembering his suicide attempts at the Sigan Harbi, Victor made great efforts to dissuade him from carrying out his resolve. He tried to tell him that even when a sharp sword is resting on his neck, a man should not give up; there was still hope. It was not certain that the Egyptians would order executions, and even if he were imprisoned for a long term, it might be shortened. However, he did not get the feeling that his words had sunk in. Binnet would only smile his sad smile.

On December 21, Binnet's lawyer told him that the following day, it would be his turn to testify. Binnet did not reply. He only asked the lawyer to get him a Bible in English.

"The following morning," relates Victor, "it was clear that something had happened. The guards had been quite relaxed in their treatment of us ever since the beginning of the trial, but now they charged into our cells, cursing and swearing; we had no idea why. We were taken out into the corridor and ordered to stand in a row, while they conducted a careful body search. When I ventured to ask why, the answer was a stream of oaths: 'Sons of bitches! Animals! Not a word, we'll kill you!'

"I noticed the absence of Max Binnet while we were still standing in the corridor, but it was only when we were led into the dock in the courtroom that I dared to whisper to Shmuel Azar: 'What's happening? Where's Binnet?' and he whispered back: 'He's killed himself. I heard his death gurgles during the night.'

"I was shocked. It was the first time that a familiar person—a man with whom I had eaten, spent time, and conducted long conversations —had departed this world. I was pale, and covered with cold sweat; I could scarcely breathe. I remembered Binnet's words on the previous day: 'I'll kill myself. If it weren't for you, I would have done it already.' My heart sank as I was overcome with a sense of defeat."

That morning, Marcelle was late in arriving in court; when she came in, all the other accused were already inside the dock and she was led to her seat without being given a chance to talk to them. "At first, I did not notice that Max Binnet was not among them. But I soon sensed that today was unlike other days. There was great tension in the air. I sat there idly, and unthinkingly scratched the bench with my fingernail. Immediately, they came to see what I had written."

No sooner had the judges entered the courtroom than the prosecutor arose to inform them that accused number six had committed suicide during the night by slashing his wrists. A sliver of razor blade had been found in the cell, and there was an investigation in progress to determine how it had reached the cell.

There was uproar in the courtroom as the journalists rushed out to report the news to their papers. When silence was restored, Digwi read out a letter from the Iraqi government, which stated that before coming to Egypt, Binnet had operated as an Israeli agent in Iraq, while masquerading as a German priest, and had been sentenced to death in absentia. The Iraqi government requested Binnet's extradition at the conclusion of his trial in Egypt.

Again there was uproar as the journalists hastened to the telephones in the corridor. In the dock, this latest piece of news was received skeptically. "We thought that this was an invention of the prosecution's, to stir up interest in the trial," relates Victor. "Binnet had never made any mention of his sojourn in Iraq."

Only years later were they to learn that Binnet knew of the Iraqi extradition application and realized that it put an end to any last spark of hope which his companions may have aroused in him. He also knew that the court intended to make the extradition request public while he was on the witness stand, to make the revelation even more impressive, and that was the "pleasure" he was resolved to deprive them of.

After Binnet's suicide, the trial underwent a sharp change of course. Hitherto, he had been the "star accused." The testimony and the harsh utterances of the presiding judge had all been directed against him. He had been marked as the scapegoat. After his death, the prosecution began to put the stress on the roles of Shmuel Azar and of Moshe Marzouk, the local commanders of the cells in Cairo and Alexandria. Outside, "spontaneous" demonstrations of angry mobs demanded that the "traitors" be subjected to the full severity of the law.

Their treatment in prison also changed for the worse. Their cells were searched in their absence, and the search was repeated on their return from the courtroom. They were no longer permitted to congregate or to receive parcels.

However, this treatment did not last long. On December 24, Gen. Digwi recessed the court while the judges and the four Alexandrian accused set off to that city to view "the scene of the crime."

Although the prisoners' escorts were ordered to keep a strict watch on them, their present trip was almost pleasant in comparison with their earlier journey from Alexandria to Cairo. Under heavy guard, the four men were isolated in a special carriage. The same train also carried the judges, the prosecutor, and the defense lawyers, as well as the journalists who were covering the trial. At the stations on the way, the latter came to the prisoners' compartment, to look at them and take pictures. In addition, they were in the custody of the ordinary police, not the Muhabarat or the secret police, and the policemen treated them like ordinary prisoners. When Philip wanted to buy a newspaper at the railway station, the officer commanding the escort merely asked: "Which one do you want?" All in all, in spite of the manacles on their wrists, the ride was like an outing.

The following day, they were taken back to "the scene of the crime."

"When the truck halted outside the American library, and I was taken off, in handcuffs, I was very agitated. A crowd of curious onlookers had assembled outside the entrance to the library, and I looked for familiar faces. We walked in and instantly Digwi yelled: 'Take the handcuffs off him! What's wrong with you?' In the courtroom in Cairo, he never displayed such anger at the sight of our manacles, but here, in the American library, there were foreigners present."

One of the latter was the American librarian, a bespectacled lady of medium age. When Robbie began to demonstrate how and where he had laid the incendiary devices, she asked him: "Why? What harm did we do to you?" and a flush of embarrassment covered his face. The frenzied activity of the photographers who were running to and fro, snapping pictures incessantly, helped him to cover up the fact that he could not answer her.

From the library, the column drove on to the post office; here, too, they reenacted the laying of the bombs. After that, they drove on to the home of Philip's parents.

Digwi, who never missed an opportunity to put on a show for the journalists, stopped at the threshold and addressed Philip with exaggerated politeness: "Do you permit me to enter your home?" Adopting the same tone, Philip replied: *"Tfadalu!"* ("Go ahead, please!")

The two dogs rushed at Philip with joyous barks, and he hugged them. Later, his lawyer would seize on this fact in his summing-up speech: "Did you see?" he said to the judges. "The only thing which interested him were his dogs. He's only a child . . ."

From there, they went on to the apartment where the cell members were in the habit of meeting. It had been rented out, and its new occupants were frightened to death at this invasion of their home. When Victor was ordered to demonstrate how he had concealed the radio in the cache above the window, he objected: "But the radio isn't here." "Never mind," came the reply, "use the radio of the new tenants."

The following day, they were taken to the Aliens Court. The courtroom was packed with Alexandrian Jews—relatives and friends (at the end of the sitting, they were all arrested and subjected to a most brutal interrogation). The table was covered with the prosecution's exhibits, numbered and sealed with the court's seal. The prosecutor began to take them out of their envelopes, and while displaying them to the judges and the spectators, he pointed out their unique traits and features like some street-corner vendor. But his attitude was as it had been at the apartment.

Philip: "The prosecutor announced: 'Here are fine scales for weighing chemicals!' Indeed, they had found scales of that kind in my home and confiscated them, but they vanished. What they displayed here was a set of ordinary scales, of the kind to be found in any vegetable shop. I was quick to remark: 'Those are scales for *fasulia* and *bandura* [beans and tomatoes].' But no one paid any attention to me. Then the prosecutor proclaimed: 'Here is the foreign currency confiscated at the home of accused number eight,' and opened up an envelope, whereupon a number of nickels and dimes rolled out. The bills which were found at my home had all disappeared. 'There isn't even one dollar there!' I said, but the prosecutor went on: 'And here is the developer, an important espionage device . . . ' And so it went on. My cheap box camera was described by the prosecutor as 'an expensive espionage camera'; a penknife found in my home was 'a dangerous weapon.' Even a fork and spoon which had somehow reached the garden storehouse were brought forward by the prosecutor as exhibits. As each exhibit was shown to them, the judges examined it and nodded in comprehension of its grave significance. Finally, Digwi realized that the performance had gone beyond reasonable bounds and terminated it. 'Enough, we've finished!' he said, and, turning to the journalists, asked: 'Have you noted everything? In that case, the session is at an end.' "

On December 26, they were taken back to Cairo, and the trial resumed. Henceforward, it would be speeded up, with the court also holding afternoon sessions. This cut down the time they could spend together, and created a doleful atmosphere. Max Binnet's death had had a profound impact upon them, and his deed was discussed at length.

In court, the prosecution presented its witnesses at a rapid tempo. The last ones to testify were the commanders of the Alexandria police, Samir Darwish and Mamduh Salem. After them, the accused themselves were called to the witness stand. They, too, appeared as prosecution witnesses; military tribunal regulations made it possible to require accused persons to incriminate themselves.

Their lawyers prepared them, trying to convince them that the main objective now was to prevent the imposition of death sentences, and with that aim in mind, it was essential for them to express remorse for their deeds, to present themselves as innocents who had been led astray by the wily Israeli emissaries, and to beg for the mercy of the court.

Victor: "But we knew instinctively that Moshe would not adopt such a line of defense. He was incapable of pretense, even if his life depended on it. The evening before he was scheduled to testify, we had

Youngsters, with their eyes on the future, Victor Levy and his fiancée, Susanne Kaufman, Israel, 1952, after Victor's secret arrival to join an army course.

Susanne and Dr. Moshe Marzouk, who also participated in the army course.

Gen. Meir Amit, whose efforts were vital in obtaining the eventual release of the four prisoners.

Pinhas Lavon, Minister of Defense, the cen[ figure in Israel's "Lavon crisis."

Avraham Dar, the Israeli agent who established the spy network in Egypt.

Benjamin Jibly, head of army intelligen whose role in "the mishap" is shrouded in r tery to this day.

(Top, right to left) Col. Digwi, president of the military court who presided over the trial of the captured spies, after he fell into Israeli hands during the Sinai campaign; Col. Samir Darwish, chief of the Alexandria police, a great believer in the power of torture; four police investigators from the General Prosecutor's office who collected testimony: Amin Abu-el-Al, Kafri Abdul-Nur, Mustaffa al-Hilbawi, Hafez Sabach.

Max Binnet, Israeli intelligence agent who took his own life in a Cairo jail.

Dr. Moshe Leito Marzouk. He believed in the solidarity of the Jewish people.

Shmuel Becor Azar; "...to be an Isr officer..."

Victor Levy's cache for his transmitter.

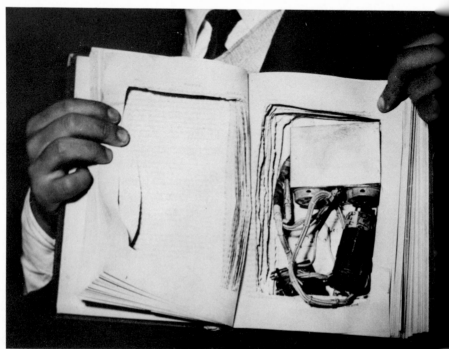

(Left to right) Robert Dassa, Philip Natanson, and Victor Levy in prison uniforms in Tura prison.

Marcelle Ninio in a posed magazine photograph in Kanather prison.

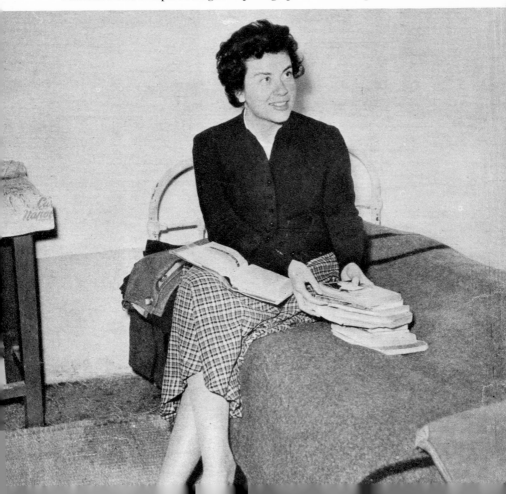

Robert Dassa receives the victory trophy for basketball in an interprison tournament.

The "spies team" of Tura prison in training; Robert Dassa with the ball.

Robert Dassa and another prisoner wit[h] sports officer of Tura.

Prime Minister Golda Meir *in loco parentis* for Marcelle Ninio at her wedding. Gen. Meir Amit stands by the groom, and the wedding canopy is held by Ze'ev Gur-Aryeh (Lutz).

חורש לזכר
**קדושי קהיר**
אשר נפלו על משמרתם
בשנת תשט״ו
קרן קימת לישראל

A silent and moving testimonial, an eternal monument for those who did not return. The inscription reads: "Grove sacred to the memory of the CAIRO MARTYRS who fell in the line of duty in the year 1952."

a long argument. He contended that if he took responsibility for the cells' operations, it might reduce our sentences. I tried to dissuade him, but when the guards came to take him back to his cell, I didn't have the feeling that I had succeeded."

Indeed, when Moshe Marzouk mounted the witness stand, he began by declaring openly: "I was in command, and responsible for everything that was done . . . "

Digwi was so surprised that he told him to repeat his words, and Marzouk reiterated: "I was responsible . . . " After that, he replied courageously and frankly to all the questions the prosecutor put to him. Only on one point did he give in to his companions' pleas: He did not disclose that he had undergone military training in Israel. However, he found it so hard to utter a lie that when the prosecutor questioned him about his meetings in Israel, and the circumstances in which they took place, he admitted that he had met Avraham Dar, who was then wearing a uniform.

The prosecutor, wishing to terminate his examination on a dramatic note, flung at Marzouk a question which contained an accusation: Did he not regard himself as having betrayed his homeland? "I was born in Egypt," replied Moshe. "I have lived here all my life, like my parents. But all the same, you never regarded us as Egyptians. In consequence, I came to the conclusion that Israel is my homeland, and the home of all Jews."

After Marzouk's words had "spoiled the show," Digwi, embarrassed, muttered angrily: "All right, all right, go back to your place."

Robbie's testimony also stressed his sense of being a second-class citizen. "I requested Egyptian citizenship and it was not granted. I applied to Egyptian universities and I was turned down. I sensed that this is not my country."

"As for me," recalls Victor, "I made no complaint. My parents were facing me, awaiting my every word. I did not wish to say anything which they'd interpret as likely to make things worse for me, thereby increasing their anxiety. I answered the questions, taking advantage of my poor knowledge of Arabic to dodge the more awkward ones. Since then, I have often asked myself if I would have behaved differently had my parents not been present in the courtroom. I can't answer that. But I do know that throughout the trial, and during my long years of imprisonment, never for one moment was my belief in the justice of my deeds shaken. I was resigned to the sentence I would receive, and my captors' opinion of me was of no importance to me."

Marcelle had been in a state of profound depression ever since she learned of Max Binnet's death. For days now, she had stopped following the proceedings, which, being conducted in high-flown literary Arabic, she did not understand anyway, and sat there drearily indifferent to what was happening about her. When the presiding judge asked her whether she had anything to say to the court, she replied indifferently: "No." But her lawyer, al Gariani, bent over her in a blazing fury: "Have you gone crazy? Don't you know that we are living in a lawless country? Your silence could cost you your life! Get up immediately! Say that you committed your deeds for money."

Lacking any will of her own, she did as he told her. In an apathetic voice, she said that she needed large sums of money to pay for her mother's treatment, and she was tempted to serve as Avraham Dar's contact by the salary he promised her. However, she denied any connection to the acts of arson, and also claimed that she did not know Max Binnet.

"But you told a different story during your interrogation!" the prosecutor flung at her.

She explained that her knowledge of Arabic was so sparse that she apparently had not comprehended the questions, or perhaps the interrogators had not comprehended her replies.

"Why did you attempt to kill yourself?" the prosecutor asked triumphantly.

"Because awful things were done to me. I was tortured . . . "

The prosecutor did not let up. Furious that she had mentioned torture in the presence of foreign journalists, he endeavored to present her as a woman prepared to do anything for money.

"Did you meet Avraham Dar on your own, at his apartment?" She was obliged to reply in the affirmative.

"And did you meet Moshe Marzouk at the cell's apartment?"

"Yes."

"Who else?"

"Eli Na'im."

"Alone?"

"Yes."

"Observe," said the prosecutor, turning to the journalists' benches, "this woman knew how to entrap men with her charms."

Cairo's newspapers displayed banner headlines: MARCELLE IN BACHELOR APARTMENTS!

## The Long Path to Death

The show came to an end on December 31. The prosecutor delivered a three-hour address, an exercise in venomous vilification such as few courts of law could ever have heard. He conducted a "character analysis" of each one of the accused, quoting every derogatory reference to the Jews to appear in the Koran. "The Jews are cunning, deceptive, treacherous by nature, swift to bite the hand that feeds them— Egypt—which opened its arms to them, offering them refuge. Before the court they masquerade as innocents led astray; but this is nothing but a mask. . . . Marcelle? What can one say about a woman who closets herself in an apartment with strange men? She tried to commit suicide, but the very attempt testifies to the weight of her guilt! It proves that she knew further secrets, and feared interrogation. . . . "

The defense counsel was given a total of three hours "to prove that the court is impartial," as Digwi put it. They repeated one another's words, asking for consideration for the immaturity and naiveté of the accused; for the fact that their deeds had not resulted in loss of life; and pointed out that the state of emergency prevailing in Egypt was not a state of war. They asked the court to be merciful in its judgment.

The presiding judge declared that the verdict would be handed down in good time, and would be made public only after its final confirmation. There would be no appeal.

The trial had come to an end.

Twenty-seven days passed before the verdict became known.

The long wait did not create tension in Istianuff prison's "death row." "The people around us—prison officers, our parents who kept up their weekly visits—told us that the long wait was a favorable indication, showing that the judges were undecided . . . " The five prisoners adopted this optimistic view. However, unconsciously, they began to sense the approaching calamity.

Victor: "Death, and the possibility of death sentences, began to creep into our conversations. We did not refer to it outright. We said 'it.' Moshe would say: 'I am prepared for "it." ' And Shmuel would say: 'I am not afraid. "It's" nothing. But the walk to the execution chamber is so long . . . ' We would pass by the execution chamber whenever we were allowed out of our cells to the washroom on the ground floor. The chamber was to the left of the stairway, and we would steal a glance in that direction and think: 'That's the room.' I swore a secret oath: I would never reach it. Inside the heel of my shoe there was half a razor blade which I had found in the washroom at the military prison. In the course of the months of suffering I had endured since then, I was never once tempted to take it out of its hiding place and make use of it. But now, thinking of it gave me a sense of tranquillity. I knew that I would not let them do 'it' to me. . . . "

The twenty-seven-day wait did not testify to any indecision on the part of the judges, as the accused tried to believe. The length of the sentences had been decided two days after the end of the trial, perhaps previously. On January 12, 1955, information reached Israel which led Premier Moshe Sharett to write in his diary: "We have received reports which are worse than we had earlier, and we have decided to take vigorous steps. Gideon Rafael set off for Paris this morning for the second time in connection with this mishap. Yesterday I cabled the Israeli embassy in London to request Maurice Auerbach, M.P., to come to Paris and stand by to fly to Cairo immediately."

Auerbach met Nasser, but his mission was unsuccessful. Gideon Rafael met with even less success; in the course of his secret contacts for the purpose of arranging an informal meeting between Israeli and Egyptian government representatives, he presented his Egyptian counterpart with the demand that no death sentences be imposed in the Cairo trial. He proposed exchanging the members of the network for a group of Egyptian students who had crossed the Israeli border at the Gaza Strip, and been sentenced to five years' imprisonment. Above all, he employed threats: If death sentences were passed, the secret meeting could not take place. At a later date, Sharett's diary records grave criticism of the manner in which Rafael conducted the negotiations. Another senior Foreign Ministry official, Ziema Dibon, accused him of arrogant and boastful behavior toward the Egyptian representative.

However, on the strength of what is now known, it is very doubtful whether the behavior of the Israeli representative could have had any effect on the outcome of his mission. The fate of the accused had already been decided by the dictates of relationships within the Revolutionary Council and of Egyptian internal policy.

On January 27, the accused were again brought to court.

It came about unexpectedly. As on previous days, they awaited the morning in tense expectation; but when the guards began to tour the cells with the daily rations of pitta, the tension relaxed. The five Istianuff prisoners were in the washroom, enjoying their weekly shower, when the guards came and ordered them to get dressed: "You have been summoned to court!"

At the Sigan el Mahata, Robbie was quick to sense that something was afoot, but he did not know what it was. At ten o'clock, he was ordered to put on his blue prison uniform. Afterward, two police officers arrived and carried on a loud argument with the prison's duty officer, after which Robbie was ordered to remove the uniform and put on his civilian clothes again. When his companions were also led out of their cells and ordered out to a waiting car, he comprehended: Today the verdict would be handed down.

By midday, when Robbie and his companions from the Sigan el Mahata reached the courtroom, the five Istianuff prisoners were already in the dock, and Marcelle was seated on her bench in front. "In the courtroom, I saw my father, and I was surprised: How did he know? Victor's parents and sister were also present."

They only had time to smile at one another before the court official roared: *"Mahkameh!"* and everyone stood up.

Only one judge appeared—Bichbashi Ibrahim Saami, the lowest-ranking officer in the tribunal. Without any preamble, without even sitting down, he began to read out the verdicts, giving no court reasons. The verdicts in full were only made public a week later, on February 6.

Robbie: "Before I had time to steel myself, the words descended like hammer blows: 'Accused number two shall be hanged by the neck till he is dead; accused number three shall be hanged by the neck till he is dead. . . .' After that, I heard nothing more. Everything went black before my eyes. I thought to myself: 'Shmuel! That's impossible! This is a continuation of my nightmare. . . .' For several nights, Shmuel had been appearing to me in my dreams, and each time, he would vanish at the end of the dream, and I woke up in a cold sweat. . . . I stared straight ahead. I did not dare look at him. I did not even hear my own sentence. . . ."

The verdicts came in matching pairs: two of the accused, Dr. Moshe Marzouk and Shmuel Azar, were condemned to death; two more, Victor Levy and Philip Natanson, life imprisonment; two others, Marcelle Ninio and Robert Dassa, fifteen years; two more, Meir Meyuhas and Meir Za'afran, seven years; the last two, Eli Na'im and César Cohen, were acquitted. Whoever worded the verdict was guided less by considerations of justice than of symmetry.

The judge terminated his reading, and immediately walked out again. For a moment, the courtroom was silent, and then, the silence was broken, as police officers closed in around the dock. Robbie: "Their words and the expressions on their faces indicated that they too were taken by surprise by the severity of the sentences. One of them said: 'We never guessed it would be like this. . . .' and another added apologetically: 'It's out of our control.' "

Victor turned to the two men to his right, who had been condemned to death. "Both of them were standing there, silent, apparently indifferent. I said: 'Don't even imagine the possibility of the sentence being carried out. . . . They can't do it . . .' But Moshe replied: 'Don't be naive, Victor. I know them better than you. But never mind, I'm ready for "it." A woman approached, a representative of the French consulate who attended the whole trial; she, too, said: 'Dr. Marzouk, don't worry. They won't carry out the sentence . . .' I said: 'Did you hear? She also thinks so!' But Moshe only smiled and said, in Hebrew: *'Od lo avda tikvateinu!'* ['Our hope is not yet lost!'] His expression indicated that he was resigned to his fate.

"They began to lead us out of the dock. My parents broke through the cordon of policemen and flung themselves to embrace me. The policemen tried to stop them, but Mamduh Salem intervened, saying: 'Let them say good-bye.' Later, after my parents were taken away, he approached me, saying: 'I am truly sorry. I didn't expect the sentences to be so severe. Hold firm!' His words had the ring of sincerity."

The prisoners were still under the shock of the sentences on their way back to prison. "I hadn't yet grasped the full significance of the verdicts," says Robbie. "My mind had not taken in what the judge said after reading the sentences, that they had received confirmation. I was convinced there would be an appeal. It was inconceivable that they could condemn a man to death, and finish. . . : In the car, Za'afran and Meyuhas sobbed bitterly. César Cohen, who returned with us to pick up his belongings, sat silent, as though undecided whether to rejoice or to mourn. As for me, I just kept mumbling: 'It's impossible, the verdict can't be upheld . . .' "

At the Sigan el Mahata they were expected. In the courtyard, a jumble of prison uniforms lay on the ground. The uniforms were particularly filthy and ragged, of the kind reserved for an *irad* (newly convicted prisoner). The convict barber awaited them with his instruments. "Sit down, *hawaga*," he said, giving the title clear overtones of contempt.

"We looked at one another—at the shaven heads and the filthy uniforms, trousers which left our ankles showing, crude rope belts, a collarless tunic with a number on the chest, all gray with filth—and our hearts fell."

They were not permitted to bid farewell to César Cohen. They were put on a truck and taken to the Istianuff prison.

Victor: "When we arrived at the Istianuff prison, while we were striding along the corridor to the inner courtyard leading to 'death row,' I walked alongside Marzouk and Azar. Shmuel looked sad. On the way, he repeated what he had often said before: 'I'm not afraid of "it." But I don't like the way. The way to the scaffold is too long . . .'

"I remained insistent. 'Don't believe it! Stop thinking that the sentences will be carried out!'

"But they did believe. When the guards ordered us to halt before the door to 'death row,' Marzouk said to me: 'You know that my brother Yossi emigrated to Israel. If you get the chance, go to him and ask him to plant a tree in my memory. And if he will father a son, let him be named after me. And tell our friends that I did my best, and I bear no grudge.'

"With that, the guards closed about them and led them into 'death row.' I tried to follow them, but I was stopped. 'What about our possessions?' I flung at the officer. But he replied harshly: 'Stop playing the fool, you are not allowed in there. Your possessions will be brought out.' "

Henceforth, they were no longer in the situation of detainees facing trial; they were now convicted prisoners. The first consequence was that their civilian clothes were taken away, and they were given prison uniforms. Beside the clothes store, the barber shaved their heads, and in a nearby hut, heavy chains were placed on their feet.

"We stood there like horses having their hooves shod, as a convict hammered the soft lead nail which fixed the chains to our legs. But we paid no attention to that. Our eyes were fixed on the barred door behind which Moshe and Shmuel had vanished. In our hearts, we entertained one sole wish: to see them again, if only once. Then the gate opened and three prisoners entered wearing torn and filthy uniforms. They looked like strangers, until suddenly, we recognized them: Robbie and the two Meirs. How prison uniform alters a person! Robbie approached and asked me in a whisper: 'Where are they?' I pointed toward the door leading to 'death row.' "

## Liman Tura

During their imprisonment following the trial, Tura prison had become more than a mere name. Robbie heard a lot about it from the guards at the Sigan el Mahata; and Philip, from his robber neighbors in Istianuff's death row. They knew it was a penitentiary for prisoners sentenced to hard labor and that it contained a large quarry. Some held that it was a better place than the other penitentiary, Abu Za'abal; others said that Tura had once been far worse than it was now. Now, as they stood beside the Istianuff prison workshop with chains on their feet, waiting for the vehicle which was to take them to Tura, they were surrounded by prisoners who showered them with good advice: they should ask their parents to send them long woolen underpants, because in Tura, they would be sleeping on the cold stone floor; and they should take plenty of cigarettes, which were of priceless value at Tura.

"But nothing of all this penetrated my consciousness," says Victor. "For some reason, I confused Tura with a-Tur; I was sure we were being taken to Sinai, and the only thing I could think of was: How would my parents be able to come and visit me there? And then, when we were placed aboard the truck and set off on our way, I discovered that we were driving along the promenade highway along the banks of the Nile."

Half an hour later, they arrived.

Tura prison is a large complex of buildings near the Nile, about 20 miles from Cairo. There were four enormous four-story blocks, each housing over a thousand prisoners. Each of the blocks was surrounded by a wall, beyond which were the prison workshops and service buildings (kitchen, bakery, laundry, washhouse, and mosque). A second wall encompassed the whole complex, which also included office buildings, a hospital, and solitary confinement cells. Beyond the wall was a fenced-in area, bordering on the Nile on one side and on the other, stretching as far as the *gabal,* Mount Tura—an elongated chalk ridge riddled with caves which served the British army as military stores during World War II. The hill also contained the quarry where men sentenced to hard labor were employed. South of the prison, but within the fenced-in area, was a squalid "housing estate" constructed for the two hundred fifty or so guards and their families. The whole complex comprised a "town" with five thousand "residents"; it was self-contained in its services and, consequently, there was little coming and going, as at other prisons. Anyone who came to Tura came to stay, usually for an extended period.

On the wall above the main gateway, there was a sign: "Liman Tura 1878" ["Tura Penitentiary"], below which, in smaller letters: *"Thadiv* [punishment] *Thahziv* [correction] *w'Islah* [and reform]."

The truck halted outside the gate. The officer in command of the escort pressed a bell and a guard opened a small door in the gate. (The gate itself was only opened in honor of the *mudir*—the prison governor —or other important guests.) They entered.

Robbie: "The first inmate of Tura we chanced upon was an enormous convict, dressed in prison uniform which was clean but faded almost white. His bare legs were in chains and his eyes had no lashes. 'Perhaps his eyelashes had been eaten away by working in the quarry?' I thought to myself in alarm. I asked him in a whisper: 'For how long?' 'Fifteen years,' he replied."

The guard escorting them halted before the office building. He ordered them to squat down and wait. Squatting was the standard prison pose for waiting. When the prisoners were led out to *tabor* (parade) they were ordered to squat; when they had to wait, outside the office or on sick call, they squatted; in the quarry, at rest breaks they squatted. Squatting is common among Eastern people, but in prison, it took on a further subtle meaning: The prisoner squatted while the guard stood over him. "What's more, what was natural for the other prisoners was unnatural to us. In Egypt, *hawagat* do not squat!" In consequence, when ordered to squat, they objected. This was their first clash with prison customs.

The second one was not long in following. A guard came out of the office, accompanied by a prisoner, to conduct a *taftish* (search) among their belongings. "Prisoners at Tura go barefoot!" he barked, ordering them to take off their shoes and pack them with the rest of their belongings to be deposited in the prison storeroom. They had heard of the ban on shoes while still at the Istianuff prison, but the story reached their ears in different versions. One of the prison veterans told them that shoes were permitted, but without laces; another old lag said that only black shoes were permitted, whereupon Philip vulcanized his brown shoes and used tar to dye them black. But to walk barefoot? That too was something the *hawagat* did not do in Egypt.

The guard entered the office to report their refusal.

Robbie: "We feared that we would soon be made to suffer for our refusal. We stood there, silently wondering whether we had acted wisely. To this day, I wonder what got into us. The only way I can explain it is by our shock on hearing the severity of the court's verdict. Perhaps we felt guilty that Moshe and Shmuel were 'wearing red,' while we were here. . . . Perhaps we sensed an unconscious craving for punishment."

Be that as it may, their fears were not realized. The duty officer— Mulazem (Lieut.) Naasef Mukhtar—was not unduly concerned to hear of the prisoners' refusal to take off their shoes. "Bring them in as they are," he ordered.

He was a Copt. In time, when the members of the network became more knowledgeable in the ways of Egyptian society, as reflected within the prison, they would observe the subtle differences between the various groups, and learn to make use of them. The Copts, who adhered to the ancient form of Christianity prevailing in Egypt before the Moslem conquest, were the country's largest minority. Since the beginning of the nineteenth century, when Egypt became a *de facto* British colony, they were the first to cooperate with the foreign rulers and to adopt a life-style borrowed from Europe. In consequence, their social and economic standing rose. But when the nationalist wave struck Egypt, they were left on one side. They took no part in the upheavals which preceded the officers' revolution, nor in the revolution itself. As a result, they were suspected after the revolution of inclining toward the *ancien régime*. Many Copt army officers were dismissed or transferred to the prison service. Aware of the injustice they had suffered, they were less prone to ill-treating "enemies of the regime." Many of them became cynical and strove only to fill their pockets before their ultimate dismissal. They competed with one another in an effort to get a posting to a "good" prison, namely, one housing well-educated or wealthy convicts who could be expected to pay well for privileges.

Tura was not one of these prisons. The vast majority of its five thousand inmates were peasants, poor and illiterate. Robbie: "One of the most depressing things at Tura was the primitive nature of our fellow convicts. Many of them had never seen a city, never seen a film or a railroad. Things which seemed elementary in the twentieth century, such as personal cleanliness, were utterly foreign to them. There were times when I felt that I had been picked up and flung back into the caveman era, without taking into account the deeds for which the other prisoners had been sent to Tura: murder, principally in blood feuds or 'defending the family honor'; brutal acts of robbery for a few pence; family conflicts in remote villages. The atmosphere was charged with violence. A man's life or honor had no value, and ill-treating the weak was a customary form of amusement. Tura was a huge ant-hill, with thousands of predatory ants scuttling about, each one concerned only for itself, always prepared to swoop down on anyone weaker than itself, and cringing in fear and self-abasement before those stronger . . ."

The prison was a faithful reflection of the society that had produced its inmates. Powerful prisoners strutted about with white cloths on their heads, like village headmen. Privileged prisoners exploited their privileges as a means of extortion from those in need of them. Nothing was given for free. Robbie: "If you had a cigarette but couldn't light it (because matches were *mamnuat,* forbidden), you were obliged to beg a light from the owner of a flint lighter, and his fee was a number of *shahtat* (draws) from your cigarette. Cigarettes were the prison currency with which you could buy anything, from a servant to additional food. You could hire yourself a killer or a bodyguard for cigarettes."

The guards and their officers conformed to this ruthless atmosphere. But when they encountered convicts of a different nature, as the members of the network must have appeared on arriving in prison, they were thrown off-balance, uncertain how to deal with them.

Mulazem Naasef Mukhtar, the Copt duty officer, treated them with distant politeness. He ignored their refusal to remove their shoes and to bow their heads when standing before him, as was the custom; he even overlooked it when one of them sat down in a chair without being asked. Quietly, he noted down their names and terms of imprisonment in the prison register, and even encouraged them: "It'll be all right, don't worry. Relatives are allowed to visit you, and your parents can bring you things. . . ."

"He regards us as potential clients," whispered Meir Meyuhas, as they marched away. "It's worth keeping up contact with him."

Robbie: "Leading out of the office building, there was a barred door, where a guard noted the names of those entering. The door opened into a large courtyard, with two shady avenues of trees planted along it, ending at the kitchen building. This was the section of the prison which visitors saw; prisoners receiving visits were brought to the prison office. To the right of the kitchen was the entrance to the hospital, and beyond that, a wall with a sign: *'Ta'adib'*—the punishment cells."

The guards led them past the punishment cells and knocked on a large wooden gate. A small door was opened for them and they passed by a duty guard, entering a closed courtyard which led to a block.

Again, their names were registered. They were each given a number and issued a *borsh* and two blankets, by virtue of which they became fully fledged inmates of the block. After that, they were taken up to the second story and locked into separate cells.

They arrived just before the *"kardal* procession." Before they had time to spread out their *borsh* and look around, the cell doors opened and the convicts stepped out into the corridor, carrying their toilet buckets.

Robbie: "I immediately picked out familiar faces. They were Brotherhood members from the military prison. They recognized me, too. Ignoring the guards who were urging them to hurry, they stopped outside my cell to fling greetings; one even shoved half a pitta through the bars. They were encouraging: 'This isn't the Sigan Harbi. . . . Do you need anything? . . . Don't worry, we'll look after you . . .' "

The fear with which every prisoner is familiar—the fear of any new place—began to recede. Philip: "The cell was light and airy. Through the bars on the door I could see a patch of sky, and from the window I could make out treetops in the distance, near the Nile. After the darkness and gloom of the Istianuff, it looked encouraging. The atmosphere also seemed freer. Convicts returning from the *'kardal* procession' stopped outside my cell to ask: 'How much?' 'For what?' They took no notice of the cursing guard who was urging them to hurry. I told myself: 'I can hold out here . . .' "

After the *"kardal* procession," they, too, were allowed out to relieve themselves and fill their jugs of drinking water. In time, they were to learn that emptying the *kardal* and bringing water were regarded as lowly occupations. Any self-respecting prisoner who possessed the necessary means hired a *nabatshi* to do them for him, in exchange for a few cigarettes.

"We didn't know that. Anyway, we were glad of the opportunity to leave our cells and look around." What they saw was a building which resembled that of the Istianuff prison. Here, too, they were in a rectangular, four-story building, with cells along all four sides, around the central "well." Unlike Istianuff, however, the central courtyard was not roofed in, and the cells were consequently lighter and better aired, and also hotter in summer and colder in winter. There was no electric lighting inside the cells, and at this time, with the winter nights falling early, they were illuminated only by the light which filtered in from the corridor. The cells were tiny. ("I remember the measurements precisely: 220 centimeters. The *borsh* was 70 centimeters wide, and when we spread out three of them side by side, there wasn't enough space left to put your foot down. . . .") But every story contained one larger cell, originally designed to serve as a storeroom but later taken over as an additional cell.

"That first day, when we met by the water faucet, we resolved to try to get ourselves housed together. When we asked one of the guards if we could arrange to be transferred to one of the large cells, so that we could be together, he shrugged his shoulders in surprise. Of course it was possible; if we asked the officer, he would surely give his permission. But why request such a thing? All the prisoners preferred the small cells, where they were confined singly. In the large cells, there were constant quarrels over sleeping places, with the favored spot—the *maraya* [corner] furthest from the door and the *kardal*—falling to the strongest or wealthiest inmate. Aside from that, there were the thefts! That was a veritable plague in Tura. Everyone stole from everyone else. Consequently, the prisoners preferred to be confined singly, or together with *baladiat* [fellow townsmen] they could trust. The guard found it hard to comprehend how five men who were neither related nor even from the same city could trust one another sufficiently to wish to live together. . . ."

The following day was Friday and the officers did not appear. Aside from prayer parade and the *"kardal* procession," the prisoners were not allowed out of their cells.

Or so it was in theory. In practice, various "privileged" convicts were allowed to wander quite freely within the bounds of that story, and even to visit other stories. They would call to the guard at the end of the corridor, who did not even trouble to bestir himself; his *nabatshi* would open the gate and collect the appropriate "fee." That day, the network members received numerous visitors. The Brotherhood members came down from the fourth story. So did two Alexandrian *baladiat*, Salah Fahim and Issam, who, at the age of nineteen, already had a murder to their "credit." They belonged to a group of high school students, sons of respectable families, who had banded together to steal the matriculation examinations from the Education Ministry offices in the city. The guard caught them redhanded, whereupon they murdered him.

Their visitors were very informative about Block 1, where they were confined. It was Tura's "transit block," where *irad* were confined for a "period of observation" which usually lasted about a month. During this time, the *irad* underwent a medical examination which settled his fate: to the *gabal* (the hill—in other words, the quarry) or to one of the workshops within the prison confines. If sent to the *gabal*, the prisoner would be transferred to another block. The ones to remain in Block 1 were the "privileged" prisoners who had succeeded in finding "professional" employment in the workshops, or gaining permission to complete their studies (which entitled them to a fourth-story solitary cell with electric lighting), or acquiring a *mulahza* (medical certificate), as well as long-term prisoners who had completed their quota of hard labor on the *gabal*.

Everyone feared the *gabal;* there were terrifying tales of the hard work and the harshness of the guard supervisors. "When you go to the doctor, pretend to be ill. Heart disease is the 'most suitable.' The doctor has no way of diagnosing it, and if you slip him something, he won't even try. . . ."

In addition to this good advice, there were offers, too. The first of these was to free them of the heavy leg irons with their irritating lining.

Philip: "That was the surprising thing. When the convicts passed by our cells for the '*kardal* procession,' they were all dragging leg irons, but when they came to visit us, they came unshackled . . ."

Issam, the French-speaking student, told him: "You can do it too." He explained that prison regulations required a convict to wear leg irons for the first ten years of his sentence. For the first seven years— as a grade A prisoner—there were heavy five-kilo chains. After five years' imprisonment, he was released from work in the quarry, and after a further two years, he was promoted to grade B, whereupon he wore lighter chains, weighing only three kilos. In his tenth year, the prisoner advanced to grade C, and was relieved of his chains. But Issam explained that a "system" had been invented in the prison workshops, whereby the process was speeded up. The lead nail which attached the chains to the prisoner's ankle was replaced by an iron nut, making it possible to remove the chains by night, and, when there were no officers in the block, by day, too. "The price is a packet of cigarettes, and if you haven't got it, credit can be arranged."

"It was a great temptation," concedes Philip, "particularly after our first night in irons, when we didn't sleep a wink. Each time I wanted to turn over, the chains would cut into my ankles and awaken me. But we were afraid. We were warned that a convict caught without his chains was considered as attempting to escape, making him liable for a flogging. On top of that, we were afraid it was a trap. . . ."

In consequence, they endured a sleepless night.

That Friday, with the officers away and the prisoners—or, at least, those who could afford to pay for the privilege—free to wander about, was an eye-opener for the members of the network. It was "market day." The prisoners employed in the service sections and workshops offered their wares for sale, after smuggling them into the block, usually with the knowledge and cooperation of the guards. Robbie was escorted by his friends from the Brotherhood, who brought him to their *murshid* (spiritual leader), el Hudeibi, housed in the "royal cell" on the fourth floor, after his death sentence had been commuted to life imprisonment. Robbie returned astonished. "On the way we passed a convict offering tea bags for sale; this was one of the most sought-after commodities in the prison, and the price was half a packet of cigarettes per bag. Another convict was selling sugar. During the coming days, while we were still *irad* and not obliged to work, we could wander around the block freely, and we soon learned that there was nothing which could not be bought. The convicts employed in the kitchen stole meat, eggs, and dry rice and offered them for sale; there was even fresh bread. Those working in the carpentry shop made wooden clogs; in the sewing shop they used the coarse cloth supplied for prison uniforms to sew clean, 'made-to-order' uniforms, with a long shirt hanging down to the ankles, making it into a kind of *galabiyeh,* of the kind that village notables wear. . . ."

The following day, Saturday, Victor and Robbie were favored with a *ziara* (visit).

Robbie: "We looked so awful, with our shaven heads and our filthy uniforms, that I was tempted to refuse the visit. I did not want my parents to see me in my miserable state. But Salah Fahim, one of the two students from Alexandria, quickly took off his uniform and gave it to me. His was 'made-to-order' and clean. Later on, when we got ourselves organized and found a way of smuggling in money, one of our first purchases was a set of clothing which had been resewn and dipped into blue dye until the cloth appeared new. This became our 'uniform for visits.' We deluded ourselves into thinking that it made us look less depressing. . . ."

The visit took place in the duty officer's office, with Victor and his family near the desk, and Robbie standing in the corner of the room with his family. As they entered, the officer said: "Speak Arabic, so that we can understand . . ." but they soon slipped into French, and he did not rebuke them.

Victor whispered: "If you have any money, take it out carefully, so that he doesn't notice. . . ." His sister dropped her purse to the floor; as she bent to pick it up, he felt her stuffing something into the chain belt around his ankle. In his cell, after the visit, he found seven pounds there, a fortune!

Their conversation was uncomfortable.

"My first question was: 'What about *them?*' Even with all the upsets and upheavals of adapting to prison life, Moshe and Shmuel remained our principal concern. My father replied: 'Don't worry, there is a storm in the world, all the powers are intervening. They won't dare . . .' I seized on his words and endeavored with all my heart to believe. . . ."

### The Point of No Return

Their request was granted. They were taken out of their single cells and all five were housed in Cell 16, the largest cell on that floor. This was to be their home for many months.

The next two days were fairly relaxed. Every morning, the cells were opened and each convict went off to his work. As *iradin* who had not yet been allocated to places of work, they were free to wander about the courtyard or to go up to the fourth story, to the "privileged" prisoners who, for various reasons, were not obliged to work. Robbie and Philip were invited to the cell of Salah Fahim, the young murderer; they came back, wide-eyed. Salah occupied a cell on his own, like all those prisoners who had received permission to continue their studies, and his cell contained a table. But that was not all. He had eight blankets and a white sheet; in the corner stood an electric hot plate and can for heating water. "It's a proper Hilton!" cried Robbie. "How did you get all this?" Salah replied: "With money, and time. . . ."

The two young murderers from Alexandria showered them with marks of affection. "They simply pampered us." The other prisoners in the block were also particularly friendly toward them during those first two days. The members of the network did not comprehend the reason for this treatment and tried to attribute it to the strange loyalty which the Egyptian displays toward fellow townsmen. It was only later that they discovered a further reason: A Sunday newspaper brought into the prison reported that Moshe Marzouk and Shmuel Azar were to be executed on the following day.

Robbie: "They hid the paper from us. They told us nothing. It was only at lunchtime on Monday, a few hours after the hangings, that Salah and Issam walked up to us in the courtyard and whispered the news: Moshe and Shmuel had departed this world. . . . Immediately, we locked ourselves into our cell. Each of us sat in his corner without saying a word. Each of us alone with his memories, in silence.

"That day, we made our first purchase in the prison 'market.' For two cigarettes, we bought a small dish of cooking oil. When the cells were locked up for the night, we lit two memorial candles. Each of us offered up a silent prayer and we remained sitting on our mats until the oil burned up and the candles went out. Then we went to bed, still without saying a word . . ."

In the course of the three days which had elapsed since the sentences were publicized, the Egyptian government was flooded with clemency appeals from public figures and governments all over the world. President Eisenhower intervened, as did Nehru and the Pope. In his diary, Moshe Sharett relates that the Israeli government considered publishing an official statement denouncing the death sentences, but decided in the negative. Perhaps Nasser would issue a reprieve after all!

Yigal Yadin, appointed by Moshe Sharett as the Israeli emissary who was to travel to Cairo for a secret meeting with the Egyptian authorities, was in London, waiting for the green light. He was given instructions to postpone his journey. "We shall not meet in the shadow of the scaffold!" Moshe Sharett affirmed.

On January 29, the Egyptian government published its reply to President Eisenhower's plea: Egypt would treat its spies in precisely the same manner adopted by the United States. In his diary, Moshe Sharett wrote: "Clearly, it's all over. . . ."

The following day, the Egyptian authorities instructed Cairo's Jewish and Kara'ite communities to send rabbis to the Istianuff prison for final prayers with the condemned men. The instructions were accompanied by the terse comment: "This request is to be treated with the utmost secrecy."

Nevertheless, the rumor spread like a forest fire. A number of synagogues held special midnight services and at dawn, a large crowd filled the square outside the prison.

Before dawn, the rabbis were brought to the condemned cells. The Kara'ite rabbi Ovadia Masliah remembers: "Moshe Marzouk was dressed in a red robe, and his face was pale and frozen. I said a prayer with him. After a time, about a dozen policemen entered the cell and took him out into the corridor. Shmuel Azar was also led out. Both of them were manacled. The prison governor read out the sentences once more. Then he turned to them and asked: 'Do you have any final requests?'

" 'No. Nothing,' " said Marzouk quietly. Shmuel Azar merely shook his head.

"As they began to march toward the execution chamber, Marzouk turned to me and said quietly: 'All of you, go *there*. You have no future here . . .' Those were his last words. I walked behind him, reading the confession prayer.

"And then the noose was looped around his neck."

Unlike the common Egyptian practice—possibly from a wish to avoid arousing world opinion even further—no journalists or photographers attended the execution. Subsequently, too, the Egyptian authorities endeavored to tone it down. On their instructions, the two men were buried secretly, and no gravestones were permitted to be erected on their graves.

However, nothing could halt the chain reaction set off by the hangings. The secret meeting between representatives of the Egyptian and Israeli governments, which might perhaps have altered the course of history, was called off. Relationships between the two countries were now imbued with such suspicion and hostility that henceforth matters would run downhill, out of control.

Pinhas Lavon, the Israeli defense minister, was forced to resign. But David Ben-Gurion's return, from his voluntary exile in Sdeh Boker, to the Defense Ministry, did not halt the escalation of hostilities. On the contrary, Israel too came under the domination of those calling for "an eye for an eye." Border incidents became more frequent and massive, and the casualty lists lengthened.

The two states were now on a collision course.

# 5

## ONE SOLITARY WOMAN

*The Women's Prison*

To this day, Marcelle Ninio remembers that final session of the Supreme Military Tribunal, where the sentences were read out, as a stunning experience whose details remain blurred.

"On the face of it, I should have been ready for the severity of the sentences. After all, ever since the day of my arrest, I expected nothing but execution, even without trial. But when the trial began, I began to hope. All those around me—my companions, the lawyers, even the police officers who chatted with us during the intermissions—all encouraged me to hope. One of them—I don't remember who it was—told me that the heaviest sentence hitherto passed by a military tribunal on a woman for a political offense was eight years' imprisonment. His words sank in, remaining in my mind as a kind of subconscious yardstick whereby to gauge my chances. I recall that when I was led into court, I paused by the dock and said to Victor: 'If they give us five years, it won't be so bad.' To tell the truth, I believed they would 'give' us more, possibly even eight years, like the sentence they imposed on that woman Communist 'record holder.' . . .

"But the moment the judge said: 'Accused number two, rise!' and then immediately read out the terrible sentence: 'The court sentences you to be hanged by the neck till you are dead,' everything whirled before my eyes. I thought I was going to faint. Out of the corner of my eye, I saw Moshe sit down without a word. Shmuel Azar, the next, remained on his feet as though thunderstruck after hearing his sentence. 'Is it possible? . . .' he muttered. I don't remember hearing Victor's sentence being read out. I was still dazed when it came to my turn. Mechanically, I rose to my feet and sat down again. It was only after the judge departed and uproar broke out in the courtroom that my mind began to take in what I had heard: fifteen years. But the words were still meaningless. Who can grasp the meaning of fifteen years' imprisonment?

"My officer escort was stunned. All the way back to the Sigan Misr, he did not cease muttering: 'Who would have expected it? . . . Such a thing!' Piously, he added: 'There is no help or salvation other than from the hands of God . . .' "

The shock waves set off by the severity of the sentence preceded Marcelle on her arrival at the prison. The duty officer—a tall, slim junior lieutenant who later became a basketball instructor in the men's section —asked her escort: "How much?" On hearing the answer, he turned pale. Addressing Marcelle, he said: "Sit down. Would you like a cup of coffee?" It was strictly forbidden to give coffee to the prisoners, but he sensed a need to express his shock and, perhaps, his feelings of pity.

Marcelle remained seated in his office until the arrival of a guard from the women's wing. No sooner was she brought to the wing than all the "politicals" swooped down upon her. For the moment, she was forgiven for being "an enemy of the people and servant of imperialism." Everyone showered her with expressions of sympathy. Aliya Tawfik said: "Are you afraid? Don't worry. You'll see, the time will pass . . ."

Marcelle: "To tell the truth, I did not yet feel frightened. Those first hours were filled with activity, leaving me no time to digest the meaning of the sentence. At a single stroke, I had been transformed from a detainee into a convicted prisoner. All the minor concessions which had made prison life tolerable were taken away from me: the mattress, civilian clothes. It was only when I had been dressed in prison uniform and taken back to my bare cell that my heart contracted with misery. But then the journalists and photographers arrived and I fought down the tears which filled my throat, to prevent them seeing my weakness. One of them asked me: 'What do you think of the sentence?' Cautiously, I replied: 'I think it is too severe.' Whereupon the guard broke in: 'What are you talking about? You were certain you were going to be sentenced to death. You got off lightly!' The thought crossed my mind that she might be right.

"All the same, I did not sleep much that night. My bones ached from the contact with the hard floor, but that was not the reason for my sleeplessness. Before my eyes, I saw the features of Moshe and Shmuel.

I did not believe that the death sentences would be carried out, but I thought: 'And what if they are commuted to life imprisonment? Is that any comfort? Spending a lifetime behind prison walls?' From here, I went on to another thought: 'And fifteen years, isn't that a lifetime?' My twenty-four years flashed before my eyes. I had lived so little! I had missed so much! My heart sank."

Marcelle's sentence was fifteen years' imprisonment with hard labor. But she was *mulahza*—under medical supervision. The following day, she reported to the doctor who, despite his unconcealed fear, renewed her *mulahza* and gave orders to give her back her mattress. He was a Copt, a good man and a good doctor, an ear, nose, and throat specialist who never ceased complaining that his medical career was in a blind alley but was too weak to break away from the prison service and begin anew. In his frustration, he sought comfort in drink, and was perpetually drunk and irritable; but he was affectionate toward Marcelle. It was only a year or more later that Marcelle discovered the reason: World War II caught him while he was studying in France and before he could get back to Egypt, the Germans occupied France. One day, he was arrested by the Gestapo on suspicion of being a Jew. He was flung into a concentration camp for Jews about to be sent "to the East." He spent only a few days there before he managed to prove his identity. But those few days sufficed to open his eyes to the fate of the persecuted, helpless Jews. Although openly terrified of what would happen if his deeds were discovered, he helped Marcelle as far as he dared. On two occasions he had her admitted to the small hospital in Sigan Misr's women's section, a privilege to which all the women prisoners aspired. Even after Marcelle was transferred to another prison, he kept up his contacts with her.

However, the *mulahza* was valid for no longer than one week. When it expired, before she had time to renew it, the *ma'amur* (deputy director) entered her cell: "Now you have to go to work."

He was one of the veteran officers in the prison service. In the past, he officiated as supervisor of the Sigan Misr, but after the revolution, being suspected of loyalty to the old regime, he was replaced and demoted. As *ma'amur*, he was in charge of the women's section. He was embittered, but more than that, out of fear for his own fate, he was anxious to survive the few remaining years before he was pensioned off. Having been instructed to keep an eye on the "Zionist spy," his insecurity made him overstrict in fulfilling his orders.

"But none of the 'politicals' goes to work!" Marcelle protested.

"You aren't a 'political'!" he replied, ordering her to leave her cell on the ground floor and move to the "criminal" section. But Marcelle, having already caught a glimpse of the revolting existence awaiting her there, resisted with a courage born of despair. "Up there? I won't go!" she shouted, threatening to declare a hunger strike. Either because he was unsure of himself or because he "didn't want any fuss," the *ma'a-mur* gave in. Taking their cues from him, the women guards also gave up their attempts to harass her into going to work. A tacit agreement was reached: Marcelle was a "political."

The status of a "political prisoner" was of great significance in Egyptian prisons. On the whole, political prisoners were educated persons, and throughout the Middle East enjoyed less stringent conditions of imprisonment. Furthermore, the political prisoner was not regarded as a hardened criminal and his imprisonment was not considered a punishment, but as a way of protecting society or the regime. Consequently, society contented itself with putting him/her behind bars; there was no need to extract vengeance. "Politicals" were not obliged to work in prison, and if they could but afford them, they were permitted to purchase all the minor comforts which the prison service proffered to prisoners of means: a bed, a sheet, food from outside, books. During the monarchy, even the man who assassinated the prime minister, Nukrashi, was granted the status of a political prisoner.

Early in 1955, only a few weeks after the members of the network were sentenced, reforms were instituted in Egypt's prisons. Their most obvious manifestation was the abolition of leg irons. In Tura prison, the network members had already given way to temptation and resolved to have their chains fixed by a nut, so that they could be removed. After paying the regular price—a packet of cigarettes per head—they went up to Issam's cell, one at a time. The "expert," a convict employed at the metal workshop, was waiting for them with his tools. Breaking the lead nail which fixed the chains to their legs, he replaced it with a nut which he had prepared in the workshop. Henceforth, they would be able to take the chains off at night, before going to sleep. But they only had a few days to enjoy the comfort stemming from the new attachment. "One morning," relates Victor, "we awoke to the sounds of a great uproar. The guards had come to notify the prisoners of the reforms and to unlock the chains. But those prisoners who had fixed nuts to their chains did not await their turn. With loud cheers, they took off their shackles and flung them down into the courtyard."

Abolition of the leg chains was only one feature of the reforms, which were quite far-reaching and designed to convert the prisons from punitive institutions into rehabilitation and reform centers. The new *laiha* (regulations) called for the establishment of vocational schools and libraries in the prisons. Loudspeakers were installed to transmit broadcasts from Radio Cairo, and the prisoners were even permitted to subscribe to newspapers. Furthermore, the *laiha* defined prisoners' rights, going so far as to specify the precise amounts of food to which they were entitled. It even gave prisoners the right to submit complaints against their guards, laying down the procedures for exercising this right.

The motives for instituting the new *laiha* were not purely humanitarian. A close examination of its innovations will show that most of the new regulations were designed less to alleviate the convict's lot than to bring him under the influence of official propaganda, which had hitherto bypassed the inmates of the prisons. Furthermore, whenever the *laiha* ran counter to existing realities—dictated by guards adhering to previous customs—the *laiha* came off second best. For example, the *laiha* allowed the prisoner to purchase an additional blanket. But the *ma'amur* at Tura, horrified by this pampering, vetoed the new ruling on the grounds that an additional blanket would make the cells intolerably overcrowded.

There were sections of the *laiha* that pertained directly to members of the network. One ruled that Jewish prisoners were permitted to observe their religious festivals, that they were to receive wine and matza at Passover, and that they were entitled to the spiritual ministrations of a rabbi once a week. "But when we demanded a rabbi," relates Victor, "our request was not met. The only occasion when we received a visit from a rabbi was when we declared a hunger strike, and even then, the rabbi only came to persuade us that hunger-striking was categorized as suicide, and therefore prohibited by the Torah. . . ."

As for the rule sanctioning complaints, this was only designed to encourage informers. The officers' regime made denunciations into one of the cornerstones of its rule, and this was not confined to the prisons alone. Everyone informed on everyone else, and informing became a reliable way of forwarding one's career—in the government services, in the army, and in the nationalized industries.

However, the reforms did have one concrete effect: When they were instituted, they were accompanied by far-reaching changes among the prison directors. Veteran officers, disciples of "the old methods," were pensioned off. Among the new directors, there was a handful who genuinely desired to apply the "revolutionary spirit," or at least to appear as reformers and innovators. One of these was the new *mudir* of Sigan Misr, Liwa Mahmud Sahb. (In time, he was to be promoted to head of the prison service throughout the whole of Egypt.) He was a conscientious prison officer who displayed an interest in the reforms instituted in Western prisons, and in novel projects to rehabilitate prisoners. He translated into Arabic *The Birdman of Alcatraz*, the story of a man serving a life sentence on an island prison off the coast of California. Adopting a sparrow which enters his cell, the convict domesticates it, relieving his loneliness and ultimately being reformed.

Marcelle: "At his arrival, there was tension in the prison, as always happens whenever a new officer appears. Furthermore, the rumor soon got around that he was 'hard' and could not be bought."

It was not long before she ran into him. She was caught committing a grave offense: Communist literature was discovered among her possessions; what made it worse, the books were in Russian!

"I fell ill. I had bouts of diarrhea and high temperature, and the doctors were unable to diagnose the cause. At first, they suspected me of faking it by secretly swallowing pills to push up my temperature. To keep a better watch on me, they took me up to the sick bay. After a time, they were convinced that my illness was genuine, and they began to treat it. I was given injections and put on a special diet: clear soup, rice, milk, and sometimes even liver, a genuine delicacy! But it was all in vain. My sickness lasted for about three months, until it vanished in the same way that it had appeared and the doctors still didn't know what I had been suffering from."

While she was hospitalized, two more women accused of being Communists were brought to the prison—Awataff, sentenced to a year's imprisonment, and Thiah Abu'l Nas, who was serving three years. Before their arrest, both of them were employed as teachers; Thiah was a university graduate. She was a fanatical Communist who treated Marcelle with considerable reserve, and—after Soviet-Egyptian relations improved—even with open hostility. But when she fell ill and was hospitalized, occupying the bed next to Marcelle's, she changed her ways, and for some time, the two women became friendly. Thiah endeavored to convince Marcelle of the justice of the Communist ideology, lending her Communist literature she had succeeded in smuggling into the prison. Two or three of the books were in Russian and Marcelle resolved to combat her boredom by making use of them to learn Russian.

Marcelle's deed was considered so grave that the director himself was called to the sick ward. He leafed through the book and then flung it to the floor in anger.

"Aren't you satisfied with the fifteen years you got for being a Zionist spy?" he shouted. "D'you want further punishment for being a Communist?"

Marcelle did not reply, and Mahmud Sahb continued his shouting until he had given vent to his anger. Then he said: "I shall take the book and destroy it, and that will be the end of the affair. And remember, if you must read prohibited books, at least make sure they're not in

Russian! Is that clear?" And he stalked out furiously. But he kept his promise; he did not report the discovery, and there were no further consequences to the episode.

Only a few weeks later, everything changed: Russia was no longer a frightful monster. In fact, the switch was not so sudden. For over a year, there had been a schism between Nasser's Egypt and the West, ever since American Secretary of State John Foster Dulles began to work for the creation of the Baghdad Pact in the face of Egyptian opposition. Relations deteriorated progressively until Dulles, as a means of exerting pressure on Nasser to abandon his opposition to the pact, prohibited the sale of arms to Egypt. Whereupon Nasser set off to the Bandung Conference, where he held talks with the heads of the Soviet delegation, paving the way for the "Czechoslovakian arms deal." This was the first of a series of fateful events. Dulles "punished" Egypt for the arms deal by withdrawing the aid promised by the United States for the construction of the Aswan Dam, to which Nasser responded with the nationalization of the Suez Canal, setting the scene for the 1956 Suez operation.

In the middle of 1955, all these developments were still a matter for the future. The "Czech deal" had just been signed, and Egypt flung itself into an orgy of national pride: Nasser had stuck out his tongue at the American giant! All over the country, "spontaneous" appeals were launched to collect money for the "arms fund." In the Sigan Misr's women's wing, the prison officers headed the appeal, and everyone contributed, even the "criminals."

"But when they came to me," recalls Marcelle, "I said: 'I don't have any money, and even if I did, I wouldn't give it for such a cause. . . .'"

The guards' first reaction was to lock her in her cell. The story soon made the rounds of the prison.

After Nasser attended the Bandung Conference, the Egyptian Communist party no longer regarded him as "an enemy of the people," and called off its opposition to his regime; there were even rumors that all the Communists would soon be released from prison. Some of the Communists in Sigan Misr now crowded around Marcelle's cell door, shouting that she had now displayed herself in her true colors. Yet again she was taking up a position of opposition to the Egyptian people. Mahmud Sahb arrived and dispersed them. Then he entered the cell and planted himself in front of Marcelle.

"Why did you refuse to make a contribution? Don't you understand that your refusal will harm your prospects of receiving a pardon?"

She tried to evade the issue by claiming that she had no money.

"If that is the reason, I'll give you some."

She refused, saying that she was not prepared to assist in buying arms with which human beings would be killed.

"Nonsense!" he shouted. "I shall make a contribution on your behalf, and that's all. There's no point in your objections."

With that, he marched out.

## The Chasm of Loneliness

What had she done to win his favor and enjoy such unusual treatment on his part? At first, it was her misery which attracted his attention; later, when he began to take an interest in her, he discovered her as a person and behaved indulgently toward her.

Without any doubt, she was in a particularly miserable state, even by comparison with the miserable women who made up the prison's population. Almost throughout the whole of her first year in prison, she was undergoing medical treatment. A long time passed before her smashed thigh healed up and she overcame her limp. But she was still troubled by back pains and prolonged standing or sitting caused her great suffering.

She was lonely, with the loneliness which can only be experienced in a crowd. Her relationships with her fellow prisoners varied from "chilly" to "hostile," in accordance with the fluctuations of the political barometer. The same applied to the attitude of the women guards.

No one came to visit her from outside; neither did she receive any letters. Logically, she justified her brother for not coming to visit her, but her feeling was of having been forgotten. "And that was the worst feeling of all."

She was also the poorest of the inmates of the "political floor." At first, all she had at her disposal was the tiny sum deposited for her by her attorney, al Gariani. Not knowing when or whether she would get any more, she restricted herself to spending one Egyptian pound a month. This sum was primarily spent on buying cigarettes. "After all, I had to pay the *nabatshia* for cleaning out my cell, and I had to offer a cigarette to the women guards from time to time." She spent what little money remained on livening up the monotonous prison diet. Once a month, each prisoner was permitted to order up to three pounds' worth of provisions—at first, only canned foods—from the prison canteen. Marcelle could not afford to take advantage of the full allocation, but she felt duty-bound to buy something, a few cans of sardines or tuna. It was not for herself alone. No less important was to be able to offer a morsel to her fellow prisoners and to contribute her share to the joint "feasts" they held from time to time. "It was good for the soul not to be the one who was always on the receiving end."

A further five months passed by before her brother Yitzchak overcame his apprehensions and came to see her for the first time, in June
1955. As it was his first time, the *ma'amur* gave permission for them to
meet in his office, instead of the noisy visitors' courtyard.

"For a whole year—ever since my arrest the previous July—we had
not seen one another. When I was led into the *ma'amur's* office and
found him there, I burst into tears. All the agony of my solitude and
abandonment, which I had repressed till then, now broke out. He also
wept. He is fifteen years older than I, and this was the first time in my
life that I saw him crying."

He was eager to explain why he stayed away from the trial and why
he had refrained from visiting her previously. Wiping away his tears,
and his voice still unsteady, he told her that it was the lawyer who had
advised him not to come to the court, telling him that he would doubt-
lessly be photographed and his picture would appear in the newspapers, which would undermine his position at the school and perhaps
even cause him to lose his job. Probably, someone in the secret police
would recall his Communist past and he would be arrested. (They did
indeed remember, and he was summoned for interrogation, but he
succeeded in convincing the interrogators that he had nothing to do
with his sister's Zionist activities.) After all, he had a wife and son to
consider.

He brought her a fine parcel. In addition to various food preserves,
it contained a set of women's underwear. The articles were of the
simplest cotton (he had been forewarned that there was no prospect of
the prison authorities permitting anything finer), but by comparison
with the crude sacking used for prison underwear, they felt as smooth
as the finest silk. They, too, were *mamnuat*—strictly prohibited—but
the *ma'amur* was lenient and permitted them "as long as they were not
visible." In the course of her fourteen years in prison, Marcelle was not
to enjoy many experiences which could compare with her excitement
the first time she wore her new underwear. "It was as though one layer
of prison had been stripped off me."

After that first time, her brother became a regular visitor. Every
visiting day, once in six weeks, he would be at the prison gates, and he
did not come alone. His wife and son joined him. But there were no
more "private visits" in the *ma'amur's* office; they were obliged to join
the rest of the visitors in the courtyard set aside for the purpose. It was
walled in and divided down the middle by two additional fences. Dozens of visitors crowded around one side of the partition while the prisoners were led into the other half of the courtyard. Visitors and prisoners stood facing one another, shouting at one another, their words
inaudible amid the din. "Our principal pleasure was *seeing* our rela-

tives, and even that pleasure didn't last long. The *laiha* prescribed a fifteen-minute visit, but within two or three minutes of our entry into the courtyard, the women guards began to urge us to finish and go. Their shouts made the noise even worse."

After a few months, Mahmud Sahb permitted Marcelle to receive her visitors together with the "politicals." This was a great improvement, for they were fewer and more refined, and the visits were relatively quiet. But there was a drawback involved: The "politicals" only received their visitors after the "criminals" had finished. In consequence, their relatives were forced to spend hours waiting outside the prison, exposed to the rain in winter and to the blazing sun in summer. They could not come later, because the administrative arrangements— checking the visitors' book to make sure that the prisoner was indeed entitled to a visit—were conducted at the general visiting time. "Even though I looked forward desperately to their visits, there were times when I imagined them standing in the burning sun for hour after hour, and I would say to myself: 'I hope they don't come!'"

It was only years later that a shelter was erected outside the prison for the convenience of the visitors.

The visits by her brother and his family were a narrow chink in the wall of solitude which encompassed Marcelle. But they did not add to her material comforts. Knowing well how hard pressed he was, she did not venture to ask him to give her a larger allowance. She continued to make do with one Egyptian pound a month; there was no one else to request help from.

She was only saved from her penury after the arrest of Maurice Nagar, one of the wealthy members of the Cairo Jewish community. Suspected of smuggling money abroad, he was detained at Sigan Misr. "On one occasion, I saw him from the window of the sick bay, when he was led out for exercise in the men's section, and I waved to him." She was acquainted with him from the time when he officiated as secretary of the Heliopolis Hakoach sports club, where she played basketball. After the club was closed down by the authorities, she began to play in the town's tennis club, and henceforth, her contacts with Nagar were confined to occasional meetings. But when he saw her in the prison, he remembered her. Shortly afterward, he was released, whereupon, on his initiative, the Cairo Jewish community began to display some interest in Marcelle.

"One day, Mahmud Sahb came and told me that a representative of the community had come to inquire about me, and had deposited forty-two pounds to my credit in the prison office. This was an enormous sum, but my first reaction was: I don't want any favors from them! I sensed no friendship toward them; they had ignored my existence for a whole year. None of them troubled to visit me or to inquire about me, not even on festivals. But Sahb said: 'Don't be stupid! They didn't come because they were scared . . . but they brought the money of their own goodwill.' He arranged to have the money registered as coming from relatives."

In fact, this money, like other sums received in the course of her imprisonment, was sent from Israel. But Marcelle would learn of this only after her release.

Looking back over the years which have passed by since then, Marcelle finds it hard to recall her years of imprisonment, the first period particularly. Memory is naturally selective, focusing on unusual events—good or bad—like her brother's visits, Mahmud Sahb's consideration, the viciousness of some guard or other, her frustration on being disappointed in her hopes of being released after the Suez war.

But in reality, those years of imprisonment were not a series of sharp ups and downs, but a long line of dreary monotony. "That was the worst thing about those years—their endlessness. I think that it was only after five years that I began to comprehend the true significance of imprisonment for fifteen years. Previously, there were times when I yearned for a pardon, when I hoped that I would be released somehow or other; and there were periods when such hopes were dashed, like when the prisoner exchange following the 1956 war came to an end without including us. I was furious then. I was out of my mind with anger and frustration. But that was nothing compared with the depression which overtook me after about five years' imprisonment. There was no particular reason for this depression, other than the fact that five years had come to an end and there were ten more to go. I stopped believing that I would hold out. I stopped hoping, I stopped yearning, I stopped feeling. I became a 'vegetable,' withdrawn, without wishes or desires, empty of thoughts. It lasted for months . . ."

The Sigan Misr's women's section housed some three hundred and fifty to four hundred prisoners. When Marcelle arrived, the hashish dealers were the largest single group; a year previously, penalties for hashish traders were stepped up, with the courts handing down sentences of up to twenty-five years' imprisonment for possession of as little as one gram of the drug. Egypt's prisons filled up with *hashishin*. About a year after her trial, the regime launched a witch-hunt against card players of all kinds, and the campaign did not even bypass high society ladies who played bridge for pennies in their homes.

However, in between the *hashishin* and the card players, the prison's "permanent" population was made up of murderesses, pickpockets, and prostitutes. "Most of them were women who had chosen to live beyond the law, and whose ways of thought fitted them to take advantage of every situation, without consideration for anyone. They lied, stole, informed, bullied their weaker sisters, and fawned on the stronger women. You couldn't trust them for a moment. The most repulsive—and the most pitiful—were the prostitutes. They disgusted me with their coarse bestiality and their constant cursing. But when you listened to their stories—horrifying tales of innocent girls who had been seduced and become objects of exploitation by their seducers—you couldn't help feeling sorry for them. And then, there were the murderesses. They couldn't be bunched together. Some had killed babies born out of wedlock or their husbands during a quarrel; there were others who had killed one of their husband's other wives, or a bullying mother-in-law. There were also those who had killed in cold blood, poisoning a neighbor because of a dispute over a piece of land or over water rights. Some of them were monsters, but there were also generous, helpful women . . ."

In the four-story building, the *hashishin* took over the exclusive fourth floor, while the prostitutes and murderesses dominated the third. The second floor housed the dispensary and the cells nearby were occupied by prisoners who were pregnant, or mothers of young children (imprisoned mothers were allowed to bring in children up to the age of two years, who were regarded as unweaned). These women were exempted from work, and even received additional food for their children; usually, they sold the superfluous rations in the prison black market.

The "politicals" were isolated on the ground floor. They were a small group. There were five or six imprisoned for being Communists: Joyce; Marie Rosenthal, the daughter of a baptized Jew (she was married to a Moslem lawyer, Sa'ad a Din Kamel, who, despite being related to the propaganda minister Fathi Radouan, was an extreme leftist and imprisoned in Tura); there was Aliya Tawfik, whose husband was also in Tura; Amal Abdul-Nur, a Communist from Nablus; the two teachers —Awataff and Thiah Abu'l Nas; and Mimi, a young Jewess from Cairo. Additional prisoners also passed through from time to time.

The "criminals" were required to work. The women's section contained a laundry and a large sewing shop, which served all the prisons and a number of hospitals in the Cairo region. But the "politicals" had plenty of free time, spending most of the day in the courtyard—in one large group when they were on friendly terms and in two or more groups when the Communists cold-shouldered Marcelle. They argued a lot; at first, before they gave her up as a lost cause, the Communists attempted to "convert" Marcelle. They conversed a great deal, particularly about the outside world; they read. But their principal occupation was "getting organized," in other words, purchases in the prison's black market and acquiring the money to pay for them.

The black market was conducted by the *ra'isa* (head convict) in the prison laundry, a murderess from Upper Egypt, and her assistant, a hashish dealer from Cairo. Numerous outsiders came to the laundry— guards from other prisons and hospital staff who came to deliver dirty laundry or collect it after it had been washed. While doing so, they smuggled in various articles which were in demand, primarily, hashish and tea. The sentries—soldier conscripts—also engaged in smuggling, as did the contractor who brought in the meals for those entitled to outside food.

For a long time, Marcelle could do no more than watch all these activities, without being able to take part, possessing neither money nor exchangeable articles. All that time, she was dependent upon her companions and their fluctuating generosity.

It was only after her brother's first visit that Marcelle solved the problem of smuggling money into the prison. The solution was typical of the manner in which such problems were resolved in Egyptian prisons. There was a female guard who, for a sizable payment (30 percent or even 40 percent of the sum) undertook to visit the prisoners' relatives and collect the money to be smuggled into the prison. For a further payment, she was even prepared to smuggle letters, but Marcelle's brother did not dare to go as far as that.

Now that she had money, Marcelle could acquire a *tau-tau*, a primitive kerosene stove made of two empty cans whose wick consisted of strips of blanket; the fuel was the cooking oil used for frying onions, which was traded by the prisoners in charge of giving out food. The name came from the sound made by the oil as it burned. In addition to the *tau-tau*, Marcelle also bought coffee and tea, and later on, even an electric hot plate. In the end, the prison authorities decided there was no point in a prohibition which could not be enforced. In the second round of reforms, instituted in Egypt's prisons at the end of 1955, the prison canteen was opened daily; in addition to canned foods and fresh vegetables, it also sold hot tea. Followed by a prisoner carrying a bucket of steaming tea, a guard would walk along the corridor, calling: *"Chai! Min le'chai?"* ("Tea! Who's for tea?")

It was a pleasure to have hot tea to drink in the mornings, but the black market in tea and coffee persisted. "Stolen waters are sweet."

Aside from "trade," there were almost no contacts between the "criminals" and the "politicals." Although they all used the same courtyard, the guards took care to keep them apart. Nevertheless, particularly during her two periods of hospitalization in the second floor sick bay, Marcelle had a chance of a glimpse at this alien, exotic world which teemed above her head.

"It was an enclosed feminine world, with abnormal sexual relationships. There were lots of lesbians in the prison; there were endless loves and jealousies and betrayals. There were also fights and acts of vengeance over disappointed love affairs. At first, I did not notice all that. We were cut off from the 'criminals,' enclosed in our ground-floor cells. In addition, I must admit, I was rather naive. I knew of such things from books, but I had no idea they were taking place so close to me. But from the sick bay, at night, I could hear the sounds from the floor above. There were nights when we were awakened by the sound of screams and fighting. From the shouts and curses, I comprehended that these were scenes of jealousy. At times, things developed into uncontrollable hysteria, which ended with the contenders being thrown into the punishment cells near our cells on the ground floor.

"There were also 'normal' love affairs, between women prisoners and the guards, or men prisoners. That was why the sick bay was so desirable: From its window, one could look out at the courtyard of the men's section and see one's 'beloved,' or to talk to some good-looking sentry, and even fling him a love letter. These were Platonic affairs, for the two sections of the prison were divided by a high wall, and the sentries were also unable to enter our section. All the same, these love affairs were very passionate, and often led to women prisoners fighting one another till blood flowed, if one of them accused another of flirting with 'her' man.

"We, the 'politicals,' were not drawn into these turbulent passions. We subjected ourselves to the most severely puritan restrictions. We avoided any physical contact with one another, not even permitting ourselves a friendly hug, and we refrained from bad language. These rules were not adopted as the result of any discussion. We never talked about these matters. But we seemed to have a tacit agreement: We were going to preserve our humanity; we would not become like them . . ."

The days crawled by slowly, scarcely filled with day-to-day existence and experiences. These were very trifling. An argument with one of the other prisoners was capable of providing enough excitement for a whole day, and her brother's visits or a rare letter filled her thoughts for an entire week. They were perpetually busy acquiring food on the black market, and seeking ways of concealing it. Contacts with the women guards and prison officers were somewhat remote; the staff had orders to keep away from the "politicals." But nevertheless, they did come into contact with them at mealtimes, during outside visits, or during the occasional searches in the cells. Some of the guards were harsh and bullied them; others were more lenient. Some of them were resentful of the "privileged politicals" who were wealthy and well educated; others focused their hostilities on the Jewish prisoners, or on Marcelle, the "traitress."

"There was one supervisor by the name of Thawahida; she was an ugly, foulmouthed monster of whom we were all frightened to death. She was incapable of walking past a prisoner without yelling and cursing. I was so frightened of her that when she was duty officer—whose job it was to tour the cells at seven o'clock in the morning, as soon as the doors were opened—I would slip away to the washroom and stay there for a long time until I was certain that she had completed her inspection and returned to her office. Anything to avoid running into her! I even composed a poem about her, in which I depicted her as the Medusa of Greek legend. But when I showed the poem to my companions, Aliya said: 'What do you want from her? She likes you!' It was only then I noticed that beneath her tough exterior, Thawahida treated me as her favorite. When she was in charge of handing out food, I always got the best morsel of meat, the freshest slice of bread, the least dirty hunk of cheese. Imagine!"

### The Gymnasts

The days crawled by slowly; the nights were endless. At first Marcelle had great difficulty in finding a comfortable position for her battered body on the hard bed. Her sleep was restless and fitful. It became a habit for her to wake up several times during the night and lie in the darkness, listening to the sounds of the prison, with conflicting thoughts running through her mind, together with scraps of incomplete dreams. Cautiously, she changed her position, waiting for the stabs of pain. And then, one night, she noticed that her pains were not as powerful as previously. Her internal injuries had healed up; her limp gradually vanished. By the time the prison underwent the "second reform," she was almost completely fit again.

This time, it was not an official reform, like the first one, but it had a great impact all the same. At the end of 1955, or early in 1956, Liwa Zacci Shukry, one of the senior officers of the prison service, returned to Egypt after a study tour of the United States and took up his post as deputy inspector general of prisons. He was full of enthusiasm for what he had seen in the United States, and, with the encouragement of the *mudir*, Mahmud Sahb, set about altering the prison. His first step was, indeed, revolutionary: All the women prisoners were issued mattresses, not the palliasses where the straw filling always bunched up into mobile lumps, but genuine mattresses, filled with cotton and properly sewn.

After that came the beds. (In fact, they did not come; they had been in the cells all the time, but they were padlocked to the wall, but now they were unlocked and made available for use.) After that came curtains! The curtains were the product of Marcelle's "private initiative." One day she asked the guard in charge of the canteen whether she was allowed to use her money to buy material for a curtain. "I'll ask," the woman replied. After a day or two, she came back with an affirmative answer. In accordance with Marcelle's instructions, the contractor in charge of the canteen bought her a piece of simple material; the women employed in the sewing shop gave her a needle and embroidery thread. Like every other "well-brought-up" Jewish girl in Egypt, Marcelle had learned sewing and embroidery as a girl. When she had embroidered the material, she hung it up in her cell, giving it a new look. The prison officers came to see and were filled with admiration. In time, that first embroidered curtain became the foundation stone of a whole industry which flourished in the prison.

From the American psychologists, Zacci Shukry had learned the importance of a hobby of some kind to occupy the prisoners, particularly those serving long sentences. On his arrival, a circular went out to all the prisons in Egypt with instructions to foster sporting activities among the convicts; as the highlight of these activities, Zacci Shukry planned competitions between the prisons and even a proper "league." It is characteristic of the thinking of the Egyptian bureaucracy that what was planned as the finishing touch for a whole series of ramified activities became an exclusive event existing in its own right. The prisons did not foster sports, but instead, they cultivated representative teams whose success or failure in competitions reflected on the status of their prison and its director.

"Zacci Shukry wished to encourage sport in our prison, too; Mahmud Sahb told him that I had engaged in sports before my imprisonment, and the pair came to me, to consult me on what could be done. I told them that the women's section did not have adequate sports grounds. At most, it would be possible to set up a Ping-Pong table in the corridor, and perhaps, to engage in gymnastics."

They asked her if she was prepared to organize these activities, and she consented. She chose about twenty women who seemed young and healthy. Most of them were hashish dealers who had been sentenced to twenty-five years' imprisonment; some were prostitutes who still had at least six months of their sentence to run. After the first session, she approached the *ma'amur* with a request: sports clothes. It was impossible to jump or do somersaults on the floor when their legs were constantly entangled in their long dresses. There was a "council of war" and the *mudir* found the solution: One of the inmates of the men's section was a young Jewish Communist, Aryeh Zak (later transferred to Tura), whose father owned a large sporting goods store in Cairo. It was not difficult to "persuade" Zak's father to contribute a set of sports clothes for Marcelle's group. Sports shoes were acquired in a similar fashion; Marcelle wrote to her friend, Marie Blumenthal, secretary to the director of the Bata marketing network, and she persuaded her employer to donate twenty-four pairs of sports shoes to the prison. (Marie would not regret her help to the prison; a year later, at the time of the Suez war, she was among the hundreds of Jews thrown into prison for "preventative arrest" and Mahmud Sahb showed himself duly grateful for her help.)

"We began to train. Possibly the hardest part of the training was to get the girls used to wearing shoes. For most of them, it was their first pair ever. Submissively, they accepted the necessity of wearing shoes during training, but as soon as the session ended, they hastened to remove them."

For Marcelle, these gymnastics sessions were more than just something to do. They became a task and a challenge; and, furthermore, they gave her responsibility. Her life now became more than a prolonged vacuum, with breaks for eating and sleeping, and with meaningless meetings with her fellow prisoners. She had a group of twenty-four young women and she was in charge. She wanted to do more than teach them to move their limbs at a uniform tempo. She held long conversations with them, trying to implant an understanding for the importance of cleanliness. She tried to convince herself that with patience and persistence, she might even be able to set off the first spark of their rehabilitation.

After a few trials, the group made good progress. "We were now capable of carrying out a whole series of exercises faultlessly and at an even tempo and I decided to raise my sights. I planned a rhythmic show, and not just any show, but one with 'props.' At my request, the prison workshop manufactured twenty-four iron hoops which we wrapped in colored paper, attaching long paper streamers. When the hoops were whirled rhythmically, they created a colorful visual illusion which was very pleasant to watch."

Any European kindergarten would have been capable of putting on a similar show, but these were women who had never seen the inside of a kindergarten. After attending one of the rehearsals, Zacci Shukry was so excited that he decided there and then to hold a celebration on the forthcoming Revolution Day, and to present his gymnastic troupe before an audience of notable guests. He gave Marcelle twenty pounds from prison funds to make the show even more colorful, and gave her an assistant, Thiah Abu'l Nas, who, as a teacher, was experienced in conducting group gymnastics.

Marcelle was infected by Zacci's enthusiasm. She had no experience in choreography, but all the same, she planned a colorful dance performance, after the taste of the audience, with a "musical accompaniment" and "scenery."

For background music, she chose Muhammed Abdul Wahab's song "Cleopatra," which was very popular at that time. The costumes, of colored paper, were designed according to the song, in the "Pharaonic fashion" as copied from ancient Egyptian wall paintings.

"I decided that a 'great show' like this deserved to be presented on a suitable stage. Approaching Mahmud Hafez, I suggested holding the festival in the large courtyard in the men's section. At first, he was taken aback. As far as I know, ever since the construction of Sigan Misr, there was no precedent for women entering the men's section. But the more he thought about it, the more he liked the idea, until he summoned up the courage to request permission, which was granted."

With the approach of July 23, Revolution Day, the rehearsals were speeded up. At noon on the appointed day, there was a dress rehearsal in costume and on the spot chosen for the performance—the courtyard of the men's section. "The men were locked in their cells and the whole courtyard was placed at our disposal. With chalk, I marked out the place of each of the gymnasts, we put the record on, and began to dance.

"The rehearsal showed up various deficiencies, and it went on and on, under the burning July sun, until the heat softened the record and it buckled slightly.

"We didn't notice until the performance itself, which took place that evening. The courtyard was illuminated by spotlights; all the prisoners, from both wings, were brought along, with the men seated on one side, the women on the other, and the prison officers seated in the center, together with Mahmud Sahb's visitors from the prison service and the Interior Ministry. After that, we took our places on the open space, between the chalk markings. Then the record player was turned on. . . ."

The buckled record screeched and whined abominably, but it gave the tempo. After the initial shock, the troupe began to dance, and from that moment on till the very end of the performance, there was not a single hitch.

The convicts cheered wildly; Mahmud Sahb and Zacci Shukry were elated. In their excitement, they began to talk of a prisoners' orchestra, to be conducted by Mimi, who was a good violinist . . .

### The Film Star

The innovations introduced by the new *ma'amur* brought far-reaching changes to the Sigan Misr women's section. From that point

on, the canteen at the end of the corridor was opened daily, there was
hot tea available in the mornings, the bed and the curtain on the
window gave the cell a warmer appearance, and the gymnastics sessions added a little interest to the monotony of Marcelle's existence. At
times, Mahmud Sahb would come along at midday for a game of Ping-
Pong "to sweat my belly off," as he would explain. ("Not that it did any
good," Marcelle comments.) His friendly attitude had its effect on the
women guards, too, but nevertheless, Marcelle was still in prison.

"It's hard to put it into words. It wasn't just the fact of being
imprisoned and deprived of my liberty, though, of course, there was
that too. But even at the best of times, I could not rid myself of my
anxiety and nervousness. What was I afraid of? Everything. Any officer
was capable of ordering a sudden search, whereupon there would be
pandemonium in the prison as everyone hurried to conceal the few
*mamnuat* they had managed to acquire. For a little dry rice they could
have us flung into a punishment cell, and an illegal letter could lead to
a *mahdar* [interrogation], which was followed by a more severe punishment. There were constant tensions, either because of some bullying
guard or because some prisoner was trying to pick a quarrel. Not even
mealtimes passed without squabbling, especially on the days when they
gave out 'salad' (consisting of dry parsnips and leaves of *kurat,* a plant
which usually served as animal fodder). Whenever the guard went to
my brother carrying a letter from me, my heart would throb with fear
lest anything should happen; she might be caught or denounce me. And
when she came back with a few pounds, it would soon get around that
'new money' had arrived, whereupon my fears would focus on the
dependability of the hiding place I had found for them. Would it withstand a search? Or the penetrating gaze of the *nabatshia?* Throughout
my long years of imprisonment, I don't once remember myself feeling
relaxed and free of tension."

New prisoners, particularly those housed with the "politicals,"
were a sure pretext for excitement. Would they fit in? Would they make
trouble, upsetting the delicate balance within their small group?

"At the arrival of Zuzu Mahdi, the former film star, we were appre-
hensive. She came from such a different world! Of course, we all hastened to welcome her."

Zuzu was a well-known film star during the forties; she was tall and
beautiful, with a sensual look. She gained fame through the daring love
scenes in which she appeared. If gossip and her own stories are to be
believed, they were not confined to the screen. . . . Before she had time
to establish close relationships with her fellow prisoners, she was already boasting of her intimate connections with famous film producers
and managers. She also told of her "grand *amour*" with an American

pilot, for whom she was prepared to sacrifice her career, but he was killed during the final months of World War II. She was now married for the second time, and had a grown-up daughter. Her husband was a hashish dealer, who had also been arrested and was now confined to the men's section. Whenever she saw him through the window of the sick bay, she would wave to him and greet him affectionately. But when the guards were around, she would curse him terribly for the awful trouble he had got her into. In the end, after a trial lasting for a year, she was acquitted and released.

"When we first saw her in the washroom, we couldn't believe our eyes. She was dressed in a sheer nylon nightgown, over which she wore a silk bathrobe. Her face was made up and her hair set. She was still beautiful, despite her age. I did not understand how she was permitted to bring in all the fashionable clothing which filled her cell."

To the Communist prisoners, Zuzu symbolized everything they considered disgusting and abominable. "I was also accepted conditionally, with a big question mark over me; all the same, they still considered me a 'political,' motivated by an ideal, however mistaken. But Zuzu was considered by the Communist prisoners to be a deviant and a hashish dealer. They kept away from her."

But Marcelle was filled with curiosity concerning this pampered, colorful creature who had landed in this prison from another planet. But her curiosity was soon tempered by mercy.

"It was two or three days later. Suddenly, Zuzu had a convulsive attack, with the spasms getting worse by the hour. Her temperature rose, her eyes reddened, and she shook all over. I was naive; I had never encountered an alcoholic and I did not know the symptoms. I called the officer and she summoned the *mudir*. Zuzu was rushed to the sick bay, and a messenger was sent to fetch her daughter."

Her daughter—a former "Miss Egypt" and now a successful fashion designer—soon arrived, accompanied by a friend, a senior secret police officer who closeted himself with the *mudir*. After that, the daughter was permitted to give her mother the "present" she had brought, without having it examined. Henceforth, Zuzu suffered no more attacks. The stock of liquor in her cell was inexhaustible. After taking a few gulps, she would adopt the mannerisms of a *grande dame*, and start telling dirty jokes, which became more outrageous the more she drank.

Marcelle had always been repelled by bad language, and in prison, this had become a downright aversion. She would slip away to her cell with a burning flush covering her cheeks. But when Zuzu was not tipsy, she was a most amusing companion who refused to permit the gloom of prison to overcome her natural gaiety. She and Marcelle spent much time together, in defiance of the reproving glances of the Communists.

Marcelle had another entertaining companion: the cat "Mickey."

"The prison was full of cats. No one could remember how and when the first one arrived, but they had increased and multiplied, and each of us in the 'political' section had at least one cat. I also adopted one, after waking up one night and finding a large cockroach scuttling across my face. The cats would hunt cockroaches."

It was forbidden to keep animals in the cells, and before locking the cells for the night, the guards would conduct a search and shoo the cats out into the corridor. But Marcelle trained "Mickey" to come back and stand beneath her window, while she let down a strip of cloth for him to climb up and get back into the cell, until he became too fat to squeeze through the bars.

One day, an officer tripped over a cat, whereupon orders were issued to drive away all the cats; they were banished to the men's section. "I was so unhappy!"

But it was not long before the cats reappeared in the women's section. Marcelle adopted one of them, naming it "Mickey 2," and when the time came for her to be transferred out of Sigan Misr, the cat went along with her.


Her transfer took place late in September 1956. As part of the general reform within the prison service, it was decided to move the women's prison to a newer and more convenient building in the township of Kanather, some 20 miles from Cairo. The prisoners were transferred in batches, in the course of a week, with the "politicals" being the last to move.

"Our principal problem was how to take our cats along. Marie Rosenthal had two, and Zuzu also had one. As it turned out, the operation was easier than we had imagined. Our possessions were not searched, the cats behaved themselves without uttering a sound throughout the journey. The evening before our departure, we held a farewell party consuming the remnants of the 'prohibited' foodstuffs we had accumulated. But despite the ample quantities of food, the party was not overcheerful. At Sigan Misr we had established habits and customs. We knew which of the guards could be bought with money or flattery; which ones to beware of. We had installed secure caches which could withstand searches. We had found our way around the prison's black market, and invented methods of smuggling in money and provisions. Now, we would have to start all over again, in a new place."

# 6

## FIVE AMONG FIVE THOUSAND

*Punishment, Reform, and Rehabilitation*

For weeks after the hangings, the five network members in Tura prison were haunted by a continual and profound sense of horror. "There were times," relates Victor, "when I found it hard to believe that it had happened. I would tell myself: 'It will turn out to have been a mistake'. . . ." Shmuel Azar continued to appear to Robbie in his dreams. Philip was filled with a fearful anger; without pause, his mind turned over foolhardy escape plans which were an expression of his subconscious thirst for vengeance: "Let me die with the Philistines. . . ."

Gradually, as the struggle for existence occupied their attention, their shock and grief wore off. But the sense of horror remained; it reappeared each day, with every confrontation with the realities of prison—the cruelty, the bestiality, and the humiliations on the part of both guards and convicts, who displayed a treacherous selfishness and antagonism. "From the very first day," recalls Philip, "we realized that many of the prisoners would have been very pleased to see us thrown into the punishment cells."

This hostility stemmed from a mixture of motives: There was antagonism toward *hawagat*, hatred for the Jews, envy of those who had more, even though the five men were the most impoverished inmates of Block 1, without any money or contacts in the prison, and the anger of the lowly against those who preserve their dignity.

The five men did, indeed, preserve their dignity, in spite of all the indignity stemming from their status as *iradin*. They walked slowly and carefully, feeling their way without standing out or attracting attention, but refusing to humble themselves before the guards or "superior" prisoners. Above all, they were united, constantly fortifying and encouraging one another. Now that they were all housed in the same cell, it was only natural for them to establish a "commune," sharing their money and their possessions. But they shared more than material objects. "We shared a common fate," says Robbie. "We knew that our chances of survival depended on our ability to maintain our unity. And so, without talking about it, without planning it, we set up a social unit in which each individual was responsible for the group, and the group was responsible for each individual. If one of us showed signs of dejection, the others would hasten to encourage him; if someone discovered an inner weakness within himself, he would endeavor to repress it, so as to avoid infecting the others." Maintaining their unity required daily efforts and incessant concessions to one another. There were times when an individual would make demands of himself which the others would not have dared to present. "But the fact is that in the course of fourteen years of imprisonment, we didn't have one single serious quarrel. There were arguments, for sure. But someone would give in before the argument degenerated into a quarrel." It was this mutual aid, more than anything else, which kept them going throughout their prolonged imprisonment.

They were saddened by the hostility they encountered in Tura. No sooner had Meir Za'afran acquired a *tau-tau* and a little tea than someone informed on him. But they could comprehend this antagonism. During the months they had spent in the military prison, their contacts with the soldier conscripts had opened their eyes to the burning hatreds which underlay the calm, smiling surface of their country. The soldiers hated their officers, the poor hated the rich, the villagers hated the townspeople, and all of them together hated the *hawagat*, the aliens. What they found hard to digest was the enmity of the Communists.

There were about thirty individuals arrested as Communists in Block 1, having recently been transferred from Block 4, following a hunger strike they staged against being obliged to work in the quarry. They were of a much higher standard than the average convict. Their number included a doctor (Sharif Hatata) and a lawyer (Sa'ad a Din Kamel, whose wife, Marie Rosenthal, was confined together with Marcelle). The workers among them were also fine individuals, inspired with an awareness of their mission and devoted to their cause.

Robbie: "Naturally, we were pleased to meet them. These were people whose personal and cultural background resembled ours. We hoped to establish friendly relations, but we were in for a disappoint-ment. They decided to take advantage of our presence so as to demon-strate their Egyptian patriotism to the other prisoners. They boycotted us."

Dr. Hatata, the leader of the group, tried to explain matters to Robbie in a "diplomatic" manner. "Look, we and you hold conflicting views. Consequently, it will be better to avoid coming into contact, so as to forestall any friction . . ."

Unlike the Communists, the members of the Moslem Brotherhood were friendly toward the five men, remembering their helpfulness in the military prison. But even their attitude was not unambiguous.

The Brotherhood members were the largest single group in Tura. About three hundred of them were housed in Block 1, and there were another five hundred in Block 4. They were not popular with the other prisoners. In 1955, they were regarded as the most dangerous "enemies of the people," and the regime mobilized its propaganda machine to make them into detested outcasts.

Block 1 contained most of their leaders and activists, including all six members of the Maktab el Irshad (the leadership), with whom the network members maintained excellent relations. At the same time, the rank-and-file members were given secret instructions to keep away from "the Jews." The Brotherhood was also concerned about its "patri-otic image". . .

Block 1 also contained prisoners who were neither Communists nor members of the Moslem Brotherhood nor criminals. One of these was Abdul Maksud, a workers' leader from Mahlat el Kubra, the large textile center in the Delta, halfway between Cairo and Alexandria. In 1954, Mahlat el Kubra was the scene of the first workers' uprising against the officers' regime. The textile works were closed for several days while the workers demonstrated for higher wages. The authorities cracked down with an iron fist; gunfire was directed at the demonstra-tors and their leaders were arrested, with two being condemned to death and others receiving long prison sentences. Maksud was sen-tenced to fifteen years.

A sly egoist, Maksud succeeded in preserving his neutrality be-tween the Communists and the Moslem Brotherhood. He was pious in his behavior and diligently attended worship every Friday, without joining the Brotherhood; at the same time, he extolled the class struggle among the "criminals" without identifying with the Communists. All the same, both groups maintained close relations with him and helped him with cigarettes and food.

He was antagonistic toward the "Zionist spies," though that did not prevent him from taking advantage of their help. In time, when they got settled in Tura and learned how to acquire prohibited articles, they set up a small "pharmacy" in their cell, which freed them of the necessity of using the prison dispensary with its infections and its bullying, corrupt orderlies. Their "pharmacy" contained various pills, and they even had a syringe and injections. Meir Meyuhas, whose mother was a qualified nurse, taught Victor how to make injections; in time, Victor grew so proficient that the other convicts regarded him as a veritable "doctor," and preferred to have "the *Yahud*" attend to their pains and illnesses rather than go to the prison dispensary. Abdul Maksud was a frequent client of "Doctor" Victor, who gave him fortifying injections. But this did not prevent Maksud from inciting the *nabatshin* against the Jewish prisoners. It was shameful for good Egyptians to serve the "Jewish traitors," he would tell them, and, being an experienced propagandist and demagogue, his words bore fruit. One day, the members of the network discovered that all their *nabatshin* had left them. However, their strike was short-lived; their Egyptian patriotism was not as potent as the Jews with their cigarettes, and one after another, they returned to work.

### In the Shadow of the Gabal

Their *irad* status lasted for precisely one month; during this time, the members of the network were not required to work at the *gabal*. They spent the time looking around, learning prison customs and practices, and preparing their battle for existence in this hostile environment.

The cell doors were opened at seven every morning. The other blocks would then witness a frenzied bustle, for it was only a few minutes before the prisoners were paraded to be taken to work. But the inmates of Block 1 did not work in the quarries, and they had time for a *"kardal* procession" and a leisurely wash before going to work in the prison workshops and service installations at eight o'clock. Those not required to work remained free in the courtyard till ten, when they were ordered back to their cells. This was when they received their daily ration of three pittas. At twelve, they received their sole hot meal of the day—a stew of beans or lentils—and the cells were locked up. At four in the afternoon, they were allowed out into the courtyard again. The forthcoming hour, with the workers returning from their jobs, was "market time." Convicts employed in the carpentry sold wooden clogs which they had manufactured surreptitiously, sharing their profits with the guards in charge. The tinsmiths sold *tau-tau,* the small kerosene stoves made out of empty cans which gave off more stench than heat, but which could be coaxed, with a little patience, into boiling water for tea, or warming up food. The men employed in the kitchen smuggled out chunks of meat or a handful of dry rice, concealed beneath their filthy uniforms, while those working in the vegetable garden occasionally succeeded in bringing in some fresh vegetables.

However, the most sought-after articles were sugar and tea, and, of course, hashish. These were handled by a number of "wholesalers," though other prisoners also succeeded at times in smuggling in a standard 36-gram tea bag, usually concealed in the anal orifice. It was reported that one prisoner, on returning from the hospital, brought in no fewer than six such bags, wrapped in nylon. However, this was a dangerous method, for there were times when an operation was required to remove the bag; furthermore, the guards in partnership with the "wholesalers" were very severe with "independent" smugglers.

However, the traffic in tea, and even more so, in hashish, brought in a good profit which sufficed for all those involved. The fact is that even at the worst times, there was no shortage of tea or hashish in the prison.

Throughout the month that the network members learned the ropes of prison life, they were continually aware of the *gabal,* a long ridge on the horizon, divided from the prison by about four kilometers of barren flats, a somber menace. All the inmates of Block 1 feared the *gabal.* They told of the hard, backbreaking labor, of the dangers of frequent avalanches, and of the cruelty and harshness of the guard-supervisors. Ways of evading work in the quarry were the principal topic of interest for the convicts. When the network members were summoned for medical examinations to determine their fitness for work in the quarry, they were overwhelmed with advice on how to fool the doctor into granting them "grade B," which would give them permanent release from the *gabal,* or, at the very least, a temporary *mulahza.*

However, the prison doctor, the one-eyed Dr. Abdul Kader, showed a violent and bitter hatred for the convicts. Years ago, a prisoner went berserk and gouged out one of his eyes. When the network members were brought before him, he fixed his single eye on them in a furious stare and muttered: "D'you suffer from any ailment?" Without waiting for an answer or paying any attention to Philip who mumbled something about his cardiac murmur, he ordered them to undress. He weighed them, took their temperature, checked whether they were suffering from venereal disease, and that was all. "To the quarry!"

Now that their fate was settled, the other prisoners tried to console them. "It's not so bad, you can get by, even at the *gabal.* The work's hard, but for the price of a cigarette, you can get the others to do your work for you. . . ."

"To tell the truth," relates Victor, "I had no need of their reassurances. I was still shocked and numb from the executions, and I felt indifferent to everything." As for Robbie, he was filled with curiosity about this *gabal* which everyone feared so deeply. "I wanted to meet the challenge."

What really worried them was that now they were posted to work, they would be transferred to Block 4, which, they had already learned, was the prison's worst, both in its living conditions and in the human material housed there. They were housed in large dormitories, which were crowded and unbelievably filthy; they were subject to the rule of the strong-arm men who had taken control of each dormitory. The prisoners—almost all "criminals"—came from the lowest stratum of Egyptian society. Since all the inmates of Block 4 worked in the quarry, with very few employed in the service installations and workshops, there was little smuggling and the choice of goods in its "market" was scant. "We had already learned that without the addition of 'black market' food, we would have very poor prospects of keeping our strength and health during the years of hard labor awaiting us."

However, they were fortunate. The day before they were due to go to the *gabal*, the *mudir* decided that since they were "dangerous" and required "special supervision," it would be better if they remained in Block 1, with other "enemies of the regime."

They had another stroke of luck: leg irons were abolished one or two days before they were due to go to the quarry. "That was a great relief," confesses Victor."We were worried about how we'd stand up to the hard labor awaiting us if we had to carry heavy weights on our legs." Philip, who never stopped working out daredevil escape plans, was highly encouraged.

Twenty days after reaching Tura, they were taken to the prison office for *tasnia* (vocational classification). The convicts employed at the *gabal* were divided up into hundred-man work brigades, each one "specializing" in some particular task. There were the *hagra* (stones) groups, whose job it was to knock down the rock face, using explosives or sharp metal spikes; there were the *kassra* (breakers) who used sledgehammers to smash up the large rocks brought down by the *hagra;* and there were the *atlin* (porters) who picked up the quarried stones and carried them out to waiting railway cars. The *atlin*'s job was considered the hardest, while that of the *kassra* was the most dangerous, because they worked at the bottom of the quarry, where falling rocks often caused injuries and even fatalities. Most of the time they worked in the quarry, the members of the network belonged to the *kassra*. When incidents on the Israeli-Egyptian border grew more frequent on the eve of the Suez war, the prison officers openly incited the other convicts against "the Zionist spies whose brethren are killing your brethren," whereupon rock falls in the quarry became so frequent that they could no longer be regarded as accidental. "It was quite clear that the *hagra* men were out to kill us," says Victor.

In the *tasnia*, the five men were separated and allotted to different *gamlat* (work squads), depending on the severity of their sentences. The first three *gamlat* consisted of convicts serving life sentences, but *gamla* 1 was made up entirely of Moslem Brotherhood members. Consequently, Victor was posted to *gamla* 2 and Philip to *gamla* 3. Robbie was allotted to *gamla* 6, while the two Meirs were sent to *gamla* 7. From the tales of the other convicts, they already knew that the lower the number of the *gamla,* the harder the work it had to perform.

"Tomorrow you go out to work," the duty officer notified them.

The following morning, they rose early. When the cell door was opened, they were ready, each one with his pitta under his arm. Not knowing where to go, they remained standing in the doorway until a furious guard appeared: "Are you the Jews? Hurry up, the *gabal* is going out!"

They marched after him to a large parade ground at the edge of the prison complex. Thousands of prisoners were already congregated there, divided up into *gamlat,* in rows of five, all squatting on the ground. At the far end of the parade ground stood a wooden structure, the quarry office; outside it, a fleshy major was seated on a chair. Armed soldiers surrounded the parade ground. In between the rows of squatting prisoners, Capt. Hussein Zacci, the deputy commander of the *gabal,* trotted up and down on a horse. The guard halted in front of him and announced: "I have brought the Jews."

The officer flung them a glance of disdain and hostility. "What is your *tasnia?*" he asked them sharply. When they told him, he turned his horse around and galloped to the hut; from afar, they could see him in conversation with the major, and then he galloped back. "Attach the Jews to the *murkabin* group!" he ordered on approaching.

The *murkabin* were prisoners caught attempting to escape. The punishment for this offense—in addition to a murderous beating—was one or two years in the punishment cells. But even there, they were not released from work at the *gabal;* on the contrary, they were required to fulfill a double daily quota of work each day, after which they were taken back to their punishment cells for the night.

"We didn't yet know what the *murkabin* were," Victor relates. "The guard guided us to a spot where two prisoners were squatting on their own. Their uniform did not resemble that of the other prisoners; theirs was red with black stripes running crosswise to mark them out from the rest and ensure that they were under constant supervision. We squatted down beside them. We sensed that being attached to them did not presage well for us, but we consoled ourselves with the thought that at least we were together."

The guards counted the prisoners, and then reported to a *sol* (sergeant major) with a pointed moustache. The latter then roared to the captain on his horse: "One thousand five hundred men going out to the *gabal,* and five Jews, sir." Henceforth, this became a regular practice: The Jews were counted separately. When one of them fell ill and did not report for work—whereupon the *sol* reported only "four Jews"— the convicts were not marched off to work without a guard being sent to the block to bring the missing man, who would have to convince Hussein Zacci that he had the doctor's permission to absent himself. "It was clear that the commander of the *gabal* had instructions to keep us under special supervision."

With the *sol* striding at their head, the long column of prisoners moved off and marched out of the prison gateway. Mounted soldiers took up positions on both sides of the column. They crossed the Cairo-Helwan highway which passed by the prison, and the nearby railway line, and halted for a further *tamam* (count). Before they resumed their march, the *sol* proclaimed: "From here on, any prisoner leaving the column will be shot instantly. You have been warned!" He repeated this warning every morning. When they began to march again, Robbie tried to talk to the two *murkabin* next to him, but they looked unfriendly. They must have guessed that it was not to their advantage that the Jews had been attached to them.

They were right. When the prisoners reached the quarry, there was a further count, and then the *gamlat* dispersed to their various places. The *murkabin,* followed by the five Jews and an armed guard, headed for a large booth occupied by a *gamla* of stone cutters. The thatched shed was the only shady spot in the quarry, and stone cutting was regarded as the easiest of the jobs, being allotted to the veteran prisoners nearing the end of their period of hard labor. The *murkabin* were only attached to them because it was easier to keep an eye on them there.

The members of the network thought they had again enjoyed a stroke of luck. They were given hammers and ordered to hack out curb stones. But shortly afterward, Hussein Zacci galloped past the booth and noticed them. With a wave of his riding switch, he summoned the guard to report to him, which the man hastened to do. When he came back, his face was twisted in fury. "Down!" he roared. "To the pit!"

The "pit"—the lowest part of the quarry—was set aside for the *hamra* (red) squad, prisoners who had committed serious infringements of discipline, such as pilfering food or attacking a guard. The prison authorities punished these men even more cruelly than the *murkabin.*

They were issued red uniforms, a little lighter than those worn by men condemned to death, and their clothing marked them out as open to any form of abuse. Working in the "pit" was a most cruel punishment in itself. The heat in the "pit" was intense and exhausting; it induced an enormous thirst, but the *hamra* were forbidden to approach the tank of drinking water which stood under the booth. Their work was also backbreaking: They had to carry the heavy stones up the steep slope to the railway cars. On top of all that, the *hamra* were entrusted to the most vicious of the guards.

"Even in the 'pit,' the seven of us were a distinct group, with 'our own' guard. We were ordered to carry stones to the waiting railway car; every hundred-man *gamla* had to fill up one car, and the seven of us were also expected to complete the same quota. The stones were big and heavy; they cut into our shoulders, which were soon covered with bleeding cuts. Climbing up the steep slope, the soil gave way beneath our feet and we would slither backward. The guard urged us on incessantly: 'Hurry up, hurry up! The train's got to go!' When he heard us tell one of the *hamra* not to load us down with such heavy stones, the guard became hysterical. 'You want to have me put in the iron?' (There was a large iron cross in front of the prison office, and disobedient prisoners were shackled to it, the length of time depending on the severity of their offense.) 'The officer said you were to carry heavy stones!' I bit my lip to contain the curse which was on the tip of my tongue. I said to myself: 'I'll hold out, even if it's the end of me!' "

The "pit" became the arena for a silent contest between the five men and their bullying guard. The astonished *hamra* ceased their work and watched the *hawagat* groaning beneath the weight of their stones as they climbed up the slope, stumbling and slipping and climbing up again. "Their" railway car filled up with disheartening slowness. The more experienced prisoners had learned how to lay the stones in the car with empty spaces between them, thereby reducing the quota of stones needed to fill it up. But the five men had yet to "learn the trade." Fearful of the guard, they filled the car to overflowing. At midday, when they were led out of the "pit" for the lunchtime *tamam,* Philip collapsed helpless, mumbling: "It would have been better to go to the scaffold . . ."

At four o'clock in the afternoon, the convicts formed up into a column to march back to the prison. The five network members were exhausted, and each of them had large wounds on his neck and shoulders. But they had won the contest. The other prisoners gazed at them in admiration.

At the gateway into the prison, there was another *tamam,* followed by a search. The *gabal* was one of the smuggling routes into the prison.

The engine driver would bring in a newspaper and sell it to the highest bidder (this was before prisoners were permitted to subscribe to a newspaper). The quarry *boloks* (sentries) sold tea to the convicts.

"Dozens of courtyard guards were standing in the gateway, awaiting us. Each prisoner hurried to 'his own' guard, with whom he shared his contraband gains. But we were 'clean,' and so worn out that the only thing we wanted was to get to our cell and stretch out on the *borsh.*"

An hour or two of rest restored their spirits somewhat. In the meantime, reports of their hard work spread through the block and visitors began to come to their cell, to express their admiration and proffer advice. Their Alexandria *baladiat* told them: "In your group, there's an old convict, a Saidi [inhabitant of Upper Egypt] by the name of Abdul Na'im. He did thirty years for murder, was released, and immediately committed another murder. He is an *umda,* and the other prisoners respect him. Give him one pound, and he will arrange to have the *kassra* in the 'pit' break the stones smaller for you."

"We didn't want to beg for favors," recalls Victor, "and we didn't have too much money. But that first day convinced us that we wouldn't be able to hold out. Swallowing my pride, I bribed a guard to take me to Block 4, to this Abdul Na'im. I found him in a three-man cell; he had washed and, dressed in his recreation clothes, was seated cross-legged on his mattress, smoking peacefully. He was thin, his head was shaven, and he had an enormous moustache dangling down on either side of his mouth. I told him that I had come because I'd heard that he could solve problems.

"He was flattered by the fact that one of the *hawagat* was requesting his assistance. He invited me to sit down. 'Was it hard?' he asked, sympathetically. I confessed that it was hard. 'Your guard is a son-of-a-bitch!' he shouted. 'I told him to treat you gently, but that damned officer threatened to chain him to the iron!'

"You have to know how to address a Saidi. They are the most backward people in Egypt, but very proud. 'You'll know what to do,' I told him. 'Help us and we will reward you.'

"He pretended to be hurt. 'Reward? Heaven forbid! But it'll cost you one and a half pounds. Not for me! The money's for the *kassra* at the bottom of the pit, so they load you up with small stones. Aside from that, bring the guard breakfast every morning.' "

Victor returned to his cell and consulted his companions. Abdul Na'im's price sounded very excessive. But what was the alternative? They thought it over, counted their money, reckoned what they needed to keep body and soul together till the next visit by their parents, and decided that they had to pay.

The following day, they went out to work with a tin of sardines and a packet of cigarettes. Before clambering down into the "pit," they shoved one and half pounds into Abdul Na'im's hand. Up to the ten o'clock breakfast break, everything proceeded as on the previous day; in fact, it was worse, because the cuts on their shoulders were becoming inflamed.

"After the ten o'clock *tamam,* when we sat down in the shade of the booth, I brought out the packet of cigarettes and offered one to the guard. He accepted it, but with a scowl. Nor did he smile when he took the *krawana* full of sardines we offered him. We had to make do with bread and onions. Till then, Abdul Na'im had been walking around among the *kassra* and whispering to them. Now he came and sat down beside us. 'It's all right,' he told us. 'I've talked to them and they'll break the stones smaller.' Turning to the guard, he said: 'Leave 'em alone!' "

When they returned to the pit, Abdul Na'im placed Robbie among the *kassra,* while he brought the others donkey cushions to put on their shoulders, to prevent the stones from cutting into their flesh. For a few minutes, everything went well, until the guard imagined that Hussein Zacci was watching him through his binoculars, whereupon he panicked and sent Robbie back to the *atlin,* at the same time taking away the saddles."

And so it went on, day after day. They used to return to the prison in the evening, worn out and exhausted; they could scarcely find the strength to wash the dust off their faces and legs before collapsing onto their mats. It was only because they knew that they had to eat to keep their strength up that they opened up a tin and listlessly consumed its contents. Ceaselessly, they asked one another: "What can we do? We can't go on like this for long." They gave their guard an even more lavish breakfast. They even gave him cash, but it was all in vain. The guard—his name was Abdul Karim—took whatever they offered him, but his fear of the officer was greater than his avarice.

"What drove us out of our minds was the knowledge that every other prisoner could get by with five cigarettes," says Robbie. "We were the only ones who couldn't. It was humiliating."

Equally humiliating was the commiseration of the other prisoners, who came to console the unfortunate *hawagat.* "We knew that they were glad to see our suffering; consequently, we didn't complain, so as not to give them greater pleasure. When they overwhelmed us with useless advice on how to evade work on the *gabal,* we pretended that we liked being out there in the fresh air, rather than in the stench of the prison."

Among those who came to proffer advice was the Saidi *umda,* Abdul Na'im, who felt that his prestige had suffered from his failure to get the five men "fixed up." His advice was: "Do what the Communists did; proclaim a hunger strike. True, they spent eleven days in the punishment cells, but they got their way. Now, they work at stone cutting, in the shade of the booth."

They were sorely tempted to take his advice. However, after consulting among themselves, the five men concluded that it was too risky. The Communists enjoyed some backing, particularly since the Czech arms deal. But who would stand behind the Israeli spies?

Consequently, they bore their fate stoically. Gradually, without being highlighted by any dramatic event, their sufferings were alleviated. Their muscles hardened and they grew accustomed to the hard work; the guards and officers at the *gabal* were rotated, with Hussein Zacci being replaced by another officer, a Copt, who was less strict. Another favorable development occurred when Meir Za'afran fell ill, and the prison officer released him from work in the quarry; instead, he was transferred to the mat workshop within the prison, enabling him to return to the cell early and prepare supper before the return of his companions from the *gabal*. He also made contact with the "market," where he purchased tea and sugar. With the workshop's civilian supervisor returning to his Cairo home daily, Meir even succeeded in smuggling a letter out to his family; after that, the supervisor smuggled letters in and out of the prison. The families in Alexandria also took advantage, bringing their letters, written on fine paper, to the Za'afran family; every week or two, the supervisor would collect them and smuggle them into the prison in the false bottom of a matchbox. "They weren't proper letters," relates Robbie, "just a few lines. But when you got back from the *gabal* and found a letter from home, there could be no greater happiness."

Later on, Meir Meyuhas incurred a gall bladder infection, and he was also released from work, remaining in the cell to clean up and protect it from thieves.

But the greatest improvement was brought about by the passage of time. As their period of imprisonment dragged on, they gradually merged with the general mass of prisoners. They were still different, they were still *hawagat*, but their presence in the prison was no longer a sensational novelty. Guards and prisoners alike grew accustomed to them, and habit bred indifference.

But that was true so long as nothing occurred on the outside to focus the spotlights on them again. With the arrival of every new officer who wished to flex his muscles, or whenever there was a serious incident on the Israeli border, or an Israeli reprisal raid—such events were frequent throughout 1955 and 1956—everyone recalled that they were "Israeli agents." Hussein Zacci, who returned for an additional spell of duty as officer in command of the *gabal*, would gallop alongside the column of prisoners going out to work and, pointing his riding switch at the members of the network, shout: "Their brethren are murdering your brethren . . . God help anyone who gives them a hand!" At that, the frightened guards would again become cruel taskmasters; the *kassra* gave them the heaviest stones to carry; at the gateway into the prison, they were searched with particular care; and wherever they went, oaths and curses followed them.

## Escape

These ordeals and the way they faced them—without demeaning themselves or grousing, but with a quiet courage and the determination to hold out—helped the five men to establish themselves in the prison, giving them that most valuable asset in all human relations: respect.

Respect brought friendship. They made the acquaintance of Gino a week after being sent to the *gabal.* Gino, an Alexandrian of Maltese extraction, was serving a long prison term for armed robbery. He was an old-timer on the *gabal;* after completing a three-year spell there, he was accused of attempting to escape and sent back to the quarry for a further period, this time, with the *murkabin* group.

The escape attempt in which he took part was one of the rare efforts of its kind in the whole history of Tura, and the only one to succeed, at least partially. The other participants were a former Greek officer by the name of Petro, who had deserted from the British army at the end of the world war and become a daring bank robber; his Egyptian friend and partner, Fathi abu Talb, an equally bold criminal who, moreover, displayed Communist leanings (he regarded himself as an Egyptian Robin Hood, claiming that his robberies helped to bring about the downfall of capitalism); and the third member of the group, a gigantic Sudanese by the name of Bak'r, who "operated" in the Suez area, specializing in thefts from British army camps. He possessed enormous physical strength, bending window bars with his bare hands; he was nicknamed "the Suez Monster."

These three men were housed together on the fourth floor of Block 1, where they planned their breakout. Fathi abu Talb began by finding some pretext to get himself transferred to the Istianuff prison in Cairo, from where he succeeded in establishing contact with the Communist underground and preparing hiding places for himself and his companions. Sending a message to Tura that everything was ready, he immediately made his getaway. He sawed through the bars of his cell and jumped from the second-floor window. Even though he was badly bruised, he managed to make his escape and reach Port Said, where his Communist friends concealed him for two months before he was caught and brought back to Tura.

After Fathi's transfer to Istianuff, Gino was housed in the cell in his place, in accordance with the rule that a cell could house either one prisoner or at least three (so as to provide an eyewitness if one of the prisoners should kill another). Gino was also made privy to the escape plan and consented to take part.

They gained the trust of the guard on duty on their floor, from whom they got hold of the key to their cell, which they copied in soap; Petro, who was employed in the workshop, then made an additional key.

On the night of their breakout, they made sure the guard on duty slept soundly by offering him a cigarette "loaded" with hashish. Then they opened the cell door and clambered up onto the roof of the block. From here, a number of parallel telephone wires led to the prison office building, outside the wall surrounding the block. Following the plan, Petro laid a mat across the wires, laid himself down on it, and began to pull himself forward until he had traversed the thirty yards to the roof of the office building. He was followed by Bak'r, but when it came to Gino's turn, the latter lost his nerve, gave up the idea of escape, and returned to his cell.

This did not help him the following day, when the breakout was discovered. The *mudir* did not believe his story about the others threatening him with a knife to prevent his calling the guards, and sentenced him to a year and a half in the punishment cells.

(After sliding down off the roof of the office building, Petro and Bak'r immediately parted company. Petro was caught two days later; Bak'r succeeded in hiding out for two months in a Sudanese laborers' camp on the outskirts of Cairo, until he too was caught. Both men were brought back to Tura and flung into the punishment cells, and they were still there when the members of the network were similarly confined at the outbreak of the Suez war. Fathi abu Talb also joined them there, and the three men again planned a breakout, inviting the members of the network to join them. "But," says Philip, "with outsiders, we weren't even prepared to talk of escape.")

Robbie: "We liked Gino from the first glance. He was about twenty-eight, modest, quiet, and refined. Like all the Europeans of Alexandria, he spoke perfect French. What made us like him immediately was his external appearance; he was neat and clean. He was alone in Egypt (his family had emigrated to Australia, and they only reestablished contact with him years later, by means of the Red Cross) and therefore received no money from outside. Consequently, he could not afford to buy a made-to-order uniform; nevertheless, he unstitched the shabby uniform issued to him and painstakingly sewed it up again until it looked tolerable, subsequently washing it whenever he had a chance. He was in difficult straits in prison without any money. Without cigarettes and unable to supplement his prison rations with the few provisions available in the canteen, he kept his dignity. He did not beg favors, refused gifts, and did not fall for the temptation of becoming the 'mistress' of some wealthy convict.

"We made friends with him. We gave him cigarettes, and when we observed that he suffered from the cold, Philip asked his parents to bring him a polo jersey, the only article of civilian clothing prisoners were permitted to wear, so long as it was blue like the prison uniform. He repaid us by displaying exceptional loyalty."

Later, when Gino completed his sentence in the punishment cells and was transferred to Block 1—meanwhile a group of British intelligence agents had reached the prison—Victor persuaded the two Englishmen who headed it, James Zarb and James Swinbourne, to take Gino into their cell as the third inmate.

## Passover in Prison

Their first Passover in prison was drawing near.

They were so occupied with their struggle for survival that they lost count of time, and they completely forgot the ancient festival of freedom, which now took on redoubled significance for them. However, about a week before Passover, Meir Za'afran received a visit from his parents, who told him of the efforts being made by the Cairo Jewish community to permit them to observe the festival properly, and of the request sent to the prison authorities, to allow matza to be brought in to the Jewish convicts. It was thus that they learned of the date of the festival.

However, the day came and nothing occurred. On the eve of the festival, they were led out as usual to the work procession. There, however, they plucked up the courage to approach the officer and make their protest: "Today is a Jewish festival, and we're entitled to a day of rest, like the Moslems and Copts on their festivals." They could not tell the officer that they knew of the letter from the Jewish community, which had reached the prison authorities.

The officer feigned innocence. "I know of nothing. The regulations make no mention of any such festival."

They went off to work. But at midday, a runner arrived from the prison office with instructions to send them back. "Parents' visit."

It transpired that the families from Alexandria, knowing that regulations permitted prisoners to receive an extra visit on festivals, had arrived at the prison, burdened down with a festive meal, with packets of matza and Passover dishes. When they were not allowed in, they went to the prison office to complain, whereupon it turned out that the prison service had indeed sent instructions to permit the Jews to observe the first and seventh days of Passover in accordance with their religious customs. The regulations even stated that non-Jews were forbidden to touch the Passover dishes; for the first time, food was brought into the prison without being examined. "All of a sudden, we were rich. We had so much food that enough was left over to give out to other prisoners with whom we were friendly."

The episode was repeated on Yom Kippur of that year. Once again, the prison service sent a letter which was ignored by the Tura administration. Hussein Zacci, the commander of the *gabal,* scowled when he was told that the regulations permitted them to remain in their cell that day.

"I don't understand this nonsense," he said. "You have too many festivals!" Seizing on the fact that their hair had begun to grow again, he sent for the barber to shave their heads.

They went off to work. But at the same time, they were firmly resolved to fast that day, whatever happened. That evening, they withdrew into their cell and offered up a prayer of particular fervor.

Religious observance was one of the few subjects on which they disagreed. Philip and Meir Meyuhas attached no value to religious tradition, whereas Robbie and Meir Za'afran came from Orthodox homes, and they themselves were strictly observant prior to their arrest. As for Victor: "Up to the age of sixteen, I was fervently religious. I even intended to become a rabbi. But then I grew out of it."

However, in prison, they all sensed an inner need to maintain their Jewishness. Only three of them—Meir Za'afran, Victor, and Robbie—read the daily prayers from a prayerbook they had gotten hold of. But the Sabbath was observed by all five. Even though they went to work on Saturday, as on any other day of the week, on Sabbath eve, they would withdraw to their cell, where Victor read out a short extract from the French Bible he had acquired at the Sigan Harbi; after that, they sat down to a meal which was a little more "festive" than their usual suppers. Robbie was the heaviest smoker among the group, but throughout fourteen years of imprisonment, he scrupulously refrained from smoking on the Sabbath.

Their physical exertions began to make their mark on them; they lost weight progressively. Philip, who weighed 155 pounds on arrival at Tura, went down to 123; Robbie, who was shorter, reduced to 121 pounds.

Regulations affirmed that a prisoner who lost more than ten kilos (22 pounds) was regarded as sick and entitled to special treatment. But when they went to the doctor, he did no more than prescribe "special food," a thin meat soup, and that was only for one week. Even when they all contracted dysentery, they did not receive medical attention. "Some prisoners were in the habit of buying the excrement of a dysentery patient and bringing it to the medical orderly, together with a pack of cigarettes, which 'earned' them a *mulahza;* this procured them not only release from work but also better food and a mattress. But the orderly was not authorized to treat us; we had to go to the doctor himself; as soon as he realized that he was dealing with 'the Zionist spies,' he became wary. It was like that with everything: The Egyptian officer is quite capable of closing his eyes and giving tacit permission for all kinds of privileges, but the moment he has to sign his name, no matter where, he is afraid to accept responsibility."

It was at this period that the five men began to build up their "private pharmacy." Their parents brought them antidiarrhea pills and vitamin tablets; later, when they suspected that their ailments stemmed from the water drawn from the well in the prison courtyard, they also received tablets to disinfect the water. Their store of medicines grew. True, from time to time the guards conducted regular searches of the cells, and if the officer was in a bad mood that particular day, he would have the whole stock of medicines confiscated. But it was not long before they began to accumulate a new store.

Sharp-tongued and daring as ever, Philip never stopped thinking up escape plans. But these plans were fruitless. They had long ago resolved to escape, but they were determined to do so only after their parents left Egypt, so as not to serve as hostages for the authorities. At every visit, the subject was mentioned cautiously, but their parents did not want to hear of the notion. Their plans were put off.

But in the meantime, Philip continued to survey his surroundings, to learn how the prison was guarded, and also whether there were any prospects of drawing the other prisoners into an organized uprising or a mass breakout.

One day, he was given an opportunity. Tahr—one of the participants in the Mannering nightclub robbery—approached Hussein Zacci and complained that he was sick and unable to work. Zacci began to whip him with his riding switch. Instinctively, Tahr struck back, and all the guards standing in the vicinity flung themselves at him with their clubs. The other prisoners stopped work and gazed at the onslaught, whereupon Philip whispered to those next to him: "Make a noise, shout!"

The convicts began to utter belly growls, and their growling spread; within seconds, a thousand convicts were snarling, the sound reverberating like an earthquake. Hussein Zacci, panicking, ordered the guards to leave Tahr alone. Later, on their return from the *gabal,* Tahr was flung into the punishment cells, where Hussein Zacci gave him a merciless beating, but Philip had learned the lesson: Given the right opportunity, the convicts could be made to mutiny, although he was not certain how long they would hold out.

"By nature, the Egyptian tends to bow to those in authority. He hates his officer but obeys him. In all the years I spent in prison, I witnessed only one single instance of a convict telling a prison officer what he thought of him. It was an *umda* of long standing who lost his temper and shouted at an officer: 'Outside, you wouldn't deserve to be my dog!' But in that case, the officer was black, a long-service *sol* who took advantage of the revolution to attain officer's rank. However much the propagandists extol the equality and fraternity of Islam's believers, in Egypt, a black man remains a slave."

Not long after, when the Copt captain again replaced Hussein Zacci as the officer in charge of the *gabal,* Philip himself was involved in a similar incident which was within a hairbreadth of ending badly for him. He was working down in the "pit"— not carrying stones up to the railway car but collecting small stones so as to prepare the quarry for the next blast. His work was supervised by the *ra'is el gabal*—a guard who was an expert in quarrying.

Philip: "That day, he picked on me for some reason. Suddenly, he stood over me and brought his long stick down hard on my arm, shouting: 'D'you call this work? Why aren't you working?' He always bullied the convicts, but this was the first time he had ever raised his stick at one of us. The blood went to my head. Without thinking, I snatched the stick out of his hand and flung myself at him. The other prisoners dragged me off him, and the guards attacked me with their clubs. Victor appeared out of nowhere and he too jumped into the melee, lashing out right and left."

By the time the *gabal* officer, attracted by the shouting, arrived on the scene, the two men had received a thorough thrashing, but they consoled themselves at the sight of the *ra'is el gabal*—his clothes torn, covered with dust, and with one eye blackened. Furiously, he demanded Philip's blood. "If prisoners are allowed to hit me," he huffed and puffed, "that's the end of my work here on the *gabal!*"

"What do you have to say?" the officer asked Philip.

Philip had managed to calm down a little. "You see," he said, pointing at his neck, which still bore the marks of the *ra'is*'s fingers, "he tried to kill me, and I defended myself. I demand an inquiry!"

The *ra'is* denied the charge, but the officer pronounced judgment.

"When we get back to the prison, they'll go to the punishment cells. And now, back to work!"

Robbie was not at work that day, but he still remembers the state in which his two companions returned to the prison. "Their clothes were torn and their backs bore the weals left by the guards' clubs. On their way to the punishment cells, they managed to tell us what had happened, and we immediately set off in a deputation to the *gabal* officer to intervene on their behalf. He said: 'They mutinied. They can thank their lucky stars that they got off with nothing more than the punishment cells.' But we replied: 'Our lives are in danger here, and the prison authorities are doing nothing.' We threatened that we would refuse to go to work on the *gabal* and that we'd go on a hunger strike; we demanded to have our complaint forwarded to the prison service. That was a well-tried tactic. No officer wanted to get involved in a scandal, because he knew that his superiors too were not interested in making a fuss, especially when it came from *hawagat* in whom the military intelligence displayed an interest. He began to give way, saying that he would persuade the *ra'is* to withdraw his complaint. 'What about the punishment cells?' we pressed further. 'They'll stay there for the night,' he said. 'Tomorrow, when they return from the *gabal*, they'll go back to their cell.' "

The officer succeeded in convincing the *ra'is* to withdraw his complaint, but it was far harder to convince Philip. He was breathing fire and brimstone, demanding a medical examination, a commission of inquiry, the Red Cross. . . . It was very hard to calm him down.

On his return to the block the day after the incident, Philip found himself the hero of the prison. The convicts, the younger ones particularly, congregated around him in open admiration. "That's the great guy who beat up the *ra'is el gabal!*"

Philip's hastiness produced another favorable outcome: Henceforth, the *ra'is el gabal* kept away from them and never addressed them again.

Either because of the Communist prisoners' hunger strike or because of the terrible overcrowding at Tura, the Harga detention camp was set up in the desert at the end of 1955 and the political detainees were transferred there.

Even though this meant an end to their work in the quarries, the rumors of their imminent transfer caused anxiety and tension among the convicts. "The rumors had it that we would be among those transferred," Robbie recalls. "We didn't know whether to be glad or sorry. On the one hand, we wanted to get out of the *gabal*, and even more, we wanted official acknowledgment that we were 'politicals.' On the other hand, transferring to the detention camp in the desert implied a change. Like the other prisoners, we had adopted a fundamentally pessimistic philosophy. Experience had taught us that no matter how bad the existing situation, it could always get worse. In consequence, we sensed both hope and fear."

In the end, they were not among those transferred. The transfer lasted several days, with a group of one hundred fifty to two hundred prisoners being sent off each day. In the morning, they were led out of their cells, with their belongings, and subjected to a thorough search. All the "property" which a prisoner had accumulated, stolen or smuggled in over the years, was suddenly taken away from him, and he had to start all over again.

When the transfers were completed, it transpired that all of the Communists had been sent off, with the exception of four (mistakenly registered in the prison records as members of the Moslem Brotherhood; despite years of attempts to correct the error, it remained in effect). Sa'ad Kamel was brought back to Tura through the intervention of his uncle, Propaganda Minister Fathi Radouan. As for the members of the Moslem Brotherhood, most of them were transferred to Harga, with the sole exception of their six-man leadership, the Maktab el Irshad, whose members remained on the fourth floor, together with several dozen less active Brotherhood members.

The cells in Block 1 vacated by the transfers were now filled with ordinary "criminals" from the other blocks. Only the fourth floor remained a "maximum security jail," and the members of the network were transferred up there. This was a marked improvement, because the fourth-floor cells were roomier and better aired, with a larger window, from which they could look out at the Nile and, on clear days, as far as the Pyramids. (In their previous cell, the prison wall blocked the view.) "It is hard to explain how the sight of a bit of landscape seen through a barred window can change the atmosphere. We would let our gaze linger on the green strip of vegetation along the Nile, watching the sails of the *falukat* glide above the treetops, and for a short moment, we could forget the fact that we were imprisoned."

The atmosphere changed in the prison as a whole, became more relaxed. It was only after the departure of the "politicals" that it became clear how their presence in the prison had engendered tensions. This is not surprising: The "political" is usually an educated man, capable of writing letters of complaint. He is also more prepared to fight for his rights and usually has those on the outside who can back up his struggle. At the same time, he also tends to jar on the sensitivities of those who flung him into prison because they regard him as a danger to themselves or their power. As long as the prison was full of "politicals," the officers were confused, nervy, and bad-tempered. Now that they had to deal with uncomplicated murderers and robbers, they calmed down again.

The block's second and third floor now filled up with "nonproblematic" prisoners of this variety. As before, the ground floor continued to house the *mulahza*—convicts under medical treatment. "We kept away from them," relates Robbie. "Most of them were suffering from infectious diseases such as tuberculosis, scabies, and a form of boil inflammation which caused their hair to fall out. They were entitled to supplementary food rations and to vitamins, but all these things soon found their way to the 'black market.' We endeavored to avoid using provisions from this source, and whenever we bought food, we tried to find out where it came from, though that wasn't always feasible."

The overcrowding on these three floors was excessive. Egypt's judicial apparatus continued to turn out new convicts at a feverish pace, while the prison was not extended. The only wing enlarged was that containing the punishment cells. When the existing cells could no longer contain all the prisoners condemned to incarceration, the *mulahza* were pushed out of one row of ground-floor cells and all crowded into the remaining row, while the row they vacated became an "offshoot" of the punitive wing, and that too soon filled up. Things reached such a pass that a cell measuring one and a half meters by two meters, originally intended for three ordinary prisoners or one man condemned to punitive detention, now housed as many as fifteen convicts sentenced to the cells. They had to take turns sleeping, and even then, they slept "on the sword"—in other words, on their sides. If one of them turned over in his sleep, he would wake up all his neighbors.

The overcrowding and the filth did not extend to the fourth floor, but the odors did. The air was perpetually laden with "jail stench"—the stink of unwashed sweat, mixed with the sharp aroma given off by the *kardals*, and the scents exuded by unaired bedding. "From that point of view," says Philip, "it was nice to go out to work on the *gabal*. There at least we were in the fresh air."

# 7

## THE SUEZ WAR

*Rising Hopes*

The fresh air was the only favorable feature of work in the quarries.

Now, late in 1955 and early in 1956, as tension rose on the Israeli border, there was a parallel rise in the hostility toward the "Zionist spies." Since his fight with Philip, the *ra'is el gabal* ignored them, but Capt. Hussein Zacci was again ranting about "their brethren are killing your brethren," and that was quite enough to stir up the primitive, subservient convicts. Over and over again, there were rockfalls which occurred precisely as the Jewish prisoners were at the bottom of the "pit." On one occasion, Victor sustained a head injury and was almost killed. Inside the block, too, they encountered venomous hostility. During this period, they did not need the guards' urgings to withdraw into their cell and bolt the door.

Even though the rising tension on the Israeli border ought to have forewarned them of what was about to happen, the Sinai campaign came as a surprise to them.

Robbie: "During the night of October 29, 1956, we suddenly heard the wailing of a siren from the nearby village, and the prison lights were extinguished. From the window, we could see searchlight beams probing the skies from the direction of Cairo. We didn't know what was happening, and it was too late at night to find out. The block had been locked up for the night, and the guards on duty knew no more than we. We thought it was a practice alert.

"The next morning, we went off to the *gabal*, like any other morning. But at ten, a runner arrived, bearing instructions to send us back to the block. As soon as we returned, we were confined to our cell and the door was locked. Before we could find out what was happening, the *mudir*—Col. al Helwani—arrived with his attendants.

" 'You Jews, all five of you, take your *nimra* [bedding] and go down to the punishment cells!'

"We were flabbergasted. What was this all about? What had we done?"

"Don't argue!" the *mudir* silenced them. "It's for your own good. There's a war on, and the punishment cells are the only place where you'll be safe!"

They tried to take their clothes with them, as well as the satchel with the "legal" tins they had bought at the canteen, but at the entrance to the punishment cells, they were all confiscated and taken away to be stored. "Such things are not permitted in the punishment cells!" To make matters worse, they were separated, each one being confined in a cell on his own (for which purpose a dozen *hamra*—red-uniformed disciplinary offenders—were dislodged from their cells and housed together).

"We wanted to protest. We wanted to tell the supervisor of the punishment cells that we had been brought here for our own safety, not for punishment. But the tension around was so great that we thought better of it and said nothing."

For a number of days—the first few days of the war—the Jewish prisoners were confined to their cells, not allowed out other than for a hasty *"kardal* procession" in the morning. The guards were sullen and hostile, and the prisoners' questions were answered with a curse or silence. "The atmosphere reminded us of the Sigan Harbi, only this time, we weren't beaten."

There was a further difference. At the outbreak of war, work at the *gabal* was stopped, and all the inmates of the punishment cells remained confined to their cells twenty-four hours a day, crowded together. But the prison workshops functioned as usual, and one of the inmates of the punishment cells—Petro, the former Free Greek officer—went off every day to the soap workshop, returning in the evening with whatever scraps of news he had managed to pick up.

The news was not particularly heartening. For the first two or three days, the Egyptian radio and press reported nothing but spectacular victories in Sinai.

"Even before the war," Robbie recalls, "we were brainwashed by official propaganda which depicted the Egyptian army as a mighty force. But we built up 'antibodies,' telling ourselves that if the regime was making such great efforts to convince us of the strength of the Egyptian army, that meant the opposite was true. Now, hearing the 'tidings of victory' which Petro reported as he passed by the punishment cells, our confidence was somewhat undermined. All the same, we were so sure of the strength of the Israeli army, we so wished to believe, that we couldn't take the news at its face value. I remember myself repeating obstinately: 'Of course it's not true. It's probably no more than false propaganda.' And another thought began to filter into my mind. The war must surely end, and the way wars end is by some kind of settlement—a peace treaty, an armistice, a compromise. And wasn't it reasonable to believe that we would be included in such a compromise? Suddenly, in the darkness of the dungeon, there was a ray of light a spark of hope."

Even before they talked about it, that same hope arose in the hearts of his four companions. And precisely because this was their first hope since their arrest, and because their somber situation made them cling to it with the desperation of drowning men, the heartbreak was all the greater when their expectations were dashed.

On the third night of the war, October 31, they could hear the thunder of distant explosions. The British and French air forces were launching their softening-up raids in preparation for the landing at Port Said. "Those of us who were from Alexandria remembered the sound from our youth, from the raids on Alexandria's harbor at the beginning of the world war. We also recalled the enormous carnage when German bombs fell on residential quarters and entire blocks of buildings collapsed from the blast. We were concerned, but we consoled ourselves with the thought that the punishment cells were on the ground floor."

A few days later, they learned that their concern was not unfounded. Tura filled up with refugees—convicts from the other hard labor penitentiary, Abu Za'abal, which was hit by mistake when the British air force tried to bomb the nearby radio station. The explosion brought down one of the prison walls, causing casualties and a panic which the prisoners tried to exploit for a breakout, whereupon the guards opened fire. In the end, Abu Za'abal prison had to be evacuated temporarily, and two thousand convicts were brought to Tura and housed in its blocks. There was not enough room for all of them in the cells, and hundreds slept in the courtyard of Block 1.

Even before the arrival of the Abu Za'abal convicts, Tura's punishment cells filled up with new inmates. When France and Britain entered the war, Egypt came under the control of its military intelligence. Thousands of citizens whose loyalty to the regime was in question were arrested; those already in prison were placed under "strict security arrest" and they were sent to the punishment cells.

The first of these was the journalist Abu'l Hir Nagib, whose acquaintance Robbie had made in Cairo's aliens jail, before the trial. "One evening he appeared, still wearing civilian clothes and a *tarboosh,* and was flung straight into the punishment cells. When ordered to take off his clothes and put on prison uniform, he refused. It didn't do him any good; his clothes were ripped off him."

The next day, an air force captain arrived, in uniform, after having been sentenced to five years' imprisonment for stealing a radio and a refrigerator from the camp in which he served.

Gino also appeared. Some months ago, having served his sentence in the punishment cells for his escape attempt and having completed his quota of work on the *gabal,* he was transferred to Block 2. But while he was there, one of the prisoners cursed the Queen of England in his presence, and Gino, recalling that as a Maltese he owed allegiance to the Queen, arose to defend her honor. After the two men were separated, Gino realized that his life was in danger in the block, and requested a transfer to the punishment cells.

These and others gave the network members a more accurate picture of the outcome of the war. The Egyptian army had been routed, the Israeli army having taken the whole of Sinai (and thousands of prisoners) while the British and French armies were occupying Port Said. It was now beyond all doubt that there would be negotiations and prisoner exchanges. The spark of hope began to glow anew.

One day, it burst into bright flame when a group of army officers visiting Tura requested to be taken to the punishment cells to see the "Jewish spies." Capt. Maggido, one of the prison officers, who guided the visitors, was not a supporter of the regime. His father had been arrested on suspicion of sympathizing with the Moslem Brotherhood, and he himself was also suspected of the same offense. At the end of the visit, he hastened back to the punishment cells to inform the network members—with unconcealed glee—of what he had heard from the visitors: "The judge at your trial—Gen. Digwi—was also taken prisoner."

"On hearing these tidings, our hopes soared. We were now sure that our release was nigh."

## A Bitter Disappointment

The war came as no surprise to Marcelle. In her new place of imprisonment, at Kanather, the Communist convicts were permitted to subscribe to a newspaper, there was a radio in the library, and news broadcasts were transmitted throughout the prison. In consequence, she was able to follow the unfolding crisis, with border incidents growing more and more violent, while Nasser's speeches became more extreme by the week, reaching their culmination when he announced the nationalization of the Suez Canal. From that point onward, war was in the air, even though no one knew when it would break out. With the establishment of the Harass el Watani (National Guard), men and women convicts volunteered to join its ranks. To the beat of drums, the volunteers marched and drilled every day on the volleyball pitch. They were under the command of a sergeant guard with a pointed moustache, and the women—dressed in overalls and peaked caps—all fell in love with him.

"I learned of the outbreak of war from the radio. It was announced that Israel had launched an attack in Sinai (I think the first announcement was broadcast on the morning of October 30). From that moment on, the radio was on continuously, transmitting military marches and announcing victories. I don't remember all the 'victories,' nor the stages of the war, only its effects on me."

The moment war broke out, there was an upsurge of nationalist feeling which was naturally channeled against the "immediate enemy" —Marcelle, the Zionist who had spied for Israel. There were even prisoners who testified to having seen her signaling to the British and French planes which flew past over Kanather on their way to bomb targets in Cairo.

"There was a small group which remained loyal to me: With the exception of Thiah, it included all the 'politicals,' Mimi first and foremost. She became my most loyal ally, defending me at every opportunity, ceaselessly arguing in my behalf and affirming that I had nothing to do with what was happening 'on the outside.' I shall never forget her for that."

Thiah and Kamella, the hashish dealer, on the other hand, incited the other prisoners and the guards against Marcelle, surrounding her with spies to report whom she was seeing and talking to. When Kanather prison filled up with Jewish prisoners, the situation got worse.

At the outbreak of war, the plainclothes detectives raided the Jewish quarters of Alexandria and Cairo, arresting hundreds of men and women. Kanather was one of the prisons where they were housed.

Marcelle: "They arrived at night. Locked in our second-floor cells, we heard considerable uproar in the men's wing; a few moments later, it spread to our wing. It was dark and we couldn't see a thing, but from the sounds we realized that a large group of women had arrived. They were housed on the ground floor of our building. We didn't know who they were, but all night long we could hear frightened cries: 'Hugette, where are you?' 'Marie, are you here?' Years later, I met one of them, Marie Blumenthal [secretary to the director of Bata in Cairo, who had arranged to have sports shoes supplied to Marcelle's gymnastic group]. She told me that they were brought in in the darkness, without knowing where they were; they were housed in cells in groups of five, scared to death."

The following morning, the cell doors remained locked till later than usual. But from her window, Marcelle could see that a table had been set up at the entrance to the building, and one of the prison officers sat there, summoning the new arrivals one by one. She recognized her friend Marie and other acquaintances from Cairo, as well as a large number of young women she did not know. They included Annie Natanson, Philip's sister, and Eugenie (Eugette) Levy, Victor's sister. The group imprisoned in the men's wing included Robbie's two brothers. There was not a single Jewish family in Egypt from which at least one "hostage" was not taken. When they were released a few months later, it was on condition that they left Egypt immediately.

The arrival of the Jewish detainees heightened the tension in the prison, even though they were not allowed to mix with the convicted prisoners, and were particularly warned not to make contact with Marcelle. Marie Blumenthal, who emigrated to Brazil after her release, came to Israel years later on a visit. When she met Marcelle, she told her: "The day we arrived at Kanather, the *mudir* called us all together and said: 'I know that some of you are friends of Marcelle's; let me warn you, for her sake and yours, not to try and make contact with her . . .'" Similarly, he warned the "politicals" not to have anything to do with the detainees. Addressing Marcelle, he said: "Remember, you've been sentenced to fifteen years. Promise you won't make trouble." She promised.

But even though both groups kept their promise ("Only once, I waved a greeting to Marie Blumenthal; she burst into tears") there was considerable tension in the prison. The guards, regarding themselves as "responsible for the security of the state," saw imaginary enemies concealed in every corner. "On one occasion, I threw a handkerchief out of my window, to one of the detainees in the courtyard; immediately, somebody hurried to tell Thiah that I had thrown a letter. Gleefully, she reported the matter to an officer, and I was summoned to the *mudir* for interrogation. Fortunately, Mimi was beside me at the time, and she could testify that it wasn't a letter I had thrown but a handkerchief, and I hadn't thrown it to a detainee, but to one of the prisoners."

The war came to an end. The withdrawal began: First, the British and French armies from Port Said, and then, with the arrival of the U. N. Expeditionary Force, the Israeli army from Sinai. The exchange of prisoners began.

Mahmud Sahb, the former *mudir* of Sigan Misr, meanwhile appointed Inspector of Prisons for the whole country, often visited Kanather. He came at least once a week, accompanied by Zuzu's daughter, and spent a long time in the sick bay. Encountering Marcelle on one of his visits, he told her: "You'll be released soon. Your judge— Digwi—is a prisoner in Israeli hands."

"Up till that moment, I don't think I connected the war with my personal fate. True, the thought of release never left me. All the prison officers talked about it: 'Be careful, lest you harm your prospects of being pardoned. . . . Don't spoil your chances of release. . . .' I think the only hope I attached to the outcome of the war was that in view of their victory—the Egyptians depicted the war as a spectacular triumph!— there might be a general pardon. But suddenly, after all these months of suffering, there was a great ray of hope. From then on, I was tensely expectant every moment of the day."

But the days passed, and nothing happened.

Finally, Radio Cairo announced that the last of the prisoners held by Israel had been repatriated, with Gen. Digwi among them, and still nothing happened.

Mahmud Sahb, on another visit to Kanather, came to look for Marcelle. He was clearly disappointed. "I can't understand why you haven't been released. I was sure they'd release you."

She made no reply. Her disappointment was so profound, so shattering that she did not dare open her mouth, lest she burst into tears. It was only when she withdrew to her cell that she released her tears, but they brought no consolation. "There was such a burden of bitterness in my heart that it hasn't completely disappeared to this day."


The five men in Tura experienced a similarly bitter disappointment.

They were still housed in the punishment cells, but the latter were not what they had once been. They were terribly overcrowded, permitting bugs and cockroaches to multiply enormously, until all the inmates were covered all over with stings and scratches; and some of the prisoners were under severe restrictions. However, the punishment cells now housed "privileged" prisoners of various kinds, who did not come under the *ta'adib* regulations, and they managed to smuggle in newspapers, from which the five network members learned of what was happening outside. They saw Nasser converting his military defeat into a political victory by turning the whole world against the states which had invaded his country, forcing the British and French armies to withdraw from Port Said. Finally, they read that Israel had consented to withdraw from Sinai and release the prisoners of war it was holding.

"Then, for the first time, we dared to talk aloud of the possibility that we might be released, as part of the exchange of prisoners."

A few days later, someone decided that the quarry had been idle quite long enough and work was resumed. The inmates of the punishment cells also went out to the *gabal.*

"There, too, we were welcomed as though we were about to be released. Even inside the prison, the Moslem Brotherhood's information network functioned well, and they would tell us of every stage in the negotiations. When the prisoner exchange began, with Israel releasing the prisoners in batches of five hundred, they would receive us with the tidings: 'Another group has arrived! Tomorrow your turn will come, *inshallah!* '"

Another batch, and another, until all five thousand POWs had been released, in return for which Israel received one single prisoner, Lieut. Yehonatan Atek, whose plane had been shot down over Sharm el Sheikh.

The members of the network remained in prison.

The episode remains a mystery to this day. No satisfactory answer has been given to the question which tormented the members of the network throughout their years of imprisonment, and which troubles the nation's conscience to this day: Why was no advantage taken of the situation in 1957 to procure the release of the six prisoners? Is it true that they were abandoned deliberately—as has been alleged—so as to prevent the reopening of "the mishap" (which had already led to the downfall of one Israeli cabinet, putting an end to the career of a promising politician and of a number of senior officers)? Or was it just a case of neglect?

One thing is beyond doubt: It *was* feasible, in 1957, to procure their release, as part of the prisoner exchange between Israel and Egypt.

This is backed up by a number of testimonies, some of which are still classified, but one, at least, can be published. In the mid-sixties, two of Egypt's most prominent journalists—the brothers Ali and Mustaffa Amin, the editors of the widely circulated *Achbar al Youm*—lost favor with Nasser. Their paper was nationalized; Mustaffa was arrested, placed on trial, and sentenced to a prolonged term of imprisonment in Tura. His brother Ali was saved from a similar fate only thanks to the fact that he was abroad when the ax fell.

However, in 1957, they were still at the peak of their power. They were regular visitors of Nasser's, who charged them with various "delicate" missions, on top of their regular task of shaping Egyptian public opinion.

When Mustaffa was imprisoned in Tura, together with Victor, Philip, and Robbie, he told them that one of these missions was to arrange the exchange of prisoners with Israel after the Sinai campaign.

Nasser, Mustaffa Amin related, urgently desired to eliminate all the aftereffects of the war as quickly as possible. He was in the midst of his campaign which was to depict Egypt's defeat as a great military victory. The press and radio swamped public opinion with stories of the heroism of the defenders of Port Said, who had successfully withstood the onslaught of two mighty powers, with the intention of convincing the Egyptians that it was this heroism and not the intervention of the United States and the Soviet Union which had forced Britain and France to pull out of Egypt. But the presence of five thousand Egyptian prisoners in Israel spoiled the picture, serving as a reminder that the Egyptian army was not as triumphant as official propaganda was trying to depict it. Consequently, Nasser gave orders for the prisoners to be repatriated at any price. "Give the Israelis whatever they want," he said, "as long as the matter of the prisoners can be completed."

"We were certain," added Amin, "that the Israelis would demand you. After all, we didn't have any of their prisoners to give them. But the Israelis didn't demand you. We were very surprised . . ."

Why did Israel not demand that the network members be included in the prisoner exchange in spite of the decision adopted in September 1955 that they were to be regarded as captured Israeli officers? Was it really because no one cared about them?

Later on, a senior Israeli Foreign Ministry official—one of the men in charge of the negotiations with Egypt—said that "Israel could not demand that the members of the network be included in the prisoner exchange because doing so would have been regarded as admitting that the state was responsible for the acts for which they had been sentenced, thereby severely harming our relations with the United States." However, the archives contain no document indicating that the matter was deliberated and resolved in this manner. The words of the senior official therefore appear to have been a retroactive attempt to justify an act of omission. Was that act indeed inadvertent?

Indeed, however inconceivable and inexplicable, it does seem that there was an element of oversight involved. Most of the men involved in "the mishap" in 1954 had meanwhile been relieved of their posts, some being discharged from the army and others serving in other capacities. Brig. Benyamin Jibly, who had officiated as head of the intelligence branch at the time of "the mishap," was now the commander of a brigade which had fought with great heroism in the Sinai approaches. Motke Ben-Tzur, commander of Unit 131, was now a civilian.

All those who saved their careers had gotten their fingers so badly burned by "the mishap" that their sole desire was to forget that they had had anything to do with it.

As for those who conducted the negotiations with Egypt for the exchange of prisoners, they were all men who had no connection with the 1954 incident, and they were unaware that somewhere or other, it had been decided to regard the members of the network as captured Israeli soldiers. Nobody told them. The six convicts in Egypt were, quite simply, forgotten.

## Back to Routine

Life in Tura gradually returned to normal. The five men were still living in the punishment cells; every morning, Victor, Philip, and Robbie went out to the *gabal*. But the tensions slowly receded, and the hostility toward them lessened. They seemed to have been left in the punishment cells as a matter of routine, because none of the prison officers took the trouble to release them.

One of the indications of a "return to normal" was the appointment of a "sports officer." While he was still the *mudir* of Sigan Misr, Mahmud Sahb had thought up the idea of introducing sporting activities into the prison. He organized a basketball team which he fielded against the team of a Cairo secondary school, with a large party taking place in the prison courtyard at the end of the game. But then came the war and no one had time to think of prison sports; the whole matter was forgotten.

And then, one day in February 1957, as he was about to go out to the *gabal,* Robbie was ordered to report to the sports officer on the basketball court behind the prison office building. A group of prisoners was practicing shots into the net, and among them, he recognized his two Alexandrian acquaintances, the student-murderers Issam and Salah.

"I've been told that you're a good basketball player," said the sports officer when Robbie presented himself. The officer was Maj. Fuad Sa'ad a Din, a tall, athletic man; later, Robbie learned that he was once a member of the Egyptian army's basketball team.

Robbie "confessed" that this was true; during his schooldays, he had indulged extensively in sporting activities, and played on his school's basketball team.

"Catch!" cried Maj. Fuad suddenly, throwing the ball at him. "Let's see what you know."

Robbie shot the ball and it sank into the net. He was made a member of the "Tura prison team."

He soon learned that with the exception of a young Moslem Brotherhood member, he was the only one who had ever played basketball. By the end of the day, he was already installed as the captain of the team.

In the afternoon, after their day's training, the "basketball team" was led to the washhouse, where they were rewarded with something so wonderful that no convict ever dared dream of it: a *warm* shower! But that was not the only wonderful thing to happen to Robbie that day. Before sending him back to the punishment cells, Fuad, who was not enthusiastic about spending the whole day on the basketball court, told Robbie that he was thereby appointed manager of the team. For the time being, or at least until the team was prepared for the prison "league," he would not have to go to work at the *gabal.*

"This was a revolutionary change in their attitude toward us," recalls Robbie. "Till then, no officer was prepared to take the risk of showing any special favoritism toward any of us. But Fuad seems to have been under the general impression that our release was near, and consequently permitted himself to ignore the instructions to treat us with particular severity."

The prediction about their forthcoming release was disproved in the course of that month, but in the meantime, Robbie had established his position as the team's manager and star player. The other players accepted him as their leader, and when Fuad managed to get the team uniforms—white shorts and red shirts—Robbie even succeeded in convincing the Saidi players that there was nothing undignified about wearing shorts.

Robbie's status as a basketball player—released from work on the *gabal*—was confirmed one morning when the *mudir* himself, Liwa al Helwani, arrived to watch the team training. Robbie was now so self-confident that he even ventured to inquire why he and his companions were still confined to the punishment cells. Al Helwani was surprised. "Yes, why?" he asked, and there and then he gave orders to have the "Zionists" moved back to their fourth-story cell.

"That day, I waited outside for my companions to return from the *gabal.* I wanted to be the first to tell them the good news."

Their release from the punishment cells was accompanied by a further gesture which testified to a "return to normal": Robbie and Meir Meyuhas received visits from their parents, the first to take place since the outbreak of war.

It was a very doleful meeting. Robbie found himself facing only his parents and his youngest brother. His two other brothers had been under detention for three months and were released directly onto the ship which awaited them in the harbor. They were not even permitted to take leave of Robbie. A similar fate had overtaken most of their acquaintances. Victor's sister had also been deported, with her fiancé following her; Victor's brother had also been forced to leave. Philip's sister was interned for four months before being allowed to depart. Those remaining maintained a precarious existence. Most of them had lost their jobs. Those with businesses of their own had been ruined by their prolonged detention or saw them crumble under the boycott imposed on Jewish firms.

Robbie pleaded with his parents to follow his brothers. He begged them to think of what lay in store for his youngest brother, who was six. "He's got no future here," he said. "And you yourselves, what can you look forward to? It would be better if you left for Israel."

He noticed that his arguments were not new to them; obviously, they had already thought about the matter at length. But they remained undecided. They could not bring themselves to abandon Robbie to his fate. He continued to argue with them, trying to persuade them that he too would feel better if he knew that they were safe. Gradually, they came around to his viewpoint. Yes, they would go away, but not immediately. They would visit him at least one more time.

"My heart fell when I heard them give their consent. I thought: 'Who knows when we shall meet again? How will we correspond?' Indeed, after their departure in April, contact between us was broken off. I knew that they had gone to Israel. But how had they settled in, how were things with them? Only two years later did we renew our contacts by letter, by means of Eugette, Victor's sister, who had gone to live in Switzerland."

In 1961, when Meir Za'afran and Meir Meyuhas reached Israel after having served their sentences, closer links were established.

Robbie: "When the time drew near for their release, the five of us got together and worked out a simple cipher which was easy to remember. In effect, we chose a number of code words for terms of significance for us, such as 'prisoner exchange' or 'parcel' and so on. We also planned to report on what was happening in the prison, and we gave code names to those prisoners in whom Israel might find an interest. For example, with us was an Italian frogman by the name of Paccola, who had been sentenced for spying on behalf of Israel; we gave him the code name 'Fish.' "

On his way to Israel, Meir Za'afran stopped over in Switzerland, where he bought a packet of picture postcards, which he gave to Robbie's parents, instructing them how to write to their son. Their letters must contain not the slightest hint that they were written in Israel; they should not refer to the weather, or to any film they had seen. They could send snapshots, but without showing any background, and they should not bear the stamp of the studio where they were taken. The cards were sent in an envelope to Eugette in Switzerland; she stuck Swiss stamps on them and sent them to their destination. If there were letters, she would send them to her father, and he would send them to Tura by way of the Egyptian mail.

This system functioned up to 1962, when Victor's parents also left Egypt and joined their daughter in Switzerland. After that, the letters were sent directly from Switzerland to the prison. On one occasion, they nearly resulted in a calamity.

Robbie's parents used to attach international postal orders to their letters to pay for the Swiss stamps. These orders, which were bought in Israel, bore the Israeli postal stamp. One day, Victor's father inadvertently left the order among the pages of the letter when he sent it off from Switzerland.

By some miracle, the censor did not open that letter. But to this day, Robbie remembers the shudder he experienced when he saw the postal order with the Israeli stamp.

On the average, letters arrived every three months. "Every letter was a cause for rejoicing. All three of us would sit and read it together, analyzing every phrase, seeking hints between the lines and trying to make each word into a source of inspiration."

But that was not the only importance of their links with the outside. Its mere existence blunted their feeling of being isolated and abandoned.

Robbie: "As a convict in Egypt, you're not a man, you're a doormat. Every officer or guard can do whatever he likes with you. Your complaints aren't worth the paper they're written on. It's only if you have friends on the outside who are prepared to intervene on your behalf and stir up a fuss that you become a person. If a convict goes on a hunger strike without outside backing, it's tantamount to suicide. Nobody will care if he fasts to death. In consequence, a prisoner intending to proclaim a hunger strike makes preparations ahead of time: He smuggles his complaints out of the prison, and has them sent to Nasser or the prosecutor general. The same goes for any attempt to improve conditions or to gain anything else. When we wanted an additional blanket in winter, I wrote out a letter of complaint, in Arabic, to the prison service; I smuggled it out to Switzerland, from where Eugette sent it to the *mudir* as though it came from my parents. A request of this nature did have some chance of being granted. Furthermore, the fact that my parents were taking an interest in my fate and were likely to stir up trouble abroad if anything should happen to me gave me, and all of us, some measure of protection."

*Massacre*

Tura received a new *mudir,* Kaimakam Said Wali, a veteran officer, bad-tempered, and with a wooden leg. Like every "new broom," he too began to sweep vigorously. There were more frequent searches; it became harder to smuggle in *mamnuat* articles, of which there was a temporary shortage. This was particularly irksome for the five network members who had just been released from the punishment cells and were beginning to "reorganize." Even when they succeeded in acquiring provisions, it became harder and harder to conceal them from the guards.

Philip: "At that time, we were grateful that the window of our cell faced the entrance to the block, so that we could see when a search was imminent."

The searches were usually made in the morning, when the guards on daytime duty arrived.

"One of us would keep a watch on the gate. At seven, the guards would be paraded there and then disperse to the various blocks. If not more than ten guards entered our gate, that indicated that we were in for an ordinary day. But if a large group appeared —at times, as many as two hundred—we knew that it was our turn to be searched. And then, in the two or three minutes which remained before the guards arrived, there would be a frenzied rush to conceal the *mamnuat.*"

In time, they found more sophisticated hiding places. From the workshop, they bought a bucket with a false bottom, opened by a concealed spring: this served for hiding those *mamnuat* whose possession involved severe punishment, such as razor blades, a kerosene stove, and even an electric hot plate. But immediately after their release from the punishment cells, they still had to make do with simpler and more primitive hiding places, the small sum of money in their possession being concealed in a hole they drilled in the wall. However, most of the *mamnuat* could not be hidden.

"There was no way of concealing the wooden sill we had fixed on the window to keep out the winter rain. In the same way, we could not hide the additional blankets, or the new 'made-to-order' uniforms we had sewn. Consequently, we followed the principle that anything which is clearly visible doesn't arouse suspicion. For example, we put the kerosene stove inside a sock which we hung on the wall, covered with a dirty suit of overalls. It was a gamble: If they found it, we would have to start all over again. As for foodstuffs, such as rice or tea, possession of which was regarded as possession of stolen property, we simply threw them out of the window."

The six-man leadership of the Moslem Brotherhood were also permanent tenants of the fourth floor, each one in a cell of his own. They still enjoyed a favored status with the prison authorities, even though most of their followers had been transferred to the Harga camp. They were rarely disturbed, they were not taken out to work, their cells were not searched, and no one rebuked their followers who were in the habit of coming up from the third floor to hear their words of wisdom or to proffer their respectful services.

These followers were regarded by the authorities as less "dangerous." Most of them were young and had been detained in the second wave of arrests. The principal charge against them was for collecting money to pay for the trials and support the families of those arrested in the first wave. They also got off with lighter sentences than their predecessors: ten to fifteen years' imprisonment. They numbered about three hundred, and like their predecessors who had been transferred to Harga, they were a united group which functioned as a closed sect, with its own law, its own doctors, and its own supervisors for work on the *gabal.*

When the "new broom" lost some of his enthusiasm and the irksome searches ceased, the atmosphere in the prison grew more relaxed. Throughout Egypt, there was an air of optimism in the first half of 1957. Nasser had proclaimed it as "the year of victory," and the massive efforts of his propaganda machine bore fruit: A sense of triumph permeated the whole country, even filtering into the prison.

However, this atmosphere had an unforeseen effect on the young Moslem Brotherhood members. They concluded that the present relaxed period, after the external enemies had been repulsed, was an advantageous moment to renew their previous campaign to acquire the status of political prisoners, and, with particular vigor, to be released from work on the *gabal.* A further reason for this unexpected ferment may have been the fact that the *gabal* officer was now Capt. Abdul Latif Rushdi, who, proud that the prisoners had nicknamed him "The Wild Man of the *Gabal,*" did his best to justify the title. However, the immediate cause of the bloody incident which occurred in June 1957 had nothing to do with the *gabal.*

Philip: "One day, Zuzu Mahdi's husband was summoned to receive a *ziara*, returning with a large parcel of food which included a fried chicken. At the same time, thirteen Brotherhood members also received visits, but they were not allowed to accept the food parcels brought by their parents. They rioted and were flung into the punishment cells. As a further punishment, the *mulahzat* for the Brotherhood were withdrawn, and they were all ordered out to work. Tension rose."

Then a further incident occurred. On returning from the *gabal*, Abdul Latif Rushdi did not remain content with the routine search at the gateway to the block. After the convicts went up to their cells, he and his men followed and conducted a further search, finding considerable amounts of booty: more than 150 pounds in cash, illegal letters, and numerous other *mamnuat*. While he was standing there, fingering the bank notes with a triumphant smile, a group of Brotherhood members attacked him. Later, Rushdi testified that they tried to throw him from the third story.

Be that as it may, they contented themselves with taking the money, as well as his pistol, and locking him in one of the cells. Guards who tried to come to the aid of their officer were pelted with *kardals* full of excrement and beaten off. The alarm was given, the block gateway was locked from the outside, and the *boloks* took up positions on the wall.

Only when the *mudir* arrived and entered into negotiations was a compromise reached: Rushdi was released, his pistol was restored to him, and the prisoners were not harmed. It transpired that the *mudir* endeavored to keep the whole episode quiet and did not report the incident, which could have marred his standing with his superiors.

But Abdul Latif Rushdi could not forget his humiliation, and he wreaked his vengeance. He behaved savagely toward the convicts on the *gabal*, making them work till they collapsed, and beating them with a wild ferocity. His hatred was directly principally against the Brotherhood members, but all the quarry workers felt the weight of his arm.

In the end, the Brotherhood members could not stand it anymore and they proclaimed a hunger strike. At first, they refused to accept prison food, subsisting only on what they bought from the canteen. No one took any notice. Then they stepped up their campaign, refusing to go to work on the *gabal*. The lawyers among them made sure their refusal would not appear as a mutiny. Each one of the Brotherhood members reported in the morning to the "*gabal* officer," bearing a request for a sick call, written out by their companions who were medical students. Contemptuously, Rushdi proclaimed that he did not recognize these requests and ordered the men to report to the work procession. Each of them in turn refused and was confined to his cell. The *gabal* workers set off.

Robbie: "An hour later, the *mudir*, Said Wali, arrived, and went up to the fourth floor, to the cell of the *irshad*. All those remaining in the block—Meir Meyuhas and I remained that day; I think we wanted to go on sick call—were ordered to enter their cells and the doors were locked.

"Till eleven, there was a tense silence. Suddenly, we noticed that the wall facing our window was covered with armed *boloks,* several times more numerous than usual. The wooden-legged *mudir* walked past our cell and went down to the third floor. We were later told that they entered the cell of Abdul Azim Doh, one of the young Brotherhood leaders, and gave him half an hour to submit and go to work, warning him that the Interior Minister had given him a free hand to put down the mutiny in any manner he found fit. Abdul Azim tried to argue that this wasn't a mutiny, but the *mudir* ignored him. Turning on his heel, he walked out.

"Half an hour later, the block filled up with armed *boloks,* headed by the sports officer, Fuad Sa'ad a Din, and the *gabal* officer, Abdul Latif Rushdi. In the meantime, the convicts employed at the *gabal* had been brought back suddenly, with no explanation. Those of them from Block 1 were not permitted to return to their cells; they were taken to Block 2 and ordered to wait there.

"Suddenly, we heard shots from the floor below."

This was the first serious uprising which ever occurred in Tura or any other Egyptian prison, and the authorities were unprepared for it. The guards had not been trained to overcome an organized, disobedient crowd; they did not possess tear gas or even clubs and shields. All these were supplied later, when the lessons of this incident were learned. But now, they had nothing but canes—which were worthless in contending with a crowd—rifles, and submachine guns.

"Wooden Leg" gave orders to shoot.

The *boloks* opened fire indiscriminately from the corridor into the cells. Their bullets pierced the locked doors and killed numerous prisoners. Those who were only wounded and still possessed the strength to drag themselves to the cell windows to call for help were picked off by the *boloks* on the wall.

Robbie: "Confined to our cell on the fourth floor, Meir Meyuhas and I listened horrified to the sounds coming from below, and tried to comprehend what was happening. It was impossible. We heard shots and cries, the savage yells of the guards and the groans of the wounded. Somebody screamed: 'Stop shooting!' and someone else shouted: 'Fire! Kill them!' One cell was occupied by eight young Brotherhood weightlifters who tried to defend themselves with their training bells. Abdul Latif Rushdi broke his way in with a submachine gun and killed them all."

Even when the shots died down, the killing did not end. The wild-eyed *boloks* stormed the cells, dragging out the dead and wounded, and, without distinction, flung them all down the stairs.

That day, twenty-three Brotherhood members were killed—at

least six had their heads smashed in on the stairs—while thirty-nine were injured.

Philip: "That evening, when we were finally permitted to return to the block, it was all over. But the bodies still lay in the corridor and on the guard tower, where they had been brought by the guards to serve as 'proof' that there had been an attempt at a violent breakout. Other guards were removing the riddled doors from their hinges and replacing them with others, to remove the evidence that the killings had been indiscriminate."

A commission of inquiry was established, but it only arrived the following day, when the coverup had been completed. The commission found that there had, indeed, been a violent mutiny, vindicating the measures adopted by the prison governor. All the guards who had taken part in suppressing the "mutiny" received a "reward": a grant of twenty-five piastres and a packet of sweets.

The "mutiny" had additional consequences.

The prisoners with *mulahzat* who had occupied the ground floor and the "criminals" from the second floor were transferred to other blocks. The only prisoners remaining in Block 1 were the Brotherhood members on the third floor, their leaders on the fourth floor, and the members of the network. The block was placed under the command of Capt. Abdul al Saluma, transferred from the Abu Za'abal prison. He was notorious for his cruelty.

The block was closed, and purchases from the canteen ceased. No one went out to work, not even to the *gabal*. They were not even let out to the washrooms, or to the *"kardal* procession." To close the block completely, Saluma gave orders to have one of the *mulahza* cells converted into a washroom. Saluma now began to "take care" of the Brotherhood members. Together with a group of guards handpicked for their ferociousness, he would begin the day with a stringent search of all the cells on the third floor. In every cell, the inmates were ordered out into the corridor, where they were stripped naked and their uniforms confiscated. In their place, they were given the filthiest and shabbiest uniforms which could be found. Their heads were shaven as well as their beards, a bitter humiliation. At the same time, anything in their cell, even sanctioned articles and foodstuffs purchased at the canteen, were confiscated. All this was done amid incessant beatings, accompanied by curses and insults.

And so it went on, from cell to cell. When they finished, they began all over again, without stopping. The next day, the process was repeated. It went on for six weeks on end.

"All that time, their leaders remained on the fourth floor, undisturbed. We too were unaffected, but all the same, it was an awful feeling to sit and listen to the shouts coming from the floor below, by which we could follow the progress of Saluma and his group and to think fearfully: 'Perhaps they'll come to us too?' It was a repetition of the horrors of the Sigan Harbi."

But Saluma never once went up to the fourth floor. Moreover, there were times when not even the duty guard came up, and the doors remained locked all day long. This usually happened on those days when Saluma and his men were "especially busy" with the third floor. "On those days, we knew that it was just as well for us that our existence be overlooked. Consequently, we did not call the guard, and when the stench from our *kardal* became unbearable, we would empty it out of the window."

This odor mingled with the smell of blood which remained in the corridor after the massacre, combining to produce an oppressive atmosphere.

The reprieve which Saluma granted to the inmates of the fourth floor had a crafty, evil purpose.

"It was some time before we grasped it," relates Robbie. "That was when we noticed the changed behavior and mood of the younger Brotherhood members on the third floor. They stood up to Saluma's persecutions bravely, until they learned that while they themselves were suffering, their leaders continued to enjoy all their privileges, and did not even attempt to intervene on their behalf. That was when they broke down. We witnessed the process only in its early stages, because, six weeks later, all the Brotherhood members from the third floor were transferred to Kanather, only returning to Tura in 1959. By then, they were completely changed. In the past, they had strictly observed the religious ban on smoking; now they even smoked hashish and indulged in homosexual practices. Many of them had openly broken with the Brotherhood and wrote petitions in which they expressed their support for the regime. They were no different from the 'criminals.' "


After the transfer of the Brotherhood members to Kanather, the block's "exiled" former inmates were brought back and matters returned to their former routine, with work on the *gabal* being resumed. "The Wild Man," Abdul Latif Rushdi, was no longer in charge there; he had been posted to another prison. (Some time later, it was learned that he was dead; the Moslem Brotherhood claimed to have murdered him in revenge for the massacre of its members.) As sometimes happens after a particularly grave incident, the prison authorities were interested in speeding up the return to "normalcy"; the convicts were permitted to renew their purchases at the canteen, and sports were also resumed.

But the sports officer did not return to his former state. He had been profoundly shaken by the massacre in which he took part, and in particular, by the death of one of the Brotherhood members who played on the basketball team. Robbie: "He never ceased apologizing: 'I'm not to blame for his death.... I'm not to blame....' At times, during our training sessions, we would see him sitting near the playing surface, fingering his *masbacha* [prayer beads] and muttering to himself."

# 8

## A PERIOD OF CALM

*The Epoch of the Spies*

A new era now began; among themselves, the members of the network referred to it as "the epoch of the spies," because it was inaugurated by the arrival at Tura of the members of an espionage network which had worked for British intelligence. They were headed by James Zarb and James Swinbourne. At the same time, the block filled up with additional prisoners who may not have been spies, but neither were they typical Egyptian jailbirds. They included ministers, politicians, journalists, and officers, the cream of prerevolutionary Egyptian society.

Mustaffa Amin—hitherto publisher and editor-in-chief of *Achbar al Youm,* who was imprisoned in Tura—later published a book about his prison experiences; the book lists the Egyptian politicians deprived of their freedom under Nasser. The list includes one president, Gen. Naguib; one regent, Col. Rashid Muhana, a member of the thirteen-man "Officers Council" which headed the revolution; and no less than twenty politicians who had officiated as ministers in various governments, mostly belonging to the Wafd party. Not all of these men reached Tura; those with the correct contacts remained in Cairo's aliens prison. Those who reached Tura were housed in Block 1. They included: Ibrahim Abdul Hadi and Nagib el Hilali, as well as Muhammed Salah a-Din, a former foreign minister who, in this post, was one of the signatories of the United Nations Charter (two years later, he was to be joined in prison by his son-in-law, arrested in 1959 for spying on behalf of Israel as part of a network headed by two Italians, Paccola and Raymondo di Pietro).

The former ministers were, of course, not sent to the *gabal*. They were housed on the fourth floor, and within a few days, they were thoroughly settled in: They bought mattresses and white invalids' pajamas, acquired kerosene stoves, and hired *nabatshin* to serve them in the manner to which they were accustomed. "But during the first few days, while still thunderstruck by their reversal of fortunes, they were quite lost in this new world into which they had been flung. We helped them: On their first evening, we—including Zarb—put on a festive dinner for them, and did our best to cheer them up."

The newcomers can hardly be described as grateful, although they kept up good-neighborly relations with the members of the network, exchanging visits and conversing at length. But when the "Lavon crisis" struck Israel in 1960 and "the mishap" returned to the headlines, letters deploring the fact that "the Jewish spies" had not been executed were sent to the authorities by the former Wafd ministers.

Ingratitude? Such a concept had no place in the moral code of Egypt's prisons, irrespective of whether the convicts were "criminals" or VIPs. It was a "dog eat dog" existence—and worse! Dogs might eat one another to still their hunger, but the prisoners at Tura lunged at one another just for the fun of it.

One VIP prisoner with whom they established close relations, which remained firm despite the prison atmosphere, was James Zarb, the British intelligence agent.

He was Maltese, stocky, and dark-haired; a professional spy who had parachuted into Yugoslavia during World War II and later operated behind the German lines in Italy. He headed a network which the Egyptians accused of causing a collision between two ships in the Suez Canal, so as to block the waterway and prove to the world that the Egyptians were incapable of running it.

At their trial, the Egyptian intelligence agents testified that they had traced the network as a result of the collision (which indeed occurred, but was caused not by any deliberate act, but rather by the inexperience of the Egyptian pilots replacing the former European pilots who had quit after the Canal was nationalized). However, Zarb believed that his men were betrayed by an intelligence agent in Beirut, who turned out to be a double agent. All the group were arrested: Zarb's assistant, Morad; a Copt official employed in the police archives, Naasif Murcus; an Egyptian navy captain named Ahmed Lutfi, a former aide of Gen. Naguib; also arrested was Lutfi's father, and his own cousin, who was employed in the Egyptian aircraft industry—both men being denounced by Lutfi. In addition to Zarb himself, three other Europeans were also arrested: the manager of the Prudential insurance company in the Canal Zone, a former major in the Free Yugoslav army, and James Swinbourne.

Swinbourne was a shriveled-up, elderly man, a long-time resident in Egypt. He was a teacher and looked the part. For some time he had taught at Cairo University, and several ministers of the revolutionary government were his former pupils. At another period, he had worked at the Arab Information Center—one of Nasser's propaganda agencies. Hints dropped by members of the British network indicated that Swinbourne's role in it was quite marginal, and this appears to have been the view of his judges, who let him off with a very light sentence—five years' imprisonment. (He was also the only political prisoner to be pardoned after having served only half of his sentence; his pardon was obtained by the mediation of Tom Little, a British writer who wrote a biography of Nasser.) Zarb was sentenced to ten years' imprisonment. The insurance agent and the Yugoslav major were both acquitted, but the network's Egyptian members were treated with great severity. Naasif Murcus and Morad were given twenty-five years, Ahmed Lutfi got life imprisonment, and his father was sentenced to death and executed.

In prison, Zarb and Swinbourne enjoyed "diplomatic immunity." Since the Suez war, Egypt had broken off its diplomatic relations with Britain, but the Swiss ambassador, who represented British interests in Egypt, had extended his protection to the two spies who were British subjects; at least once a month, he or one of his employees would visit them in prison. Furthermore, the two men were the richest of the block's inmates, because the Swiss embassy had deposited a sizable sum of money with the prison authorities on their behalf; in addition, they received a spate of cigarettes and food parcels, and the Catholic priest who brought Zarb weekly "spiritual sustenance" made up for any deficiencies by smuggling in money or anything else he was asked to bring.

Swinbourne was chilly in his behavior toward the members of the Israeli network. "He was concerned for his own skin," says Robbie. "He was afraid that his chances of a pardon would be harmed if he had anything to do with us." With Zarb, on the other hand, they established a close friendship which remained unimpaired until his release after serving six years. Zarb was fond of cooking, but he lacked contacts in the prison. To acquire the ingredients he wanted, he needed help from the members of the Israeli network. Zarb regularly received British newspapers, which were in great demand. In addition to being a ray of light from the free world, the thin airmail paper on which they were printed was excellent for rolling cigarettes. Zarb also owned Tura's first private radio.

"In one paper, we read of the latest innovation—a transistor radio no larger than a matchbox. If only we had a radio like that, we thought to ourselves. So we talked about it with Zarb, who conveyed the request the next time he was visited by the priest. This priest, an Italian, was arrested at the beginning of World War II; being an enemy alien, he was detained in the Sudan for four years. Knowing the bitter taste of confinement, he could understand us. Being acquainted with Egyptian prison procedures, he knew how to mislead the guards. After a few weeks, he found what we had asked for, and brought the radio to Zarb." Once a week, the tiny receiver would be taken to the cell of the network members.

Their lives were now enriched by a new dimension. On "radio evening," they would withdraw to their cell and wait impatiently for the doors to be locked, whereupon they brought the radio out of its cache in the bucket with the false bottom, and tuned it to the Israeli radio or to the BBC. They had to turn the volume right down to prevent the radio from being heard outside; placing the radio on a blanket, they would lie around it on their stomachs, listening and dreaming. . . .

Later on, after Swinbourne's release, Zarb would join them for these "radio evenings," usually held on Thursday nights when there was little likelihood of the duty officer paying an unexpected visit. For a packet of cigarettes, the duty guard consented to leave Zarb in their cell till next morning.

Victor: "We would hold a festive meal, opening a can of bully beef which Zarb fried in lots of onions. After the meal, we would have a drink —the priest smuggled in a jar of concentrated liquor and we had a device for extracting alcohol from the sugar syrup now available at the prison canteen. Then Zarb would light one of the cigars brought by the Swiss ambassador and we would all lie around the radio."

Zarb was released after British public opinion was aroused on his behalf. A London newspaper published a tear-jerking article about the loyal British agent rotting in an Egyptian prison, pointing out that Zarb had not even seen his son, who was born after his arrest. The readers' response was stormy, whereupon the paper paid for Zarb's wife and son to journey to Egypt to see him.

The British press was engulfed with readers' letters demanding his release; many wrote him letters of encouragement. "He received thousands of letters and parcels, including a crate of Jaffa oranges, which arrived in their original wrappers. Sadly, we thought to ourselves: 'If only there were half as much interest in us. . . .' "

Zarb was finally pardoned and released.

*Artistic Pursuits*

A period of calm now reigned. But the term is a relative one.

"In prison, 'calm' means that there are no extraordinary events: no mutiny, no large-scale searches, no particularly tyrannical officer. But your fears remain. You still have to stand guard every morning and keep a lookout on the gateway; you are still thrown into a panic whenever you see signs of an impending search, and you are so fearful of its possible outcome that you throw valuable *mamnuat* out of the window, after expending great efforts on acquiring them. Minor afflictions also persist: An officer who gets up on the wrong side of the bed is capable of ordering a *tafnita* [change of cells]. One of them, on discovering snapshots of our parents in the cell, told us that 'a picture is like a visit; choose which you prefer.' "

During this period, Muhsein Tala'at—the *ma'amur* and one of the officers who had studied American penitentiaries—set about extending the hobbies available to prisoners, by inaugurating a painting class. Naturally, this was done in characteristic Egyptian fashion. The aim was not to teach the prisoners how to paint, but rather to pick out those already skilled and to display their paintings as a tribute to the success of the prison and to its *mudir*'s innovations.

Which of the inmates of Tura knew how to paint? Meir Za'afran, the architect, of course. Gino also turned out to have been a gifted artist in his youth. After a moment's doubt, Robbie also stepped forward; his drawings had been praised when he was at school.

The painting class met at the prison library. The three men were released from work on the *gabal*. The sports officer, in charge of all the prison leisure activities, received a five-pound allocation for the class, using the money to buy brushes and a number of tubes of paint. For canvas, they used the coarse uniform material, while the easels were constructed in the prison carpentry shop. The money ran out within a few days, but the three men had, in the meanwhile, completed two or three paintings. The sports officer, already imagining the praise which would come his way after exhibiting the works of the "Tura prison painting class," offered no objections when Meir Za'afran suggested asking his parents to "donate" paints and canvases to the prison. All the same, the officer took care to make it clear that the finished paintings would remain prison property. Za'afran having consented to this condition, the officer was present in person at the next visit, to make sure that the "donation" was brought into the prison without any hitch.

The "painting class" flourished. A number of its oil paintings already adorned the prison offices, pleasing the sports officer so greatly that when the time came for a new *tasnia* (allocation to vocational groups), he told Robbie and Za'afran: "I'll put you down for the house painters' group, and then you can go on painting undisturbed."

Robbie: "The drawing class became very important later on in our imprisonment. The amount of paints donated [Meir's parents had now been joined by Victor's parents and Philip's mother] was now so large that we could afford to paint the walls of our cell with oil paint, giving it a more tolerable appearance. When the sports officer saw this, it gave him an idea. The inspector general of the prison service was in the habit of visiting Tura once a year; in anticipation of his visit, the prison would undergo a thorough cleaning, with the walls being newly whitewashed and peeling mortar touched up. The prisoners were driven hard at such times. Then the officer came to me and said: 'Suppose, instead of just whitewashing the library walls, you did a painting on one?' Naturally, he chose the wall behind his desk.

"On a black background, which rather startled him at first, I painted a large mural depicting all the 'leisure-time activities' pursued in the prison—sports, the orchestra, painting. . . . It was rather a naive painting, but he was very enthusiastic about it, as were the *ma'amur* and the *mudir.*"

The prison officers came to express their admiration, which was followed by various hints: "Next month is my wedding anniversary. Could you do me a nice painting? All these years, my wife has yearned for a painting in the salon. . . ."

"The fact that the officers approached us with requests, and visited us repeatedly to watch the progress of the paintings they had commissioned, enhanced our status in the eyes of guards and prisoners alike. This didn't come cheap: Not one of the officers offered to pay for the canvas and the paints, and our parents were forced to step up their 'donations.' But the price was worth paying."

Their painting activities gave Meir and Robbie an opportunity to spend some time outside the prison.

Every year, an exhibition was held at the Gzira Exhibition Center, where prisoners' work was put on display. In 1958, prisoners' hobbies were to be exhibited for the first time. To help him in preparing the exhibition, its director could call on the assistance of the best prisoner artists, with Meir and Robbie among them. Their inclusion was no easy matter. At first, it was vetoed by the *mudir* of Tura. The exhibition director, having heard of the "two gifted painters" from Tura, was forced to appeal to the director general of the prison service. Henceforward, the same tussle was to be repeated every year: The *mudir* cast his veto and the director general overrode it. Every year, with the exception of the two years when the political crisis inside Israel brought "the mishap" back into the limelight, Robbie would finally find himself among the group preparing the exhibition.

"The first time," he recalls, "about twenty of us—prisoner crafts-men—traveled to Gzira in an open truck. We all stood up, our eyes wide open, gazing at the landscape flashing past. The first time we spotted a woman, everyone yelled: 'There's a woman!' Then, as we approached Cairo, silence fell as we drank in the sights of that life to which we no longer belonged. At times, instead of driving directly to Gzira, the truck driver consented to take us on a drive through the suburbs of Cairo, and then we really rejoiced, because Cairo's snarled traffic forced the driver to slow down, or stop at intersections, giving us a chance to exchange shouts with passersby or even to fling a letter. There was always some-one who picked it up and sent it to its destination."

Preparing the exhibition lasted about a month, and for Robbie, it was the best month in the year. The Exhibition Center was heavily guarded while they were working there, but all the same, "it wasn't prison, it didn't give off the stench of prison. A nearby stall owner was permitted to sell us *ta'amiya* [falafel] or a plateful of beans.

"In the evenings, on returning to my cell, I would tell my compan-ions of the wonders I had seen; about the new women's fashions, the new car models, giving them additional subject matter to replenish their dreams."


Philip also managed to get out of work on the *gabal* even before his official date for *tasnia;* in his case, too, this was indirectly due to his hobby.

At that time, the administration decided to institute a prisoners' album in every prison. Each prison in the country chose one guard, and the whole group—fifteen in number—were sent on a course to learn photography, developing, and printing. At the end of the course, Tura's photographer, accompanied by the prison's education officer, was sent to the Harga detention camp to take photographs of its four hundred detainees who were regarded as belonging to Tura. On returning to Tura to develop the film, the officer prudently ordered him first to develop a film of landscape shots and general views of Harga. His caution was vindicated: The novice photographer burned up the film.

At that, the officer summoned Philip. He did so not without a sense of foreboding; defying orders, he had already released two "Zionist spies" from the *gabal,* but the knowledge that unless the pictures came out well, he would have to make the trip to Harga again overcame his reluctance.

"Immediately, I grasped what had happened," Philip relates. "The guard photographer had no idea of developing. He could not distinguish one acid from another, and made such a mess of it, it's a wonder he only burned the film!"

Philip emptied the solution out into the basin, washed the developing basin clean, and made a new acid solution. With the officer breathing heavily, Philip placed the first film in his new solution.

It came out perfect. The officer flung a scornful glance at the photographer, who shrugged and said: "What do you want? He's a spy, an expert . . ."

"Tomorrow you will continue," the officer told Philip.

"Tomorrow I will go to work on the *gabal,*" Philip replied. "I'll be able to continue in three months' time, when I finish my quota of work there . . ."

But the officer approached the *mudir* and asked to have Philip "reallocated" and officially appointed "photographer's assistant." That was the first time a Tura prisoner ever had an official *tasnia* before completing three years' work on the *gabal.*

In the course of the forthcoming days, or, rather, evenings, for with no way of darkening the photography room, he had to work after dark, Philip developed all the Harga films. It then transpired that Tura was the only prison which had begun putting together its prisoners' album. In all the other prisons, the films were spoiled while being developed.

There was considerable uproar, an inquiry was conducted, and it was decided that all the guard photographers would undergo a further course at Tura.

On account of the course, Tura's photographic laboratory was supplied with large amounts of equipment, some of which Philip used to take pictures of prisoners and guards. But he also took art photographs, the best of which were sent to amateur competitions (one even won a prize). When the basketball games began and the Tura team started to travel to other prisons for tournaments, Philip was attached to it as its "official photographer."

"In our block, I was the first out of my cell in the morning and the last to return, well after dark, because the course was held in the evenings. Often, by the time I arrived, the lights had been switched off, and they would be turned back on specially for me, until I finished my supper. During the day, the sports officer charged me with photographing prison life. I wandered around the workshops, I went to the *gabal,* I was even taken to the *mazra'ah,* a kind of farm outside the prison walls where vegetables were raised for the prison. The *mazra'ah* was tended by short-term prisoners and it was lightly guarded. I saw a chance of making my escape, but the thought of what would happen to my companions held me back."

In January 1958, after three years at Tura, Victor, too, was released from work on the *gabal* and was henceforth employed in the carpentry shop.

## Mutiny in the Women's Prison

Gradually, like someone awakening from a nightmare, Marcelle got over the depression which overtook her after the Suez war. She renewed her friendship with her fellow prisoners, resumed her training of the gymnastics class, and when she found herself one day thinking expectantly of the next meal, she knew that she was back to normal. But her bitter disappointment continued to burden her.

By comparison with other Egyptian prisons, Kanather was now relatively comfortable. Originally designed for juvenile delinquents, the prison had been restored and adapted to its new role as a model women's prison. Indeed, except for the wall which encompassed it and divided it from the men's wing, and the bars on the windows, Kanather did not have the somber, oppressive appearance of a typical prison. It possessed an enormous courtyard, ending in a kind of amphitheater with a raised stage and a scaffold for a film screen. Once a month throughout the summer, there was a film show, to the disgust of the women guards who were obliged to remain at their posts till the performance ended. They found a way of getting even, not ceasing their cursing and swearing all through the film, whose dialogue was punctuated by cries of: "Sit down, you whore! Bitch's daughter, you'll get yours, you'll see!"

"Nevertheless, it was a wonderful experience to go out of the building, to sit in the open and see the stars. The *ma'amur*'s wife used to come to the films, too, and so did the wives of the duty officers who came to join their husbands for the weekend. We would feast our eyes on their civilian dresses and take in the changes in fashion."

However, the film shows did not go on for long. After one prisoner was caught trying to escape—somehow or other, she got hold of a civilian dress and tried to slip out with the guests at the end of the show —the screenings were stopped, only being renewed years later.

Another innovation at Kanather was that various *mamnuat* were now permitted. Electric hot plates, for example. Each of the "politicals" and many of the "criminals" possessed small electric hot plates, an essential piece of equipment under prison conditions, with the sole meal of the day being served cold and insipid and hot drinks available only when the canteen was open. All the same, the hot plates were "illegal," and they could be used only in the evenings, after the cells were locked up. The load on the electric network caused a number of short circuits; when this recurred, the *ma'amur*—Hassan al Kurdi—conducted a search and found the hot plates.

"We were all summoned to the prison office. He pointed at the plates piled up on the desk and asked: 'Are these yours?' We replied in the affirmative, saying that they were indispensable. A person needs one hot meal a day. 'All right,' he said, 'but not in the cells. The plates will be deposited in the canteen, and anyone who wants to cook will do it there.'

"But this arrangement did not take into account another use, no less important, to which we put the plates: Nothing helped to shorten the long, lonely evenings in our cells like preparing a cup of hot tea. Consequently, the hot plates were left in the canteen all day, but in the evenings they found their way back to the cells. The short circuits persisted."

Those long nights were the most depressing thing. "At first, I found it very hard to remain alone. The locked door was irksome, and I went out of my cell whenever I had the chance, to be among people. But gradually, the tension of prison took over and cast its shadow. From the moment the cell was unlocked in the morning, I knew there was a danger of a sudden search or of a confrontation with some ill-tempered prisoner or a harsh guard. I began to feel at ease only when the cell door was locked. To be alone, to read, to think, to cook, to write letters—to make another day pass. Not that I got used to imprisonment. The deprivation of my liberty provoked an internal revulsion. But while imprisoned, I preferred the peace and calm of solitude. But not at night . . ."

Night is the time of terror for those who are lonely, above all, for the lonely prisoner. "You lie on the bed and sleep won't come. Gradually, the sounds of prison die down and you're left alone with your memories."

Many of the prisoners—the "politicals" particularly—took sleeping pills. But Marcelle feared them; in her mind, they were connected with drugs, and seeing around her what drugs do, she feared addiction. Consequently, her nights were long, and often passed sleeplessly, in a fitful doze as she floated somewhere in the past. In the morning, her pillow was damp with tears.

Shortening the night, then, became one of the most important tasks, part of her struggle for existence, like staying healthy and getting additional food. For a time, a way was found.

One of the sergeant women guards was fat and old, and notoriously lazy. When she was on duty, she did not budge from her chair on the ground floor, where she sipped countless cups of tea, while her *na-batshia* massaged her swollen legs. If anything needed to be done—

summoning a prisoner, or opening or closing doors—the *nabatshia* would do it.

One of her duties was to lock the cell doors at night and reopen them in the morning. The "politicals" bribed the *nabatshia* to close the doors without locking them. They would wait until the prison fell quiet —the *nabatshia* went back to her wing and the whole building was left to the two guards on night duty—and then, very quietly, they would slip out to the cell agreed upon beforehand (usually Marie Rosenthal's, where there was a washbasin). They would spend a number of hours there, conversing in whispers, drinking tea, and eating supper together. There was no danger of the guard surprising them; every half hour, when she was supposed to tour the cells, an alarm clock would ring beside her, clearly audible throughout the building. On hearing it, the prisoners would fall silent and listen for the guard's footsteps on the stairway. She would halt, fling a glance along the empty corridor and its closed doors, and return the way she had come.

But one night, when Marcelle was on her way back to her cell, the guard appeared at the top of the stairs. For some reason, the alarm clock had not gone off.

Marcelle immediately ducked into her cell and closed the door. The short-sighted guard saw her for a fleeting moment in the half light of the corridor, but knowing that the cell doors were locked, she never even thought the vanishing shadow could have been a prisoner. *"Bismilla al rahman al rahim!"* ("In the name of merciful Allah!") she cried, and fled headlong down the stairs, screaming: "A devil! I saw a devil!"

She soon returned with the other guard. Marcelle had time to warn her companions, and they were all in bed, in their own cells, when the inspection began. But the unlocked doors were discovered.

Henceforth, the keys were not entrusted to the *nabatshia*, and that was the end of the "social evenings."


Every prisoner is lonely, but Marcelle's loneliness was particularly severe. Her nearest relative was her brother, but after her transfer to Kanather, he was not allowed to see her; his visits were only resumed in the second half of 1957, and then only after she complained to Zacci Shukry, now inspector general of prisons, when he chanced to visit Kanather. For about a year and a half, no one came to see her.

The "politicals" with whom she was friendly were released one by one, and there was a brief period, after Thiah and Marie Rosenthal were released early in 1959, when the "politicals' floor" housed only two prisoners: Marcelle and Mimi. The other cells were empty, until the *ma'amur* decided to use them to house "criminals" who were pregnant or recovering from childbirth.

A new period began in the summer of 1959, when Soviet-Egyptian relations again deteriorated. This happened after Egypt united with Syria to form the United Arab Republic and the Syrian Communist party was outlawed. The Russians were furious, Nikita Khrushchev called off a scheduled visit to Egypt, and the Communist press (not that of the Soviet Union; the task was entrusted to the Polish newspapers) began to publish "revelations" about the ferocious persecution to which the Communists were subjected under Nasser's rule. Shuhdi Attiyeh, a Communist who had been tortured to death at Abu Za'abal prison, was depicted as a martyr.

The Egyptian press hit back by describing the atrocities committed in Mosul, in northern Iraq, under the short-lived Communist regime there. But matters did not end with this war of words. Throughout Egypt, Communists were again arrested, and Kanather's women's wing filled up once more.

As usual during periods of tension, all the painstakingly gained privileges were withdrawn. But that was the least of their troubles.

The new prisoners—in effect, they were only detainees, for they had yet to go on trial—had still not grown accustomed to regarding the Nasser regime as hostile. In time, they were to curse the *ra'is* and send him to the devil, as had their predecessors prior to the 1955 Bandung Conference. But in the meantime, even though shocked by the sudden change in their condition, they still regarded themselves as fervent patriots, and, furthermore, felt bound to prove it.

"They decided that I, the Zionist spy, was unworthy of living with them. They appeared intelligent; there were a number of teachers, writers' wives, and the fiancée of a Communist poet from Gaza. As for her, I could comprehend her unconcealed hatred. But the others! They boycotted me, harassing me at every turn. They wanted me to apply for a transfer to the 'criminals'' section, and when I refused, they resolved to make my life a misery until I departed. Mary Papadopulu, a Greek woman, was the sole exception, saying: 'Outside is outside; here, we're all prisoners.' But she was the only one."

There was only one person in the prison in whom she could confide —the doctor, Dr. Sadek. He was a short, sharp-tongued man with a quick temper, "but an excellent doctor and a wonderful person. To this day, I can think of him with nothing but admiration and respect and I regret that he has departed this world, so that I can't repay him." Dr. Sadek was something of an anomaly in Egypt's prisons, a doctor who joined the prison service out of a desire to help the most wretched and downtrodden of human beings. Even when he learned to know those he wished to help, his revulsion did not overcome his ideals. He was "irritatingly" uncorruptible. He waged relentless war against the contractor who supplied food to the prison, frequently refusing to certify the maggotty meat he provided. His campaign was in vain; the prison officers shared the supplier's profits, and when the doctor refused to certify the meat, it was received without certification. Most of the prisoners also disliked him for "harming business." For example, he had the milk sweetened before it was issued to pregnant women and nursing mothers, preventing them from selling them sugar on the black market. Nor did he give out *mulahzat.*

Right from the start, he treated Marcelle with a fairness which soon changed into fatherly affection. When she felt depressed, he was her only salvation. He called her to the dispensary daily, to make sure that she had at least eaten some of her food, and above all, to console her and cheer her up. When she regained her interest in the world around, he got into the habit of "forgetting" a copy of *Life* on his desk; Marcelle would smuggle it into her cell and bring it back the next day. The journal, with its pictures which reminded her of the outside world, sustained her hopes and dreams, and helped her recuperation.

Later, he made her his assistant, charging her with giving out supplementary food rations to prisoners who were pregnant or nursing, and with weighing the dozens of babies in the prison. He needed these records for his research on the development of babies under prison conditions. Later still, whenever he performed minor operations, she served as his assistant and gave injections. "You've got a steady hand," he would point out, to encourage her when she hesitated.

After her release, when she was already in Israel, he took the trouble to contact her brother in France, by means of whom he sent her a most friendly letter. Shortly afterward, he passed away.

In her distress, Marcelle approached Dr. Sadek, telling him her troubles and explaining that the "state of belligerency" with her neighbors was sapping her strength and she was thinking of applying for a transfer.

"Don't you dare!" he shouted. "You're to remain where you are, and if they don't like it, let them ask for a transfer!" Not remaining content with that, he hastened to report the matter to the *ma'amur.* Hassan al Kurdi summoned her to his office.

"I told him that I would prefer to move to another prison or even to the 'criminals' section—anything to get away from the hostility with which I was surrounded. But he said: 'The room is yours, and you're staying in it. If you request a transfer, I won't approve it.' "

She remained, ignored and isolated.

With time, the antagonism faded. After a year or two, the Communists began to question their enmity toward Marcelle. At that, they called off their boycott and the atmosphere grew more relaxed. They were still not friendly. It was only after the Communists' hunger strike, when Marcelle, as the doctor's assistant, cared for them and secretly supplied them with vitamin tablets, that relationships really improved. When they were released in 1963—after Nasser's regime resumed its friendship with the Soviet Union and the Egyptian Communist party decided to dissolve voluntarily—one of them came to say good-bye to Marcelle, saying: "I shall never forget you."

Where could Marcelle turn for company? To the "criminals"? Since witnessing their mutiny, she found it hard to overcome the sense of revulsion she felt when facing them.

Like most prison uprisings, this one too broke out due to the excessive zeal of a new guard. She was a sergeant, Aliya Mursi, who wanted to display her prowess to her superiors or perhaps to the black marketeers, and conducted searches until she turned up a secret store on the roof, crammed with treasures: a sack of rice and a measure of beans, all stolen from the kitchen, together with some hashish. The discovery brought the prison's black market to a standstill, prices soared, and the resultant unrest soon broke out into open revolt.

It erupted without prior warning. Marcelle was sitting in her cell, reading or sewing, when the silence was suddenly broken by screams. Hurrying to the window, she saw dozens of prisoners congregated in the courtyard, screaming hysterically and hurling clods of earth at the duty officer who stood facing them, helpless and confused. Newly arrived in the prison and lacking experience, he made the mistake of summoning the *boloks* from the walls. At that, as though on some prearranged signal, the women stripped themselves naked, and bringing *kardals* out of the building, poured the contents all over their own bodies. The *boloks* drew back in disgust.

The mutiny was put down only with the arrival of the *mudir*, Abbas Kut'b. Without hesitating, he ordered the *boloks* back to their posts, and in their place, he called in guards from the men's wing, who came in swinging *korbetsh* whips whose lashes forced the rioting prisoners back to their quarters. All the women taking part were transferred out of Kanather and dispersed among other prisons, the only exception being the *rai'sa* of the laundry, who controlled the prison's black market; she was spared even though her role in organizing the mutiny was well known. The overzealous sergeant was also "rewarded" for her diligence by a transfer to the prison of Kinniya, far away in Upper Egypt.

In consequence, Marcelle had only one companion, Mary Papadopulu, who became a loyal friend. When Mary was released in 1964 and deported to Greece, she wrote to Marcelle's brother in

France: "I have been released, but I am not happy, because I left Marcelle on her own and she is like a sister to me. Why wasn't she pardoned after serving half her sentence? And has everything been done to ensure that she receives a pardon after serving three-quarters of her sentence?"

So utterly lonely, with everything around revolting and the future too unclear and somber, it is only natural for a person in search of love to think back to the only secure thing: the past. That is what happened to Marcelle. The past was her haven to which she reached back eagerly, borne on the wings of her memories, each one of which she fondled and cherished, magnifying it beyond its natural proportions.

Prior to her arrest, she never sensed any particular attachment to her brother. Fifteen years older than she, with a family of his own, he was unable to fulfill the natural role of an elder brother toward her. But now, in her solitude, he embodied everything of which she was deprived—family, childhood memories, life itself. His brief visits, sometimes accompanied by his wife and son, were milestones in the endless wasteland of her existence, the only sign of the passage of time, something to hope for. When he left Egypt in 1961, she felt as though she had been orphaned a second time. She was not certain that she could stand her loss.

A similar explanation can be found for the love she sensed toward the five men in Tura who shared the same fate as she, particularly toward Victor, Philip, and Robbie. At first glance, they were almost strangers to her. She was born and bred in Cairo, while they were from Alexandria. Before her arrest, she had met them only once or twice, briefly (she had not met Robbie at all). During their trial, when they met in the dock daily, both she and they were too overwhelmed by events to focus their feelings on one another.

But when they were separated after sentence was pronounced, and she, in her loneliness, sought refuge from the hopeless present in memories of the past, her imagination magnified their stature. They were a part of the past, they were part of the reason for her present situation. To preserve her sanity, to avoid the maddening suspicion that it had all been useless, she had to believe in what she had done, and in the people who had taken part.

Like herself, Victor, Philip, and Robbie were noble sacrifices, offered up on the altar of a lofty ideal. With the passing of time, as her sufferings multiplied, her memory endowed them with an imaginary purity. She remembered them as she had last seen them in the courtroom—young boys, thunderstruck by the verdict they had just heard who exerted all their youthful courage to prevent their lips from trembling.

She thought of them constantly. Marie Rosenthal's husband, imprisoned at Tura, wrote about them, describing their days of toil on the *gabal,* and Marcelle's sense of a common fate flared up into a feeling of great love and pity which she tried to express in the regards she sent them in Marie's letters. By the time of Marie's release, Marcelle's links with them had become a vital necessity for her, something she found quite indispensable.

At that time, a prisoner by the name of Bak'r was transferred from Tura to Kanather. He was a peasant serving a life sentence for murder; his family had severed its ties with him. At Tura, he had worked in the kitchen, until Robbie "discovered" him and added him to the basketball team. His lot greatly improved; he was boundlessly grateful to Robbie and sought ways of repaying him. He had the opportunity when the prison basketball league began to function and he returned to Tura as the star of the Kanather team.

"He searched around for me," relates Robbie. "When he found me, he whispered: 'Marcelle sends her regards. If you want to send her a letter, give it to me after the game.' I had to go out and participate, but Victor and Philip passed up the game, returning to the cell and writing a letter which they concealed in a matchbox. To this they attached two books from our own library."

At Kanather, Bak'r was employed in the canteen in the men's section; several times a week, he came to work out accounts with Mary Papadopulu, who ran the women's canteen. He found no difficulty in smuggling the letter and the books to Marcelle.

Marcelle had another contact, Mahmud, a hashish smuggler from Gaza. He was the prison's odd-job man, in charge of maintenance, with some skills as an electrician and plumber. He was summoned to the women's section whenever there was a short circuit or when there was a stoppage in the sewage pipes.

"He was friendly toward me," Marcelle reports, "precisely because of my connection with Israel. He would tell me about the Israeli occupation of Gaza, always ending his account by saying: 'The worst thing Israel did to us was consenting to withdraw from Gaza, and allowing the Egyptians to come back.' "

When the Tura team came to Kanather, he too sought out Robbie and offered to carry a letter to Marcelle.

"The two men vied with one another," says Marcelle. "Each one wanted to be the first to bring me a letter from my companions in Tura. Mahmud said: 'When you hear that the Tura team is coming here to play and you want to send them a letter, all you have to do is to cause a short circuit or block up the sewage and I'll come to you.' "

He came escorted by a guard, but the latter preferred to wait for him in the canteen, sipping a cup of tea and chattering with one of the women guards, while Mahmud was thrusting his arm into the lavatory bowl, fishing out the rag with which Marcelle had contrived the blockage. He carried the letters in the bottom of his bucket, beneath a stinking rag. None of the guards ever thought of searching there.

In this manner, a regular mail link was established between the two prisons. In time, it was no longer restricted to the opportunities afforded by basketball games. There was a regular movement of prisoners between Tura and Kanather, and each group carried a letter. Those headed for Tura knew that the "Zionist spies" paid handsomely for any letter brought to them.

This "postal service" functioned perfectly throughout their imprisonment, but it was not adequate. In time, they opened up a new channel of communication, by means of the national postal service. The letters were smuggled out, stamped, and posted. On reaching their destination, they were filched from the table of the mail guard before the officer could inspect them. There was no difficulty involved: The *nabatshi* of Tura's postman had long been cooperative, while in Kanather, supervision of the mail was entrusted to a new social worker, an avaricious woman whose principal interest was the tea traffic she conducted among the prisoners. She left the mail to her *nabatshia*, who, for a few pennies, would bring the letters to Marcelle's cell. Later on, when she had learned to forge the social worker's signature, she even sent Marcelle's letters off with the outgoing mail.

"The only hitch in this arrangement," says Robbie, "was that we had to write the letters in Arabic, in case they were opened by the censor. I used to do the writing. It was a strange feeling, writing to Marcelle in Arabic; we had never used that language among ourselves."

This correspondence, which permitted Marcelle to give vent to her hopes and fears, strengthened the sense of proximity and mutual involvement between the five men in Tura and the lone woman in Kanather.

"On one occasion, when she wrote to us about a dream she had about a small house by the sea, I sat myself down and drew her a house like that, with waves curling toward the beach and a white sailing boat on the horizon." She knitted socks and scarves for them. (Robbie: "We didn't use them; we kept them as mementos. When the time came for our release, they were among the few possessions we didn't give out to the other prisoners; instead, we brought them to Israel.") She embroidered handkerchiefs for them.

But none of these was any substitute for a face-to-face meeting. On the contrary, the letters they exchanged only heightened their desire to meet. On one occasion, they almost succeeded.

Organizing the meeting was a complex operation, launched some time before a scheduled game at Kanather by the Tura basketball team. "They wrote that they greatly wished to see me, even if only briefly, even if only from afar. On the day of the game, could I stand someplace where I would be visible from the basketball court? The tournaments were held in the men's wing, which women prisoners were strictly forbidden to enter. But the X-ray laboratory lay between the two wings, and it possessed a large window looking out on the basketball court. This was where the prison officers watched the game. I wrote back that I would endeavor to stand in front of the window before the game. My excuse for going to the laboratory was to receive treatment for some mysterious allergy I had contracted, causing my hair to fall out. The laboratory assistant—a Lebanese hashish smuggler and former Middle East Airways steward by the name of Simon—was a friend of mine."

The inmates of Cell 186 at Tura prison were overcome by a feverish excitement at the prospect of seeing Marcelle. Robbie persuaded the sports officer that the team should be accompanied by a group of supporters to cheer them on, and got Victor included. Philip went along as the team's "official photographer."

"We just got off the truck at Kanather when Mahmud approached us. Pointing at a second-floor window, he whispered: 'That's where she'll wait.' When we entered the court, Bak'r also came along to shake hands and point at the window. I don't think I've ever played so badly. I constantly turned my glance to the window, but all I saw there were officers."

Victor and Philip also kept their eyes on the window, but they too failed to see Marcelle.

"It was a bitter disappointment. Somehow or other, we won the game, but I felt no joy in our victory. All the way 'home' we sat silent and quite worried. What had happened to Marcelle?"

They only learned the answer to that question on receiving her next letter. She had indeed come to the X-ray laboratory, but when she got there, she found the prison officers already seated by the window, and she was unable to remain. She tried to approach the window and look out over their heads, but when they began to fling puzzled glances in her direction, she was left with no choice but to depart.

Another eight years were to elapse before they met.

### The Disciple of "The Saint of Helwan"

It was this yearning to see Marcelle which finally induced Robbie to overcome his reluctance and consent to be sent to the hospital at Cairo's Sigan Misr for tests. "We heard that Marcelle was suffering from a kidney ailment and that she was about to be taken to Cairo for an operation. I hoped we would be there together."

The tests which Robbie was to undergo were meant to find the cause of a strange twitch in the leg which he contracted several years earlier, in 1957, and which the doctors were unable to diagnose. "To me," says Victor, "it was a clear case of nerves. We all suffered from prison depression, from anxiety, from the constant necessity to consider one another so as to preserve our united front. This was what distinguished us from other groups of prisoners at Tura. If they fell out with one another, they could always find a way out by requesting a transfer to another cell. We had no such option. We were *obliged* to remain together. In consequence, whenever there was friction among us—and there are a thousand and one reasons for quarreling when five men are imprisoned together in a tiny, crowded cell for many years—we were forced to curb our passions and make it up. There were times when we gave vent to our feelings by cursing or pouring out our hearts to one another. But not Robbie; he had always been an introvert and became more so in prison. I remember, early in our imprisonment, how somber and gloomy he was; it was only by great efforts that I got him to tell me the reason: He was concerned about his parents, whose income had been sharply reduced, but who were obliged, nevertheless, to send him parcels and smuggle money in for him. He wanted to tell them to stop sending parcels, but he didn't dare. What would we live on? It never even occurred to him to consult us, to confide in us. Even after his parents left Egypt, his worries did not end. He wondered how they were getting on in Israel; he missed them. He was the only one of us who didn't receive visits. Again, he kept his worries and grief to himself, without talking about them. I think the last straw for him was the period we spent in the punishment cells after the Sinai war. Shortly after we were released from there, the twitch in his leg appeared."

The order to refrain from issuing *mulahzat* to the "Zionist spies" was still strictly observed at this time. After great efforts, which included bribing all the dispensary *nabatshin*, Meir Meyuhas succeeded in getting Robbie to a doctor, only to hear the latter pronounce that "this was no illness."

The twitch got worse. "We would wake up at night, and by the dim light filtering in from the corridor, we'd see Robbie sleeping while his leg twitched incessantly, convulsively. It would make us weep with concern."

When the prison entered its "calm period"—meanwhile, the doctor had been replaced by the more humane Dr. Snafero—Robbie again reported for sick call; this time, his ailment was treated. Over a period of months, Dr. Snafero tried out various sedatives, but it was all in vain.

The twitching persisted. The doctor tried to improve Robbie's condition, giving him a *mulahza* and getting him issued an additional blanket, but that too did no good. The doctor began to suspect that this mysterious ailment was a mere pretense. He put his suspicions to the test by having Robbie brought to the dispensary and anesthetized. All the doctors stood around watching and saw his leg twitch while Robbie was unconscious. After that, Dr. Snafero concluded that the defect stemmed from damage which Robbie had sustained in one of his nerve centers and ordered him to be sent to the Sigan Misr for tests and brain X-rays.

This was no easy decision, for the members of the network were registered as security prisoners under strict supervision, whom it was forbidden to allow out of the prison. The *mudir* vetoed the decision and the doctor was obliged to wage a prolonged struggle before extracting his permission.

Robbie, too, was not keen about the idea. He was reluctant to leave his companions; on top of that, he did not trust the prison service's doctors. He stuck to his refusal for some time, but when he heard of Marcelle's hospitalization, he consented to go off for tests.

In Egypt, prisoners are transferred from prison to prison on Thursdays only. When Robbie reached the Sigan Misr, the doctor had already left for his weekend leave. "The duty officer gave orders for me to be housed in one of the wings, at which I rebelled. Among 'criminals'? I'd prefer the punishment cells!"

In the end, the duty officer consented to house him in the hospital. But it was out of the frying pan into the fire.

The sick bay was a large hall, filled to overflowing. Only privileged prisoners—*umdat*—were given beds. Ordinary prisoners lay on the floor, enduring agony. Most of them were there for rectal operations; such ailments were very common in Egyptian prisons, particularly among smugglers. They were in great pain, but no one paid any attention to their suffering. The duty orderly was brewing tea for a group of *umdat*—military officers who had been caught stealing army property or smuggling hashish—only turning his head from time to time to shout *"Uskut ya wallad!"* ("Shut up, boy!") at some groaning convict.

All that night, Robbie did not shut his eyes.

It was Saturday before he reported to Sigan Misr's chief doctor, Dr. Magdi. The latter was notoriously corrupt, and it was well known that he would do anything for money, from ordering a prisoner hospitalized to recommending his release. (A release on medical grounds was supposed to be given only to prisoners suffering from an incurable disease, with the aim of permitting them to die at home. But it was related in Tura that for a suitable sum, any prisoner could get Dr. Magdi to certify that he was dying.) The doctor had excellent top-level contacts, which protected him when prisoners informed against him. But not even he was prepared to get involved in releasing an "Israeli spy." "Anyway," says Robbie, "I didn't have any money."

When Dr. Magdi learned the identity of the patient he was treating, his manner became abrupt and impatient. He ordered Robbie to receive electric shock treatment.

"But in Tura I was told I was being sent to be X-rayed," Robbie protested.

"Are you trying to teach me my profession?" growled the doctor, and Robbie fell silent.

A metal ring was strapped around his head.

"After the first shock, I said: 'That's enough. I don't want anymore.' I was warned that if I refused the treatment, I would not be X-rayed. I said: 'Very well. No X-ray!' And then I was sent back to Tura."

A forensic doctor was summoned. He made Robbie sign a statement that he had refused the treatment prescribed by the prison doctor and that he was prepared to take the responsibility for the consequences of his refusal.

On the following Thursday, he arrived back at Tura.


Victor's *tasnia* had been changed. He had spent a year in the carpentry shop, making lavatory seats. Then, one day, in anticipation of a scheduled visit by some VIP, the *mudir* gave orders to brighten up the appearance of the prison by planting a garden in front of the office. At that, someone recalled that one of the "Israeli spies" was a qualified agronomist; Victor was appointed prison gardener.

After the first garden succeeded, gaining the praise of the VIP, Victor's services were in great demand, and he was ordered to plant gardens in front of each block. Picking out a plot of land by the mosque —a handsome building whose surroundings had been neglected—Victor made it into a plant nursery. With seeds supplied by his parents and with two prisoners lugging buckets of sewage to enrich the soil, "I began to reclaim the wilderness." The nursery flourished, giving forth splendid flowers. "On completing his duty, every officer used to send his *nabatshi* to ask for a bunch of flowers to take home. At least once a week, I would also bring flowers to our cell. I also grew vegetables there, though the prisoners stole them all." (At which Robbie comments: "They didn't steal them; Victor handed them out. That's the way he is; he gave them vegetables while we had to carry on paying cash for ours.") Victor even erected a shed, which was quickly engulfed by a climbing plant.

At this time, a new officer arrived: Maj. Kut'b. His reputation had preceded him. At Sigan Misr he was regarded as the worst of the officers. He was red-haired, quick-tempered, fanatically religious, and had a bitter hatred for all convicts.

Victor: "The first time he appeared near the mosque, he terrified me. He had such a cruel face. The prisoners assisting me began to work faster. He stood there wordlessly watching us working, and then he walked away. But he soon came back, carrying a chair. Placing the chair in the shed, he sat down and beckoned to me. I went over. He asked me who I was, what I had been convicted of, and how long was my sentence. He sat there a little longer, neither rebuking nor hitting us, and then he went away.

"The following day, he returned, fingering the *masbacha* [prayer beads]. Henceforth, the shed became his regular post. He would sit there, fingering his beads and gazing around with an air of self-importance."

When Victor absented himself from the nursery for a few days, Kut'b welcomed him back like a long-lost brother. "Where were you? Why didn't you tell me that you felt bad? Still dizzy? Sit down, don't tire yourself."

He sent a prisoner to the office to bring an additional chair. Astounded, Victor sat down beside him. The fearsome redhead was all sugar and honey, like an affectionate mother. "Did the doctor look at you? What did he say? But why go to doctors? Don't you believe in the Almighty? After all, you belong to the People of the Book. You ought to know that faith heals everything. Are you a believer?"

It was a strange and wonderful situation. The prison's most ferocious officer sitting there calmly fingering his beads and talking to one of the prisoners about his religious beliefs!

"He told me that he was a disciple of the 'saint' of Helwan, Sheikh Suleiman the Miracle Maker. Gradually, he also told me the story of his life. How he grow up a mischievous, unruly youngster, how he married a beautiful dancer, how he discovered that she was unfaithful. And then, when his whole world lay in ruins, he made the acquaintance of the sheikh from Helwan, who helped him find the truth and regain his peace of mind."

At the same time, for the prison as a whole, Kut'b remained the most vicious of the officers. When he was put in charge of the *gabal,* the workers experienced a period far harder than anything they had ever endured. He would beat them viciously, overworking them and handing out severe punishments for the most minor infringements. Loyal to the shed near the mosque, it was there that he sat in judgment once a week. He would justify the heavy penalties he inflicted, saying:

"They're criminals, and they have to pay for their crimes. Right, Victor?"

And Victor, his heart beating wildly, would reply: "Right. . . ."

While he sat in judgment, he would order Victor to stand beside him. Kut'b would admonish the accused man, saying: "I have purposely brought a member of another religion here, a man who has neither stolen nor murdered, so that he may judge whether or not my verdict is just."

When he handed down his verdict—five lashes or ten—he would turn to Victor and ask: "Is the verdict just?" Usually, Victor had no choice but to nod his head; but at times, he would pluck up his courage and plead for the man: "He's a *maskin,* a miserable wretch . . ." and Kut'b would grant the request. "Since Victor has pleaded for you, I forgive you. Go, and thank your God."

He was a strange, eccentric man. The prisoners were terrified of him. The other prison officers hated him, and he avoided their company. He befriended Victor, of all people.

"He was capable of sitting there for hours. He used to say that the sight of flowers growing and the sound of running water open up the mind to comprehend the enigma of the Creation. He would talk about his sheikh and the miracles he performed, about the serenity to be found in faith. I had no doubt that he was a true and genuine believer."

Victor told Kut'b of his concern for Robbie and his mysterious ailment. Aroused, Kut'b asked Robbie to come and see him.

"Victor kept begging me to come," relates Robbie, "so one morning, I joined him. I sat before Maj. Kut'b while he questioned me. 'Are you a believer?' I replied in the affirmative. 'Good. In that case, you have no need of doctors. Your faith will heal you.' But he did not rely on my faith alone. He brought me a charm from his saint; hanging it around my neck, he ordered me to say the magic charm: *'At-ma tmissa'* out loud every day. 'Very soon you'll feel better!' "

But he did not get better. Every morning, Kut'b would ask Victor how Robbie was and whether the twitch in his leg was better. When Victor replied in the negative, he was openly grieved.

"He doesn't believe sufficiently," he would say. "He must believe with all his heart!"

In the end, Robbie's salvation came not from doctors or miracle workers but from a book on yoga sent by Victor's brother, who accompanied it with a letter, saying: "It is said to help fortify the spirit."

Victor: "We began to practice yoga. We did it as a joke or out of curiosity. But it grabbed us. We decided to spend half an hour every evening doing yoga exercises together. Philip was soon amazingly limber; Robbie mainly did concentration exercises while I did headstands.

One evening a guard glanced into our cell; he must have thought that we had gone out of our minds."

It took them two years to work through the book to the final exercise. (Philip promptly began it all over again, and kept up his yoga exercises right up to his release.) But long before that, Robbie's leg mended, and the twitch disappeared completely.

# 9

# "THE MISHAP" FLARES UP ONCE MORE

## The Capture of "The Third Man"

"The mishap" reared its head once more in Israel early in 1961. A seven-man ministerial committee headed by Justice Minister Pinhas Rosen, after examining the documents connected with "the mishap" and the reports of earlier commissions of inquiry, presented its findings before the Knesset on December 12, 1960. The committee concluded that former Defense Minister Pinhas Lavon had not given the order to institute operations in Egypt in the summer of 1954 and therefore did not bear the responsibility for their outcome. These findings were adopted by the cabinet unanimously, with Ben-Gurion alone abstaining. It was now impossible to halt the conflagration which flared up around "the mishap" and its aftermath. Despite restrictions imposed by censorship, a sharp and bitter debate soon raged across the newspapers, sweeping the cabinet, the ruling party, and the whole country. For years to come, "the mishap" was to cast its dark shadow over Israeli politics.

But the crisis had been brewing below the surface long before it broke out in 1961; in fact, it had seethed incessantly ever since "the mishap" of 1954.

In the first stage, all those connected with it were progressively removed from their posts. The first to go was Motke Ben-Tzur, head of the special task force of military intelligence. He was dismissed from his post and from the army in October 1954; documents concerning "the mishap" would henceforth refer to him as "the reserve officer." Ben-

Tzur was followed by Pinhas Lavon, forced to tender his resignation from the government on January 2, 1955, after the Dori-Olshan committee found itself unable to say more than: "We were not convinced beyond any shadow of doubt that 'the senior officer' [Jibly] did not receive orders from the Defense Minister. At the same time, we are not certain that the Defense Minister did, in fact, give the orders attributed to him . . ."

Benyamin Jibly was also swept away by the avalanche. Not long after returning from Sdeh Boker to take over the defense portfolio in the Sharett cabinet, David Ben-Gurion removed Jibly from his post as head of military intelligence, replacing him with Gen. Yehoshafat Harkabi, who had been studying abroad when "the mishap" took place.

Of all those involved in "the mishap," the only person who seemed to emerge with his reputation unscathed was Avraham Seidenberg— alias "Paul Frank," alias "Robert," alias "the third man"—the man who had given the Alexandria cell the order to act.

Having got out of Egypt after all the cell members had been detained by the plainclothes detectives, he stopped over in Germany, awaiting clearance to return to Israel.

As it later transpired, he was received at Lod Airport by Motke Ben-Tzur, who briefed him on the testimony he was to give to the Dori-Olshan committee. His testimony helped to undermine the credibility of Pinhas Lavon, and constituted an important link in the chain of circumstantial evidence which prevented the committee from adopting a clear-cut decision in the argument between the Defense Minister and the head of military intelligence.

Seidenberg got a hero's welcome, as "the sole ember snatched from the flame." The fact that he had stayed on in Egypt fourteen days after Philip Natanson's arrest—"to try to save the others," as he claimed— and that even while hunted by the detectives, he did not abandon his transmitter but managed to smuggle it out of Egypt—all these were regarded as marks of his resourcefulness and devotion.

Some time was to pass before various persons began to wonder out loud what it was that Avry Seidenberg actually did in Egypt during those fourteen days, aside from selling his car? But for the time being, his prestige was sky high. Even when it was learned that while in Egypt, he had disobeyed an express order from his superiors, the matter was overlooked. Furthermore, it was not long before he was entrusted with a new mission, still using his old alias of "Paul Frank." He was sent to Germany with a large sum of money and instructions to establish companies and create an identity as a rich businessman in anticipation of a future mission.

This plan encountered opposition from an unexpected quarter:

Issar Harel, the legendary head of the Mossad. As Harel related in a 1976 television interview, he too still did not cast doubts on "Paul Frank's" loyalty, but he was concerned over the man's personal safety.

He contended that the name "Paul Frank" was known to the enemy as an Israeli in disguise or at least as a German working for Israel. His name had been mentioned at the Cairo trial, where he was sentenced to death in absentia. If the Egyptians found out that this was the same man, "Paul Frank" would almost certainly become a target for assassination or kidnapping attempts. On top of that, he was in danger from the German authorities, whose laws he had defied by improper use of a German passport. There is a general rule in intelligence work that an agent is not to operate in the country which serves as his cover.

Consequently, Harel demanded to have Seidenberg ordered back to Israel. Finding no one to heed him, Harel approached the then commander-in-chief, Moshe Dayan, who, concurring with Harel's view that Seidenberg's cover had been blown, ordered him to return to Israel and, furthermore, to terminate his work for the intelligence service.

When Avry Seidenberg returned to Israel in January 1956, he was informed that his contract with the army had been severed, on orders from the commander-in-chief. But his superiors, wishing to soften the blow and help him through his transition into civilian life, employed him for a short time in writing reports on his activities in Egypt and Germany. For this purpose, he was given access to the archives of the unit in which he had served. Years later, it was learned that he had taken advantage of this openhanded attitude to gain possession of a sizable packet of top secret documents from the archives.

On being discharged, he had to give up his "Paul Frank" passport, and he was expressly forbidden to enter Germany. But, a short time later, when he received a telegram from Vienna, informing him that his father was ill, there seemed to be no reason to prevent him from going to Austria. Traveling on his Israeli passport, as Avraham Seidenberg, he spent some time in Austria (while there he renewed his Austrian citizenship) and then returned to Israel. Shortly afterward, he again departed for Austria. With his father's health deteriorating, he found that he would have to remain there for some time. On the recommendation of his former colleagues in Israel, he found a job with El Al; after some time, his wife and son joined him in Vienna. During this period, he flouted his orders by crossing the border into Germany several times. On one of these visits, he approached the German Ministry of the Interior, and, presenting himself as "Paul Frank," reported the loss of his passport and requested a new one.

Three years had passed since the uncovering of the network in Egypt; its members were languishing in Tura's punishment cells and breaking their backs on the *gabal.*

In mid-1957, it was learned in Israel that Bob Jansen—who had shared an apartment with "Paul Frank" in Cairo—was back in Germany. He had opened a gas station not far from Frankfurt and was in contact with the new Egyptian military attaché, Col. Nuri Otman, formerly deputy commander of Egyptian military intelligence. Contact was established with Jansen.

Jansen revealed that Seidenberg had visited Germany. Furthermore, it was learned through Jansen that one of the purposes of these visits had been to renew Seidenberg's links with Nuri Otman, with Jansen serving as an intermediary. Seidenberg asked him to contact Nuri and tell him of an Israeli prepared to sell important information to Egypt, for a sizable payment.

Jansen, well acquainted with the details of the Cairo trial and knowing that his friend "Paul Frank" was an important Israeli intelligence agent, genuinely believed the offer to have been a ruse. He adhered to this belief even when the Israelis questioned him about "Paul Frank's" activities in Germany. Highly offended, he said: "What's this, don't you trust me? Is this how you try to test my reliability? After all, I told your man that I was ready to serve as his go-between with Nuri Otman!"

When the report reached Israel, it produced consternation. Issar Harel related: "First, we contacted his former unit, to make certain that it had not instructed him to disregard the ban on entering Germany, nor to try to make contact with an enemy agent. When this was confirmed, our suspicions were aroused."

When Issar Harel began taking an interest in Avraham Seidenberg's deeds, "I learned of various initiatives he had undertaken and which aroused doubts here."

The files of the 1954 "mishap" were taken out and reexamined. All the questions which had remained unasked, about "Paul Frank's" behavior in Egypt, about the fourteen days he remained there to no purpose, about the circumstances under which he had left Egypt, suddenly took on gigantic significance.

"We came to the conclusion," said Harel, "that his unlawful contacts with Nuri Otman may have begun while he was still in Egypt."

It was now recalled that Nuri Otman—as deputy commander of military intelligence and head of the Egyptian army's security services —had been in direct charge of investigating the activities of the "Zionist network" in 1954.

All this was no more than suspicion, but, in view of Seidenberg's attempts to establish contact with Nuri Otman, the implications were so grave that it was decided to get him back to Israel before irreparable damage ensued.

But how was this to be done? A direct order was not feasible, for it might arouse his suspicions, leading him to disobey. Because he was an Austrian citizen residing in Austria, Israel had no jurisdiction.

"We got him back by a trick," Harel related.

He was permitted to continue his work with El Al, under close but discreet scrutiny. Some time later, after the ground had been prepared by a series of letters which passed through Seidenberg's hands, he was invited to come to Israel to discuss the establishment of a European subsidiary of El Al, which he would head. The offer was precisely made to measure; those who prepared it knew Seidenberg's character and his fondness for playing the role of the big businessman. To tickle his curiosity even more, the projected company was to operate in spheres which any enemy agent would give half his pension to discover.

He swallowed the bait. At the end of 1957, he arrived in Israel.

He was watched constantly from the moment he got off the plane. At first, he was allowed to move around freely; he did nothing which could arouse suspicion. He visited his sister, went to his former flat in Haifa, met friends—many of them officers whom he visited in their camps—but there was nothing out of the ordinary about that. Till recently he had been a soldier himself, and it was no wonder that most of his acquaintances were still in the army, serving in senior posts and key units.

Finally, he seemed to grow suspicious. When meeting fellow officers—not necessarily close friends, but men known for their courage and their readiness to stand up against any apparent injustice—he began to hint that he was "in trouble," that some people were "out to get him" for his testimony which had caused the downfall of Pinhas Lavon.

At this point, it was decided that he had been given sufficient rope and he was summoned for an interview. As a matter of prudence, the senior officer who invited him was one whose tasks included recruiting manpower for intelligence missions. If Seidenberg should wonder about the purpose of the meeting, he could reassure himself with the thought that he might be reemployed. His pride would make him accept the invitation, if only to turn the offer down. On the other hand, if he was indeed working for the enemy or intended to offer his services for sale, he would jump at the offer.

Two other senior intelligence officers concealed themselves in the neighboring room with the door slightly ajar.

When Avry Seidenberg settled in his chair, the interviewing officer presented the first question: "Tell me, Avry, could you swear by everything holy that you have never acted against the state of Israel?"

Avry hesitated for a brief moment before launching on his predictable string of denials. That moment sealed his fate.

Under interrogation, he denied everything. With regard to his meetings with Bob Jansen and his attempts to meet Nuri Otman, he explained it all away by his desire to provide Israeli intelligence with a set of links to the senior Egyptian intelligence officer in Europe, thereby proving that he could still make himself useful and confuting those who had removed him from the intelligence service on the grounds that his cover had been blown. Challenged as to his acquaintance with Nuri Otman in Egypt in 1954, he replied coolly: "Of course, I reported the fact."

Searches through his belongings, his hotel room, and his brother-in-law's home turned up nothing. But when they were about to leave, a random remark by one of the members of the family sent them speeding to Avry Seidenberg's former apartment in Haifa. There, in an attic, they found a shabby old suitcase containing a veritable treasure trove: fifteen envelopes stuffed with classified, top secret material. Apparently, Avry had gained possession of documents stolen from the unit's archives two years earlier, but some of it was new and could only have been taken from one of the intelligence bases where he went "to visit friends."

Indicted on charges of possessing this material and of attempting to set up contact with an enemy agent, Seidenberg went on trial in camera before the then president of the Jerusalem District Court, Dr. Benyamin Halevy. Seidenberg denied everything. Furthermore, he told the full story of his false testimony before the Dori-Olshan committee in 1954, claiming that his present trial was an attempt by Israeli intelligence to silence him by sending him to prison for the rest of his life. He alleged that the whole trial and the evidence against him were nothing but a plot to frame him, with everyone—military intelligence, the Mossad, the witnesses from Europe and Israel—in collusion against him, while he was the only one telling the truth.

His allegations were so grave that, departing from usual practice, Mossad chief Issar Harel himself mounted the witness stand to refute them.

The court did not believe that all of Israel's intelligence services were in collusion to persecute an innocent Avry Seidenberg. Dr. Halevy (later appointed to the Supreme Court and afterward a member of Knesset) handed down his verdict in which he proclaimed his conviction that there were no grounds for the accused's contention about being the victim of a sinister plot. On the contrary, the accused was making skillful use of his past perjury, so as to distract the court from the charges against him and so as to exert pressure on his former superiors to intervene on his behalf. Dr. Halevy said he did not believe the accused's "crooked contention" about distortions and fabrications brought up against him. He sentenced Avraham Seidenberg to twelve years' imprisonment (an appeal to the Supreme Court got it reduced to ten).

But the court also ordered Seidenberg's testimony to be forwarded to the attorney general, Gideon Hausner. Among those who learned details of the trial was a senior intelligence officer, the man who had replaced Motke Ben-Tzur as commander of the special task force. This officer—known in documents relating to "the mishap" as "the man"— had long been aware of the irregularities arising from "the mishap," which had poisoned the atmosphere in his unit; he hoped that, in view of Seidenberg's testimony, an inquiry would now be ordered with the aim of finding out what really happened in 1954.

After waiting in vain, he took the initiative and contacted the then director general of the Finance Ministry, Pinhas Sapir, one of the powerful figures in the ruling Labor party, and told him the whole story.

In April 1960, Sapir met Lavon, now secretary general of the Histadrut trade union confederation. Three months later, after conducting a private investigation which dredged up further proofs, Lavon approached Ben-Gurion and revealed his findings.

There were further investigations. Ben-Gurion charged his military aide, Col. Haim Ben-David, with conducting an unofficial investigation. Later, Supreme Court judge Haim Cohen was appointed to conduct an official inquiry, in secret; the attorney general, Gideon Hausner, then undertook a further investigation.

All these inquiries found that witnesses had been induced to commit perjury in 1954; they discovered that important documents connected with "the mishap" had vanished, with Hausner finding that at least one document was forged.

In consequence, a seven-man ministerial committee was set up under Justice Minister Pinhas Rosen; when its findings were presented, the dam burst, releasing a flood of testimony concerning lies and forgeries by heads of the intelligence services.

Amid all this upheaval, no one paid any attention to a further commission which was studying "the mishap." It was headed by Col. Ariel Amiad—later deputy mayor of Tel Aviv—and charged with reexamining all the relevant material to determine whether there was room to indict Avry Seidenberg on charges of betraying the two cells in Cairo and Alexandria to the Egyptian police. The commission found that there was insufficient legal material to bring Seidenberg to trial.

Seidenberg was imprisoned at Ramleh jail. He was a model prisoner, and the prison's governors noted his positive influence upon his fellow convicts. Like Robbie Dassa at Tura, Seidenberg excelled at sports and was the star of Ramleh prison's basketball team. All the same, he failed to get his term of imprisonment reduced for good behavior, as is customary. He served the full ten-year term.

On being released—still claiming innocence—he briefly engaged in selling television sets in Tel Aviv. In 1972 he emigrated to the United States, settling in California.

### Hunger Strike in the Punishment Cells

The border between Israel and Egypt is fenced off on both sides by barbed wire, minefields, and military patrols. The same goes for Israel's other borders, making the state into a beleaguered isle in the Middle East. Nevertheless, whatever happens in Israel, whatever is said or written there reverberates as far as Cairo and Damascus, Beirut and Amman—and vice versa.

"At first," Victor relates, "there was only talk of some governmental crisis in Israel, connected to some mysterious episode from the past. No details were given. We were not mentioned, and it never occurred to us that we had anything to do with it. Philip was the only one who said, right from the start: 'This is our affair.' "

Philip's sharp intuition also made him the first to mention the possibility that their arrest, six years earlier, was no mere mishap.

"Among the books I chanced upon, there was a detective story about an aging boxer who is hired to assassinate a politician. The assassination itself was carried out by someone else; but when the boxer was caught, he could not deny the deed, because he had agreed to perform it. He was imprisoned, and poisoned. It was a cheap novel, without any literary pretensions. I read it the way I read any other detective story, skimming through it in one session. But after I finished reading, for some reason I couldn't forget the story. I would wake up at night, searching for analogies between our fate and that of the old boxer. We too had taken it upon ourselves to commit a deed, and because we were caught while doing it, we thought it self-evident that we were caught because of what we had done. But was this the case? I would lie on my bed, with my companions sleeping around me, and reconstruct the events of that fateful Friday, July 23, 1954, and of the preceding days. One after another, I picked out weak points in the story. Why were the police waiting at the entrances of Alexandria's cinemas? Why were passports not prepared beforehand so that we could make our getaway in case of some misfortune? Why was nothing done to save those who could still have been saved? And why did 'Paul Frank' remain in Egypt fourteen days longer?"

Remembering "Paul Frank," Philip's thoughts ran in a different direction. "Frank's" dallying in Egypt after the capture of the network was not the only puzzling thing he had done. Philip recalled his own pleas to remove the laboratory from his home before they began their operations. It was "Paul Frank" who decided against it; it was he who also ordered that messages received and transmitted should not be destroyed.

"One night," Victor recalls, "Philip woke us and proclaimed dramatically: 'We were sold!' We silenced him, not wishing even to consider such a possibility. If we had held out till now, it was due in no small measure to our awareness of having acted on behalf of our country. Without that faith, we would be deprived of the only vindication for our sufferings. Better to be deprived of our lives. . . . But Philip persisted, and when he is obstinate, he is capable of being a nuisance. In the end, we adopted an unfair device, telling him: 'It was all your fault: the bomb went off in your pocket, and that's why you're trying to blame others.' Only then did he withdraw into an offended silence."

A few weeks later, when the first rumors of the revival of "the mishap" in Israel caused Philip to cry: "That's our affair!" the others again lost their tempers with him.

It was not long before he was proved correct. This was confirmed by the sudden change in the attitude the prison authorities adopted toward them. Once again, they felt as though they were bearing the mark of Cain on their foreheads: the prison officers scowled at them, they were bullied by the guards, and the more compliant convicts, trying to conform with those in authority, began to display hostility toward them.

Robbie: "We were literally in danger of our lives. Wherever we turned, we encountered curses. 'Here come the traitors!' We had to be wary of being caught in some corner on our own. I presume that neither those who initiated the publicity in Israel nor those who sanctioned it had any intention of harming us. They simply didn't think of what it might cause us."

Matters got worse when the Egyptian press discovered the link between events in Israel and the five men in Tura. The 1954 "mishap" reappeared in the headlines, and journalists came to Tura to interview them.

At first, they refused to grant interviews, fearing that further publicity would make things worse. "But the man from *Al Ahram* said: 'Whatever happens, we'll write about you. If you refuse to answer our questions, we'll make up the replies ourselves.' At that, we decided that we really had nothing to lose. On the contrary, perhaps the publicity would cause those 'on the outside' to remember our existence."

They were photographed in the library, in the shed near the

mosque, and in their cell. Numerous questions were asked. One of them was: "What will you do when you are released?" They replied: "We'll go to Israel, of course. That is our country."

"Supposing Israel is no longer in existence by then?"

They responded with mocking laughter. The journalist, angered, published a vicious article, depicting the "presumption" of the Zionist spies who had yet to learn their lesson; even after seven years in prison, they still dreamed of Israel. He added a broad hint that they might be too well off in prison, sitting in a shady shed amid the fragrance of flowers, with access to a fine library and housed in a roomy fourth-floor cell with a wonderful view of the Nile . . .

The hint was taken. Two officer convicts arrived in Tura at that time precisely: Maj. Aziz al A'akad (a nephew of Hamza from the Sigan Harbi) and Capt. Kazem al Atrabi. Both were taken prisoner by the Israelis in the Sinai campaign; later, they got involved in smuggling hashish and were sentenced to a prolonged term of imprisonment. Thanks to the influence of Hamza el Bassiuni, they had hitherto been confined to the hospital in Sigan Misr, where they did as they pleased. But they apparently went too far; after being caught conducting a drunken orgy with prostitutes brought in from outside the prison, they were sent to Tura. They were soon followed by el Bassiuni, who came to intercede on their behalf. The *mudir*—now al Helwani once more —took the opportunity of killing two birds with one stone, by fulfilling el Bassiuni's request while at the same time making life difficult for the "Zionist spies" whom the spotlights of publicity had shown up as "dangerous." Since they were dangerous, he decided, they must not be housed together. He gave orders to have them removed from their roomy cell, which would now house the two officers, while the five of them were to be dispersed among various cells.

The two officers were already waiting outside in the corridor, with their possessions. But the five men refused to leave their cell, and demanded to see the *mudir*. Finally, he arrived, puffing and blowing furiously.

"I am in command of this prison," he roared. "It's my right to decide where to house you!"

They reminded him that he himself had given orders for them to be housed together, for their own safety. "We are Jews," they said. "We have our own religious laws, we pray together. If you house us together with Moslems, it will cause friction. And what's more, some prisoner who lost a relative on the Israeli border might take his revenge on us."

"I don't care if they kill you!" al Helwani shouted. "I'm in command of the prison, and I'll decide where to house you!" Turning to the guard, he said: "Make sure they vacate the cell immediately."

They were given time to pack; when left alone in the cell, they resolved not to give in. They would go on a hunger strike.

But knowing from experience that a hunger strike had no prospect of success without prior preparation on the outside, they decided that only four of them would strike; Meir Meyuhas would not go on strike with them; instead, he would ensure that news of the strike got out.

When the guard returned to lead them to their new cells, they told him: "We're not going. We've decided to go on a hunger strike."

Under Egyptian prison regulations, a prisoner who goes on a hunger strike is immediately committed to the punishment cells. He enters without his possessions, taking only his *borsh* and one blanket, and these too remain outside in the corridor all day, being given to him only in the evening.

At least they could console themselves that they were imprisoned together, but that lasted only one day. At that time, the punishment cells housed a group of Syrian convicts. Ever since the union between Egypt and Syria, there had been an increase in the number of Syrians imprisoned at Tura, primarily for smuggling hashish and gold. They were a troublesome group, constantly complaining (they claimed that the union had brought Syria nothing but poverty like that of Egypt) and demanding to be transferred to Syria. Now, hearing of the hunger strike, they decided to join in. They only held out for a few hours, but an infuriated al Helwani, accusing the Jews of inciting the Syrians to strike, ordered them separated in the punishment cells, too.

A hunger strike is principally a demonstrative act. In consequence, most hunger strikers remain content with proclaiming their strike; afterward, they secretly eat the food smuggled in to them. But the four men resolved to refuse all food; they also chose the most severe form of hunger strike, refraining from drinking water. They only smuggled in salt tablets, to avoid excessive damage to their health.

For three days, no one took any notice of them. Every day, the guard entered, took out the canteen which remained full of food, and replaced it with another; he likewise replaced the water jugs. He said nothing. At the same time, Meyuhas was smuggling letters out to their parents, notifying them that they had decided on the hunger strike as a last resort "because if we give in and consent to be separated, we won't hold out; we'll die." Their parents were asked to send telegrams to the Red Cross, to President Nasser, to the Interior Minister, and to the director general of the prison service, asking them to intervene. This was no small request. The authorities were likely to strike back, and by this time, those Jews left in Egypt retained few illusions about the degree of protection they were offered by the law. They knew that they were at the mercy of any person in authority. Consequently, the parents argued among themselves anxiously. In the end, they sent off the telegrams, and Philip's parents were even granted an interview with the director general of the prison service. But it was in vain; he refused to intervene, growling: "I don't care if they croak!"

On the third day of their strike, while they were still capable of standing up, they were taken to the prison office and interviewed by a representative of the prosecutor general, who had come from Cairo. They told him they were fighting for their lives; if separated, they were liable to be murdered. They complained of being discriminated against. "For seven years, we've been model prisoners, without a single infraction. But we're still treated with hostility and we're deprived of our rights. Of all the prisoners, we are the only ones denied 'spiritual succor' from a clergyman."

The official thought he saw an opening for compromise, and promised to clarify the matter. Two days later, a rabbi arrived in Tura.

This was Rabbi Siddess from Heliopolis—an elderly Jew, widely educated and speaking both Hebrew (he was born in Jaffa) and French. "But in the presence of the duty officer, he was obliged to stick to Arabic. For this reason, we thought he may have been carrying out orders. Most of the time, he told us that the Jewish religion forbids its adherents to endanger their lives; that we were in the Diaspora and must therefore bow our heads before the laws of the country, and do as we were told. We replied that we preferred to die."

The rabbi was accompanied by Philip's parents. Although prisoners confined to the punishment cells are not permitted to receive visitors, he was allowed to see them. His mother burst into tears on seeing how he looked, and both his parents added their pleas to those of the rabbi. But the four men kept up their strike.

"We realized that we were at an impasse. The *mudir* could not give in to us without losing face. But we too were unable to give in."

On the seventh day, they were no longer capable of standing on their feet. Various prison officers came to them to mediate. "You must understand: the *mudir* can't withdraw. In the whole history of Tura, it's never happened that a hunger strike has achieved its objective. You must give in. It will only be for show. After a short time, you'll be housed together again."

When they remained adamant, a further proposal came up: "Very well then, you won't be separated completely. You'll be housed in pairs, with an Egyptian as the third man in the cell." Still, they refused.

On the eleventh day of their strike, Meir Za'afran's condition deteriorated; his pulse was up to 140 and he was on the verge of losing consciousness. He was taken to the hospital and he broke his fast. When he came around, he asked to be taken back to the punishment cells, to persuade his companions. He told them: "The doctor says that if you don't end the strike today, from tomorrow on, you'll be force-fed."

Wishing to hold a consultation, they asked to be carried to one of the cells. Victor said that the strike had gone as far as it could; whatever they had not gained would not be gained by going on. Philip and Robbie were more obstinate: "We decided to fast to the end, and that's what we're going to do."

The following day, Rabbi Siddess came again. "My sons," he implored them, "consider what you're doing to your parents. They are outside, weeping and distracted from worry. You are shortening their lives."

Unable to withstand this reproach, they announced that they were ending their strike.

They spent three days in the prison hospital. When they were recovered, they were taken back to the block. The officers were so pleased at the termination of their strike that they permitted them to choose not only their new cells but also their Egyptian fellow inmates. Za'afran, Philip, and Robbie chose Abu'l Yazid, the laundryman. He was a gigantic, blue-eyed Saidi, a murderer. Victor and Meir Meyuhas chose the block's barber, Amin. Hailing from Mansura, Amin, too, was a murderer, but quiet and clean. It was some time before they learned that he took advantage of their absences from the cell to rummage through their possessions. After a time, Philip, tiring of his incessant cough, persuaded him to report for sick call, whereupon it transpired that he was suffering from tuberculosis at an advanced stage. "It's a wonder we weren't infected."

Later, when the time drew near for the two Meirs to be released, Victor and Meir Za'afran changed cells. When the two men left the prison, Philip, Victor, and Robbie again remained together. The Saidi laundryman had long since moved to another cell and no one paid any attention.

## The First Releases

Hopefully, but with no little anxiety, the five men awaited the date when Meir Meyuhas and Meir Za'afran would complete their sentences. Right up to the last moment, they did not believe they would be released. No wonder, they had experienced so many disappointments whenever they dared to hope.

Egypt's prison regulations state that a prisoner is entitled to a reduction of one quarter of his sentence if his behavior is good. In addition to this concession, which applies to all prisoners, a prison governor is empowered to recommend the release of a prisoner after he has completed one half of his sentence. On top of that, festive occasions or dates such as Revolution Day may be marked by pardoning individual prisoners or certain categories.

Philip: "Whenever such dates approached, we would experience a feverish optimism. Would our names appear on the list of those receiving pardons? But we quickly learned that we had nothing to hope for. The official proclamation announcing the pardons would state expressly that they did not apply to those convicted under the 'Atrin 10' file. All the same, we continued to hope, though with no great conviction. In the same way, we counted the days until the two Meirs completed half of their sentences; but when our hopes were dashed again, we were disappointed but not shattered. But we looked forward quite confidently to having the last quarter of our sentences reduced. After all, hadn't we been model prisoners? When five years had elapsed since our arrest, leaving only two or three months till the two Meirs completed three-quarters of their sentences, we were again on edge. We were incessantly engaged in trying to guess: Would they or wouldn't they be pardoned? We would try to encourage ourselves, saying: 'How could they possibly avoid issuing a pardon? After all, it's written in the *laiha!*' All the same, there was no pardon. Once again, the proclamation appeared on the notice board, with the disheartening phrase: 'With the exception of those convicted under the "Atrin 10" file.' "

There were other times when their hopes soared; for instance, whenever someone important fell into Israeli hands.

Robbie: "In 1957, a Copt priest was arrested in Israel and charged with espionage. The press reported his arrest with great indignation and we began to dream: If he's so important, maybe they'll exchange us for him? But some time later, it was reported that he had been sentenced to ten years' imprisonment."

A year later, the Egyptian journalist Ahmed Ossman, a former major with close links to the Revolutionary Council, was also arrested in Israel on charges of espionage. This time, they had more concrete grounds for their hopes: Ossman's wife was related to one of the *bolok* officers, and the latter boasted widely of Ossman's prominent status and of his contacts with the regime. He repeatedly told the members of the network: "The President won't abandon Ossman in an Israeli prison; he's certain to procure his release. Maybe in exchange for you people. . . ."

They believed him. Although the Egyptian press gradually toned down its reports of Ossman's arrest and he was forgotten, the five men in Tura still adhered to the belief that their prospects of release depended upon him. As the two Meirs prepared for their release, one of the missions with which their companions charged them was to urge those in positions of responsibility to offer to exchange Ossman for the network members.

Years later, Ossman again made the headlines. This was when he organized the mass breakout of dozens of Arab security prisoners from Shatta prison. He himself did not succeed in getting away; he was severely injured in the attempt. Egypt's newspapers were filled with stories of his heroism "and we decided to take advantage of the fact. We smuggled out a letter, signed with a fictitious name, addressed to one of the newspapers; in it, we complained that no effort was being made to get the national hero Ahmed Ossman repatriated to Egypt, even if it was in exchange for the Jewish spies eating Egyptian bread in Tura prison. But the letter wasn't published."

When the union between Syria and Egypt disintegrated, the blame was placed on Mushir Abdul Hakim Amer, who served as High Commissioner in Syria. Personally, he suffered no harm, but several of his followers fell victim in the behind-the-scenes struggle between Amer and Ali Sabry, who vied for second place after Nasser. Some of these men found themselves in prison; they included Amer's secretary, Col. Daud Aawiss; Maj. Wahid Ramdan, the air force's representative on the Revolutionary Council; and Col. Lutfi Waked, a member of parliament. The latter made friends with Victor, Philip, and Robbie, regaling them with inside stories of the years when he was among Nasser's intimates. When he heard from them of the letter they had smuggled out and of the hopes they attached to Ahmed Ossman, he waved his hand disparagingly. "That's a waste of time," he said. "I knew Ahmed Ossman when I was serving as military attaché in London. He's no more than an adventurer and a dreamer. Nasser doesn't take him seriously at all. If he's your only hope, I'm afraid you're going to spend many more years here."

He turned out to be right. Ossman was only released in 1966, as part of a package deal which also included the Armenian spy Ya'akov Yakobian and two *fedayeen*, in exchange for a Jewish family which had inadvertently crossed the Gaza Strip border.


Meir Meyuhas was the first to be released. The days preceding his release saw all five men engaged in feverish activity. They composed an innocent-looking poem, filled with the outpourings of a convict lamenting the loss of his freedom; Meir Meyuhas was to take it with him as a memento. In effect, this was the key to a cipher which they intended to employ henceforth in their letters, with each word conveying an additional meaning. They charged him with various missions: he was to visit their families (Robbie's parents in Israel and Victor's sister in

Switzerland); he was to arrange for parcels to be sent (from now on, the parcels contained far more cigarettes, and customs duty was paid in advance); in Israel, he was to stress the feasibility of an exchange of prisoners—for Ahmed Ossman or others; alternately, he was to arrange for "noise" abroad, so as to mobilize pressure for their release. If these prospects failed, they gave notice that they intended to try to escape.

Meir Meyuhas left Tura on August 5, 1961, precisely seven years after his arrest. Meir Za'afran was released six days later. He, too, left exactly seven years after the day of his arrest. But a further seventeen days elapsed before he was permitted to leave Egypt. Later, it transpired that his release had set off the old debate between the "extremists" and "moderates" among the ruling circles in Egypt. Some contended that even though they had served their full sentences, the "Zionist spies" must on no account be permitted to leave Egypt. The disagreement was brought before Nasser, who decided in favor of having them deported.

However, a few days more passed before their passports were prepared, and a European country (in the case of Meyuhas, Italy) expressed its willingness to grant them visas. In the meantime, Meyuhas was confined to Kanather prison where he tried in vain to make contact with Marcelle.

Finally, he departed, and postcards began to arrive—from Italy, from Switzerland, from Italy again. They were addressed to Ali Rashidi, the *nabatshi* of the mail guard. The contents of the postcards again lit a spark of hope among the three remaining prisoners. Meyuhas wrote expressly: "I am not continuing my journey as planned, for the time being. I have decided to remain in Italy to await you."

"If he's decided to wait for us," the three men told one another, "there must be something behind it. It means he knows that we are soon to be released!"

There was, indeed, something behind it.

Egypt's relations with the Soviet Union had deteriorated again, and for the umpteenth time, Nasser repeated his favorite trick of playing the two sides off against one another, by wooing the Western powers. He was particularly successful in his overtures toward Italy, and the two states were on close terms. Aminatore Fanfani, then serving as Italian Foreign Minister, chanced to visit Israel at that time, and promised his hosts that he would take advantage of his contacts with Nasser to persuade him to pardon the four remaining network members.

Hearing of this, Meir Meyuhas believed that they would soon be released.

Fanfani kept his promise, but Nasser turned him down, causing another heartbreak to the three men in Tura (Marcelle did not receive the optimistic tidings and was therefore spared the disappointment). In 1964, when Fanfani paid a further visit to Cairo, he was "compensated" by Nasser for the earlier refusal, when a pardon was granted to two Italians, Paccola and Raymondo di Pietro, who had been convicted of spying for Israel.

Before his arrest, Paccola served as a diving instructor in an Egyptian navy frogman unit. After consenting to work for Israeli intelligence, he recruited an Italian resident of Alexandria—Raymondo—to help him. After a time, Paccola's contract ran out and he returned to Italy, where he kept up his contacts with Raymondo, sending letters written in invisible ink. In 1959, the Egyptian police searched Raymondo's postal box, finding a letter from Paccola which they succeeded in deciphering. Raymondo was arrested. Paccola was also lured into returning to Egypt; he was offered a new contract as a frogman instructor and arrested as his plane touched down. He was sentenced to fifteen years' imprisonment; Raymondo got ten.

Robbie: "When Paccola and Raymondo arrived in Tura, they approached us directly. While they were still in the Sigan Misr, the Egyptian prisoners told them: 'When you get to Tura, you'll be better off; the Jewish spies will look after you.' "

They did, indeed, look after them. Raymondo was rescued from the *gabal* because Robbie made him a member of the basketball team. (In time, all five leading players on the basketball team were, without exception, spies.) Paccola also got himself settled in. "Both of them were grateful and even sensed a strange kind of guilt toward us. They had broken down under interrogation, revealing everything they knew, and now they felt obliged to justify themselves to us, as though we were official representatives of the state of Israel."

When the two Italians were pardoned, the network members were the first to learn of it, via a letter from Victor's father who had read about it in a Swiss newspaper. "When we brought them the news, they wept for joy. They wept again when they took leave of us. As for us, we were glad for them, but we were also sorry at their departure. In Tura, there were few men like them, with a European background, with whom we could converse on matters beyond day-to-day prison life; we could even play chess with them."

During this period, from 1959 onward, five more cells of spies who had operated on behalf of Israel were uncovered. There was no link between them, beyond the fact that they employed the same invisible ink.

One of these cells consisted of two Greek residents of Cairo—George Stymatio, the headwaiter of the famous Groppi café, often summoned to cater parties in the homes of leading members of the officers' regime; and Nicola Kois, a decorator and exhibition designer whose work often took him on trips abroad. These two were also taken under the protection of the network members. After Za'afran's release, Nicola replaced him in the group preparing the annual exhibition.

Another spy cell uncovered at this time was "Dr. Katz's cell." Dr. Katz was a German-born doctor who became one of the most renowned surgeons in Egypt, treating the royal family before the revolution and Nasser's brother subsequently. In effect, he was one of the minor members of the cell, which operated primarily in Alexandria. One of the cell members, an Egyptian employee of the Ford corporation, was sentenced to death; others got prolonged prison terms. Dr. Katz was also sentenced to ten years' imprisonment, but immediately after his conviction, he was pardoned through the intervention of the West German government, and left Egypt.

Then there was a cell consisting of noncommissioned officers in the Egyptian air force, employed at a military airfield.

In 1963, another network was uncovered; most of its members were Greeks and Cypriots. They stated at their trial that they had no idea they were working for Israel; they were convinced that they were spying for NATO. Their arrival at Tura provoked a storm, because they were all homosexuals. This was the first time that Tura encountered *hawagat* who were "gay," and everyone hastened to see them and point them out. Their arrival seemed to restore the Egyptians' dignity. . . .

The Cypriots in the group were pardoned some time later, as their country's closer relations with Egypt led Archbishop Makarios to visit Cairo.

One of them, Yorgo, was a music teacher prior to his arrest. By this time, Tura already possessed a complete orchestra, composed of convicts, which appeared on holidays and festive celebrations. But its instruments were all Oriental—flutes, cymbals, and drums. Robbie, seeking ways of getting the spies released from work on the *gabal,* approached the recreation officer with the idea of adding an accordion, to be played by Yorgo, the music teacher. The officer brought up the problem of the expense, but Robbie undertook to solve it. "The families will pay," he said. (At that time, only Philip's parents still remained in Egypt.) The officer still hesitated, and made it conditional: "The accordion will become prison property," he insisted. Robbie consented.

The request was forwarded to the *mudir.* Even before it was approved, Yorgo began to teach Robbie how to play. After going over the scales, Yorgo drew a diagram of the keys, marking each one with its own tone. By the time the accordion arrived, Robbie was able to play a simple tune.

About a month later, the Cypriots were pardoned and the accordion was passed on to Robbie, who now took Yorgo's place in the prison orchestra. Gradually, he began to alter the group's repertoire, adding songs he had picked up from the European hit parades he heard during the nighttime radio sessions. The tunes were somewhat changed by being accompanied on the cymbals, and their composers might have found them hard to recognize. But they pleased the other players, who were eager to learn more *"hawagat* tunes." On one occasion, Robbie playfully taught them to play "Hatikvah," the Israeli national anthem, and the melody caught on.

After Egypt's intervention in the civil war in Yemen, the prison filled up with Egyptians who had deserted from the army, for fear of being sent to fight there. At the same time, Tura was also visited by delegations from that primitive, mountainous land; they came to learn how to conduct a "modern" prison. On one occasion, the prison orchestra entertained them with . . . the Israeli anthem. The Yemenites applauded vigorously along with the prison officers.

The melody now became part of the orchestra's regular repertoire. Robbie was afraid of what would happen if it was heard by someone who could identify the tune, but he had a ready-made excuse prepared: The tune was not the Israeli anthem, but rather a French song by the name of "Keep Hoping," which resembled "Hatikvah." Sung by Delida, it was a very popular song, often transmitted by Radio Cairo, until a sharp-eared listener wrote to the broadcasting authority, complaining of its similarity to the Israeli anthem. At that, Cairo radio no longer played the tune, and Robbie too was forced to omit it from the program.

The accordion was kept in their cell, and in the evenings, after the door was locked, Robbie would take it and practice quietly. Gradually, his memories flooded back. He played songs he had learned in the Zionist youth movement and tunes he had learned during his brief stay in Israel. On Fridays, when the block was locked up and the officers went off on leave, he would present a "request program" for the other inmates of their floor. "D'you know this one?" Raymondo would call from his cell, singing the first few notes of the song he wished to hear. Robbie recognized the song and played it, with Raymondo singing along with him. Then came the turn of Gino, and of Yani, one of the Greek spies; and so it went on until they were all engulfed by memories.

# 10

## GOLDFISH, PARAKEETS, AND DUCKS

*"Jerusalem the Golden"*

With the release of the two Meirs, the three remaining men felt much better; today, they will admit the fact, though somewhat guiltily.

In such a small community—five men crowded into one cell—there was no lack of pretexts for friction. Victor recounts: "Each of us had his own habits. One slept later; another got up at dawn to do his exercises; a third couldn't rest till everything in the cell was in its place, while another might be more indolent. I, for example, hated to do the cooking. When my turn came, they had to make do with salad, and not everyone was prepared to accept that."

There were problems right from the start. Robbie and Victor smoked, the others did not. Philip, constantly hungry, wanted the equivalent of the cigarette money to buy more halva. They quickly learned that things would not work out unless they displayed joint responsibility and obeyed majority decisions. They pooled their money and did their buying jointly; everything was shared equally—one sardine, five olives, and five cigarettes per person every day. But that did not put an end to the arguments. During their years of work on the *gabal,* they realized that they would not hold out without supplementary food purchased on the black market. However, the principal source of supply came from the convicts suffering from tuberculosis, who were housed on the first floor. They were issued supplementary food rations (two eggs a day, milk, rice, sugar, and tea; and, twice a week, a portion of chicken) which they then promptly sold for cigarettes. Victor refused to take advantage of these supplies—"for fear of being infected," as he explained to his companions. There were a hundred and one pretexts for arguments. In winter, when they hung a piece of material across the tiny window to keep out the cold wind, the kerosene stove would fill the cell with a stifling cloud of smoke. The question then was: Which is better, a hot meal or fresh air? And in summer, what was better than a drink of cold water? But the only way to cool water was to fill a bottle, wrap it in a damp cloth, and hang it in the breeze which came in through the window. But possession of a bottle was forbidden, and there were those who said that it was not worthwhile taking the risk for a bit of cold water. And the water dripped down from the cloth, evoking complaints from whoever slept beneath the window.

For Victor, reading was more important than anything else. The books were donated to the prison library by their families, but he kept his favorite books in the cell, wrapped in the sack where they kept their provisions. He read the books over and over again (by the light of a smoky candle, another subject for the complaints of his companions). His literary tastes ran to novels, and he identified completely with their heroes. "I read *Dr. Zhivago* twice in English and then a third time in French. To help me remember the numerous characters, I made out a list of names and sketched out a kind of family tree which depicted their roles in the plot. At night, I would dream of packs of wolves galloping across the snow-covered steppes of Siberia."

But books attract insects, and his companions demanded that he take the books back to the library. In the end, they gave in to him, but only on condition that he slept next to the sack of books.

Robbie: "Every matter was settled by a majority decision. But there were issues which could not be resolved by voting. For example, we decided to refrain from relieving ourselves into the *kardal*, to avoid fouling the air in the cell. But what could a man do if he was suffering from diarrhea? In addition, we tried to avoid overfilling the *kardal*, so as to leave room for the water from our morning wash. But suppose we had forgotten to wash the vegetables before the cell was locked? Philip was crazy about fresh vegetables and fanatical about washing them. We were quite prepared to do without salad in the evening, but he wasn't! He would wash them in the cell, filling the *kardal* completely; in the morning, we were unable to wash."

There were some rather noisy arguments about the width of their bedding space. The cell was very crowded, which was particularly irksome in the blazing summer heat of the Nile valley. The only way to restore the peace was to measure the cell and calculate the precise width to which each one was entitled: 62 centimeters when they were in the larger fourth-floor cell and 57 on the second floor, where the walls were thicker.

But the most vigorous arguments centered on subjects which might be categorized under the label of "security." Should they purchase an extra blanket for the winter, running the risk not only of having it confiscated but perhaps being punished on top of that? Was it worthwhile smuggling out a letter of complaint and thereby risk incurring the wrath of the prison officers? The two Meirs—the eldest members of the group—always preached prudence and care. "As long as they were with us, we didn't dare even to mention the idea of escape. They never gave up hope of a pardon: at first, after serving half their sentences, and then, they hoped to be let off the last quarter. They always had a date to look forward to and we couldn't bring ourselves to do anything which might harm their prospects of being released. Only after their release did we begin to think in earnest about acquiring a radio of our own."

Their lives were now running placidly. After "reclaiming the wilderness," Victor tended the garden and the plant nursery near the mosque; Robbie painted and did decoration work, as well as playing in the orchestra and on the basketball team; and Philip the photographer attended every event in the prison. Whenever some important visitor arrived (George Brown, the British Labour leader, came to see Swinbourne and Zarb; delegations of prison governors came from various countries, as well as groups of senior Egyptian officials), Philip would be summoned to chronicle the event with his camera. If the visitor was a foreigner, he also served as interpreter.

But now, after seven years in prison, they felt more and more cut off. More and more, their dreams centered on a radio receiver of their own, to break through their isolation and bring the outside world into their cell.

But how? They found no solution until the arrival of Kaimakam (Col.) Ali Abdu, an elderly police officer, chubby and genial, who, to his distress, had been transferred to the prison service in his old age. He did not feel at home in his new post.

"All day long," Victor relates, "he would wander around the blocks, complaining to anyone prepared to listen to him: 'What am I doing here? I wasn't made for this, to tyrannize a group of wretched convicts.' Whenever he ran into us, or any of the other Europeans, he would stop and ask: 'Don't you find it hard in this hole? Is there anything I can do for you?'

"At first, we didn't trust him. We suspected him of putting on a show, but we wondered what he was driving at. But he kept it up.

Whenever he served as duty officer, he would come to us and say: 'I'm on duty today. If you have a visit, tell me. I'll let anyone in.' Indeed, the days when he was on duty were holidays in the prison. Some prisoners informed on him to the *mudir*, who rebuked him, but Abdu didn't care. He used to say to us: 'Let him shout! The main thing is, did you enjoy yourselves? Share things out among yourselves? Fine, give something to my *nabatshi.'*

"He never asked for anything for himself, with one exception. He had a hobby, breeding goldfish, to which he was devoted heart and soul. He constructed a magnificent aquarium in his home, and every now and then, he would ask us, by way of our parents, to get him something that wasn't available in Egypt—special fish food or an oxidizer for the aquarium. My parents ordered the things from Switzerland and he was very grateful. When he learned of the illness of my eldest sister, Mireille, he invited my parents to his home, to make the acquaintance of his family. It was his way of cheering them up.

"There was something else he asked for, some of Robbie's paintings. He began modestly, bringing a snapshot of his children and asking Robbie to paint them in oils. Then he brought a nude photograph he had cut out of a journal, which he wanted as a large oil painting for his bedroom. In time, he accumulated twenty-two paintings, at a considerable cost in paints and canvas. But Robbie painted them willingly, because the man was good to us. He would stamp our letters without even reading them, and frequently took them with him, to drop in a civilian postal box."

After prolonged indecision, they decided to put their trust in him.

"Before deciding," recalls Robbie, "we argued endlessly. We said: If he were corrupt, if he took bribes, we would take the risk. And then, I think it was Philip who said: 'But he takes paintings, and that's also prohibited. The frames are prison property, the canvas is prison property, and the paints are our property. If he squeals on us, we'll squeal on him!' "

And so, one afternoon, Robbie bribed the guard to take him to Abdu's office. The office was near the kitchen so that the officer could supervise the allocation of meat from his window. Robbie waited patiently for the office to be vacated, so that he could be alone with Abdu.

Robbie continues the story: "That day, he had received another painting from me and he was in a good mood. Pleasantly, he asked: 'And what can I do for you?'

" 'I want a transistor radio,' I replied.

"Instantly, his smile froze. 'What?'

" 'A transistor radio,' I repeated. 'A small radio, working on batteries.'

" 'Have you gone crazy?' he shouted. 'You were convicted of espionage! If they find it in your possession, you will be suspected of keeping up your contacts with Israel. I don't want any trouble!'

" 'We won't let on that we got it from you. You know you can depend on us. And as for the danger, nothing could be worse than the present situation. My parents have gone away, I have nobody, and I'm going crazy from loneliness.'

" 'But where will you hide it? Under your hat? What will happen when the batteries give out? How will you pay?'

"When he touched on the matter of payment, I knew that we had won. This was shortly before the date of the annual repostings among the prison staff. He knew that the *mudir* didn't like him, and that he would soon be transferred to another post, in another prison, and this knowledge blunted his fears. I said: 'Find out which is the smallest transistor radio available and how much it costs. Don't worry about the payment.' "

A few days later, Abdu summoned Robbie to his office and said: "I've found it. It'll cost you twenty pounds."

This was an enormous sum, but they could still afford it. For the past two years, since 1959, the Cairo Jewish community had begun paying into their account every month; the money came from Israel, and the sum was larger than they were permitted to spend at the canteen. They already had a sizable sum to their credit, but how could they get it out in cash?

They also had cash, smuggled in by their parents, but that was too precious to them. In the end, it was Abdu who came up with the solution.

"Next month," he said, "my daughter is going to London to study. Write to your parents to forward the money to her. I'll send the letter."

And so it came about.

A few more days passed before it was Abdu's turn to serve as duty officer again. Inadvertently, as it seemed, he passed by the plant nursery, and whispered to Victor: "Tell Robbie to come to me at the end of the day."

"All day long," Robbie relates, "we were kept guessing: Had he brought it, or did he want another painting? That evening, when everybody had finished work and the guards were about to lock up the cells, I stood up and went out. 'The *kaimakam* Ali Abdu is asking for me,' I told the sentry at the gate. I knew that when someone was summoned to the *kaimakam*, he wouldn't be searched on his return. I came to his office. He found some errand for his *nabatshi*, and when we were left on our own, he held out the transistor radio to me, saying: 'But be careful.' Without even looking at it, I hid it on my person."

Victor: "When Robbie entered the cell with a big smile all over his face, we knew: He'd got it!"

Everything had been prepared for the "newcomer": There was a piece of blanket to cover the window and a jam can with a false bottom where the radio would be concealed, wrapped in cotton wool. They waited impatiently for the cell doors to be locked for the night.

Victor continues: "And then, from its hiding place in his trousers, Robbie brought it out. I have never seen anything more beautiful in my life. It was a simple Egyptian-made set, but to us, it was the world's most fabulous apparatus. It was gilt on one side, black on the other, and when you turned the knob, it spoke! The whole world was now within reach!"

That night, they did not sleep a wink. And in the years to come, that radio was to deprive them of many nights' sleep.

In the past, there had been tranquil periods when they tried to draw out the day as long as possible and spend a little more time with others, but now, they waited for evening impatiently. In festive fashion, they would take off their working clothes, put on their pajamalike white recreation suits, and eat their supper. Then they waited for the turmoil of the day to die down, while the duty guard got ready to go to sleep. And then, reverently, they would slip the radio out of its hiding place.

They listened to every station they chanced upon, but above all, they sought out the "Kol Yisrael" frequencies—in English, Hebrew, or Arabic. At periods of tension, or whenever the Egyptians stepped up their disruptions of the Israeli broadcasts, they would listen to the BBC or the "Voice of America." Mainly, they looked for news or commentaries, hoping to hear something which might have some bearing on their fate. For fear of the radio being heard through the door, they kept the volume down to a minimum, each one taking his turn to press the radio to his ear. Whoever was listening was required to tell the others what he heard, but only Robbie and Victor managed to do so. Philip claimed that listening and speaking at the same time was beyond his powers. "To tell the truth," Victor concedes, "when it was my turn, I didn't grasp what it was I heard and passed on. When the news broadcast ended, my companions had to repeat to me what I had just told them."

In the same manner, they used to listen to musical programs, later arguing whose song was the best. On the eve of Israel's Independence Day, in May 1967, while listening to the Israeli song festival being broadcast from Jerusalem, Victor heard a song which brought him to the verge of tears. Breathlessly, he told his companions: "What an extraordinary song that was!" But however hard he tried, he could not repeat the tune. However, they would all hear it again soon, more than once.

It was "Jerusalem the Golden."

Listening to "Kol Yisrael" brought Israel closer to them. They began to recall the Hebrew which they had almost forgotten. When the radio mentioned place names, it reminded them of spots they had seen briefly many years ago. They wondered what changes had taken place there and whether they would recognize these places when they saw them again. Astounded, they heard the news which depicted Eilat as a town with a harbor and hotels and industrial plants. They remembered Eilat as a shed and two tents, with a refreshment stall, a few mud huts, and several dozen workers sleeping on the beach. They resolved that the first thing they would do on reaching Israel would be an outing to Eilat.

Although they endeavored to use the radio as little as possible, so as to save its batteries, they gave out within a few months. But by that time, they had found a guard who consented to go to Victor's aunt in Cairo and pick up the batteries she had bought in response to their request. Kaimakam Abdu had meanwhile been transferred to another prison, but a year later, when he came to visit his "sons," he brought them a surprise for which they are grateful to this day: On finding himself alone in the shed with Victor, he thrust a paper-wrapped bundle into his hand, whispering: "Take it and hide it!"

The parcel contained a dozen batteries.

*The New* Mudir

Indirectly, Ali Abdu was the cause of the most radical change in their status.

He was so attached to his hobby of raising goldfish that he brought a pair to the prison and kept them in a bowl on his desk. To please him, Victor built a small concrete pool in front of his office, where the fish were left free to swim about. Within a short time, the pool was filled with fish. The officers from the other blocks, envious of Abdu, now also asked for pools to be constructed in front of their offices and a larger one was built in front of the office building for the *mudir*.

One day in 1964—Abdu had long departed and the *mudir*, al Helwani, had been replaced by Gen. Abdalla Immara—a large white goose flew over the wall and landed in the goldfish pool, where Victor caught it.

He guessed that the goose belonged to one of the officers, whose quarters lay beside the prison wall. Victor went to the prison office, to find the owner; there, he ran into the *mudir*.

"What's that?" the *mudir* asked, pointing at the goose. Victor explained.

"If its owner can't look after it," said the *mudir*, "he has forfeited his right to it. It is now prison property." Victor built a cage for the bird in the plant nursery. In time, it transpired that the bird was a female.

Victor had a "personal guard," the same man who had gobbled up their sardines so greedily during their first days at the *gabal*. In the meantime, he had grown old, and was found to be suffering from tuberculosis, whereupon he was given an easier job: He was put in charge of the convict gardeners. Well aware that his comfort now depended entirely upon Victor, he courted him and did anything he wished. Victor now made the man an offer: "Bring a gander to mate with the goose, and we'll share the goslings."

Two months later, the goose began to lay eggs, and six of them hatched out. When they grew a little, the guard took his three, leaving three others and the mother. They became the pets of the *mudir*, who gave them all names and came every day to feast his eyes on them. Orders were given to the kitchen to keep the scraps for the geese.

This gave Victor an idea. He told Immara: "In the stores, I noticed an old incubator; it must have been lying there for years. I think I can patch it up. If you can get hold of some fertilized eggs, we can start a small poultry farm. After all, there are more than enough food scraps."

The *mudir* liked the idea and procured fifty eggs from a friend who ran a state farm. In the meantime, Victor got hold of a book on poultry farming and the incubator was put to work.

"Twenty-one days passed—that is the incubation period for chicken eggs—and nothing happened. I began to fear that I had not adjusted the incubator properly or that the eggs were unfertilized. But when I examined them by lamplight, I thought I saw some signs of life. Full of doubt, I left the incubator working. On the twenty-eighth day, they began to hatch out. What the *mudir* had brought weren't chicken eggs, but duck eggs. Forty-four ducklings hatched out."

These were the modest beginnings of a project which was to take on gigantic proportions. "Immara was enthusiastic. Anything I requested for the ducklings was provided. No sooner did I see that a rearing house was needed than carpenters were summoned and the structure went up before my very eyes. Two convicts were placed at my disposal, to grind up the food scraps from the kitchen. When the ducklings grew feathers and their time came to leave the rearing house, Immara ordered the orchestra to vacate the two rooms behind the amphitheater where it used to hold rehearsals. The rooms were converted into duck runs."

Victor learned the technique of duck farming by trial and error. Only when the ducklings began to lay ("They laid like crazy!") did he learn that chance had provided him with ducks of the Peking variety, which are excellent layers.

"After a year or two, the duck farm ran the whole length of the prison wall. Tura contained a school building, constructed during the campaign against illiteracy. Immara ordered the pupils out and placed three of the classrooms at my disposal, to serve as rearing rooms, this time, equipped with electric stoves. The incubator hut was now fitted out with three up-to-date incubators operating simultaneously. The kitchen scraps no longer sufficed, but Immara did not hesitate to requisition the convicts' bran to feed the ducks."

The duck farm built up Immara's prestige. His slogan, "At Tura, we don't throw away scraps," was in keeping with the spirit of austerity which the regime was trying to bring to the country. Important visitors hastened to Tura to see the duck farm, and governors of other prisons came to learn how to convert garbage into meat; they bought ducklings to found duck farms of their own. Abdalla Immara's prestige soared.

Immara was a unique character. He was an ambitious man, of peasant stock, for whom his commission in the prison service was a breakthrough to a higher social class. He soon recognized the opportunities which the officers' revolution had opened before him, and became a fanatical disciple of Gamal Abdel Nasser.

The news of his appointment as *mudir* struck terror into the inmates of Tura. The arrival of any new officer was always accompanied by a wave of rumors and guesses, "But with regard to Immara," says Victor, "there was no need to guess; we knew him well. He was the *gabal* officer when we first reached Tura. He was tough, cruel, abusive . . ."

From the *gabal*, Immara was transferred to the prison *mazra'ah*, the vegetable farm. Later he was appointed commander of a prison in Alexandria, where he achieved even greater notoriety. He made that prison into a purgatory. He was particularly detested by the Communists, toward whom he displayed great cruelty: some of them were crippled, and there were rumors about prisoners he had tortured to death. In Kanather, hearing of his appointment as the *mudir* of Tura, Marcelle wrote to her three companions: "I'm very worried about you." They too were worried. Immara knew them as *irad*—novice convicts — as "hard laborers" without any privileges. It seemed probable that he would find it hard to accept their present status and would make things hard for them.

It may have been the arrival of the new *mudir* which finally convinced Robbie to go to the hospital. He had long suffered from hemorrhoids and the doctor recommended an operation. But Robbie had seen quite enough of the hospital during his brief stay when he was suffering from the twitch in his leg; he refused to entrust himself to the surgeons there. Now he reconsidered. When he left the cell, leaving only two inmates there, Philip was transferred to the cell occupied by the Greek spies while Victor was left on his own.

One night—it was nearly midnight—when the prison had fallen silent and Victor, beneath his blankets, was completely immersed in listening to the radio, "I suddenly heard a hoarse voice from the corridor, a voice with which I was familiar from the distant past." It was Abdalla Immara, marking his entry into his new post with an unconventional act, a midnight search.

He went from cell to cell with his attendants. In each cell, the inmates were ordered to take their possessions out into the corridor, and then strip naked. Victor heard Immara's hoarse voice shouting: "What is this, a prison or a hotel?" and then his order: "Confiscate everything! What is this, a fashion parade? When I'm here, you'll wear prison uniform, and not 'made-to-order' suits!" At the end of the search, there was nothing left in the cell beyond the *nimra*—mats and blankets.

He was coming nearer. What was to be done? Victor's first concern was for the radio. Its usual cache—in the jam tin with the false bottom, among all the other tins of food in the sack of books—had hitherto withstood all searches. But from the shouted commands, Victor learned that this time food sacks were also being taken out into the corridor. For a moment, he was at his wits' end, and then he decided. He hid the electric hot plate in the cache at the bottom of the *kardal;* as for the radio, he slipped it into the pocket of his overalls, which were hanging on the wall. "I thought to myself: 'When I'm ordered out, I'll take the overalls and go outside. Perhaps they won't search through them.' "

The door was flung open, with a shout of: *"Inteba! Hadrat el basha!"* and Abdalla Immara entered.

"He recognized me instantly. 'Are you still here?' he said in surprise. I replied: 'Yes. We didn't have any luck. The Italians, the English, the Brotherhood—they all got pardons. But not us.' He nodded his head and asked, 'How many years have you been here?' 'Don't you remember?' I said. 'We worked on the *gabal* under you. Over ten years ago . . .' "

Immara looked around, and his glance rested on a cage hanging from the ceiling; it housed a pair of parakeets. This was the latest craze in Tura, and thereby hangs a tale.

One day, a blue-winged parakeet landed in Victor's garden. He caught it and brought it to the cell, where it turned out to be a female. Philip fell in love with it from the first glance; he named it "Pepita," ordered a cage from the carpentry shop, and planned to ask his mother to bring him a male bird of the same species on her next visit.

These plans were brought to an abrupt halt the next time there was an inspection of the cells. Keeping animals in the cells was strictly forbidden, and Philip was ordered to hand "Pepita" over to the prison hospital.

But by now, he was so attached to the little blue bird that he was ready to face the officer in command of the hospital—Capt. Fathi Draz, one of the toughest and most vicious guards in Tura—and propose a deal: His mother would donate a similar pair of parakeets to the hospital in exchange for which he would be permitted to keep "Pepita" and bring her a mate.

Draz consented. On her next visit, Philip's mother brought three parakeets—a pair for the hospital and a yellow-winged male, named "Pedro," to relieve "Pepita's" solitude. The cell was filled with the birds' cheerful twittering, and Philip grew even more deeply attached to them. He asked his mother to bring him a book on rearing parakeets, studying it carefully. When "Pedro" was sufficiently well trained to be released from the cage and alight on Philip's shoulder, running his beak through his hair, Philip's joy knew no bounds.

One thing he did not learn from the book was the rapidity with which the birds multiplied. "Pepita" laid eggs at a furious pace, sitting on them with great devotion. Soon, the cell was full of fledgling parakeets. As soon as they grew a little, she began laying again. At the end of the first summer, the cell contained no fewer than twenty-one parakeets, who, chirping, irritated Robbie no end.

It was essential to reduce their number. Some of the birds were transferred to a cage which was put up in the garden shed, but that did not suffice. They began to give the birds to prison officers as bribes, each such gift provoking a quarrel with Philip, who was devoted to his birds and did not want to give away a single one. Tura prison filled up with parakeets.

But Immara's first visit took place at the beginning of this whole episode, when there were only the two birds in the prison hospital, and "Pepita" and "Pedro" in their cell.

Immara broke into a smile on observing the birds. "Have you read of the prisoner of Alcatraz?" he asked. Victor was startled. Not having read *The Birdman of Alcatraz,* he imagined that the *mudir* was hinting at some famous prison escape. But Immara, noticing that his officers' faces also showed their incomprehension, told the story of the convict at Alcatraz who made friends with a sparrow which flew into his cell; he became famous throughout the whole world as an expert on birds, and a film was made about him.

Then he turned to Victor again. "Where are your friends? Where's that fellow who plays basketball?" While in charge of the prison in Alexandria, Immara had organized and supported a basketball team of his own. When the Tura team came for a game, he would growl, half-playful, half-serious: "Where's that Jewish star of yours? Put him in the punishment cells so he doesn't play!" Victor told him now that Robbie was in the hospital and Philip in another cell.

"All right. Keep going." And away he went, without conducting a search or confiscating anything. Furthermore, the next day he went to the hospital to visit Robbie and remind him that he was to blame for the team's failing to win the cup.

"The next day," Victor recalls, "all the prisoners in the block were gloomy and mournful. Everything they had managed to accumulate in the course of years had vanished overnight. They hoped to console themselves by finding that the Jews had suffered a similar fate, but here, too, they were disappointed."

Immara had come to Tura determined to "break" the prisoners. On his second day there, after his nighttime search of Block 4, he turned his attentions to Block 2. One thousand inmates were ordered out into the courtyard and ordered to strip naked. In this state, they were taken to Block 3, where they were issued with new *nimra* and uniforms from the prison stores. Their places in Block 2 were taken by prisoners from Block 3.

Then he came back to Block 1; all the inmates of the fourth floor were moved down to the first floor, with the exception of the Jews.

"Hitherto," Victor says, "no one dared to show favor toward us, certainly not in such an open and demonstrative fashion. We were branded as 'enemies of the state,' and anyone who helped us immediately fell under suspicion. But Immara was so renowned for his cruelty and his loyalty to the regime that no one thought of suspecting him." There were some prisoners who complained. Immara was in the habit of calling the prisoners together in the courtyard and asking them to submit any complaints about prison conditions, promising them immunity from punishment. There was a convict by the name of Said Lutfi, a journalist who supported the old regime and fled to Iraq. During Nuri Said's rule, he broadcast attacks on the Nasser regime from Radio Baghdad. After the 1958 revolution in Iraq, he was arrested and handed over to Syria, and after the union with Egypt, he was transferred to Egypt. The network members tried at first to make friends with him and to help him, but he was openly envious and informed on them whenever he had the opportunity. On one occasion, Lutfi stood and addressed Immara as follows: "You are well known for your nationalism and your loyalty to the revolution. In that case, why do you permit the Jewish traitors to receive parcels without any restriction while others are forbidden to do so?"

"Very simple," Immara replied without a moment's hesitation. "They have received permission from a higher authority. If you are as smart as they and you also get permission, I'll allow you to receive parcels as well."

Of course, this was no more than a pretext. For a long time, the three men believed that Immara's generosity toward them stemmed from his dependence upon the medicines they procured for him. Immara was a diabetic, and had an unbounded faith in Swiss-made medications, which were unavailable in Egypt. On one occasion, he hinted to Victor that he would be grateful if he would ask his parents to send him some rare drug, and Victor fulfilled his request. Henceforward, every parcel from Switzerland contained medicine for Immara. Victor: "Previously, receiving parcels involved great difficulties. On receiving notification from the post office that a parcel had arrived, we had to find an officer who would sign the permit for it to be brought to the prison. He then searched it and released it. This was a costly affair. But now, we would notify Immara that his medicines had arrived and he personally made sure that the parcel was forwarded to the prison and brought in without a search."

Only years later, on the eve of his release, when Victor went to Immara to say good-bye, did the *mudir* reveal a further reason for the change in his attitude toward them. His brother-in-law, while serving as an army doctor at El Arish, had been taken prisoner during the Sinai campaign, and was treated well by the Israelis. "To this day, he tells me how well your people behaved toward him." Immara took it upon himself to repay in kind.

All the same, he had not lost his old fears of the "Zionist spies." While saying good-bye to Victor, he told him how he used to think about them during his first period as *mudir* of Tura. He would lie in bed at night and think: What are they up to now? One day, he heard a rumor which was circulating among the convicts that Robbie's accordion contained a concealed transmitter. He sent a guard to borrow the instrument on the pretext that the *mudir* was holding a party, and had it thoroughly searched.

Even though he was flattered by the renown he attained by virtue of the duck farm, Immara resented the fact that Tura's model project was directed by a "Zionist spy," who received all those coming to visit the duck farm. In consequence, he put Hamza el Bassiuni's nephew, Maj. Aziz al A'akad, in charge of "egg-counting," making him the senior convict employed at the farm. Victor soon noticed a marked drop in the number of eggs. The reason was not hard to find, because, at the same time, there was a similar increase in the number of eggs available on the black market. "I wasn't prepared to be an informer," says Victor, "but neither did I want to overlook the matter." Approaching the guard in charge of the duck farm, he handed over his keys, saying: "From now on, you and Aziz are in charge."

But the guard also knew what was going on and why egg production had dropped. But he was less conscience-stricken. He reported to the *mudir* and informed him: "Victor isn't prepared to take the responsibility, nor am I. Aziz is stealing eggs."

Aziz was dismissed. Immara had complete confidence in Victor. Matters reached such a point that even guards punished by the *mudir* for some offense would plead with Victor: "He docked me ten days' pay and I don't have enough to feed my children as it is. Please, do something for me."

One man who found Victor's privileged status intolerable was the *ma'amur,* Yusuf Tumraz. "He was a thoroughly evil man," Victor says of him, "with a particular hatred for us Jews." Whenever he saw Victor outside the block in the afternoon, when the cells were locked up, he would order him to halt, call a guard, and send him to his cell. Tired of this, Victor one day reported to the *mudir* and notified him that he would not go on working in the duck farm. "The incubators are full of eggs," he complained. "They have to be under constant supervision. But whenever the *ma'amur* sees me working, he locks me up. The eggs can be ruined, and then you'll come to me and want to know why. I don't want trouble."

Immara considered the matter for a moment. Then he picked up a red card, wrote something on it, and held it out to Victor. "This is a permit, allowing you to be outside when the cells are locked. Now we'll see if anybody dares to make trouble for you." But he was no fool. To avoid any pretext for complaints that he was favoring a "Jewish spy," he issued ten additional permits of the same kind, for all the *nabatshin* of the offices.

### Escape Plans

It was this red card—their crowning achievement as convicts—which brought their escape plans to fruition.

Their status was higher than that of the other convicts. They were trusted by the *mudir.* ("There was one thing he could be certain of: We weren't thieves.") Each of them was employed in some occupation where he enjoyed a position of exclusivity, with considerable freedom of movement. No wonder their renown extended far beyond the walls of Tura! In Cairo's Sigan Misr, which served as a transit station for prisoners sentenced to hard labor, old lags would advise *irad* prisoners on their way to Tura: "When you get there, try to contact the three Jewish spies. They're the *mukhtars* [headmen] of the prison. If they want to, they can be of great help to you."

Their status and renown deprived them of the anonymity which had protected them hitherto, leaving them exposed to envy, hatred, and denunciation. The guiding principle of Egyptian society and, even more so, of Egyptian prisons—the higher your position, the greater the number of people below you who will try to drag you down to their level—was fully confirmed in the case of the three men. On the surface, everyone played up to them and tried to approach them. Former ministers invited them to dine; the famous journalist Mustaffa Amin spent much of his time in their company, airing his wisely cynical views on the Egyptian people and its rulers and the conflict with Israel; and they were regaled with amazing anecdotes about the life of the European aristocracy by a prince of the royal blood (Prince Namuk, a direct descendant of the last Ottoman sultan, extradited by the revolutionary rulers of Iraq to stand trial in Cairo for his part in a plot to restore the Egyptian monarchy). They also found themselves being wooed by the guards, not only those who wanted Victor to intervene with the *mudir* on their behalf. Officers also came round to receive an injection or some medication from their "private pharmacy," or to "borrow" a pack of cigarettes, and, incidentally, to gossip pleasantly about events in the prison, or about the trio's plans after their release from prison. "They were no longer amazed when we told them of our intention to emigrate to Israel," relates Robbie. "Some wondered. One of them said: 'Whatever for? There is hunger and poverty there, and anyway, the state is doomed. And after all, you have a good profession. You're a painter and you can make a living anywhere.' But when we told them that they did not know all the truth about Israel, and that anyway, this was our country, for which we had gone to prison, they were not offended the way they would have been in earlier years. One or two even said: 'If you had answered otherwise, you would have forfeited our respect.' "

At the same time, not a day passed without some prisoner or other attempting to get them into trouble by informing on them or smuggling complaints out of the prison, or without some officer or other placing obstacles in their way.

"We were under constant pressure. True, now it was psychological rather than physical, but it was no easier to bear. We felt exposed up there, and from the peak, the chasm looks deeper and more terrifying." This was one of the reasons for their decision to make practical preparations to escape.

The other more direct reason was Victor's "red card," which permitted him to spend several hours alone in the incubator house while all the other convicts employed there were confined to their cells and the guards were enjoying a siesta.

The incubator house was a mere fifteen paces from the prison wall.

Truthfully, they had not stopped thinking about escaping ever since their first day in Tura, when, rousing themselves from the shock of their conviction, they began to grasp the implications of the heavy sentences imposed on them.

"But during the first years," Victor says, "we were forced to put off our plans because of the two Meirs, and out of consideration for our parents' welfare."

Their concern for their parents, their regrets for the sufferings to which they had already subjected them, and the fear of further suffering to which they would be exposed should their sons attempt to escape weighed heavily on their thoughts.

"Even though we looked forward to seeing them, each of their visits was a painful event, causing us severe pangs of conscience. Counting the newly appeared wrinkles on Mother's face . . . consoling myself with Father's erect bearing . . . watching them pretend to be cheerful so as to encourage us, and seeing the worry behind the pretense. We did the same: We pretended that prison was a recreation camp, that our crime was only a youthful prank, that our life sentence would end in a year or two . . . and the inner awareness that our masquerade was no more convincing than theirs. After each of their visits, I would remain upset and gloomy for days."

Each of them did his best to persuade his dear ones to leave Egypt, but only Robbie succeeded. Victor's younger brother, Roger, and his sister Eugette did leave after their internment in 1956, but that was only because Mamduh Salem, head of Alexandria's aliens police, urged their father: "Send them away; your son looks too English. He'll have a lot of trouble." But Victor's father would not heed his pleas. How could he abandon his son? "In 1959, when he told me that my eldest sister, Mireille, had decided to join Eugette in Switzerland, I was overjoyed. But I was surprised that Father had let her go, and even more surprised that she hadn't come to say good-bye to me before leaving." His wonder grew when he received no letters from her. His father hinted that she had gone to Israel and that he should therefore not expect to hear from her, but Victor remained unconvinced. After all, Robbie did receive letters from his parents. He experienced a sense of foreboding, but he stopped inquiring about her. "I saw how hard it was for them to lie, and I didn't want to make them suffer anymore." It was only after his release that he learned the bitter truth: Throughout this period, when Mireille was supposed to be in Israel, she was wasting away in the cancer ward of an Alexandria hospital. All this time, his sister's illness was kept concealed from him. His parents, knowing how attached he was to her, did not want to add to his distress.

This was an awful time for Victor's father. His family was dispersed: one son in prison, a son and daughter overseas, and another daughter dying slowly. He lost his livelihood; the chemical export firm which he directed had been nationalized and he was dismissed. He tried to earn a living as a clerk at a small Jewish bank, but that too soon closed.

Then, early in 1962, he was told that the only chance of saving Mireille was by a complicated operation which could probably not be performed in Egypt. This overcame his obstinate refusal; he consented to take up the wanderer's staff and leave Egypt. However, it was in vain. Two months after the family reached Switzerland and Mireille was operated on, she passed away.

Henceforth, the elder Levy devoted all his energies to caring for his son and his companions in prison in Egypt. He took over responsibility for sending parcels and letters. His own letters—lengthy, perfectly typed without a single erasure—remained an inexhaustible source of encouragement to them. He did not miss a single opportunity to stir up interest in their case. When Abba Eban—then Israeli ambassador to the United Nations—visited Switzerland, the elder Levy wrote him a long and angry letter, with detailed proposals for a political campaign on behalf of the imprisoned members of the network. The letter is filed away in Israel, together with an unsigned recommendation that "it should be explained to Mr. Levy that he ought not make a nuisance of himself."

Philip's parents were even more persistent and obstinate than Victor's. Even after their daughter left Egypt, they did not give up their fight on behalf of their son. They continued to come on every visiting day, paid for most of the "requests" sent from the prison with their own money, and remained an obstacle to the trio's escape plans.

But in 1964, Dr. Natanson suffered a heart attack and died while walking down a street in Alexandria. Only his wife remained in Egypt. "We were resolved that before carrying out our escape plans, we'd make sure she left the country."

Their escape plans were now coming to the fore. "We felt that we had nothing to lose. We had no hope of a pardon. The two Meirs did not have a single day deducted from their sentences. The Egyptian government was not prepared to exchange us for prisoners held by Israel, and a further opportunity, like the one which arose after the Suez war, did not appear likely. When Abdalla Immara gave Victor his 'red card' which permitted him to remain in the incubator house while the whole prison was locked up at noon, we began to plan a tunnel in the direction of the wall."

The plan was daring but not unfeasible. While he was alone in the incubator house, Victor managed to dislodge one of the floor tiles, so as to examine the soil beneath. It was sandy and easy to dig. If he could get one of his companions appointed to assist him in the duck farm, they could complete the 15-meter-long tunnel under the prison wall within three or four months.

They had yet to fix a date for their breakout, or even for beginning to dig, but Victor began to prepare the ground. Whether or not it was necessary, he withdrew into the incubator house for hours every day, locking the door and strictly forbidding anyone else to enter. "Some people are *nahus* [impure]," he explained, "and their presence would prevent the eggs from hatching." Guards and prisoners alike were so deeply steeped in superstition that they swallowed his explanation.

The tunnel was only the first part of their escape plan. It was quite clear to them that they could not succeed without outside assistance. At the same time, they did not want to endanger anyone. When the time came, they intended to make contact with Israel (by means of Victor's uncle in Cairo, who took over the visits to the prison after his parents' departure) and ask for passports and tickets. Victor's uncle would also be asked to rent an apartment for them in Cairo, leaving it fitted out with civilian clothes, suitcases, and provisions for a prolonged stay—and then immediately leave Egypt.

They intended to make their getaway in the morning, immediately after withdrawing into the incubator house and locking its doors. Then, after emerging from the tunnel exit, they would head for the apartment in Cairo, change clothes, and set off for the airport. Foreseeing the vigorous manhunt which would be launched when their escape was discovered, they hoped to be on board the plane by that time.

However, in case this did not work out, they had an alternative plan: If they were unable to leave the country immediately, they would remain in the apartment for weeks, or perhaps even months, until the hunt died down.

The starting point for the plan was to get either Robbie or Philip appointed to help Victor in the duck farm so that they could dig the tunnel together. This was now the objective toward which they directed all their efforts.

However, the escape plan was again fated to be postponed.

A new prisoner reached Tura: the "German" spy, Wolfgang Lutz. After they made his acquaintance and he revealed his secret—he was an Israeli, a major in the Israeli army, and his true name was Ze'ev Gur-Aryeh—they invited him to join them in the escape attempt.

Lutz agreed without hesitation. He had been sentenced to life imprisonment, and he was under continual danger if the Egyptians learned his true identity. But his consent was conditional on the escape being staged only after the release and departure from Egypt of his German wife, Weltrude (Naomi), who was serving a three-year sentence at Kanather prison.

# 11

## BATTLES IN KANATHER

*The Embroidery Plant*

When her brother came to say good-bye before leaving Egypt in the summer of 1961, Marcelle felt as though her capacity for bearing her sufferings had reached its limits. She would now have no one left in the country.

However, well aware how important his visits were to Marcelle, Yitzchak Ninio did not rest content until he found someone to replace him: their aged aunt, Mathilda Goldstein, their father's sister. She was over seventy years old, a childless widow who lived alone in an old-age home maintained by Cairo's Jewish community. Marcelle remembered her from her childhood and she loved her, but hitherto, it never even occurred to her to trouble the old lady. However, after her brother's departure, she was the only person entitled, by virtue of their family ties, to visit Marcelle. She took up the task without hesitation.

"In spite of her advanced age," Marcelle relates, "she was effervescent and full of life. Mahmud Subhi, the new *ma'amur* at Kanather, fell in love with her at first sight."

This Subhi, a large, fleshy man, "as fat as Farouk," was of Turkish extraction. He was very strict, beginning his service at Kanather with a thorough search of Marcelle's cell. However, a few days later, Marcelle's aunt came on her first visit, and Subhi discovered that she too hailed from Turkey and still spoke the language. From then on, Marcelle's meetings with her aunt took place in his office. Instead of letting the two women talk to one another, Subhi dominated the conversation as he prattled away cheerfully in Turkish. Marcelle did not resent this, because he conducted no more searches in her cell; on the contrary, thanks to her aunt, he altered his treatment of Marcelle.

"My aunt was a regular old battle-ax," Marcelle recalls, smiling at the memory. "Until my release, she didn't miss a single visit, in the heat of summer or in the winter rains. When she learned how badly off I was, she didn't hesitate to give the heads of the Jewish community a piece of her mind, even though she herself was dependent on the community for her livelihood. 'Marcelle needs this or that,' she'd say, and when my aunt demanded something, there was no getting out of it."

In her efforts to help her niece, Aunt Mathilda found a loyal ally in Maurice Nagar. Ever since his brief meeting with Marcelle at Kanather, he had spared no effort to help her. Now, he joined forces with her aunt, and under their combined pressure, the community set aside a special budget to help Marcelle—five, and later ten, Egyptian pounds per month. This at least reduced her financial straits. On learning that Marcelle had been admitted to a Cairo hospital, he took her aunt there and handed out generous sums of *baksheesh* to open up the way to Marcelle's room. From then on, until she returned to Kanather, he brought her aunt to the hospital twice a week; his presence, and his generosity, made life much easier for her there.

Marcelle was hospitalized a few months after her brother's departure, when her health suddenly deteriorated. "I couldn't understand why. All of a sudden, I experienced pains and nausea; white blotches appeared on my face, and however long I spent in the sun, I failed to develop a tan. I suspected that I was suffering from a vitamin deficiency, and each time my aunt came to see me, I presented her with a list of medications to get me. But none of them was any good. I had alternating periods of being unable to sleep and of being fit for nothing but dozing on my bed."

She gave up her gymnastics class, which then disbanded. But she still endeavored to exercise in her cell one hour a day until, one day, while doing her exercises, she suffered severe bleeding accompanied by sharp pain. She thought she had ruptured herself, but when Dr. Ibrahim Zacci came to see her, his diagnosis was either kidney stones or a cancerous growth. Immediately, he sent her off for tests to the urological department of the Kasser el Eini hospital in Cairo. An X-ray revealed a stone blocking the exit from her kidney, causing it to swell up. The doctors ordered an immediate operation.

Since Marcelle was a security prisoner, the prison governor notified the Muhabarat of her transfer to the hospital, whereupon officers of the secret police arrived to make sure her ailment was not feigned. Two policemen, relieved every eight hours, were posted at the entrance to her room.

This "interest" should have had a prejudicial effect on her standing in the hospital; but Nasser's Egypt was in terror of the secret police, and the mere fact that the Muhabarat was taking an interest endowed her with a privileged status. She was given a private room and treated by the finest doctors in the hospital.

One of the doctors in the ward was a young intern, the son of a teacher who had once been a colleague of Yitzchak Ninio. "He entered into conversation with me, telling me that he knew a teacher by the name of Ninio, who was a friend of his father's. When I told him that he was my brother, we became friends. His father sent me cookies, and he himself didn't budge from my bedside. When I came round after the operation, he was bending anxiously over my bed. During the next few days, he rescued me from the inexperienced nurses by coming personally to give me injections of painkillers. Even after his transfer to another department, he used to come and see me whenever he had the chance, to make sure there was nothing I needed."

The operation was successful, but Marcelle was in no hurry to return to the prison. "During the first few days, I felt uncomfortable. There were too many people around me—doctors, nurses, patients who dropped in for a chat. Having to talk to them all was a burden, and I longed for the solitude of my prison cell." But later on, particularly after her aunt's "takeover" of the hospital, the idea of returning to prison became less and less attractive.

Marcelle was strictly forbidden to receive visitors, and the first time they came, Maurice and her aunt went to the neighboring room, which was occupied by a paralyzed patient, and talked to her through the open door. But Maurice Nagar soon found a way of bribing the police guards, who henceforth remained in the corridor where they did not trouble her. They even performed small errands for her, such as buying *kabab* from the nearby Hati restaurant, or *ta'amiya* from the refreshment stall facing the hospital.

Her aunt brought her parcels of goodies, while Maurice Nagar supplied her with a radio and books, and, in response to her request, with writing paper and envelopes. She wrote many letters—to her brother, to her friend Mimi who had recently been released, and to her companions in Tura. She made friends with some of the patients in the ward, as well as some of the nurses. There were some who kept away from her, calling her *gassussa* (spy) to her face and behind her back. But some, particularly the young student nurses, made her into a mother-substitute, pouring out their hearts to her, telling her of their secret passion for the medical students training at the hospital, and asking her advice on how to win their affections. When the time came for her to return to prison, some of the nurses were in tears as they bade her farewell.

She put off her return to Kanather for as long as she could. When the doctors pronounced her completely recovered from her operation, she complained of eye pains, and later asked to have her teeth treated. But after four months, she ran out of excuses and she was taken back to Kanather.

It was as though she had never been away. She returned to her own cell, which had been kept for her, with Mary Papadopulu carefully cleaning it at least once a week. She went back to her work as Dr. Sadek's assistant in his research on preventative care of children under prison conditions; once a week, she weighed the babies, checking on their development, taking care that they were well nourished, and giving them inoculations. She shared their mothers' grief at being separated from their offspring (the same law which permitted women prisoners to have their babies with them in prison also proclaimed that at the age of two, they were to be taken from their mothers and handed over to their families, or put up for adoption). Marcelle was quite surprised to discover that these women—for all their bestiality and a viciousness which made them capable of committing any crime—were equally capable of a genuine, passionate mother's love, and their parting from their children was heartbreaking. Marcelle knew of only one single case in which this parting was not final, and hence, all the more tragic. This was the case of an El Arish hashish dealer, who gave birth to a baby daughter while she was in prison. Her family took no notice of her, never once visiting her, and when the baby was two years old, she was adopted by a wealthy childless couple in Cairo. Shortly after the adoption, the foster mother—hitherto barren—got pregnant, but instead of the foster parents reconsidering the adoption, the precise opposite occurred. They regarded their adopted daughter as a *barka* (divine blessing) and raised her as their own daughter, without, however, concealing her true origins. Every six weeks, they brought her to visit her mother. It was a touching sight. The little girl, now six or seven years old—pretty, clean, well dressed—facing her mother in her filthy prison garb. Even more touching were the mother's silent sobs at the end of the visit. "What will happen when I'm released?" she would moan, lying in Marcelle's embrace. "Will my daughter want to return to me? She's a little lady and what am I?"

Marcelle's work as Dr. Sadek's assistant came to an end a year later, when he was transferred to Tura. "He was too kind," says Marcelle. "The prisoners took advantage of his kindness to squeeze medical certificates and supplementary rations out of him; in the end, the *mudir* got tired of him and sent him away."

For a time, she remained idle. She was known to be in poor health, and was therefore not harassed. She would spend her days reading or writing letters which she had smuggled out by her aunt or one of the women guards. She also renewed her interest in handicrafts. She would spend hours embroidering or knitting while she daydreamed. One day, the *mudir* suggested that she make her hobby into a vocation, and instruct the other prisoners.

"Idleness was beginning to get me down," she admitted years later. "I myself was looking for something to do. For the past three months, I had been teaching English in the prison's 'anti-illiteracy' school. Some of my pupils were truly gifted, with a natural talent for study, and working with them gave me great satisfaction. They were also pleased with their attainments. But as soon as the matter reached the *diwan* [prison administration], orders were given to stop the lessons. They were afraid I'd have a bad influence on the prisoners." Consequently, when the *mudir* made his offer, she consented willingly.

When Kanather prison moved into its permanent quarters, in a building originally designed as a juvenile prison, a knitting shop had been set up, as part of the reforms which aimed at taking advantage of their periods of imprisonment to endow the prisoners with a trade. But, like all other good intentions with regard to Egypt's prisons, this one too soon collided with realities.

Knitting machines were brought to the prison, and a number of prisoners were taught how to operate them. The end results—mostly scarves—were sold at the annual exhibition of prisoners' hobbies. Later, they were marketed through a contractor who purchased the entire output. The prisoners shared in the profits, their pay coming to one Egyptian pound a month, or even more, a sizable sum for most of them. This sparked off competition for the right to work there, and there were those who made money out of this rivalry.

Two muscular women, serving sentences for murder, gained control of the knitting machines; they were appointed *umdat* (supervisors) and took their share of the other women's pay. On the side, they also traded in hashish.

The workshop also contained a second wing, for embroidery, employing women from Gaza and El Arish, who learned their skills at home. Mostly, they embroidered tablecloths, and their work, being quite good, was in great demand. But the patterns they knew were few and crude, and Marcelle was requested to teach them more complex embroidery, like that she did herself.

The chance of keeping herself busy and helping the time go by made her throw herself into her new job with great enthusiasm. The *ma'amur* gave her permission to write to her sister-in-law in Paris and ask for embroidery books containing instructions and embroidery patterns, with which she added variety to the prisoners' work.

This soon caused friction with the two *umdat*. She recalls: "They were very angry at the *ma'amur* for putting me in charge of allocating wool, which they were in the habit of stealing to sell to mothers who wished to knit clothes for their babies, and giving me the key to the store. As for me, I couldn't stand the stench of hashish which constantly filled the workshop. On one occasion, when I came in and found them all smoking placidly, while one of the *umdat* was selling stolen tea, I got furious and said: 'If this doesn't stop, I'll tell the *ma'amur!*' But they knew I wouldn't inform on them, and the party went on.

"I went to the *ma'amur*, but I was incapable of informing on them. I just told him: 'I'm not prepared to go into that filth anymore!' He asked me why, but I didn't tell him. I just took the cleaner women and led them to another wing of the workshop building. One of the *umdat*, Paula, tried to appease me, but I refused to make up. I engaged solely in hand knitting and embroidery."

But even so, she could not avoid treading on some toes. When her trainees completed their first project, an enormous tablecloth embroidered in a mass of colors, Marcelle brought it to the *ma'amur*, who showed his admiration. Casually, he asked her how many packets of thread she had used.

"Twenty," she replied innocently, and he was astounded. Hitherto, similar tablecloths had been estimated to require fifty packets, the estimate being made by the prison service instructor, who took the remaining packets for herself and sold them, through a convict intermediary, to the other prisoners who used them to decorate their *tarha* (veil).

"Without realizing it, I ruined their business," Marcelle relates. "The *ma'amur* was furious and he didn't rest until he caught the intermediary and flung her into the punishment cells. But he did not suspect the civilian instructor, thinking innocently that she was just a victim of the prisoners' guiles; he just rebuked her for her carelessness. To tell the truth, I didn't suspect her at that time either."

She had scarcely commenced her work, and she had already angered two or three "women of influence."

The two *umdat* from the knitting shop waited for an opportune moment to revenge themselves on Marcelle, who sensed the tension in the air.

For the time being, however, she did her job diligently. It was her job to copy the patterns out of the book and etch them on the material, to instruct the women how to do the embroidery, and provide them with thread. As the patterns grew more complex, the prices fetched by the tablecloths soared. A tablecloth which took a week's work was sold for three pounds, almost all clear profit, 40 percent of the money going to the women. Their work was now highly profitable and the women were grateful to Marcelle, particularly as she refused to take any share of the profits. "But even though they were devoted to me, that didn't stop them from stealing my thread. Theft was a way of life in the prison and everyone indulged in it. Even the more honest women who wished to remain law-abiding, or were afraid of getting into trouble, came under the pressure of the women guards or the social workers, who demanded pieces of embroidery as payment for a visit or for permission to bring in a parcel, leaving them no alternative but to steal."

The struggle to prevent themselves from being dragged down into the whirlpool of corruption all around was one of the hardest tests faced by the members of the network during their fourteen years in prison. It was even harder for Marcelle, on her own. "I held out only because I was meticulously strict with myself. I think that my refusal to take money for my work stemmed from the same reason, the unconscious desire to stay clear of financial dealings, though to myself, I said I didn't want *their* money."

Be that as it may, since she received no pay for her work, she enjoyed a considerable measure of freedom in the hours she worked. "I would never come to the workshop before ten. If the women needed me earlier, they had to come to my cell." This apparently minor detail was of great significance, pointing up Marcelle's special status in the eyes of prisoners and guards alike. It proved that she was not just an ordinary convict who could be pushed around.

*Relief from Solitude*

Everything was a struggle: a struggle for status, a struggle against the depravity all around her, a struggle over every parcel, every visit, every letter; struggles against her solitude, struggles for her privacy, for her humanity, for her hopes. Looking back today at her years in Kanather prison, Marcelle sees nothing but a long series of confrontations whose cumulative effect was a despairing weakness, and that too was the subject of another struggle.

She recalls no more than two rays of light amid this endless gloom: her radio and the arrival of Weltrude Lutz, proving that her hardest struggle was with her solitude. The radio was the first to arrive.

In April 1964, Mary Papadopulu completed her sentence and was released for deportation. Over the past years, Mary had been Marcelle's closest—in effect, her only—friend. They forgot their earlier political disagreements; now, they were just two young women coming from similar backgrounds, well educated, and possessing strict principles and philosophies in the midst of an ocean of crime, filth, and ignorance. In each other, they found refuge from their environment; they shared conversations about literature or theater or made jokes about the latest women's fashions as displayed by the officers' wives; they shared their memories of yesterday and their dreams of tomorrow.

Now, they were about to separate. Looking ahead at the years of imprisonment still awaiting her, Marcelle felt lost, as she had felt when her brother came to say good-bye.

During those last few days prior to Mary's departure, they worked out a list of things for Mary to do on reaching Europe (she was to be deported to Greece). She was to contact Yitzchak Ninio, to approach Amnesty International and request its intervention, she was to try to evoke interest in other quarters, possibly the press, in Marcelle's fate. Trying to postpone thoughts of what would happen after Mary's departure, Marcelle flung herself into this planning with great enthusiasm. As for Mary, possibly motivated by her guilt at leaving her friend, she never stopped asking Marcelle: "What else? What else can I do for you?" Whereupon Marcelle expressed her secret wish: a radio.

Portable transistor radios were no longer a sensational innovation. Marcelle had seen one on the desk in the *ma'amur's* office when she chanced to enter, and the prison doctor also had one. "But I've heard that there are smaller sets in Europe," she told Mary, "so tiny they can be hidden in a cigarette packet."

Mary promised—and the promise was kept. She contacted Yitzchak Ninio; she wrote to Amnesty International, fruitlessly, like the Israeli organizations which preceded her in the attempt; she talked with a number of Greek journalists in an attempt to sell them the touching story of the "Zionist spy" confined alone to an Egyptian jail for the past ten years.

Finally, she bought a Japanese-made transistor radio—the tiniest available, a little larger than a matchbox—and sent it to Egypt, to a relative who had remained there; the latter passed it on to Marcelle's aunt, and she found a guard who, for a liberal payment, smuggled it into the prison and subsequently provided Marcelle with fresh batteries every month. This was her salvation from her solitude.

The "political" wing was now empty, the neighboring cells now serving as doctors' reception rooms which were unused at night. But if this isolation frightened her initially, after Mary's departure, she was now thankful for it, because she could listen to the radio without fear of detection.

"Without fear" is a relative term. "During the first two days after I got the radio, I was scared to death, not so much of being punished if it were found as of having it confiscated. I concealed it in the only safe place I could find—on my person. For the first week, I didn't dare to take it out and use it."

She tried hiding it in the cache where she kept her *tau-tau*—in the flush tank in the washroom. There were two lavatories in her wing; in one of them, she deliberately caused a stoppage in the flush tank, so as to put it out of action and use it as a hiding place. When Mahmud of Gaza came to repair the defect, she hinted that it would be better to leave it as it was and rewarded him with a packet of cigarettes. However, one day, the stoppage—a hunk of sticky rice—opened of its own accord, and the tank filled with water. Miraculously, she managed to rescue her radio before it was damaged.

In the end, she found a suitable place to conceal it—inside an English cigarette tin, which she had received in a parcel. She placed the tin in a box under her bed, where she stored her food provisions. Henceforward, she took care to use the box only for storing tins of the kind on sale at the canteen, and with which the women guards were familiar. As it was, her heart fluttered wildly whenever some guard rummaged among the tins, and she needed every ounce of willpower to hold back her cry of alarm, saying instead, with a show of indifference: "What are you looking for down there? Those are only tins of food from the canteen . . ."

But the radio was worth the trouble and risk. "It gave me the feeling that I was still part of the world," she says. Impatiently, she awaited the evening, when the wing emptied and the doors were locked and she could give herself over to the "cult of the radio." Radio Cairo's "Second Program" gave her much pleasure; this was the "intellectual" station, transmitting classical music accompanied by commentaries, or good popular music, as well as plays—from Shakespeare to Brecht—literary criticism, and discussions of the work of well-known authors such as Samuel Beckett, all the things which nourish the mind and the soul and which had previously played such an important part in her existence.

Before long, she "discovered" the Israeli radio, becoming a regular listener to the seven o'clock program in basic Hebrew, which gave her that which Victor, Philip, and Robbie had gained during their brief stay in Israel: raw material for her dreams. Even though she had given everything she had for Israel, the state was something vague and featureless to her. She had never been to Israel and her knowledge of the country did not even compare with that of her peers who regularly attended youth movement activities. "It was years after my arrest before I had my first sight of the *menorah*, the official emblem of the state of Israel. This was when I got hold of a copy of *Life* containing several pages of pictures from the Eichmann trial. How excited I was! To see

that courtroom, so distinguished-looking and imposing, with the judges
and the policemen; and the accused, small and despicable in the glass
cage. But above all, the emblem of the state on the wall. . . . I couldn't
sleep all night."

The radio now gave her the exciting experience of getting acquainted with Israel; she heard Hebrew songs, place names, and news
of what was happening. She would lie in bed with the radio pressed
closely to her ear as she endeavored to convert the words and music
into visual images, telling herself that the day would come when she
would see them with her eyes and not her imagination alone. Strangely
enough, she too was intrigued and excited by the name "Eilat"; her
mind conjured up a splendid sight of red hills dotted with white houses
and green palms, around a blue bay sparkling in the sun. How she
longed to go for a dip in the water and allow it to caress her skin as she
darted about like a dolphin. She swore that whatever happened, she
would not forgo the experience.

For ten months, from Mary Papadopulu's departure in April 1964
up to late February or early March 1965, Marcelle lived in "glorious
isolation," on her own in the "political" wing, filling up her days with
her work, supervising the women doing embroidery, and with her
clandestine correspondence with her companions in Tura, while her
nights were given over to the radio and her dreams.

And then, abruptly, her solitude came to an end; another Israeli
*gassussa* arrived in Kanather: Weltrude Lutz.

*The Champagne Spy*

"By this time," Marcelle relates, "I was getting a newspaper regularly [she was not allowed to receive it herself, but she got it by way of
a 'criminal' prisoner, in return for a liberal reward] and I knew of the
arrest of a German couple on charges of spying on behalf of Israel. The
paper also carried their pictures, with a shot of Wolfgang Lutz pointing
to the pocket transmitter which had been discovered in their apartment, and I knew that, sooner or later, his wife would arrive in
Kanather.

"Obviously, my curiosity was aroused. I was astounded by the com-
bination of a German couple [the papers stressed that Wolfgang Lutz
had served as an officer in Rommel's Afrika Korps during World War
II, and had been taken prisoner by the British in the Western Desert]
and espionage for Israel. I thought to myself that they were a couple
of adventurers who had worked for money. All the same, I identified

with them; after all, they had served Israel and now they would suffer for Israel. I awaited Weltrude Lutz's arrival with great impatience."

However, when she arrived, the *ma'amur* gave strict orders to the prison staff to prevent any meeting between the two *gassussat*. In consequence, whenever Weltrude was brought to the showers or the washroom near Marcelle's cell, the guard would first make certain that Marcelle was either locked in or outside the building.

Weltrude Lutz had been in Kanather for a week and Marcelle had yet to meet her. "But the grapevine constantly kept me informed about her doings. She was the sensation of the jail, both the 'criminals' and the guards being quite entranced with her. She was so beautiful, this German woman! Tall, fair, and so elegant! And she made up her face every day!"

Being a detainee awaiting trial, Weltrude was permitted to bring in, in addition to her civilian clothes, her cosmetics (she was the only prisoner permitted to use makeup) as well as a box full of canned foods. Guards who had the good fortune to enter her cell came to Marcelle extolling the wonders they had seen there. "She's got two suitcases full of dresses! And a suitcase full of perfumes! She's even got artificial eyelashes!"

She was taken every day to the *ma'amur*'s office to meet her husband, who was confined to the neighboring men's wing. These meetings also aroused astonishment: "They're so much in love! Whenever they meet, they embrace and kiss, like in the movies! They're not at all bashful if strangers are present." (This last comment conveyed more disapproval than admiration. To the ordinary Egyptian, only errant women displayed their affection for a man—even their own husband— in public.)

After a week, the duty guards were changed. Either because the tension surrounding the new *gassussa* had slackened or because the new guard was less strict than her predecessor in fulfilling her instructions, Marcelle's cell door was no longer locked whenever Weltrude walked along the corridor. The door was closed, but the guard did not reprimand Marcelle when she opened it a little to peep at the German woman as she walked past on her way to the showers. However, when Marcelle said she wished to speak with Weltrude, the guard was horrified. "Madame, what are you trying to do to me?"

The next day, however, when Marcelle was doing her shopping in the canteen, Weltrude appeared. The guard escorting her noticed Marcelle and ordered her to leave, but Marcelle rebelled. "It's my right to be here!" she shouted. "If you don't want us two to meet, don't bring her into the canteen!"

Weltrude did not understand Arabic, but she sensed that she was the subject of the exchange. "What's the matter?" she asked in English. "They say we're not permitted to meet," said Marcelle angrily. Weltrude made no reply. But that evening, as she walked by Marcelle's cell on her way to the showers, she stopped and asked: "Who are you?"

"I've been here for eleven years," Marcelle replied. "I was convicted for spying for Israel." Noticing the German woman's expressionless features, she added: "My name is Marcelle Ninio. When you meet your husband, tell him you saw me. Will you remember? Marcelle Ninio."

When they met again the next day, Weltrude was highly agitated. Her husband remembered the name and was familiar with the whole story. "We became sisters-in-arms," Marcelle relates. "It was only some time later that I learned that Wolfgang Lutz, even though he identified me, advised her to be careful with me. 'After eleven years in prison,' he said, 'who knows, she may have become a collaborator.'"

At first, their relationship was rather restrained and reticent. On her way to the showers, Weltrude would halt at the entrance to the washroom while Marcelle stood in the doorway of her cell; they would exchange a few sentences, to the great concern of the guard, who kept flinging frightened glances along the corridor. Their conversations gradually grew longer, but the ice was not broken until Wolfgang Lutz —either advised that Marcelle was to be trusted or wishing to put her to the test—smuggled a short note to her by way of his wife. It contained no more than a few general words of encouragement in English, but it ended with a sentence in Hebrew.

"This told me that he had been to Israel. I did not yet suspect the truth—that he was an Israeli. But in itself, the fact that he had been to Israel was proof that he wasn't what I had initially taken him to be— a common adventurer and a former Nazi. I replied with a short letter, in which I wrote: 'Your knowledge of Hebrew is surprising and astounding.' From then on, till his trial ended and he was transferred to Tura, we exchanged letters. Weltrude would bring them, concealed inside a matchbox. When we met in the corridor, I would offer her a cigarette, and she would hold out the matchbox with the letter. The next day, we would reverse the procedure: She offered me a cigarette, while I held out the matchbox with my reply. Even after his transfer to Tura, Wolfgang Lutz was occasionally permitted to see his wife, opening up a further channel for my correspondence with my companions." Gradually, the prison grew accustomed to the presence of the German woman, and the tension surrounding her relaxed completely. The guards no longer rebuked her when she and Marcelle exchanged visits.

When their trial began, "Teddy"—though anxious—was not aware of the gravity of their situation. She did not understand the testimony; and the friendliness of the prosecutors and prison officers together with her faith in her husband convinced her that "he will find a way out." "As for me," says Marcelle, "I was very concerned. I followed the trial in the papers, and at night, on the radio. I feared the sentence would be very severe, possibly even death. I endeavored to prepare her, but nothing could penetrate her shell of optimism."

The day Teddy was taken to court to hear the verdict, Marcelle stood at her cell window. "I waved to them and gave them an encouraging smile, but inside me I was praying."

Before Teddy's return from court, the verdict had been broadcast by Radio Cairo, and was transmitted throughout the prison: Wolfgang Lutz, life imprisonment; Weltrude Lutz, three years' imprisonment.

"She was completely dazed when she returned. She was not concerned for herself, but rather for her husband. 'He's sick, he's got kidney trouble,' she mumbled over and over again. 'How will he hold out? Life imprisonment . . .' I tried to encourage her, telling her of all the foreign spies who were pardoned shortly after being sentenced. I said: 'You'll see, the German government will intervene on your behalf. . . . Both of you will be released even before your own sentence is completed.' Indeed, I really believed it. And if I wondered regretfully: 'And who will intervene on my behalf?' I endeavored to repress the thought."

Teddy was a strong woman. After she got over the shock of the verdict, she did not blink an eyelid when the guards took away her civilian clothes and dressed her in prison uniform (Marcelle had taken care to prepare a clean white uniform for her). She faced up to her new status with great courage. The following day, she asked the *ma'amur* to have her transferred to the cell adjoining that of Marcelle. For the next two and a half years, right up to the Six-Day War, they were neighbors, sharing their meals and spending their free time together. "She received lots of books from the German embassy and we spent much of our time reading. At night, I would listen to the radio and tell her the news the following morning. When she was taken to Tura to visit Wolfgang, she took along the socks and scarves I had knitted for my companions, as well as letters."

For three months, the trio in Tura "awaited" the arrival of Wolfgang Lutz, the German spy whose trial filled the newspapers. "We waited for him," says Victor, "with the same degree of curiosity we felt toward any prisoner of European extraction who seemed likely to extend our narrow circle. But in addition, he had spied for Israel; in other

words, he was an ally. And yet, he was German. We didn't know how
to treat him. We decided to wait and see what he was like. But when
the time passed and he failed to arrive, we began to think: 'Perhaps he's
been sent to Abu Za'abal?' "

In fact, Lutz spent all this time at Kanather, waiting for the verdict
to be confirmed by the president. "But then, one day, a rumor was
passed around," Victor continues. "The German had arrived and had
been taken to the punishment cells. We had a friend in the punishment
cells, the *nabatshi* of the *shawish* in charge, a man by the name of
Fatuh. He was a tough old convict who boasted of having once taken
thirty lashes without uttering a sound. We made his acquaintance when
we were confined to the punishment cells during our hunger strike; we
became friends. Now I went to look for him.

" 'A *hawaga* has been brought in to you,' I said. 'Look after him.'

" 'Is he a friend of yours?' he asked.

" 'No,' I replied. 'But he's a good man. Look after him, and you
won't regret it.'

" 'All right, I'll look after him the way I did for the English spies.'
He went straight to Lutz, bringing him tea and cigarettes and saying:
'Hawaga Victor sends his regards. Is there anything else you need?' The
next morning, he came back to me, very self-satisfied: 'All night, I made
him tea,' he told me, 'and in the morning, I made chips.' The English
spies, Swinbourne and Zarb, were very fond of fried potatoes; ever
since, Fatuh had regarded chips as the height of luxurious indulgence
to which a *hawaga* could aspire.

"I knew that the day after Lutz's arrival he, like every new prisoner, would be taken for a medical examination. So I found something
to do in the garden outside the dispensary and when Lutz was led past,
I said to him in English: 'I'm Victor Levy.' He halted. 'Oh, hello,' he said.
'Regards from Marcelle.' He appeared afraid to stay in my company too
long, but I accompanied him nevertheless. 'If there is anything you
need, tell Fatuh. And when you report to the doctor, tell him you're
sick. Tell him you're suffocating in the punishment cells. Whatever
happens, ask for a mattress.'

"I waited till he came out and he told me that my advice had been
useful: The doctor permitted him to receive a mattress, but he did not
release him from the punishment cells. 'Never mind,' I consoled him.
'You'll be out of there within a few days.' "

Indeed, a week later Lutz was released from the punishment cells
and brought to the fourth floor, where he found that Victor and his
companions had smoothed his path, preparing a one-man cell which
had been cleaned and decorated; the shabby mattress he brought from
the punishment cells was replaced by a new one. They bought a kero-

sene stove for him, stocked up the cell with provisions, and found him a trustworthy *nabatshi*.

"We did everything we could for him, regarding him as having fallen into captivity while working for Israel. All the same, we still considered him an ex-Nazi, and we found it hard to overcome a sense of antagonism his appearance aroused in us."

But Lutz clung to them and they could not find a way of keeping him at a distance without offending him. "He would spend the whole afternoon with us, staying until the cells were locked up. He was a very cheerful fellow, vivacious, the jokes rolling off his tongue. We enjoyed his company, though at times, he tended to be overcheerful. But beneath his cheerful exterior, we noticed that he was very anxious and in need of encouragement, and that was another reason for not rejecting him. He was madly in love with his wife, very concerned about her, and missed her greatly. In the end, we couldn't bear to see him suffer, so we brought him into the secret of our 'clandestine mail' to Kanather. He repaid us by telling us about Marcelle, from what his wife had told him and from what he had seen with his own eyes. When he told us of his sole meeting with Marcelle—who walked past as he was bidding farewell to his wife—we found it hard to believe. Had he really seen her? We inundated him with questions about her appearance, about the state of her hair (we were concerned over the rumor that it was falling out), about her health."

As yet, Lutz did not dare to reveal his true identity, even though the temptation was very great. Victor: "The first evening after his release from the punishment cells, we held a party in his honor. Robbie played the accordion while we sang and Lutz told jokes, and then we sang some more. And then suddenly, Robbie began to play 'Hatikvah.' We watched Lutz's face, but his expression did not change. It was only some time later that he told us how close he had been to bursting into tears."

Lutz's identity was revealed a few months later, quite by accident. "We were sitting in our cell, arguing about something—I think it may have been the risk involved in sending a letter to Kanather. Robbie disagreed with me, and suddenly, I blurted out, in Hebrew: *'Al tafriz'* ['Don't exaggerate'], whereupon Lutz broke in—in Hebrew! We were thunderstruck, and he was surprised, too. 'Don't you know that I'm an Israeli? I'm an officer in the Israeli army!' "

At that, the ice was broken. Wolfgang Lutz (or, to use his Hebrew name, Ze'ev Gur-Aryeh) was adopted into their "family." They let him into the secret of their radio receiver, and, once a week, they passed it to him for the night. He repaid them with his accounts of Israel, "though we were not always grateful for that; we were naive and we wanted to regard Israel as a unique state, without any defects. His stories of strikes and crime, of the storm around 'the mishap' did not fit in with the picture we had drawn in our imaginations."

Lutz was very quick to learn the ways of prison life. He won over the guards with cigarettes and their officers with smutty jokes. He had the doctors eating out of his hand; never before had they shown up for duty so regularly as when he was hospitalized after a light heart attack. Abdalla Immara, the *mudir,* did not like him, but Lutz had highly placed patrons in the prison service. The German consul came to visit him once a month, his lawyer came over from Germany every few months, he received numerous parcels. Furthermore, without any precedent in the chronicles of Tura, his wife, Weltrude, was brought from Kanather to see him!

Thanks to his numerous visitors, Lutz was sometimes the first to pick up some important piece of news. For example, he told his companions what he had heard from his lawyer, Kral-Orben: that they had not been forgotten in Israel, and there were continuous efforts to bring about their release.

These efforts were stepped up when Gen. Meir Amit became head of military intelligence, and, later, of the Mossad. He initiated a number of approaches to the Egyptians, with the aim of getting them released, either in exchange for Egyptian prisoners, or for ransom, or else by international pressure. Even though all these approaches were rejected by Nasser, the Israelis did not give up.

However, the three men in Tura did give up all hope of being released. When Robbie completed three-quarters of his sentence without being paroled, they decided that there was no point in continuing to hope and that their only prospect of regaining their freedom was by escaping. They shared their secret with Lutz, who showed no hesitation in agreeing to join them, but only after the release of Weltrude, at the end of her sentence, in the spring of 1968.

They began to count the days.

# 12

# THE SIX-DAY WAR

*A Religious Leader, a Prince, and Other VIPs*

The years 1964 to 1965 were a turbulent period in Egypt. In the internal struggle within Nasser's entourage, the leftists under Ali Sabry gained the upper hand, and relations with the Soviet Union again grew close. As a direct consequence, the Communist prisoners were released from detention, in keeping with a promise to Nikita Khrushchev. (But the Egyptians tricked him; some of the detained Communists were released, but those serving prison sentences continued to rot in jail until two Communists—one of them a Jew—managed to escape from the Harga detention camp. On reaching Paris, they disclosed the Egyptians' deception. Khrushchev was so furious that he called off a scheduled visit to Egypt. In the end, Nasser gave in, the Communists were released, and Khrushchev's visit took place.) At the same time, the Moslem Brotherhood was subjected to renewed persecution; their *murshid al am*, Hassan el Hudeibi, was brought back to Tura, and Said Kut'b, released a few years earlier because of a heart ailment, was rearrested. Kut'b was one of the world's greatest Moslem theologians, and his arrest provoked considerable uproar. Iraqi president Aref intervened on his behalf, but to no avail. Kut'b's books were burned, he was put on trial charged with plotting a coup, and sentenced to death.

There were also arrests among prominent public figures known for their pro-Western sympathies. The chief of these was the journalist Mustaffa Amin; Dr. Az-a-Din Abdul Kader was also lured back to Egypt, and immediately flung into prison.

Dr. Az-a-Din was of a lineage which should have granted him a privileged position in revolutionary Egypt. He was the great-grandson of Ahmed Urbi Basha, the first nationalist leader to hoist the banner of revolt against the British as long ago as the end of the nineteenth century. But aside from his ancestry, he was a well-known revolutionary in his own right. He was one of the founders of the Misr el Fatah, a pro-Fascist nationalist movement which operated in Egypt up to the end of World War II (one of its members was Anwar el-Sadat, later to become the third president of Egypt). In 1936, after an unsuccessful attempt to assassinate Nahas Basha—the premier and leader of the Wafd party—Abdul Aziz was obliged to flee, finding asylum in Canada, where he completed his studies. He submitted his doctoral thesis, married, and fathered four children. In the early fifties, he settled in Morocco, where he wrote another book attacking the officers' regime in Egypt. Egyptian nationalists detested him, but when Nasser met him while on a state visit to Morocco, he embraced him and kissed him demonstratively, promising him the earth if he would return to Egypt. Dr. Az-a-Din believed him. However, no sooner did he walk off the plane than he was surrounded by policemen. That same night, he was brought to Tura.

In prison, he became a close friend of Mustaffa Amin (whose ancestry was also nothing to be ashamed of; his grandfather was Zaglul Basha, the founder of the Wafd party and the man who took Egypt on its first steps toward independence).

Whenever the two men strolled arm-in-arm around the courtyard of Block 1 in their white pajamas, deep in conversation, men would point at the pair and say: "There goes the history of Egypt."

Mustaffa Amin suffered from diabetes; nevertheless, Abdalla Immara flung him into the punishment cells, like any other *irad*. But he could not keep him confined there for long. Even after his downfall, he still retained too many friends outside. One of these was Hassanin Heikal, who, despite succeeding Amin as Nasser's press adviser, did not forget that Amin was his teacher and that it was under him that Heikal began his career as a journalist. Heikal came to visit him at least once a month, bringing a large packet of newspapers. Being at the height of his power at this time, he was allowed to be alone with Amin in the visitors' courtyard, but without being separated by the fence. The two men—Amin, tall, and Heikal, short and stocky, the two most prominent journalists in the country—walked back and forth, arguing passionately. What were they arguing about? About politics or the press, most probably; none of the convicts came within earshot.

Aside from newspapers and cigarettes, Heikal brought Amin nothing; he never took advantage of his position to intervene on behalf of his mentor. But Amin never complained.

"He was an altogether unusual character," Robbie says of him. "One of the few Egyptians I have known who really absorbed Western culture and didn't just let it run over him. His father served for many years as Egyptian ambassador to Washington, and Mustaffa spent his boyhood and youth in the United States. It was there that he got his education. That may be the reason. He was amazingly modest, a rare trait among men of his position; his curiosity was insatiable. He was capable of sitting down with his *nabatshi*—an illiterate villager from the Delta—and questioning him about his life in the village and about his aspirations, as though they were of the same class.

"He refrained from taking sides in the political arguments which sometimes broke out in the prison. Under pressure, he would put on a show of adopting the views of his collocutor. But underneath this conciliatory mask, there was a tough man with a clear eye and a clear mind, who regarded everything somewhat cynically. On Fridays, the prisoners would ask him to help them decipher the hints between the lines in Hassanin Heikal's weekly column; at this time, Heikal was the oracle of the regime. But Amin would wave his hand disparagingly. 'What hints are you looking for? Heikal writes whatever he's told to write.'

"He was very friendly toward us, often coming to our cell to talk. He always said that common sense would triumph and then there would be peace between Israel and Egypt. 'What disrupts relations now,' he would say, 'is the mutual lack of trust. It is necessary to create a situation in which we can get to know one another better. Familiarity will bring trust.'

"When the war broke out in 1967, before its outcome became known, he was the first to come and congratulate us. 'Now you'll be released,' he promised, and told us the story of the opportunity missed in 1956 to procure our release. When we were in fact released and came to say good-bye, he was genuinely pleased for us. I'm sure that if we had the opportunity to meet now, he would embrace us as friends."

(After the members of the network left Egypt, Amin was transferred to the Kasser el Eini hospital in Cairo; shortly after Sadat took power, he was pardoned and restored to his position as the editor of one of the most important newspapers in the country.)

One of the few prisoners of whom they retained pleasant memories was Prince Namuk, a scion of the Ottoman rulers. Namuk was in Baghdad, a guest of the court, when the 1958 revolution broke out, and he was imprisoned. He witnessed the wholesale executions which marked the early days of the revolutionary regime, and he was not far from the scaffold himself. But in the end, the Iraqis preferred to hand him over to the Ba'ath rulers of Syria. He was imprisoned there for a number of years, in the fearsome al Mazeh jail, until the Syrians passed him on to the Egyptians. He was put on trial for plotting to restore the Egyptian monarchy and to crown an Ottoman prince, one of his relatives. He was sentenced to ten years' imprisonment. (In prison, he denied the charges against him, but he admitted to the members of the network that he had worked for British intelligence—not against Egypt, but in connection with the conflict between India and Pakistan.) He was about forty-four, so enormously fat that he was unable to stand up without support. He was always feeding himself frantically, a habit which ultimately brought about his death.

He was a frequent visitor to the trio's cell for marathon chess tournaments against Philip and Robbie, the champions of Tura, and also because he was sure of being invited to a meal.

It was a trifling price for the pleasure he gave his hosts. He was an excellent guitar player (boasting that he had learned the skill from one of the greatest Spanish guitarists) and an even better raconteur. He had an enormous fund of entertaining and amazing tales about the ways of the aristocracies of Europe and the Middle East, whose palaces he frequented prior to his arrest. There was nothing more soothing, no better way of forgetting gloomy realities than to listen to him. "It was like immersing ourselves in a legendary world with beautiful princesses and gallant princes, with splendid palaces and festivities and imposing titles. When he finished his stories and got up to return to his cell, we would all let out a deep sigh, regretting the necessity of returning to reality."

His highly placed acquaintances endeavored to procure his release. Even United Nations secretary general Dag Hammarskjöld intervened on his behalf, and was rumored to have received Nasser's promise to pardon Namuk. But he did not live to see the day.

One evening, after completing a sizable meal in the trio's cell, he withdrew to his own cell with five portions of canned beans he had bought that day in the canteen. He had a heart attack while he was eating. He managed to call for help, but by the time the guard opened the door, he was lifeless.


There were other prisoners who dropped in on the trio—to talk, to seek advice, to argue. Robbie gave accordion lessons, Philip taught French, and Victor gave English lessons to the younger prisoners who were studying for their matriculation examinations. The trio were widely respected, with undertones of envy and even hatred, "but we were treated with respect. In their eyes, we represented Israel. Not the

Jew from the caricatures—cowardly, treacherous, double-dealing—but rather the Jewish state which everyone hated, while yet respecting its strength.

"Prison," says Philip, "is a reflection of Egypt as a whole. All classes and strata of society, every community was represented within the prison walls. In the course of time, we held conversations with them all, giving us a chance to learn their views.

"Those without any education took no interest in Israel or the conflict with her. They knew about it vaguely, but they did not wish to learn more. Their behavior was influenced by the general mood, by what the officers said, by the propaganda on radio and television.

"The most extreme in their attitude toward Israel were the semiliterate prisoners and the young men who had grown up under the Nasser regime, swallowing the anti-Jewish propaganda which was poured out continually. Even among them, we occasionally came across some exceptional individual who agreed that the Jews also had a right to exist. But on the whole, they were of the view that the Jews were not a people, that they did not have a history, and that the Holocaust had never occurred.

"We found a common language with the older men who had received their education before Nasser came to power; they were acquainted with Jews, and knew they didn't have horns.

"Among the prisoners there were army officers who had been taken prisoner by Israel during the Sinai campaign. Even though they did not love Israel, they were prepared to concede: 'In Israeli captivity, we were treated better than we are here.' But there were some men —including some of the guards—who came round to a strange kind of affection for Israel, out of their enmity toward the Palestinians. Many of the convicts were Palestinians, men who had smuggled hashish from Jordan to the Gaza Strip, and a number of spies and double agents who had worked as mercenaries. Paradoxically, we were on almost friendly terms with them. Some of them helped us and we endeavored to help them too. We were looked upon as 'Israelis' and the Palestinians were also regarded as foreigners. In consequence, we regarded one another —and the Egyptians also treated us—as *baladiat* [fellow countrymen].

"The Palestinians were almost universally detested. The Egyptians continually flung at them: 'All our troubles are on your account!' (On the other hand, the head of the Shawa family from Gaza, who was imprisoned with us, once said: 'There is one thing for which the Israelis can never be forgiven, for letting the Egyptians back into Gaza!')

"The Egyptians hated the Palestinians and vice versa. The prison also housed Sudanese and Syrians and Lebanese—who all hated one another. The Moslem Brotherhood hated the Nasserites who hated the

Communists; the guards hated their officers and the prisoners all hated
Abdul al Saluma, the sadistic commander of our block.
"And we were right in the middle."

The vague feeling of being "right in the middle" sharpened into an
active threat as the crisis erupted in the spring of 1967.

Robbie: "In spite of some improvement in our material conditions,
for some time we had been exposed to the frequent upheavals in the
political mood. Every time Nasser made a speech on the radio—the
broadcasts were now transmitted throughout the prison by means of
loudspeakers—we had a sense of danger. Nasser was in the habit of
devoting a considerable portion of each speech to Israel, which he
reviled and denounced at length; nor did he spare the Jews as a people.
We always wondered how the prisoners would respond to this incitement. For a day or two after every speech, we would keep ourselves
apart and refrain from arguments."

However, as 1967 advanced, their reticence was no longer sufficient. The Nasser regime's ramified propaganda apparatus was now
reaping the fruits of years of endeavor. In the public consciousness,
there was a growing sense of Egyptian might as against Israeli feeble-
ness and there was an upsurge of national pride. Listening to the radio
and reading their newspapers, the Egyptians began to regard themselves as a powerful nation, equaled only by the Soviet Union and the
United States; nothing was beyond their reach. In contrast, Israel was
depicted as a crooked-nosed dwarf, suffering from internal conflicts and
divisions, from unemployment and destitution. As soon as the Egyptian
army began to march, Israel would crumble like a clay doll.

"We couldn't even argue with them," says Robbie. "True, we knew
that the real Israel was quite unlike the descriptions carried by the Arab
media. But how could we convey the fact to our adversaries? We
couldn't say: 'We heard it on the radio.'

"What was more, every day we heard and read the numbers of
tanks and planes the Arab armies possessed. On returning from leave,
the guards would tell of city streets filled with soldiers, about tanks
driving through the towns. They didn't all intend to provoke us, but all
of them displayed an air of self-satisfaction and pride. All this began to
have its effect upon us. Not that we lost our faith in an Israeli victory.
But when we got hold of a Lebanese paper brought to Mustaffa Amin,
which published tables showing the arms and manpower at the disposal
of the Arab armies in comparison with those available to the Israeli
army, we asked ourselves: '*How* would that victory be achieved?' At
night, we would seek the answer in the Israeli radio's transmissions, but

their restrained tone, when compared with the arrogant trumpeting of Radio Cairo, only multiplied our worries. It wasn't easy to be a Jew in Egypt at that time, particularly not in prison."

After Israel's Independence Day, when the situation began to deteriorate rapidly and harbingers of war appeared on the horizon, some of the convicts tried to show off their patriotism by harassing the Israeli spies, and they were encouraged by many of the prison officers. The *ma'amur*, Col. Tumraz, had not forgotten the humiliation he suffered when he came off second best in his confrontation with Victor. In the meantime, he had another account to settle with the Jews: A nephew of his was brought to Tura after having been convicted of spying on behalf of Israel. Tumraz did not know how to hide his disgrace. But now he found a way of getting his own back. Calling one of the most violent of the "criminals," he told the man: "If you hit Victor over the head with an iron bar, I'll make sure you come to no harm." Having said that, he straightaway went home, to provide an alibi for himself should the man take the hint.

The attack on Victor did not take place, for a reason characteristic of Egyptian convicts: Someone informed the *mudir*, not so much out of love of the Jews as to spite the *ma'amur;* or else, in hope of being rewarded. Abdalla Immara acted swiftly.

"In the middle of the day," relates Victor, "a runner came to me with an order: 'The *mudir* commands you to enter your cell and stay there.' We did as we were told, without knowing the reason why. The following day, 'my' guard—the man in charge of the gardens and the duck farm—told me that the *mudir* had called together the officers and *shawishin* and addressed them as follows: 'A rumor has reached me that there are certain persons in the prison who wish to harm the *hawagat.* I don't know whether the rumor is correct or not, but if anything happens to them, that means there is an absence of discipline in *my* prison. That is something I won't tolerate, and I will punish it severely.' "

A day later, when they were permitted to return to their work, he summoned Victor to his office. "He wanted to warn us," says Victor, "but he could not state expressly that we were in danger, so he said: 'I dreamed that someone hit you over the head with an iron bar. The dream frightened me, and that's why I gave orders to lock you in your cell. It was only a dream, but times are hard. Be careful. Don't walk around on your own.' "

They heeded his advice. The preparations for their escape—which required Victor to remain alone in the incubator house at midday—were temporarily shelved. "Each of us hastened to complete his work, so that by ten o'clock, when the morning paper arrived, we were all back in the cell. 'Rusty' Lutz was already there, waiting for us. He would come in in the morning, as soon as the cell doors were unlocked, and ask us for the news we had heard on the radio the night before. When we left, he took it upon himself to guard the cell till our return, and then he remained with us till the cells were locked up for the night. We ate together, we read the newspaper together, comparing its contents with what we had heard on 'Kol Yisrael' and the BBC. Rusty was our military commentator, explaining difficult points and resolving contradictions. He was as firm as a rock, overflowing with confidence and optimism. We endeavored to imbibe his optimism."

As always occurred in moments of tension, everyone kept away from them, particularly the "politicals." Amin was one of the few who did not abandon them. He would come and ask their opinion about the outcome of a war, should it break out. When Philip told him confidently that Israel would win, he nodded his head skeptically. "The question is, will Israel dare to go to war?" he said. But after the war, forgetting his earlier skepticism, he was in the habit of boasting: "The day Nasser blockaded the Straits of Tiran, I knew that Israel would have to go to war, because the southern waterway is a vital artery for her."

At Kanather, the approaching war with its accompanying tensions and hatreds was felt with equal force.

When the Egyptian army started to move into Sinai and the radio began to broadcast Um Kultum's endlessly long nationalist songs, a number of women prisoners formed themselves into a "walking choir" which accompanied Marcelle wherever she went, singing: *"Allah hu achbar!"* and *"Nar! Nar!"* ("Allah is great" and "Fire! Fire!"—two war songs which achieved overnight popularity), backing up their singing with threatening gestures.

They were headed by a woman from Gaza by the name of Salma, who also rebuked Marcelle's *nabatshia* for "serving that Jewess."

Marcelle: "The poor woman would come to my cell in the morning in tears. As it was, she felt like an outsider among the other prisoners on account of being a Christian, and now she had the further sin of being my *nabatshia*. We decided to take advantage of Teddy's status as 'the lady of the prison.' Everyone knew that the German ambassador was keeping an eye on her and that she enjoyed the protection of the *mudir*. She received frequent visits from embassy employees, from her lawyer, and from a Protestant clergyman. Aside from that, she was big and strong, and in her halting Arabic she was capable of conveying such a degree of authority and disdain that the other prisoners bowed to her. Together, we approached the officer-supervisor, notifying her that unless she put a stop to the harassment of the other prisoners, we would complain to the *ma'amur*, Teddy would summon the German ambassador, I would appeal to the Red Cross, and there would be trouble."

In consequence, Salma's enmity did not become less venomous, but it was toned down. The "walking choir" dispersed.

"All the same," says Marcelle, "even though things calmed down, inwardly I sensed no calm. Unlike my companions, I had no clear picture of my own of the state of Israel. After all, what did I know about Israel? Whatever I heard on the radio—and 'Kol Yisrael' was very subdued in the tone of its broadcasts. There was something reassuring about this quiet tone, but nevertheless, it did not make them into an effective counterweight to the venomous propaganda of the Egyptian media. I was terribly worried."

The formation of Israel's Cabinet of National Unity somewhat dashed Egyptian self-confidence. When Moshe Dayan and Menahem Begin joined the cabinet, it opened the eyes of the better-educated prisoners, dashing their hopes of a bloodless victory and indicating that war was inevitable. They withdrew inward; silently, they awaited what the morrow would bring. It was now too late to halt the stampede of events.

*Back to the Punishment Cells*

When war broke out, at eight o'clock in the morning of June 5, 1967, each of the three men was at work: Victor was in the duck farm, Philip in the library, and Robbie on the sports ground. Suddenly, there was a long, drawn out siren.

Robbie: "We thought it was yet another siren test, of the kind which had been upsetting our repose at least once a week ever since the tension began. We were only surprised that it came during the day. But half an hour later, the order came over the loudspeakers: Everyone was to return to their cells and the doors would be locked. The quarry workers were also brought back.

"Another half hour passed and then, from afar, we heard dull explosions. No one knew what they were, but a bizarre kind of gaiety overtook the prison. The prisoners cheered. The officers vanished and quickly returned, wearing battle dress and with pistols in their belts. An officer announced over the loudspeakers: 'I have good news. We have shot down seventeen enemy planes.' There was still no word of the outbreak of war, as though this were no more than an ordinary border incident.

"Shortly afterward, the same officer reported sixty enemy planes shot down. From the cells came cries of joy, as well as calls of: 'Give us the Jews! We'll slaughter them!' " Immara now decided that the atmosphere was overheated and gave orders to stop transmitting the broadcasts from Radio Cairo over the loudspeakers. From now on, he took it upon himself to "edit" the news transmitted to the prisoners. He came to Block 1, to the trio's cell, and gave orders to have them transferred to the punishment cells.

"He apologized to us," Robbie relates. "He explained: 'It's for your own safety. You know that you're better off in the punishment cells at a time like this.' He permitted us to take part of our provisions with us, telling us to leave the rest in our cell, which he then ordered the guards to lock up. 'You'll be back,' he promised, 'and then you'll find everything as you left it.' "

They were not surprised at being transferred to the punishment cells. For days now, as indications increased that war was on the way, they had considered it probable and made the necessary preparations. "We never dreamed that Immara would give orders to have our cell locked, with all its contents. But when it happened, we resolved that we could not leave our most precious possession, the radio. Consequently, we stuck to our original plan, entrusting the 'tin of jam' where the set was concealed to Nicola Kois, the Greek spy with whom we were close friends. As camouflage, we made him a present of some other cans of ours."

Like Victor, Nicola was one of Immara's favorites, and his cell was rarely searched. Furthermore, he occupied a one-man cell, further reducing the danger of denunciation. But as it turned out, precisely because he was alone in his cell, Nicola feared to keep the radio, and he passed it on to an Egyptian friend, who lived in a five-man cell. There, the set was discovered. The Egyptian did not inform on Nicola, even though he was given a severe beating on the soles of his feet. But Nicola could not bear his friend's sufferings. Of his own accord, he approached the *mudir* and confessed that the radio was his. Not only did Immara refrain from punishing him, but he gave him back the radio, telling him to "give it back to its owners." They gave the set to Philip's mother, who brought it with her when she emigrated to Israel.

Taking their *nimra* and a few possessions, they went down to the punishment cells. It was two o'clock in the afternoon, and Immara's voice came over the loudspeakers, announcing that ninety enemy planes had been downed, "whereupon we began to cast doubt upon the veracity of the reports. An hour later, the number of Israeli planes downed had reached two hundred and four and then we knew clearly that it was all a lie; Israel did not even possess that many interceptors."

They were housed in the first cell in the punishment wing. Uri was confined there with them, but not Lutz, since he was a "German," not a Jew. They heard the incessant crackle of the radio belonging to the officer in charge of the punishment cells. Apparently not satisfied with listening to Radio Cairo, he also tuned in to foreign stations. "He was the first man in the prison to have his triumphant expression wiped off his face. That evening, he came to talk to us, and we could already observe that he was uneasy. 'Who needs this war?' he asked, his face clouded over with worry. 'After all, it is possible to live in peace. But at least here, in the punishment cells, you're safe. If there's a bombing raid, you won't be harmed.' Then we knew that the war was not going well for the Egyptians. That night we listened to the conversation between the *bolok* on the roof and the guards down in the courtyard. The following morning we heard a guard who had just come on duty asking: 'Well, have we reached Tel Aviv yet?' (Um Kultum had promised to give her next recital in occupied Tel Aviv!) Somebody replied: 'Not yet, but we will soon be there!' But our hopes were soaring, and we told one another: 'The punishment cells are nearer to the gateway. Let's hope we don't have to go back to the fourth floor.' "

When war broke out, Marcelle was sitting in Teddy's room; the two women were trying to forget their worries by concentrating on their embroidery. Then a guard arrived at a run, saying she had orders to lock the doors. "She wanted me to return to my cell," Marcelle relates, "but we argued with her, and in the end, she left us alone. The radio was not switched on that day, there were no prisoners to be seen in the courtyard, and there was a spooky, scary silence hanging over the whole prison. Suddenly, the sound of muffled explosions came from the direction of Cairo.

"We knew that there was something going on, but we hadn't been told anything yet. In the end, we couldn't stand the tension anymore, and we decided that I should return to my cell and try to listen to the radio. If I had any news, I would knock on the wall separating our cells, and this would be a signal for her to go to the window."

Before long, a knocking on the wall sent Teddy scurrying over to the open window, where she heard Marcelle's excited voice calling: "It's begun!"

Radio Cairo was transmitting military marches, broken off every now and then for "army communiqués" heralding stunning victories. By six o'clock that evening the radio was boasting of five thousand Israeli prisoners, including five hundred women. "I knew what awaited women who fell into Egyptian captivity and I was terrified lest the report be true." She tried to pick up "Kol Yisrael," but there the news was highly vague. "Hard fighting is in progress." Marcelle did not possess sufficient military knowledge to read between the lines.

That whole night, she sat glued to her radio, alternating frantically between "Kol Yisrael," Radio Cairo, and the BBC. Then, at some hour of the night, she began to grasp that something great and wonderful had occurred: The Arab armies had suffered heavy punishment. She still did not fully comprehend it all, she was still troubled by doubts, torn between the triumphant statements from Cairo and the laconic announcements on "Kol Yisrael," but her heart filled with joy—and hope.

The next morning she and Teddy were summoned to the office of Mahmud Subhi, the *ma'amur.* "I'm sorry," he said, in a genuinely apologetic tone, "but I must confine the two of you together. It's for your own good, so that we can protect you better."

They tried to object. "For over thirteen years, I had been in a cell on my own," says Marcelle. "I couldn't stand the idea of having to share my room with someone else all of a sudden." But the *ma'amur* insisted. Since Marcelle's room was larger, Teddy moved in there, while her own cell now housed three Israeli women prisoners—Sima, Ofra, and Rina —who had crossed the Gaza Strip border a year previously, and soon regretted their act.

"I have given orders," said the *ma'amur,* "that the other prisoners are not to be allowed near your wing."

The order may have been superfluous. "There was no open hostility toward us," says Marcelle. "There was tension; Salma continued to incite the 'criminals' against us, while Kamela, my old adversary from 1956, now back in Kanather after her exile in Qena, used to stand under our window and curse us, but we ignored her. I stopped working in the workshop, almost never leaving the cell."

The cell was filled with Teddy's possessions—her bed, her shelves, and a table and chair she had been given. "It was crowded, but after we got used to one another it was quite pleasant. I listened to the radio whenever I had the chance—I no longer waited for nighttime—with Teddy on guard at the entrance to the washroom, watching out for the approach of a guard. Afterward, I told her everything I had heard. And we talked. I hadn't talked that much for thirteen years! We talked about the prospects of release, about our dreams and hopes."

On the second day of the war, the atmosphere in Tura changed completely. Philip: "On the morning of the first day, the military communiqués reporting victories were broadcast every ten minutes. Later, every hour, and later still, every two hours. But the successes were still astounding. Over two hundred Israeli planes had been shot down. Five thousand prisoners. On the second day, when the guards of the punishment cells came on duty, they reported having personally seen Israeli prisoners being marched to Cairo's radio station, surrounded by secret policemen who shouted to the crowds: 'Here are the Israelis!' Later it transpired that these were Egyptian Jews who were again detained en masse, as they had been in 1956.

"Suddenly, we became very popular with the prison officers," Philip recalls. "One after another, they dropped in on us, supposedly for a chat; but they soon blurted out a question which was repeated several times: 'What is "a second line of defense"?' This term began to be heard with increasing frequency in Radio Cairo broadcasts, which reported that the Egyptian army had taken up 'a second line of defense,' from which it was inflicting severe defeats on the Israeli army."

That evening, there was uproar in Block 1 when the *ma'amur*, Tumraz, caught Lutz smoking near his cell window and accused him of signaling to the Israeli planes (a strict blackout had been imposed in Tura since the outbreak of war, and even the searchlights on the wall had been switched off). At eleven o'clock at night, the "politicals" were all led down from the fourth floor to the first floor, the din reaching as far as the punishment cells (when Immara arrived the next morning, they were taken back to their cells). Robbie: "The convicts clung to the windows of their new cells, shouting into the darkness: 'Dayan, come and save us!' But we also heard other shouts: 'Let us have the Jewish traitors, we'll slaughter them!' In this atmosphere of terror, Tumraz burst into their cell, seething with anger and hatred. 'You think the Israeli paratroopers will come and save you?' he bellowed at the four men. 'I'm telling you, we'll kill you in the cells! You won't get out of here alive!' "

The following day, Wednesday, the third day of the war, Victor was summoned to the *mudir*.

"Till then, we were quite anxious," Victor relates. "We knew that the Israeli army had gained the upper hand, but Tumraz's outburst the previous night had presented us with the possibility that an Israeli victory would not necessarily bring *us* salvation. On the contrary, perhaps. Then the door opened and the guard shouted: 'Victor, the *mudir* wants you!' I found him seated in the courtyard, surrounded by his officers. To my surprise, he greeted me pleasantly. 'How are you? Got any complaints? Has anyone hurt your pride? I'm not asking about the conditions; I know it's unpleasant in the punishment cells. I'm asking you about your pride. Has anyone offended you?' Somewhat surprised, I mumbled that everything was in order. 'All right,' he said contentedly. 'I wanted to hear that from your own mouth. How are things in the incubators?'

"I replied that I didn't know. I had been confined to the punishment cells for the past three days.

" 'Well then, go there and save the situation.'

"I hurried to the incubator house. Some of the eggs hatched out that day, but since no one had taken the trouble to turn them over, the ducklings were weak and died immediately. The incubator was full of dead ducklings. I began to curse. I called the guard in to help me and we spent the next hour in feverish activity. There wasn't much left to do, but at least, I wanted to remove the bodies. Later on, when I was washing in the courtyard, I was approached by Yusuf Magali. He was serving a life sentence for espionage, having been a member of the Suez Canal network. There was a broad smile on his face.

" 'Victor,' he said, 'Al Kuds [Jerusalem] is in our hands!'

"I felt exhilarated; I wished to believe, but I didn't dare. 'Really?' I murmured.

" 'I swear it, by my life!' he cried. 'I just got the news from outside. Jerusalem is in our hands!'

"I was beside myself. Tears sprang from my eyes and I couldn't stop them, nor did I want to. I mumbled to myself: 'Mireille,' calling my sister who had passed away years previously. I don't know why it was her name that came out at that moment. 'Mireille, d'you hear? Jerusalem is ours . . .'

"This was too great a piece of news to keep to myself; I had to tell my companions! 'Enough,' I said to the guard. 'Take me to the cell.'

" 'But we haven't finished,' he objected.

" 'We've finished!'

" 'What's the hurry?' he urged. 'Stay outside a bit in the fresh air. Are you in a hurry to get back to the punishment cells?' It was only after he extracted a promise that I would come back in the afternoon that he agreed to take me back to the punishment cells.

"Arriving there, I could scarcely restrain myself till the door was locked behind me, before I blurted out: 'Friends, Jerusalem is in our hands!'

"They didn't believe it. We had no idea that Israel was fighting on three fronts. True, on the eve of the war, the radio said something about Egyptian commando battalions being sent to Jordan, but the moment the fighting began, everyone's attention was fixed on the Sinai front, and no one mentioned the battles on the West Bank. My companions began to question me: 'What did Magali say precisely?' I repeated his words. They were not satisfied and asked me to repeat them again. Perhaps I had made a mistake? Perhaps he had made a mistake? But in spite of our doubts, our hearts were filled with joy."

(Marcelle: "That evening, I chanced on 'Kol Yisrael' at the precise moment when it was transmitting the scene at the Western Wall. The announcer's voice was trembling. Then there came the sounds of jubilation, the sounds of the ram's horn, Rabbi Goren's prayer, 'Hatikvah,' and 'Jerusalem the Golden.' As I listened, I cried for joy. I tried to explain to Teddy what I was experiencing. I told her: 'Just imagine, the Western Wall is in our hands!' But she didn't comprehend.")

In the punishment cells, the three men grasped the full extent of the Israeli victory when they heard the *boloks* on the walls wailing with grief. "It was in the evening," Robbie relates, "at the end of Nasser's speech in which he announced his resignation."

The following morning, the mail *nabatshi* slipped up to the punishment cells and flung the newspaper in through their window; the paper carried the full text of the speech. Yet again, the Egyptian president demonstrated how well he could play on the feelings of his people. The speech was a masterpiece! Nasser took it like a man, accepting full responsibility for the debacle (even though the speech was full of broad hints that the blame fell, not on him, but on the military commanders who had betrayed the trust placed in them). Nasser announced his resignation, nominating a temporary successor: Interior Minister Muhi el-Din. There was a crafty thought behind the choice. As the man in charge of the secret police, Muhi el-Din was widely detested. Egypt's few underground newspapers had long referred to him by the nickname "the Beria of Cairo."

The moment the speech ended, "spontaneous" demonstrations erupted in support of Nasser. Even though this "spontaneity" was well organized initially, there can be no doubt that it appealed to the feelings of the masses. Within an hour, the number of demonstrators had reached a million or more. They wailed hysterically, calling for the blood of "those really responsible for the debacle, the traitors!" Like children abandoned by their father, they called upon Nasser to withdraw his resignation.

The following day, at noon, Nasser announced that he was taking over the reins of power again, "until the situation returned to normal" and "until the uprooting of the weeds which had taken root in Egypt."

It did not take long for his meaning to be made clear. The early setbacks in the Yemen war also led to generals being dismissed and flung into prison. But this time, the knife cut into the very flesh of the revolutionary regime. Ministers, widely respected generals and military commanders, heads of the military revolution, and members of the Officers' Council which had led it were all imprisoned. Even the Mushir Abdul Hakim Amer, the army commander and vice president, was placed under house arrest.

The wave of hysteria reached Tura, where it turned—or rather, was directed—against the "Jewish spies." Lutz, now on his own on the fourth floor, heard such violent words directed against the trio that he was horrified. "We'll drink their blood when they come back! We'll tear them to shreds!" These threats made such a deep impression upon him that when the three men were released from the punishment cells two weeks later, he hastened to warn them. (He was astounded to see the hostility evaporate completely. No sooner did the trio enter the block than all those who only yesterday planned to "drink their blood," now courted them with ingratiating smiles.)

The purge did not rest content with the heads of army officers. The powers of the secret police were now unlimited, making it the effective ruler of the country and presenting it with the opportunity to settle accounts with other "enemies of the regime." Hundreds—possibly thousands—were arrested. Hassan el Hudeibi was brought back to Tura in retribution for having his name mentioned on "Kol Yisrael." One hundred and sixty-seven members of the Moslem Brotherhood, hitherto confined in the fearsome Sigan Harbi, were now transferred to Tura; on arrival, they were all placed in the punishment cells, which filled to overflowing.

Robbie: "To make room for them, all the other prisoners were removed from the punishment cells, with the exception of us, but that was not sufficient, so the *mudir* gave orders to transfer us, too, not to our cell on the fourth floor, but to the first floor, under strict supervision and closely guarded. We were both glad and sorry to be leaving the punishment cells. We had cherished the hope that 'the way from the punishment cells leads to the gate,' and yet, there we were, returning to the block, not even to our own cell, and furthermore, under 'strict supervision.' "

### *"Israel Wants You!"*

They had one consolation: On their return to the block, they renewed their postal links. No sooner was the cell door locked behind them than the mail *nabatshi* appeared, carrying a bundle of letters from Switzerland. "If you want to send off a reply," he whispered, "I'll be back in an hour." He brought them paper and pencil.

"We wrote hurriedly," says Robbie, "just a few lines: 'We hope to be seeing you soon.' "

For the first week after their release from the punishment cells, while Victor returned to his work in the duck farm, Philip and Robbie were kept under "strict supervision"—in other words, complete isolation. They were only taken out for half an hour a day, to "exercise" on their own in the interior courtyard. But the strictness of their isolation was gradually relaxed. A week later, a few enterprising prisoners found various excuses to go out into the courtyard while they were out there "exercising."

Robbie: "Only then did we begin to hear details of the Israeli victory. Prisoners who possessed radios or who had received visits from relatives came to tell us what they had heard. We collated the facts until we had pieced together the whole picture—and it was wonderful! The Israeli army was on the Suez Canal and Mount Hermon, and we held Judea and Samaria! But what about *us?*"

Among those approaching them was Mustaffa Amin, friendly as usual, and this time, optimistic, too.

"You'll certainly be released now!" he said. "It's one hundred percent certain. There's nothing to argue about."

"With all our hearts, we wished to believe him," says Robbie, "but we had suffered so many disappointments! We were afraid to cultivate our hopes. We argued with him: 'Where did you get the idea?' Then he told us for the first time that Israel held five thousand Egyptian prisoners, including numerous senior officers. He had heard it on the BBC. All the same, we tried to play the matter down. We said: 'In 1956, Israel also held five thousand Egyptian prisoners . . .' "

"Then, too," said Amin, "if Israel had demanded you, you would have been released." He went on to tell them the story of the 1956 prisoner exchange, when Nasser ordered him to get the Egyptian prisoners released at all costs, saying: "Give the Jews whatever they want, as long as you get our prisoners back quickly." "However," Amin added, "Israel didn't demand you, to our great surprise."

"And what makes you think that Israel will demand us this time?" asked Robbie.

"Because Israel has already announced it," said Amin triumphantly. "Last night, the BBC announced that in exchange for the five thousand Egyptian prisoners it is holding, Israel demands the release of ten Israeli soldiers who were taken captive and, in addition, six civilians. Who are they? You, of course! This time, you'll be released!"

"Our knees shook with agitation. We were glad when our 'exercise' ended and we were led back to our cell. We had to sit down, to overcome our agitation, and to give clear-headed consideration to what we had just heard. How bitterly we regretted that we no longer had our radio, making us dependent on crumbs of secondhand information.

"We began to wonder: Who were the six? There were the four of us, but who were the other two? To tell the truth, we never even thought of Wolfgang Lutz and his wife. We thought they meant Nicola Kois and Uri.

"But the days passed and turned into weeks, and nothing happened. We were still under 'special supervision' on the first floor (after a time, the 'special supervision' was called off, and we were transferred, not to our old cell, but to an ordinary cell on the second floor). The subject of a prisoner exchange was swallowed up by silence.

"For us, it was a nerve-wracking, maddening period. We began to fear that we had again been forgotten."

They were not forgotten. Before the guns fell silent beside the Suez Canal, a firm decision was adopted in Israel: This time, the members of the network would be released! There can be no doubt that the decision owes much to the Israeli intelligence community and to Gen. Meir Amit. "The mishap" occurred years before he became head of the Mossad, or before he commanded military intelligence, and Amit could, therefore, have washed his hands of the matter. But he contended: "They acted on instructions from Israel and under the command of an emissary sent from Israel. Even though the instructions are a subject of disagreement and the emissary was a dubious person, Israel is responsible for their fate." Years before the outbreak of the Six-Day War, he sought ways of presenting various proposals to the Egyptians, with the aim of gaining the release of the four prisoners. One suggestion was to pay ransom. Every now and then, there were proposals for a direct exchange—the release of Egyptian spies or terrorists from the *fedayeen* groups in exchange for the four members of the network. In 1965, when the Mushir Abdul Hakim Amer paid his first official visit to Paris—which marked France's first steps toward the Arabs—a delegation from the French Jewish community offered him as ransom the enormous sum of one million dollars per head, four million dollars for the four prisoners. Surprised, Amer said that such a tempting offer would have to be presented to Nasser, who, however, rejected it, saying that Israel's presumption in daring to represent residents of Egypt was offensive to Egypt's national honor.

"But now," said Amit, "with Israel holding five thousand Egyptian prisoners, we have a rare bargaining card, and we can insist that our people be repatriated."

At first, no one disagreed with him. Unlike 1957, "the mishap" was no longer an episode shrouded in mystery. It had taken a heavy price and left deep and painful wounds, and there were many well-known people in Israel who felt that it would continue to poison Israeli public life until justice was done to its victims. In consequence, in the first unofficial talks on an exchange of prisoners, Israel insisted that the four network members be included.

The Egyptian response was in the negative. Now, in 1967, Nasser was not prepared to pay the price which, according to Amin's testimony, he had been ready to offer in 1957. This may be explained by the fact that thirteen years of contention over the fate of the network members had made the issue a matter of principle. Around "the mishap," Nasser had built up a ramified propaganda campaign, by which he tried to present Israel as responsible for undermining relationships between Egypt and the United States and forcing Egypt into the arms of the Russians. He stated this expressly in a letter he sent to John F. Kennedy when the latter was elected president. In propaganda for domestic consumption, too, "the mishap" was depicted as the root of all evil; there was not a single espionage trial in which the prosecution did not attempt to dredge up the 1954 episode and show the analogy with the case under discussion. In consequence, Nasser, entangled in his own lies, was unable to withdraw without arousing questions. He was also affected by the polarization of his own attitude toward Israel after the 1967 defeat, when he proclaimed at Khartoum that the Arabs would never recognize Israel, never make peace, or conduct negotiations with her.

Whatever the reason, when Israel demanded that Egypt release six spies in addition to the ten Israeli soldiers it held, the Egyptian reply was a resounding "No!"

Israel responded by breaking off the talks.

But the Egyptians dug in their heels. They seemed not to care if their prisoners remained in Israel forever. Perhaps they were not, indeed, interested in repatriating another five thousand eyewitnesses of the worst defeat Egypt had ever suffered. In Israel, on the other hand, there were those who did care. Although the Israeli prisoners of war, who had received some hint as to the true reason for the delay, sent off a message that they were prepared to suffer an extension of their captivity "as long as the objective was attained," their families in Israel were less patient and exerted pressure on the Defense Ministry to procure the release of their dear ones. Furthermore, winter was approaching fast, and it would soon be necessary to equip the five thousand prisoners with winter uniforms and additional blankets, and the Israeli army's quartermasters did not welcome the idea.

At one stage, Defense Minister Moshe Dayan was inclined to give in and relinquish the repatriation of the "spies." He himself conceded as much to the members of the network on meeting them after their arrival in Israel. He told them how matters had unfolded, describing the day when Meir Amit approached the prime minister—the late Levi Eshkol—asking him to adhere to the demand for the repatriation of the network members, even if he only kept it up for one week more. "I was opposed," said Dayan frankly. "I didn't believe that we would manage to soften Nasser up and I felt sorry for our fellows. I was prepared to undertake the prisoner exchange without you."

But Eshkol gave Amit the extension he asked for and even consented to make a gesture toward the Egyptians. Five hundred prisoners, headed by one of the six captive generals, were to be released immediately and gratuitously, as a mark of Israeli goodwill. Amit asked the general: "Will you see Nasser on your return? We would like you to give him a message for us. Tell him that we're prepared to release you all, but we insist on the repatriation of the six civilians. Tell him we won't make any further overtures. If your colleagues remain in captivity, it will be because your government doesn't want them."

The five hundred prisoners were driven to Kantara, on the banks of the Suez Canal, and ferried to the other side. It is not known whether the general met Nasser on his return or whether he transmitted the message. But the negotiations remained at a standstill. A week and another week . . . the winter rains began to fall.

In the end, Nasser's opposition was broken by the intervention of Gunnar Jarring, the emissary sent to the Middle East by the secretary general of the United Nations. The tall Swede went to Cairo to meet Nasser and returned to Tel Aviv.

"He still refuses to exchange civilians for soldiers," he reported to Gen. Amit.

"They are not civilians!" Amit exploded. "Each one of them is an officer in the Israeli army!"

"If only Nasser could be persuaded of that!" the Swede muttered. Amit seized on the opening. He wrote a letter to the Egyptian president, informing him officially that the members of the network had been Israeli officers since 1953. He even gave their military numbers, adding: "They have suffered more than enough. Israel is interested in their release on purely humanitarian grounds and to prove it, she is prepared for them not to be handed over directly as part of the prisoner exchange. Israel will be content if they are released from prison and allowed to leave Egypt for any other country. Furthermore, Israel undertakes to keep their release secret."

Dr. Jarring returned to Egypt with the letter and the ice was broken. Nasser read the letter and said: "In that case, all right. I agree."

On the strength of his verbal consent, Israel began to release the prisoners.

Nothing of all these developments reached Tura or Kanather. The imprisoned members of the network alternated between hope and despair. Kept in the dark, sensing that their powers of resistance were running out, they feared that they would be unable to face a further disappointment.

Marcelle's memories of this period are largely concerned with the

major events, most of which reached her by way of her tiny radio: the
speech by Israeli Commander-in-Chief Yitzchak Rabin on Mount
Scopus ("I didn't understand most of his words, but I felt that I was
participating in a sublime event. When he completed his speech and
the orchestra began to play 'Hatikvah,' I stood at attention, with the
tears pouring down my cheeks"); Nasser's resignation speech ("I felt
rather sorry for him. I even said out loud: 'Poor man, all his illusions
have been shattered.' But Teddy, the outsider, had a better understanding of him. She immediately said: 'He's a liar, he's pretending!' ");
Nasser's return to power; and the first time that the radio reported
Israel's demand for the release of six civilians, in addition to her ten
soldier captives.

"The day after the broadcast, the prison doctors came to our cell
to congratulate me: 'Mabruk [Congratulations], you're going to be
released.' A few days later, Teddy's lawyer arrived from Germany. He
confirmed that we four, as well as she and her husband, comprised the
six prisoners demanded by Israel. But time passed, month after month,
and nothing happened."

Suddenly, the prisoner exchange began, and her hopes soared
again. "We were told nothing, but I heard the broadcast of the exchange ceremony at Kantara. Talking to Teddy, we let our imaginations
depict us arriving at Kantara, where our companions would be waiting
for us. Together, we would go down to the ferry and cross the canal to
the eastern bank, where the Israeli flag was fluttering. . . ."

But the prisoner exchange went on and on, and, as nothing happened, the two women grew increasingly anxious. Then the exchange
ended. "On 'Kol Yisrael,' I heard the description of the last Israeli
prisoner arriving. I remember the announcer describing his shaven
head, and the prisoner—it was the pilot Yair Barak—saying cheerfully
that this was the latest fashion in Egypt. And then I said to myself:
'That's it. We're not being released.' And Teddy, who had been so
strong till now, broke down and burst into tears."


At Tura, the torment of waiting was even worse.

Philip: "At first, the papers reported that Israel had released the
Arab consuls taken captive in eastern Jerusalem. We regarded this as
a favorable omen, and it was quickly followed by others: The Jordanian
prisoners were released, followed by the Syrians. Only the Egyptian
prisoners remained, but everything was at a standstill, and we didn't
know why."

No longer under "special supervision," they were now housed in
a second-floor cell. Victor had returned to his work at the duck farm,

"but we," Philip relates, "remained in the cell. There were no sports now, and the library had not reopened either. We sat in our cell, dolefully awaiting the news. Lutz often came to visit us—he gave the guard a cigarette to permit him to come down to our floor—but he had no news either. We would pass the time by playing chess or trying to fathom the reasons for the delay in the prisoner exchange."

"Each day," Robbie recalls, "Lutz would arrive with the 'tidings': 'Fellows, we're soon going to be released!' It was his lawyer who kept up his optimism. At first, we were tempted to believe him, but in time, our hopes began to fade. Only Lutz continued to believe. We played a chess marathon, and on one occasion, he said: 'When I beat you ten times, we'll be released.' The trouble was, chess wasn't his strong point.

"At first, I didn't go out to work," Robbie remembers, "because I didn't want to be out of the cell when the news of our release arrived. But the days passed and the time drew near for the annual exhibition of prisoners' handicrafts. The exhibition manager wanted me and Nicola to come and prepare it. For some time I refused, more out of bitterness and disappointment than for any other reason.

"That was probably the worst time of all our years in prison. The air of depression is hard to describe. I found refuge in working. I would get up early, while my companions were still asleep. On my return, I found them immersed in a game of chess. They were silent; they didn't even greet me when I entered. But they looked up at me to see whether I had any news. When my expression told them I had nothing to relate, they turned their eyes back to the chessboard, without a word.

"One day, as I was walking to the duck farm, I was stopped by Immara. 'Why doesn't Robbie go to work? He's needed for the exhibition.'

" 'He's incapable of working,' I told him. 'He's waiting to be released.'

" 'Stop thinking of your release!'

" 'But Lutz's lawyer told him he would soon be released.'

" 'You aren't Lutz. Tell Robbie to go to work!'

"I returned to the cell, dejected and despairing. I had brought news —but what news!"


Off Port Said, the Israeli destroyer *Eilat* was sunk; in a severe reprisal raid, Israel destroyed the oil refineries in the city of Suez.

"That's it," the three men told one another. "That's the end of our release."

Despairing, Robbie decided to go back to work.

Another month passed and their hopes rose again. Paradoxically, they were aroused by an article in *Al Ahram* containing a sharp attack on Israel for her obstinacy which was delaying the prisoner exchange. It was Mustaffa Amin who brought them the newspaper. "See what's written here," he said cheerfully. "You are going to be released!"

They read, but they failed to comprehend. "But it says here that Egypt will never consent to release civilian spies."

"You don't know us," he replied. "Why do you think permission was given to publish this article? They want people to know that because of the six of you, the return home of five thousand Egyptian prisoners is being delayed. How do you expect the average Egyptian to react to that? He'll say: 'Give them the six spies and bring our men home!' That's exactly what Nasser intends. He wants to release you, but he wants to do so under the 'pressure' of the people, so that no one can blame him for it afterward."

At first, they did not believe him. But before long, the first part of his prediction came true. Army officers, some of them high-ranking, began to visit the prison "to see the six traitors who are to blame for our colleagues rotting in captivity."

"Around us, the atmosphere was unpleasant, but, paradoxically enough, it was this which rekindled our hopes. We told one another: 'So far, Amin's analysis has proved correct. Perhaps the rest of it is also correct?' Once again, we began to court the prisoners who owned radios, asking to borrow them for a night so that we could hear the news."

Then their hopes faded again. It was when the radio reported that Israel had released five hundred prisoners, including two generals, receiving nothing in return. "Our hearts sank. Till then, we had envisaged the prisoner exchange as a ceremony in which we would all be brought to the banks of the canal, with the Egyptian prisoners on the other side, and we would be exchanged. And now the Egyptian prisoners had been released, and we were still here."

A further period of inactivity ensued.

# 13

## FREEDOM

*New Clouds of Uncertainty*

And then, one day in December 1967, Robbie returned from his work at the Gzira Exhibition Hall, and while the guards were searching him at the gateway, the mail *nabatshi* came toward him, shouting from afar: "Robert, you're being released!"

"I was sure he meant immediately," says Robbie. "I raced for the cell, but when I arrived, I found my companions sitting there, still wearing prison uniform. What a terrible disappointment!"

"That morning," Victor recalls, "I was summoned from the duck farm. 'You're wanted by the head doctor.' I didn't know what this meant. At the entrance to the dispensary, I was joined by Philip and Lutz. My heart began to thud violently. We were led in, to be greeted cheerfully by all the medical orderlies: *'Mabruk!* You're going out!'

"The forensic doctor arrived. (He was employed by the government to issue official medical documents, principally death certificates.) I knew him from his previous visits to the prison, and I recalled that after each of his visits, some prisoner was released on medical grounds. Mostly, these were men suffering from fatal sicknesses, and their release was little more than permission to die at home. We were taken in to see him. He looked at us furiously, and, without any preamble, he barked: 'Name? Age?' and scribbled something on a yellow form. Only Lutz was treated somewhat more courteously. Then we were led out, still without being told anything. But outside, we were again surrounded by medical orderlies. 'Congratulations! He's signed a recommendation for your release on account of illness!'

" 'What illness?'

" 'A fatal illness. What's the difference? The main thing is that you'll be released within a few days.'

" 'And Robbie?' "

There was no reply.

The recommendation for release on medical grounds stemmed, as they learned later, from Gamal Abdel Nasser's vigorous refusal to sign a pardon for Israeli spies. He was determined that future historians would not find his signature on a document of *that* nature. Consequently, it was arranged that Philip, Victor, and Lutz, who were serving life sentences, would be released "on medical grounds," on the recommendation of the prison service's chief doctor. As for Marcelle and Robbie, they would receive the routine release from one-quarter of their sentence, to be signed by the head of the prison service administration. In this way, Nasser's name would not appear on the documents connected with this "fraud."

When Robbie returned from work that evening, they still did not know what to tell him. "I demanded to be taken to the office," Robbie relates. "I asked Immara: 'What about me?' He replied: 'They are being released, but you aren't. Those are the instructions I have received.'

"I was completely dazed. I didn't understand what was going on. Only that evening, when the prisoners came pouring into our cell to congratulate us, did Dr. Az-a-Din Abdul Kader come up with an explanation for why I had been overlooked. 'You,' he said, 'have served almost the whole of your sentence, and therefore, you don't require a release on medical grounds. You'll get the usual parole for good behavior.'

"I seized on his words like a drowning man clutching at a straw."

Days passed and again nothing happened. "Immediately after our return from the forensic doctor," Victor relates, "Philip and I wrote to our parents, telling them the good news. I wrote to my uncle in Alexandria, with whom my parents had left my civilian clothes, and asked him to bring them to me. Philip wrote to his mother with a similar request. When they arrived carrying the suitcases, and we asked the duty officer to allow them to bring them in, he replied: 'I have no such orders.' We approached Immara, and he too declared: 'I have received no orders. . . .' He gave instructions to have the suitcases taken to the prison stores.

"Once again, we were shrouded in clouds of uncertainty."

On January 15, 1968, a series of prisoner exchanges was inaugurated at Kantara. Every day, five hundred prisoners crossed the canal in the westward direction, and one or two eastward.

On January 27, everything was terminated. The last prisoners had been repatriated.

At Kanather, Marcelle felt as though icy fingers were clutching at her heart. "It was worse than in 1957." She did not have the strength to hearten Weltrude Lutz, who was crying bitterly.

At Tura: "I heard the news from the BBC, on a radio belonging to one of the officers," says Victor. "I heard the announcer say: 'The prisoner exchange between Israel and Egypt has been completed.' Darkness descended upon me. On returning to the cell, I didn't have the heart to tell my companions, but my face gave me away."

Within a few hours, a stream of prisoners came to "console" them. "They came to our cell to tell us how sorry they were, but in fact, they were there to enjoy our discomfiture, even those who considered themselves to be friends of ours, and those who were to inherit our possessions when we were released."

(When their release appeared imminent, the trio began to "assign" the property they had accumulated in the course of the years. They decided they would take with them nothing but the woolens which Marcelle had knitted for them. They did not want any mementos of their fourteen years in prison; only Philip, finding it hard to relinquish "Pedro" and his offspring, wanted to take them with him, and they had a hard job persuading him to relinquish the idea. They told him: "What if it should turn out that you need licenses to take birds out of Egypt or bring them into Israel? What will you do with 'Pedro' then? Let him loose to die in the desert?" At that, he gave in.)

They endured six awful days of depression and uncertainty, until suddenly, on February 3, without any forewarning, Lutz was summoned to the prison office, and informed that he was free. The same day, Weltrude Lutz was also released.

"I was left alone again," Marcelle says, "and even though the room was emptied of Teddy's possessions and furniture, it looked narrow and stifling to me. I strode up and down, like a caged animal, unable to read, unable to sit and do nothing, unable to do a thing. Around me, everyone talked of my imminent release; the doctors used to tease me every morning, saying: 'Are you still here? Go away!' I received a letter from Victor, in which he wrote: 'You are probably very sad now that Teddy has been released, but cheer up. Our turn will come soon.' Indeed, I sensed it in my bones, I felt that the nightmare was coming to an end. But I was so frightened of a further disappointment that I drove the thoughts of release out of my mind. Those days were endless."

It was the same in Tura, where the torments stemming from their doubts were sharpened by the hypocritical "consolations" they received from the other prisoners.

"After Lutz's release," Robbie relates, "the 'politicals' showered us with pity and feigned commiseration. 'Why was the German released, of all people?' There were also some who flung away all pretense and, with open glee, said: 'What did you think, that the whole dispute was on account of you? The whole performance was put on because of *him*. As for you, you'll continue to rot here!' Others vented their anger and disappointment on Israel. 'You never knew how to finish the job,' they said, 'just like 1956! Why did you halt at the canal, instead of taking Cairo? Look, Nasser's back on the horse!'

"We did not want to give them any pleasure. We hid our sufferings, and pretended indifference."

During this period, Mustaffa Amin proved himself to be one of their few true friends. He would come to their cell carrying food he had cooked, saying: "I know you don't have the heart to do any cooking, but you've got to eat something." Then he would sit down and talk—about Egypt, about Nasser's virtues and weaknesses, anything to take their minds off their troubles.

Immara also came one day. "I have received no instructions concerning you," he said regretfully. "It's bad luck, but what can you do? Stop thinking about your release, go back to work, and you'll feel better."

When the order came, on the evening of February 8, he wanted to inform them, but, not wishing to appear to be showing them any special favor, he sent his runner, at ten o'clock at night: "Go and ask the Jews if they all have civilian clothes."

That night, none of them slept a wink. But the following day, there was a further disappointment. Nothing happened.

Victor: "That day, my aunt came to visit me. We were so torn by uncertainty that I asked her to contact the Red Cross and inquire what was happening with us, and when we would be released. No sooner did she depart than I was summoned to the office. 'You are being released today,' I was told. 'And my companions?' I asked. 'There are no instructions concerning them.' I didn't know how to tell them."

In the meantime, the rumor spread through the prison. By the time he left the office, Philip, Robbie, and Nicola were waiting outside. They accompanied him to the clothes store.

Robbie: "We felt very peculiar. On the one hand, we were overjoyed by his release. On the other hand, we had been dreaming of the day when we would all leave the prison together. And here he was leaving on his own."

Victor looked as though he regretted his release. He was given his suitcase, but he was in no hurry to take off his prison uniform. "You'll see," he repeated, over and over again. "You'll soon follow me," until Philip rebuked him: "That's enough! You have to get dressed!"

After fourteen years, the clothes in the suitcase were small on him, so he put on Robbie's, while Nicola, the last of them to be imprisoned, helped him knot his tie. He stood before them, elegant in his gray flannel jacket, dark trousers, and pointed shoes. ("I was sure that I was the height of fashion—until I left Egypt. . . .") They smiled at him, and he stood there, looking doleful. It was a strange situation: They, who were to remain behind in prison, were obliged to cheer him up on his release. "Perhaps they intend to release us one at a time," they told him. "Our turn will also come. Don't feel sorry for us."

He was called to the office again, to settle his accounts and receive the money outstanding.

"There were a few pounds to my credit, and I had just whispered to the clerk to put them into Nicola's account, taking something for himself, when a secret policeman came in carrying a bundle of documents which he laid on the desk. Out of the corner of my eye, I saw that they were Red Cross forms and the names of Philip and Robbie were printed at the top. I went outside to my companions and told them: 'Friends, your documents have arrived. I've seen them!' They didn't know whether to believe me or not. But I felt better."

His aunt returned. She had not gone to the Red Cross; instead, she visited the Greek embassy. There she was greeted with some surprise. "What? He hasn't been released yet? But we were requested to issue him a passport, and it's already been sent off to Tura! He'll probably be released tomorrow or the day after." She returned to bring her nephew the good tidings and found him already dressed in civilian clothing.

She stayed with him till five o'clock, when the gates were locked. "You are to fly out tomorrow," she told him, having learned of this at the embassy, which bought the tickets. "I'll come to the airport to see you off."

The prison was locked up, the convicts were confined to the blocks, and Victor was left waiting. When darkness fell, he requested permission to return to the block to say good-bye. He went straight up to the second-floor cell and sat down. When his companions expressed their surprise, he said: "I'm hungry." Philip handed him a sandwich. He ate it and remained seated. "He was very pale, and it was obvious that he didn't want to go," Robbie recalls. "If a guard had not come to summon him to the *mudir*, who knows how long he would have stayed there."

"I sensed no joy as I left the block which had been my 'home' for the past ten years," Victor relates. "This wasn't the way I had envisaged my release. In the *mudir*'s office, I found an 'officers' convention'—about four or five of them, with Immara seated in the middle, smiling all over. '*Tfadalu,*' he said, 'come and sit down. Have something to drink. Bring him some tea!'

" 'What about Robbie and Philip?' I demanded to know.

" 'You have a passport,' he explained. 'It was issued by the Greek embassy. They don't possess passports. They're stateless, and they have to have travel documents prepared for them. That takes time.'

"I sat there for an hour or more and we chatted. He asked me: 'Well, Victor, what now?'

"I answered frankly. 'First of all, I'll go to see my family in Switzerland. And then I'll go on to Israel.'

"He drew back and for a moment he seemed uncertain whether to be indignant over my frankness. But he soon broke into a smile.

" 'I'm glad you're completely frank,' he said, and then he turned to the others. 'Did you see? He could have lied, but he didn't. He's incapable of lying. This is a man I wouldn't hesitate to invite into my home!' Then he turned to me again. 'You were model prisoners. Honest, hard-working, well behaved. I wish our people would take your example. After all, it was harder for you than for the others.'

"He turned to his companions again. I soon observed that he wanted to address some parting words to me, but prudent to the end, he pretended to be addressing them. Now, he said: 'You see, he fell into captivity while serving Israel and now he's returning there. Don't think it's hell there. My wife's brother, the doctor, was in captivity there in 1956, and to this day, he praises the Israelis. It's really incredible.'

"For four years, he had been the *mudir* of Tura. During this time, I met him almost daily; he was always more courteous toward me than to the other prisoners, but throughout, he never permitted me to forget for one moment that he was the all-powerful *mudir* while I was a worthless prisoner. All this time, I had never permitted myself to forget how crafty and cruel he was capable of being. But now, he seemed to have become a different man. To this day, I wonder which of the two was the true Abdalla Immara."

At eight o'clock that evening, a group of detectives arrived, charged with escorting him to the airport. Immara told their officer: "I am entrusting you, not with a prisoner, but with a friend. Take him without handcuffs and treat him well."

All that night, Victor was obliged to wait at Cairo's deserted airport, with the detectives taking turns to guard him. Then, at ten o'clock the following morning, the officer escorted him to the gangway leading up to the Olympic Airlines plane.

For the first time in fourteen years, he was walking as a free man.

Victor left Tura on Thursday. The same day, the papers arrived for Philip and Robbie. Under Egyptian law, when a man's sentence is completed, he may not be detained in prison even for one additional day. He is not allowed to attend the prisoners' *tamam* (count) held every morning. But in the case of Philip and Robbie, the law was not observed. They were told nothing, and the following morning, they went out to be counted together with the other inmates of the block. Only later were they informed, not that they were being released, but that they required photographs. But it was Friday, and the official photographer had not arrived; he would only appear for duty on Saturday.

In honor of the photograph, they were permitted to put on their civilian clothing—new clothes Mrs. Natanson had bought on learning that their release was imminent. "But when we had to take them off again and get back into our prison uniform, it was awful. We went back to our cell. Now we no longer had Victor with us to go sniffing around the offices and bring back news. We sat there gloomily, and time didn't budge."

In the end, Robbie could not stand it anymore. He persuaded the guard to let him out for a "walk" near the offices, and, as he hoped, he ran into Immara.

"Is there anything new in connection with us?" he pleaded. "Anything encouraging?"

Immara shrugged his shoulders. "What can I say? When there is any news, you'll be told."

But Robbie did not give up. "Suppose the notification comes in the evening? How will we receive our money?"

That day, the *mudir* was in a generous mood. He gave orders to summon the guard in charge of the money accounts, and in Robbie's presence, instructed him: "Even if the release order comes at four o'clock in the morning, open up the cash desk and give them their money back." Then, to Robbie: "There, are you *mabsut* [satisfied]?"

Robbie had no further pretext to dally and he returned to the cell. Nicola Kois now lived there in place of Victor. In spite of being broken-hearted after having deluded himself for weeks that he was one of the six prisoners whose release Israel demanded, he looked after Philip and Robbie most maternally, cooking for them and coaxing them to eat. "He almost fed us the way you feed babies."

At dawn, they were already up, with their possessions packed, and prepared to hand in their prison issue equipment. But the clock read eight o'clock and nothing happened.

"We were in despair. We got up and walked out and the guard

allowed us to walk past him without even rebuking us. We approached the office of the duty officer. What was happening?"

"I don't know. I haven't received any notification."

"All right. In the meantime, can we put on our civilian clothes?"

"Go ahead . . ."

At eleven o'clock, they returned to the block wearing their civilian clothing ("We felt that we were the best-dressed men in the world") and everyone came to admire them. Their "heirs" were already standing by to receive their tailored prison uniforms. "We refused to part with them till the last moment—for fear of the 'evil eye.' " Again, time crawled by with a maddening slowness. "We looked at one another, and in our hearts, we prayed silently: 'Let them not tell us to get undressed again!' "

At long last, a secret police officer arrived and closeted himself with Immara; then the *mudir* came out.

"Well then," he said. "You're leaving. But someone else is coming in" (he was referring to a Spanish sea captain who was on trial for spying for Israel, but he had yet to reach Tura) "and don't forget Nicola . . ."

They did not forget him. He "inherited" most of their possessions —the kerosene stove, their stock of provisions, and their ready money, as well as the accordion. They had intended to entrust the canaries to one of the convicts who was a bird fancier, and who had undertaken to take good care of them. For the past few days, Philip had been taking "Pedro" to his cell for a few hours each day, to give him a chance to get accustomed to his new master. But when Abdalla Immara expressed a desire to receive the parakeets, they could not refuse him. Marcelle's woolies were the only things they took with them; and then, at the last moment, Robbie plucked up the courage to take a sketchbook containing his drawings of prison life and conceal it under his clothes. His heart thumping, he headed for this final *taftish* (search), which was conducted by their old "friend" Tumraz.

Unlike his usual custom, Tumraz flung no more than a casual glance at their belongings. On opening Robbie's bag, he found several packs of cheap cigarettes there. "You are the first man who's ever taken cigarettes *out* of prison!" he growled. "What d'you need them for? Give them to those remaining behind." Without making any objections, Robbie handed the cigarettes to the *ma'amur's nabatshi*, and Tumraz, mollified, broke off his search.

They went back to the block once more to bid farewell, up to the fourth floor, but most of the "politicals" had withdrawn into their cells. Only Mustaffa Amin came toward them, giving them a friendly hug and promising, "Some day, we'll meet outside and have a serious conversation about fraternity between peoples." Hudeibi, the spiritual leader of the Moslem Brotherhood, sent to call them to his cell. "Don't be angry at them," he said, indicating the neighboring cells which their inmates had bolted from the inside. "They are sad to see you going out while they remain behind. Forgive them."

They were ready to forgive anything, as long as the gate was opened. Finally, it was opened. Placed on a barred prison truck, they were soon making their way through the streets of Cairo.

Marcelle was summoned to the photographer on Thursday. She went with her heart thudding as she grasped that her release was approaching. But the next two days crawled past with a maddening sluggishness; she was told nothing. It was only on Saturday morning that she was summoned to the duty supervisor.

"I'll tell you something," she said, "but keep it to yourself, because you're not supposed to know: Tomorrow, you're being released."

She was very grateful, for the advance warning gave her a chance to pack her belongings and hide Victor's letters and the transistor radio, the only possession she wanted to take with her.

At noon, the sergeant also came along: "Marcelle—tomorrow! But hush, no one must know!"

That evening, before locking the cell door, the night guard also brought the same tidings.

That night, Marcelle needed sleeping pills to get to sleep.

The following morning, she was summoned to the *ma'amur:* "Marcelle, I have good news for you. You are leaving. Immediately."

"Why didn't you tell me before?"

"Because I wasn't certain, and I didn't want to disappoint you again."

Returning to her cell, she put on the civilian clothes she had prepared the day before. She left almost everything else to Fauzia, who had never been so rich in all her life, but cried bitterly all the same. "She was a good girl," says Marcelle, "and genuinely attached to me."

The farewell ceremony was brief. Only two of the women from the Moslem Brotherhood, occupying the last cell in the wing where Teddy Lutz had spent her first days in Kanather, came out to bid her farewell. The three Israeli girls had vanished a day or two earlier (they were repatriated to Israel) and there were no other "politicals" in the prison. As Marcelle crossed the courtyard, the inmates of the murderesses' wing waved to her.

The *ma'amur* was extremely gallant and courteous. "Sit down, sit down. Will you drink a cup of tea? No? But you must!" He clapped his hands and called: *"Chai* for Marcelle!" At long last, when the police escort arrived, the *ma'amur* said good-bye: "I wish you all the best. Forget the bad things and remember only the good times."

And then, the tensions of the past few days and the tormenting doubts of recent months all vanished. She sat in the little van, beside the officer who was driving. It was the first time she had left Kanather since her return from the hospital, six years previously. All around, Cairo's teeming traffic streamed past, while her gaze took in the houses fleeting by, while she looked out in vain for familiar spots or faces.

Beside the district court, in the center of the city, the van halted behind a parked prison truck, and her glance rested on the two men in civilian clothes sitting at the back. Even though fourteen years had passed since she last saw them, she recognized them instantly: Robbie, grinning broadly, and Philip, his long forelock dangling down his face as he waved vigorously.

She asked the escorting officer to permit her to move over into their truck. Women prisoners were not allowed to travel together with men, but they were all—theoretically at least—free citizens, and, after a moment's hesitation, he gave his consent.

She found it hard to clamber up the back of the truck, and Philip and Robbie had to haul her up. Her first question was: "Where's Victor?" They had written notifying her of his release, but the letter had not reached her. "He'll be waiting for us in Israel," they replied.

The journey to the airport lasted three-quarters of an hour. Their route passed by Heliopolis, which was connected with many of Marcelle's childhood memories, but she never even noticed it. She could not take her eyes off her two companions, and they looked at her eagerly, affectionately. They did not talk much. "What could we say? Everything was clear: At long last, we were free and together."

They had yet to imagine how long would be their path to a true freedom, when they had shaken off the spiritual bonds and ways of thought of the convict. This was a gradual process which was to last many weeks and months. It consisted of getting used to a phone ringing, of learning to sit on a chair, to drink from a glass, to use a European-type washroom, to find their way and preserve their sanity amid the splendors of a department store. In many ways, they resembled babies, learning to take their first steps. But they were middle-aged babies, whose life stories lacked an entire chapter which is essential to a person's development—their youth. They were to grasp what it was they had forfeited when they tried later to give vent to their feelings of joy and playfulness and found that they did not know how. "On our first Purim in Israel, we walked through Tel Aviv, through the noisy, festive crowds, and we were beside ourselves with joy. At the same time, we felt like outsiders. We wanted to merge into the rejoicing around us; we too wanted to play tricks, hitting passersby over the head with plastic hammers, to let off yells of joy, but something within us held us back. Fourteen years of forced restraint, of repressing our feelings had deprived us of the ability to let go."

## A Fourteen-Year-Old Dream

They reached the airport at midday, with several hours yet to wait. Outwardly, they were free to do whatever they wished, but their release had been conditional: It did not apply on Egyptian soil. This condition was enforced by their guard, an elderly *sol* policeman, who retained their passports and watched their movements.

They had a little Egyptian money, from their prison accounts, which they were unable to convert into foreign currency. They led the *sol* to the washroom, and there, out of sight, they slipped a five-pound note into his palm, after which he allowed them to wander around the terminal building, while he watched them from afar. They now began their first lesson in civilian life: shopping. To walk into a shop and buy anything they wanted—that was an old dream of theirs. But at Cairo airport, the wares offered for sale were poor and meager. They bought key rings; at the bookstore, Marcelle purchased Françoise Sagan's latest novel, of which she had heard on Radio Cairo's literature program, while Philip bought *The Spy Who Came in from the Cold*. Suddenly, they lost their desire for a shopping spree. They went to the mail counter and sent the rest of the money to Philip's mother and Marcelle's aunt.

They boarded the plane at three o'clock in the afternoon. They were the last to mount it. The *sol*, together with a number of secret police officers, escorted them right up to the gangway, and it was only there, one minute before takeoff, that they handed the stewardess their papers—Red Cross travel documents, containing a Swiss transit visa valid for forty-eight hours.

They sat together with Marcelle in the middle, and looked around. For all three, this was their first flight, but the "butterflies" in their stomachs soon calmed down. Another thought began to engage their minds: What would they do on arrival? Where would they turn and what would they do? They did not have a penny in their pockets.

Philip said: "At worst, we'll take a taxi to the Israeli embassy; they'll pay the fare."

They were the last ones to disembark at Geneva. They wandered around in the arrivals hall, hoping that someone would approach them. But no one came. Deciding there was no point in waiting any further, they went out. Philip and Robbie were carrying crude canvas bags manufactured in Tura, while Marcelle lugged an enormous suitcase, as well as a blanket tied up with string. "Suddenly, we sensed how we stood out in our pointed shoes and 1953-style wide trousers, and our old fear, which every prisoner knows—the fear of prominence—flooded us." Their fear was mingled with a sense of shock: That year, particularly bright colors were in fashion, and there was the shock of seeing the horizon without encountering walls. Marcelle felt the shock of being among a crowd, unescorted. All three felt weary, in body as well as soul. It was weeks since they had slept peacefully, untroubled by their quivering nerves.

"We clung to one another, sensing that our security lay in being together. All these other people all around, they were strangers, not our people . . ."

Two elegantly dressed men detached themselves from a wall and approached them, politely removing their hats before Marcelle. "Mademoiselle Ninio? We are from the Red Cross."

"I introduced Robbie and Philip. The smug look on the two officials' faces provoked me into asking: 'And where were you until now?' I meant, where were they when we needed them, in Egypt, but they took my words at their face value.

" 'We were not permitted to pass the passport control,' they replied, 'so we preferred to await you here. We will take you to Red Cross headquarters, where you will meet those who dealt with your case, but for whom you have hitherto been nothing more than numbers.'

"They were very courteous, taking us on a short tour of Geneva, pointing out the League of Nations 'Palace of Nations.' On the way, a little snow fell, the first I had ever seen. At Red Cross headquarters, we were offered refreshments—sandwiches, biscuits, and tea—but who was hungry?

"They asked whether we wished to contact our families. Robbie did not know where his parents lived in Israel, nor whether they owned a phone. I wanted to speak with my brother in Paris, but there was no answer. We also tried to contact Victor's sister Eugette, but there was no reply there either. Philip was the only one who managed to make contact with his sister in Paris.

"And then, after coughing and clearing their throats in embarrassment, the Red Cross officials brought up the subject which had been bothering them. 'You understand, it's a delicate matter. Israeli representatives wish to meet you. But if you don't want to see them, if you don't want to go to Israel, tell us, and we will arrange for your transit to another country. You are completely free.'

" 'Of course we want to go to Israel. What are we waiting for?'

"However, the Red Cross officials remained 'neutral' right up to the end. They did not take us directly to the Israeli representatives; instead, they left us in the foyer of a hotel in the center of Geneva, and the embassy employees came to us there."

Twenty-four dizzy hours.

Marcelle: "We were taken to the office of the Israeli delegation to the United Nations institutions in Geneva. Our first thrill: On the wall, facing the door, was the *menora* emblem. Hitherto, I had only seen it once, in a copy of *Life* magazine I chanced upon at Kanather.

"We were received by the ambassador, Mordechai Kidron. Then we were taken to the home of the head of Geneva's Jewish community, M. Brunswick. Did I say home? A palace! And it was all at our disposal, including the servant and the chambermaid. There was a bathroom attached to each room, a fourteen-year-old dream. Philip was a perfect gentleman, preparing my bath with his own hands, pouring in a whole bottle of bubbly soap. And the beds! They were so soft, we couldn't fall asleep . . ."

They dined at the ambassador's home. Afterward, they listened to records. Marcelle requested to hear "Jerusalem the Golden," while Philip asked for the other Six-Day War hit, "Nasser's Waiting for Rabin." Their hosts were astounded: "How did you come to know these songs?" And that was the cue for stories, well into the night.

The following day, the delegation's secretary, Lily Kastel, went with them to buy clothes. They felt like children in a candy store: Their eyes tried to gobble it all down, but when it came to choosing, they could not make up their minds. Finally, they settled for a costume and shoes for Marcelle, and a jacket, trousers, and shirt each for Robbie and Philip. There was no money for anything more. But when they passed the toy counter, they could not resist buying a present for Victor, a multicolored toy duck, "to console him for the ducks he had left behind at Tura."

The same day, they flew to Zurich, and from there, via El Al, on passports bearing fictitious names, to Lod.

When they walked down the gangway, Victor was there with arms stretched out to embrace them.

Victor had landed at Athens four days earlier. On the flight, he too wondered what to do on arriving at his destination. He decided that if no one contacted him at the airport, he would go on into the city and find the way to the Israeli delegation.

Indeed, no one contacted him. His passport was stamped and he boarded a bus; as it was about to move off, a policeman appeared at the entrance, calling: "Victor Levy?"

His deeply rooted fear of anyone wearing a uniform made it impossible for Victor to reply. But the policeman boarded the bus and asked to see the passengers' passports.

Victor's heart sank when he was ordered off the bus. He was led to the airport police station. He tried to think what they could have found wrong with him, but with no success. None of the policemen spoke any language other than Greek. He was led into the officer's room where he tried out all the languages he knew. English? French? The officer only shrugged his shoulders and indicated the bench in the duty police-man's room. He was to wait.

"I sat there for about an hour and nothing happened. I found a porter who could speak a little English and asked him to inquire why I was being detained. But the officer only said: 'I don't know. He must wait.'

"I waited another hour, and then an elegantly dressed man with a moustache—to me, anyone with a moustache looks like a secret police-man—walked in and addressed me: '*Shalom!*' I was so dazed that I couldn't put the syllables together into any word I was familiar with. I replied: 'I don't speak Greek. Do you speak English?'

"Then he said in English: 'I have regards for you from your friends.'

"Suddenly, I realized that he had said *Shalom*—Hebrew!

" 'I am the Israeli consul,' the man continued, and answered my unasked question: 'I asked my friends in the police to keep you till I came. You are expected at my home.'

"All of a sudden, the police officer also 'understood English.' He said: 'Do you want to go with him? You are free to go into town, if you prefer.'

"The consul drove me to his home, where a magnificent lunch was awaiting us. We held a short conversation. I told him that I wished to go to Switzerland, to see my family. But I was told that in Israel it had been decided that I should go there first for a few days. It was not desirable that news of my release should be publicized before my companions were released; it might harm them.

"Naturally, I consented without making any objections. But I asked to phone my parents.

"At four o'clock, I was back at the airport, this time, with an Israeli passport and a first-class ticket. At six, we landed at Lod. I took my possessions and got off the plane. It all seemed perfectly natural. I was returning home."

Victor was taken to an isolated building in the vicinity of Tel Aviv, where Wolfgang Lutz and his wife had already been staying for the past few days. "Our meeting was emotional. Then I had a hot shower, using lots of soap. Then we had supper together, with roars of laughter as Lutz fired off his jokes in bursts. At ten, Meir Amit arrived.

"He told me that an emissary had been sent to my parents, to explain why I was unable to visit them at first, and why my release had to be kept secret.

"The next day, Father arrived. I was taken to the airport to identify him, so that he could go through passport control without attracting attention. From the VIP lounge overlooking the tarmac, I saw him approaching, a bent old man in a raincoat, not the vigorous, optimistic man I remembered. He was brought to me. It is not customary to weep in our family. All the same . . ."

Victor's father was given a room next to his son's. "For three days, we didn't go out. We talked and talked. On the first day, Father told me of the death of my sister Mireille. I was not surprised. In my heart of hearts, I had known for years that she was no longer among the living. But I did not dare to inquire about the circumstances of her death. Only a month later, when I was permitted to go to Switzerland, was I told."

From the moment of his arrival, Victor wanted to go to see Susanne. During the early years of his imprisonment, an occasional letter from her reached him—sometimes a book as well; then the letters stopped coming. He did not know that she had married—though he guessed it—nor did he know that she had since divorced. In his mind, she remained a precious figure from the distant past. But whenever he asked to see her, he was told: "Not yet. Wait till they get out."

The day the other three reached Geneva, he was told: "They're out. Now you are free to phone Susanne. Here is her number."

He phoned, but there was no reply. Before he had time to try again, Avraham Dar appeared. Their meeting was an emotional one. When they calmed down, Avraham said: "Come to my place. You're allowed out now. I have a surprise for you." Nothing could make him reveal what it was.

"Together with Father, he took me to an apartment on Gordon Street, which Avraham had rented for his stays in Tel Aviv. We had a drink, we chatted a little, and then Avraham told me: 'I invited Susanne as well. She'll soon arrive.'

"No sooner had he said it than the doorbell rang.

"Susanne entered. We flung ourselves into one another's arms. She cried. Later, we went to have dinner at the Trayana restaurant. She had dried her eyes, our first reticence had worn away, she was cooing with joy and caressing me with her glance. Looking at her, I felt as though the past fourteen years had never happened.

"The next day, we all drove to the airport, to welcome the others on their arrival from Switzerland."

The deal which had brought about their release was still kept secret, and measures were taken to prevent the news from leaking out. They were given passports with false names—Robbie arrived on a passport bearing the name Robert Dasseau. Immediately on getting off the plane, they were taken to a waiting room, while an official took their passports to have them stamped at passport control. However, the policeman on whose desk Robbie's passport was laid was none other than his brother Yossi. "When he saw my picture peeping out at him, he almost lost control. But when he noticed the 'doctored' name, he understood that there was something afoot, and regained his self-control." He did not even say anything at home, until an official messenger came and addressed his father: "Mr. Dassa, are you capable of controlling your feelings like a man? Robbie has arrived. I want to take you to him. But without any fuss!"

They were dazed as they got off the plane at Lod. Marcelle and Philip were locked in an embrace with Victor ("The few days we had been apart had brought about such an enormous change in him! He was vigorous and happy, and looked as though all the imprints of his imprisonment had been wiped away") while at the same time, wondering what awaited them in their alien homeland. Robbie sensed a vague anxiety as he contemplated his imminent meeting with his parents and brothers after their prolonged separation. "I thought: How will the first meeting go? How will I find a common language with my brothers? How will I know their children?"

His parents arrived at eleven o'clock at night, and Robbie's fears vanished. His mother flung herself at him, while his father stroked him with a shy smile, and Marcelle stood nearby, weeping for joy. A few days later, Robbie was taken secretly to his brother's apartment. The whole family had assembled there, and even though they were forced to exercise restraint, for fear of attracting attention, Robbie soon learned that his fear of lacking a common language with his brothers was groundless.

"We were always a united family."

A day or two later, Marcelle experienced the joy of being reunited with one brother, whom she had not seen since he emigrated to Israel in 1952, with his two sons, whom she recalled as babies, and with his daughter, who had been born in Israel.

They stayed at that military hostel for a month, gradually peeling off the gloom of prison. Robbie: "There was only one thing we didn't get rid of for a long time, and that was our fear of remaining on our own. We would awake at night, and when we found ourselves alone, we were overcome with fear. We would hasten to Victor's room, or go and knock on Marcelle's door, so as to be together."

Throughout that month, there was a party every day. "The day after our arrival, we met the Defense Minister, who told us that he had been on the verge of giving up the demand for our release. We were received by President Shazar and his wife, both very charming to us. And Levi Eshkol—so human! Each of the ministers, and all of them together. We ate so much—three meals a day and a party in the evening. After the reception at the president's residence, we were taken to dinner at the Mandarin. We couldn't bear to see so many people. We were taken on tours all over Israel. I was so exhausted that my memories of this whole period are completely mixed up and confused in my mind. But despite my weariness, I couldn't fall asleep at night."

Meir Meyuhas returned to Israel especially so as to meet his four companions, and Meir Za'afran arrived from Haifa. "It was a wonderful evening for all of us. We slipped out and they took us for a stroll along Dizengoff Street, without any speeches, without any handshakes, just a group of young people swallowed up in the crowds."

When Philip's sister reached Israel, and Marcelle's brother, they decided that the time had come to realize an old dream: a trip to Eilat. "Our stay was arranged for three days, which we extended into a week. We were on our own, just us and our families—totally anonymous. Nobody stared at us and nobody asked 'How was it?' Eilat matched up with everything we had imagined. Red hills and yellow desert and blue sea—and it was wonderful to find out that I could still swim!"

There were other imposing events; the ceremony where they, together with other returned prisoners, were granted the Six-Day War medal (later, in a separate ceremony, they were also given the Sinai campaign medal). "And the ceremony in the office of Gen. Shmuel Ayal, the head of the army's manpower division, where we were each promoted to the rank of major. And most imposing of all, the day when, in uniform and bearing our insignia of rank, we watched the military parade in Jerusalem—the victory parade."

But the greatest experience of all was their meeting with David Ben-Gurion. "We were taken to see him at Sdeh Boker. We were told that he did not feel well, and that therefore we should not prolong our stay. But in the end, it was he who wouldn't let us go. He talked on and on. He expressed a desire that we should Hebraize our names. He brought up the name of Moshe Marzouk, saying: 'In my eyes, he was a saint. I shall perpetuate his memory.' He said that we should meet for a freer conversation. Then, as we got up to leave, he said suddenly: 'There is one thing you ought to know. You were sold. And Lavon lied. You should write a book. Don't let what happened to you be forgotten.'

"With that, he reopened the old 'Pandora's box' which we had imagined was closed forever."

# AFTERWORD

Many years have passed since that day in 1968 when three men and one woman arrived in Israel, the homeland for whose sake they had sacrificed so much, bearing hopes of beginning their lives anew.

Their hopes have been realized. Even though it took them a long time, they found repose for their bruised souls (and Marcelle, after undergoing an operation, was relieved of her physical sufferings). They rebuilt their lives. All of them got married. Victor married Susanne, the sweetheart of his youth; Robbie, Philip, and Marcelle found maturer passions after reaching Israel. Their children are growing up in a sovereign Jewish state, free of the fears and frustrations which tormented their parents in their youth.

They all live in the Tel Aviv area, and even though each of them has turned to his own vocation, they still maintain close links and meet frequently to recall days gone by.

They frequently recalled the past, but were not permitted to tell their story. They had to contain their memories, and even more, their desire to justify the deeds for which they fell into captivity and their friends mounted the scaffold.

But they were condemned to remain silent. Every promise exchanged between Israel and Egypt has long been broken; only the promise to Nasser to keep their release—and, consequently, their story —secret, remained binding. Even after Nasser died. Even after "the third man"—Avry Seidenberg—completed his sentence and was released from prison. Even after all those involved, directly or indirectly, in "the mishap" stepped off the stage of history.

They remained anonymous, and unheard. They felt that they were condemned to silence because of all the murky overtones which had become associated with "the mishap," and because of which it was considered best forgotten.

But they were unable to swallow this injustice. As far as they were concerned, "the mishap" consisted of: Moshe Marzouk and Shmuel Azar, who, pure and saintly, mounted the steps to the scaffold for a precious ideal; Max Binnet, who committed suicide for the sake of human dignity and for the honor of the Israeli army; Yosef (Armand) Karmona, an innocent victim; and they themselves, young Jews fired by the ideal of the distant Jewish homeland, ready and willing to offer up their lives and liberty in any task that Israel required of them.

In this "mishap," there was nothing dishonorable. It was all honest, pure, and innocent. That is what they wished to shout from the rooftops, but they were not permitted to do so.

Until, twenty-four years after they were condemned to silence, they were set at liberty to tell their story, and they told it.

This has been their story.

# INDEX